WHO'S
HAD
WHO

WHO'S HAD WHO

An Historical Rogister Containing
Official Lay Lines of History
from the Beginning of Time to
the Present Day

Written and compiled by
SIMON BELL • RICHARD CURTIS •
HELEN FIELDING

WARNER BOOKS

A Warner Communications Company

A DOVE BOOK

First published in England by Faber and Faber Limited.

Warner Books Edition
Copyright © 1990 by Warner Books, Inc.
Copyright © 1987 by Simon Bell, Richard Curtis, and Helen Fielding
All rights reserved.

This Warner Books edition is published by arrangement with
Faber and Faber Ltd., 3 Queen Square, London WC1N 3AU.

Warner Books, Inc., 666 Fifth Avenue, New York, NY 10103

W A Warner Communications Company

Printed in the United States of America
First Warner Books Printing: June 1990
10 9 8 7 6 5 4 3 2 1

Library of Congress Cataloging-in-Publication Data

Bell, Simon.
  Who's had who / by Simon Bell, Richard Curtis, Helen Fielding.—
Warner Books ed.
     p.   cm.
  1. Sex—Humor.   2. Celebrities—Sexual behavior—Humor.
I. Curtis, Richard.   II. Fielding, Helen.   III. Title.
PN6231.S54B37   1990
818′.5402—dc20   89-70564
ISBN: 0-446-39042-9 (pbk.)   CIP

Cover design by Syndi Becker

Cover photos by AP/Wide World Photos

Book design by Giorgetta Bell McRee

Dedicated to our nephews and nieces,
Christian, Clare, Justine, Oliver, Rosie and Toby.

CONTENTS

PREFACE

Malthus, the clergyman and economist, once observed that if you placed a grain of rice on the first square of a chess board, then doubled it for the second square, and then continued to double it square by square, by the time you reached the 64th square, you would have enough rice to feed the world three times, with enough left over after that to open a medium-sized Chinese restaurant.

If you transpose this sort of arithmetic to the world of rogering, you get a picture of sexual profligacy on a world-wide scale that amazes and confuses the mind. The authors of this book did just that, and it threw our minds into such amazement and confusion that we have made it our lives' work to formalize that most informal of human activities, rogering: to bring some order to the chaos of carnal coupling that is all around us.

Our intentions are not salacious, but rather to show the foolishness of salaciousness. If so many people are rogering and so many always have, what matter another pair? The book is neither a condemnation of, nor an invitation to promiscuity, but rather should be thought of as a billet-doux to the promiscuous, bearing the simple motto . . .

'you are not alone'

INTRODUCTION

This book of rogers is not comprehensive. If it were comprehensive it would be a book as big as the whole world, including Taiwan. It is rather a smorgasbord of delights picked from the rich kitchen of couplings that is history.

The major working principle of the book are lay lines, lines of people who have lain with each other and not just fallen asleep.

Starting with Henry VIII, a fairly cataclysmic rogerer if ever there was one, we have followed these lines through European history up to the present day. When we reach the start of this century, the lay lines spread out, to show more of the variety and curiosity of the rogering of our time. It does indeed seem that you can get from almost anyone to anyone else. Every time you roger someone you leave a bit of yourself behind. Then:

**If you've rogered anyone you've rogered everyone
in the history of the world.**

Whether or not there is any deeper meaning to the lay lines, whether the people in them are bound together by some mysterious force, we are not in a position to say. Let each reader judge for himself or herself. What is true is that the lines tie together the great and the humble, the beautiful and the ugly, the talented and the talentless in one great spider's web of lust and tenderness, marriage and adultery, polite fumbling and good, hard rogering-the-living-daylights-out-of.

The text has been extensively annotated to give all the relevant information about all the rogers and those involved. On the whole the notes are true. Where they are not, they are obviously not.

We hope that you, the reader, will find a variety of uses for the book, something like the variety to be found in rogering itself. Sometimes you can use it for just a quick dip, and other times have nice long sessions with it. Sometimes you can treat it with care and attention and love, and at other times, just casually exploit it. One day investigate it in loving detail, looking into all its private little nooks and crannies, the next day just go for the quick cheap thrill.

And at the end, perhaps some readers may compile their own series of lay lines, seeing where they, their friends and their rogering partners past and present fit into the complex puzzle. It was after just such an experiment, sitting on a sofa working out that we had not only slept with each other but, indirectly, with everyone else we knew and Sheena Easton, that we three authors decided to embark on this long journey through the stained sheets of time.

THE NO BANG THEORY

It is generally thought by Christian philosophers that God is omniscient, knows everything there is to know. A small group of Dutch theologians, however, in the early part of this century posited a theory called **Omniscience Minus One**, in order to explain the mess that the world is in.

The theory ran like this. What if God knows everything except ONE THING. What if He has a blind spot: there is no one around as intelligent as Him to put Him right, and He doesn't know He doesn't know it because that is the one thing He doesn't know. The developers of the Omniscience Minus One Theory then gave this rather graphic example.

What, for instance, if God has always pushed a red button to send people to Hell, and a blue one to send them to Heaven. And what if the one thing God doesn't know is that He is colour-blind. And sees red for blue, and vice-versa.

Chaos.

Having put forward the possibility of Omniscience Minus One, the question immediately arose: what is the Minus One? What is the one thing that God knows absolutely nothing about? Almost as soon as being posed, the question was answered.

God knows absolutely nothing about rogering.

It is not the job of this book to present the full proof of this startling assertion. But here are some of the major damning pieces of evidence:

1 From the very start, God showed a complete lack of knowledge of how rogering worked. Consider the evidence:
God made Adam and Eve.
'Adam knew Eve his Wife'. (Genesis 4.1) and then 'Adam knew Eve his wife again'.
They had two sons: Cain and Abel.
The next thing we hear is that Cain 'knew his wife and she conceived and bear him Enoch'.
But where does the wife come from?
The brutal truth is that God had forgotten to put an extra woman on Earth. Cain and Abel had to roger Eve, and poor old Eve had to agree in order to keep the family going. **MISTAKE.**

2 Not one to learn from His mistakes, because He didn't know they were mistakes, God did *exactly the same thing* a few years later, wiping out everyone on Earth except Noah's family. Again, compulsory incest. **MISTAKE.**

3 Then, when He finally did get around to sending His blessed Son to Earth to sort out the mess created by the rogering He didn't understand, God went and did it via the virgin birth, *a ludicrous misunderstanding of how babies are born*, that no one except God could have got away with. **MISTAKE.**

4 After that, Mary continued to be called the Virgin Mary for eternity, even though she quite clearly wasn't because Jesus had a brother, James. **MISTAKE.**

5 Then, once the Church was founded, God decided to keep some people away from sex, to be as in the dark about it as He is: He called them nuns and monks. *And yet*, if He wanted people not to desire nuns, why did He dress them in nun's habits which are the *most startlingly erotic clothes ever invented*, and if He wanted monks to be celibate, why not put them in trousers like the rest of us, instead of tempting them with the facility of the quick up-and-in afforded by the monk's tunic. **TWO MORE BIG MISTAKES.**

6 The final proof is less specific, but perhaps most damning. From our own experience, we know that anyone who has never had sex doesn't really know what it's all about. *God has never had sex.* **MISTAKE.**

This refinement of the Omniscience Minus One Theory is known as the **No Bang Theory.**

In His Big Game Plan for Earth, God obviously took *no account of rogering whatsoever*, and allowed for no bangs whatsoever.

It is this that has thrown human history into utter chaos from the very beginning.

Comparative mythology confirms this theory. Greek legend has the Chief God, Chronos, having his penis actually cut off, and thrown into the sea by his enemies. And likewise Christian mythology from the Middle Ages speaks of the Devil, who certainly knows more about rogering than God, having a two-pronged penis so he could commit fornication and sodomy at the same time. The truth of the matter is clear: in the battle for Supremacy, which God, thank God, won, the Devil *actually stole* God's penis and has been using it ever since.

As a result of this blind spot with God and rogering, the whole carefully planned plot for the world went wrong. Even when we join the full story with Henry VIII, rogering is still causing a lot of trouble. But before then . . . chaos.

THE BIBLE

Soon after Noah, things are quite out of control. David, son of Solomon, one of God's real favourites, had 700 wives and 300 concubines.

Elsewhere in the Bible rogers caused cataclysms left, right and centre. For instance, the case of Shechem, who rogered Dinah, the daughter of Jacob. Dinah's brothers weren't pleased, and devised a brutal revenge. They asked Shechem and the Shechemites if they would agree to be circumcised as part of a future marriage contract. The Shechemites foolishly agreed: and when they were at their sorest from the circumcision, the brothers of Dinah attacked and slaughtered the lot of them.

THE ROMANS

After the Bible, the next important block of history is Rome, and trouble once more.

The Roman roger really careered out of control shortly after Julius Caesar and Mark Antony both rogered Cleopatra. The taint of the Egyptians finally sent the system mad because the Egyptian rulers slept with all their brothers and sisters and then were expected, if male, to marry their mothers as a matter of course. This carelessness about family ties, known as the Egyptian roger, soon became the Roman roger. Suddenly gone were the boring Roman matrons of republican days and on came the freewheeling emperors and their crazy women.

Emperor Tiberius kept a swimming pool stocked with boys to 'nibble' him as he swam.

Caligula rogered all three of his sisters and married one of them. He also encouraged his boyfriends to roger his sisters too. In the end, as well as his sisters, he rogered all the other women of rank in Rome: two of them at their weddings.

Claudius first rogered his niece, then set himself up as the Henry VIII of Rome, divorcing three wives and executing one, Messalina, for running a brothel in which she was the only thing on the menu. His daughter then went and married his stepson, Nero.

Nero, for starters, rogered his sister, and married his step-sister. He then rogered his mother and raped a Vestal Virgin. Finally he fell for a boy and tried to have him turned into a girl by castrating him: after which he married him. It was hoped that things might then cool down with

Otho, but he in his turn rogered Nero and Nero's wife. The Imperial power was then handed on to

Domitian, who rogered his niece and then kept the dynasty going by rogering his successor as well, the future emperor, **Nerva**.

Shortly afterwards, the Roman Empire ceased to exist. With so much rogering to do, they simply did not have time to rule the world. God by now was starting to panic, and the world drifted towards . . .

THE DARK AGES

Being so dark, this was obviously a time of almost ceaseless rogering. Just as in New York on a night in the 1960s when the electricity failed and nine months later there was a rash of new-born children, so the Dark Ages encouraged rogering. What few values and standards the Bible and the Romans had at least pretended to have went out of the window once and for all.

In 610, the women of Ulster and their Queen came to meet Cuchulain naked above the waist and raising their skirts 'so as to expose their private parts'. It was this kind of welcome rather than religious zeal that made the Crusades so popular.

By the eighth century, according to Boniface, the English 'utterly despise matrimony, live in lechery and debauchery'.

In the ninth century, Alcuin writes: 'the land has been absolutely submerged under a flood of fornication, adultery and incest'. Values were so upturned that the word 'bastard' was starting to be a mark of distinction.

By the eleventh century, bastards were doing so well that the country was actually invaded and ruled by one.

God's plan was skidding out of control. If he had hoped the Kings of England would help him get things right again, he was mightily mistaken.

THE KINGS OF ENGLAND

They were as bad as the rest.

William, the Conqueror, who was a bastard himself, defeated England for the first and only time on her own soil, and ruled.
    Henry I had twenty bastards.
    Henry II had to rely upon a bastard son to put down a rebellion inspired by his real son and was himself a major rogerer. He rogered, amongst others, Eleanor of Aquitaine, Princess Nesta of Wales, and Bellebelle, a prominent prostitute. Eleanor, in her turn, also rogered Louis VII of France, Raymond of Tripoli, Geoffrey of Anjou, Geoffrey of Rancon, and Raymond of Poitiers. Henry was so adept at rogering that he rogered a Breton nobleman's daughter while he was himself being held hostage by the father. It was generally accepted that he 'scorned no filthiness'.
    King John, further down the line, raped so many of the barons' wives and daughters that they forced him to sign the Magna Carta to defend their rights.
    Edward II, William II and Richard I were all gay, for which Edward paid a heavy price in terms of a poker and a red hot bottom.
    Edward III was soon back on the straight and narrow, however, sleeping with women again. His particular favourite was Alice Perrers, famous for her 'weasel's body and lecherous eye'; when the King died she ripped the rings off the corpse and lived in luxury on the proceeds.
    Henry VI looked as though he was, at last, going to start cooling things down. He married Margaret of Anjou, and didn't roger outside wedlock, or in it indeed: when Margaret announced she was pregnant, Henry couldn't

work out how it had happened. The fact is that Margaret had been making up for his restraint: she had rogered most of the important lords of England.

Edward VI followed hot on Henry's heels and got quickly back to business. 'He was licentious in the extreme', and a master of the fine art of the Roger with Promises. He promised all the girls he rogered that he would marry them, and then married none. He kept three whores, 'the merriest, the wiliest, the holiest harlots in the land'. Jane Shore, 'the merriest' had her great year in 1494, when she rogered the King, the Earl of Dorset and Lord Chamberlain Hastings.

Then came Henry VIII and dynamite.

God had long ago given up trying to control anything at all. His blind spot had left Him impotent. What chance did He have to control things, when He didn't allow for rogering, and just one roger can change the world. For instance . . .

A ROGER THAT CHANGED THE WORLD

At the age of sixteen, Henry VIII rogered a prostitute.

As a result of this, he contracted syphilis. The syphilis went to his brain, disordered his behaviour and led him to change his wife five times in ten years.

As a result of the divorce with Catherine of Aragon, England left the Catholic Church. This instituted the major shifts in English religious life which led to the founding of the Puritan movement, which eventually left England to colonize America.

As a result, America became English, rather than Dutch or German, and was tied firmly to England and English-speaking Europe.

As a result, this led to the crucial American involvement in the defeat of Hitler in 1945, and the saving of the free world.

Thus, it is because of a single roger by Henry VIII one hot summer afternoon when he was sixteen that the world as we know it now exists. Without that one roger, there would be no Church of England, no English-speaking America, no free Europe. Also, presumably, no East–West confrontation, no Star Wars, and no McDonalds.

With this terrifying thought of the power of the roger ringing in our minds, let's go . . .

WHO'S
HAD
WHO

PRAYING MANTIS

FROM	**HENRY VIII**
TO	**MARY, QUEEN OF SCOTS**
IN	**5 ROGERS**

This unhappy line covers a time when it was extremely risky to roger anyone. Life between the sheets was a dangerous thing, and, like the praying mantis, many lovers found themselves dying a grisly death as a result of a simple roger. The head upon the pillow found itself soon upon the block, and 'I love you' was too often a polite way of saying 'I'm about to have you killed.'

The Royal Family in particular seemed to be taking rogering a lot too seriously. At least anyone who sleeps with a Royal nowadays is only hounded by the press, not by the hounds of death.

3

HENRY VIII

Born	**1491, in England.**
Occupation	**King.**
Hobbies	**Rogering, divorcing and beheading.**
Distinguishing Features	**'Extremely excellent calf'.**
Romantically Linked With	**Catherine of Aragon (m), Anne Boleyn (m), Jane Seymour (m), Anne of Cleves (m), Catherine Howard (m), Catherine Parr (m), Anne Hastings, Mary Boleyn and Jane Popincourt. And a prostitute with syphilis.**
Nickname	**Bluff King Harry.**

Henry is the font of most great English sexual and romantic traditions (see Footnotes) and one of the most decisive and impressive of all royal rogerers. The Zsa Zsa Gabor of the sixteenth century, he got through six wives[1] and numerous other lovers, divorcing some, abandoning others and cutting off the heads of the rest.[2]

He was thought of as being good-looking and clever in his time, and would have been a pleasant surprise to Catherine of Aragon in those days when you married who you married, no matter what they looked like. In fact, Catherine was probably a remarkably relaxed bride: the other great fear, not getting on with the groom's family, was also no worry to her:[3] she had already married Henry's brother, so she knew the score. However, after the initial euphoria, things didn't go well, and Henry began to sleep around[4]: amongst those he chose for his big Royal favours were Jane Popincourt,[5,6] a visitor from France, and Mary Boleyn, who had a pretty little sister.[7]

Eventually, poor Catherine failed to produce a male heir,[8] and Henry began the outrageous behavior that was to take up so much of his time in the years to come.[9] He left the Catholic Church, started a new one, and got himself a new bride.[10] The new bride was Mary's little sister, Anne Boleyn, but, like Catherine, she couldn't bear Henry a male heir and so, soon enough, he couldn't bear her either. She became rude and overbearing, people started calling her 'the goggle-eyed whore',[11] and before you could say 'Henry's an utter bastard', Thomas Cromwell had got 'evidence' together that she had been sleeping around, and she and her 'suitors' were executed.

Eleven days later, Henry married Jane Seymour, who at last gave him a son, but died in childbirth doing so. Next came Anne of Cleves, who was apparently unbelievably ugly, and then Catherine Howard, who was tried and executed for treason, the treason being rogering a subject.[12] So she got the chop, and finally Henry settled down with Catherine Parr. Sadly, however, it was all too late for his tired manhood, and he died of syphilis, alcoholism and bad temper, deeply resenting the amount of money that actors, writers and film producers were going to make out of his life story 400 years later.

FOOTNOTES

1 It is most certainly from Henry VIII that the British derived their abiding passion and lust for Royal Weddings. Were it not for the sense of rampant splendour and gay abandon with which Henry married almost everyone under forty that he met, it is likely Fergie and Andy would have had a quick registry wedding and popped off unannounced to the Falklands for their honeymoon.

2 Henry is the man who can be said to have started the now popular practice of rogering a woman with a bag over her head. Although, of course, instead of the rather tame bag arrangement, Henry actually cut the head off completely.

3 See Sylvester Stallone, and Appendix: Mothers' Page.

4 A sadly well established tradition.

5 This started the great tradition of the man of the house rogering the French au pair.

6 Jane had also been the mistress of François I of France, of whom it was said when he died, 'Ladies more than years, caused his death.' There was a strange correlation between sex and death in Tudor times: the peak of the sexual act was often represented by the word 'die' and dead people were often euphemistically described as being 'well': because they were in Heaven, with God, and therefore better off than on Earth.

   The resulting confusion was enormous. If you asked your mother at breakfast how your father was, and she replied, 'He is well', it meant that he was dead. On the other hand, if you asked how your father was, and she said 'He is dead', it meant that he was perfectly all right and had had sex before he went off to work. If you expressed surprise, saying, 'Dead?' and she replied impatiently, 'Yes, dead, dead, dead!!!', it meant that not only was he alive, but also at the peak of sexual fitness, still upstairs, relaxing after a three-fold pre-breakfast bout.

7 Another tradition: although he didn't sleep with her, our Prince Charles was a good friend of Princess Diana's sister before he started to cast the royal eye over young, fresh-faced Di herself.

8 See Ronald Reagan and Jane Wyman: 'All that time, Dutch, and only a girl'.

9 Another great English tradition, careers thrown down the drain worrying about love. See Byron, Edward VIII and Britt Ekland.

10 Again, another fundamental British tradition: using church to pick up girls, as many an eager chorister will tell you. Or using the church to pick up boys, as many an eager choirmaster will testify.

11 The tradition continues, although nowadays it is normally the men who look really grim, with puffy red eyes from the stag party and blood-spattered skin from the over-hasty shave in the car.

12 Catherine's answer at the trial to the accusation of rogering Thomas Dareham, is a testimony to the unchanging nature of the human spirit: anyone who has ever been accused of sexual infidelity, and been guilty, will recognize the confused logic behind this statement: 'Sometimes in his doublet and hose, and two or three times naked, but not so naked that he had nothing upon him, for he had always at least his doublet, and, as I do think, his hose also, but I mean naked when his hose were put down'.

HENRY VIII & CATHERINE PARR

This roger doesn't really bear thinking about. Medical records from the time show that when Henry married Catherine he was fat and arthritic and, having syphilitic ulcers, had to wear bandages around his suppurating legs. He was also an alcoholic and probably had malaria. If Catherine gave him a good time, she was quite a woman. And, of course, if he gave her a good time, he was quite a man.

CATHERINE PARR	
Born	**1512, in England.**
Occupation	**Wife and survivor.**
Distinguishing Features	**Outliving a marriage with Henry VIII.**
Romantically Linked With	**Henry VIII (m), Lord Seymour, two men who died (m) (m).**

When Catherine married Henry she was thirty-one. He had been widowed five times, and she had already been widowed twice. When Henry asked her to marry him, she screamed and begged to be his mistress. Despite her long hooked nose, she was fond enough of her own head not to let it go without some kind of struggle. However, his failing health and her own moral uprightness finally encouraged her to say 'Yes, all right, Hank, it's a deal' and they tied the happy knot at which both their hands were already relatively adept.

Four years later, she nursed him at his death, and calmly acquiesced to his final request that he be buried next to Jane Seymour, the wife he had really loved, 'The woman who died in order to give me a son.' Many will see in the touching story of her years a premonition of the final years of another great king.[1]

FOOTNOTES

1 See Clark Gable and his final wife, with Carole Lombard acting the demanding role of Jane Seymour.

CATHERINE PARR & LORD SEYMOUR

After the death of Henry, Catherine was still an attractive woman of under forty. Even if she had not been, the novelty of rogering someone who had been married to Henry VIII, and not being killed for it must have been quite irresistible: many had been the man who *hadn't* rogered someone married to Henry VIII, and still been killed. In the end Seymour asked to marry Catherine, and she thanked him for not having legs covered in sores, and for not looking like Keith Michell covered in BBC make-up, and agreed.

LORD SEYMOUR	
Born	1508, in England.
Occupation	Lord High Admiral and schemer.
Hobbies	Sailing and scheming.
Distinguishing Features	Brotherly hatred.
Romantically Linked With	Catherine Parr, Elizabeth I.

Almost everything that Thomas Seymour did in life was motivated by hatred for his brother, the Duke of Somerset, who, being a duke, was much more powerful than Thomas, who was a mere lord high admiral. Every day, Thomas woke up and thought to himself: 'God, I hate my brother.'[1]

In Tudor times there were many ways of grabbing power: the way that Thomas picked on was popular at the time, and very demanding: he decided to roger his way to the top of the tree.[2] First stop was Catherine Parr, who as Henry's widow still wielded some power. Unfortunately for Thomas, though, Catherine died a year after he married her, so he was forced to move on. Who to move on to was simple. Henry's non-Catholic heir was Princess Elizabeth and so Lord Seymour got to work on her.

The one drawback was that Elizabeth was only thirteen years old: but this did not stop the lord high admiral.[3] He and Elizabeth grew increasingly intimate but, as time passed, Thomas' brother still lorded it over him. So Thomas set his sights even higher than Elizabeth: he turned to King Edward himself. The problem was, Edward was a little boy, so rogering was out of the question[4]; and this is where Thomas made his big mistake. He turned from what he was good at, to something he hadn't tried before. He quit rogering and tried kidnapping. It was like Bjorn Borg trying to play snooker, or Diego Maradona having a go at presenting an afternoon television programme about country cooking. His plot was foiled and his head was off before he could say 'April Fool!' But his memory did live on. Elizabeth immediately disappeared, and rumours that she was pregnant by Seymour grew and grew. When she returned after six months, she loudly protested her innocence of the ugly rumour; it was generally considered that she protested a little too much.

FOOTNOTES

1 See Bobby and Jack Kennedy for another way of getting on with your brother.
2 The importance of rogering in the pursuit of power and influence cannot be under-estimated, particularly in the historical section of this book (for a modern example, see Eva Peron). It is worth stopping a while to look at the career of Philip II of Spain.

   Philip was a man who knew full well that the penis is mightier than the sword. He ruled Spain when Spain was at its greatest and he was obsessed by a desire to put Catholic rulers on all the thrones of Europe. He was also determined to use every roger of his life to that end.

   First, he rogered and married Maria of Portugal—and inherited Portugal. He then rogered and married Mary I of England, Elizabeth's sister, and inherited England.

   When Mary died and Elizabeth took over Philip simply tried to roger her instead.

   When he failed, he immediately turned his attention to rogering France in the person of Elizabeth of Valois, daughter of France's Henry II and by doing so he ended all wars between France and Spain for a generation. After that, it was Austria's turn to play host to Philip and his rogering: he soon married Anne of Austria, daughter of Emperor Maximillian XI and made Austria Catholic. Philip treated Catholicism as though it were some kind of sexual disease: as long as you rogered someone they would become or stay Catholic.

   And during his lifetime, he was right: through marriage he got Naples, Sicily and the Netherlands, too. For Philip, as for so many since, power was something you popped into your underpants.
3 The connection between sex and the sea has always been strong. Frank Sinatra says of making love:

> *Deeper than the deep blue sea is,*
> *That's how it's got to be*
> *If it's real.*

and many great lovers have been seafaring men: see Jack Kennedy; also Edward VIII, who first made love to Mrs Simpson on a sea-cruise, and Rod Stewart, who hasn't spent much time out at sea, but did have a huge hit with a song called 'Sailing', which is partly about the sea. See Appendix: Unusual Places to Roger.

4 Although, of course, being rogered by older men was soon, with the establishment of public schools, to become a crucial part of education for all male British aristocrats.

LORD SEYMOUR & ELIZABETH I

Any tale told about Elizabeth and sex must always remain a tale, because almost everyone involved died for it,[1] and those who didn't sure as hell weren't going to boast about it. But the tales that are told of Elizabeth and Seymour are of playful capering in the carefully cut gardens of Tudor England[2]: kisses stolen behind rose bushes, embraces in the shadows of great oaks, lip touching lip under the green curtain of the bending willow, hand touching breast amidst the lush foliage of the rhododendrons: and who knows what illicit delights deep in the heart of the mazes of Hampton Court.

ELIZABETH I

Born	**1533, in England.**
Occupation	**Queen.**
Hobbies	**Not rogering.**
Distinguishing Features	**Red hair, white face and big crown.**
Romantically Linked With	**Lord Seymour, Earl of Essex, Sir Robert Dudley, the Duke of Norfolk and Sir Walter Raleigh.[3]**
Nickname	**The Virgin Queen.**

The question of Elizabeth's virginity, or lack of it, is one of the most vexed questions in history. Many the learned scholar, accustomed to assessing the use and abuse of rotten boroughs, who has found himself slap bang diddle in the middle of a row over Elizabeth's virginity and been mightily vexed by it. Colleagues remember the tragic case of Dr Hadley of Nottingham University who, at his death, was discovered stark naked in bed with a Holbein portrait of Elizabeth I and a packet of contraceptives wedged tight into Trevelyan's *Kings and Queens of England*. We do not wish to get into such dangerous waters, but what follows is some of the evidence that leads us to believe that, in the court of the 'Virgin' Queen, Sir Roger was definitely one of the most favoured of courtiers.

1. At the start of her reign, Parliament tried to make Elizabeth marry: to no avail. But when presented with the assertion 'seeing your Majesty declares yourself resolved to die a virgin', Elizabeth replied: 'I am resolved never to marry'. A careful distinction.

2. After Lord Seymour, and the strong rumours about their sexual involvement and her possible confinement, she gave Sir William Pickering rooms in her palace so they could have 'long conversations'[4]: it then became a habit to install her favourite courtiers in the palace. Most notable of all was Sir Robert Dudley.

3. The French Ambassador was one of the many convinced she and Dudley were lovers: he actually picked out a definite day when they rogered: New Year's Night, 1565: and when one considers the awful New Year's Night indiscretions we all harbour, it seems pretty likely he was right. Most Englishmen were convinced as well: 'Lord Robert doth swive[5] the Queen' said the crowds of Totnes. Elizabeth was certainly known to visit his rooms late and long and eventually his wife was found dead at the bottom of the stairs when the servants had been given a day off: and what would Hercule Poirot have made of that?[6]

4. When Elizabeth was again pressed to marry, again she refused with the interesting qualification: 'I am no angel'.

5. Finally there was the Earl of Essex. Contemporary reports speak of how after visits to the Queen the Earl of Essex 'cometh not to his lodging till the birds sing in the morning.' Essex, however, lost Elizabeth's favour, and was executed. In her condemnation, she said, 'I put up with much disrespect to my person,[7] but I warned him that he should not touch my sceptre'.

In short, Elizabeth seems to have done as she pleased, as long as she stuck to her firm determination to stay single. England's 'Virgin' Queen was really just England's unmarried Queen. And it is no wonder that marriage didn't appeal. Her mother and her stepmother both had their heads cut off, and then the first man who expressed a desire to marry her had his cut off too.

Politically, however, not marrying was the best move Elizabeth ever made. For the rest of her life, all other business in European diplomacy was put in the pending tray while *everyone* tried to marry Elizabeth. Most of the English court spent most of its time explaining to exasperated foreigners why the Queen wasn't keen to tie the knot with their favoured Luigi, Pierre or Sven. Philip II of Spain asked for her hand. So did Charles IX, Henry III of France, Eric XIV of Sweden, and the Duke of Savoy: the Duc D'Alençon she kept hanging on a string from 1558 to 1583, writing him lovey-dovey letters, addressing him affectionately as Dearest Frog, but never actually shoving on the whites and getting down that aisle.[8] Meanwhile, she collected the most massive number of presents—another good reason for not marrying (apparently the King of Sweden she fleeced particularly rotten[9])—and England's power grew ever greater.

By the end of her life, Elizabeth was no longer much of a looker[10]—her striking pale, aquiline features and red golden hair now giving way to half an inch of make-up and quite a few inches of baldness—but her power was unabated. As she had promised from the first, she had never married and never given birth—but her marriage to her kingdom had certainly born fruit.

FOOTNOTES

1 In fact, Elizabeth's lovers are one of the few examples of men giving head in history. You made love to her, and then gave her your head.

2 Making love in gardens has always been a romantic idea, indulged in by few because of the practical difficulties and obvious discomforts. As with unconventional rogering sites indoors the crucial thing is to come prepared. If possible, when intending to make love in the great outdoors, wear a thick fur coat, which can double as a rug later. If this is not possible, and your partner points out that a large fur coat is odd clothing for a summer's day, then try to let your passion strike when near an item of garden furniture, the cushion from which can be neatly popped into place at the crucial moment. If there is no garden furniture about— if you are for instance in a municipal park—then all you can do is make sure, when it comes down to it, that you are on top: let your loving partner be the one to end with grass stains on his/her shoulders, bee stings on his/her thighs, mud in his/her hair and quite a few daisies up his, or her, delightful behind.

3 Raleigh is himself a very important figure in the history of rogering because of his introduction of tobacco into English society. Since then, the cigarette has become one of the most important of erotic tools. Seduction by cigarette is one of the most tried, tested and effective means of attaining a roger. The steps are simple:

    a Offer, or ask for, a light.
    b Smoke the lit cigarette.
    c Run out of cigarettes.
    d Go to the room to find some more cigarettes.
    e Have sex in the room.
    f After it, light another cigarette.

Cigarettes have had a lot of bad press recently, people saying how awful it is to kiss someone who has been smoking heavily. But as with so many things, it is all a question of training and experience. Many is the man who, first having been in love with a heavy smoker, finds any kiss without the tang of nicotine, any passionate embrace which does not end with a little exhalation of smoke, a grave disappointment.

4 See Appendix: Names for Rogering.

5 See Appendix: Names for Rogering.

6 Robert tried very hard to get Elizabeth to marry him: but eventually in exasperation decided to marry a certain Lettice Knollys, Viscountess Hereford*. When Elizabeth found out, she was distraught, and she and Robert were united in tears: she stayed faithful and loving then until his death.

7 See Appendix: Names for Rogering.

8 This poor Frenchman's ordeal is an example to those today who complain if someone doesn't roger them after twenty-five minutes, let alone twenty-five years. The Duc does, for all his failure, sound a pleasant cove: someone wrote sweetly of him: 'The pock marks are no great disfigurement. They upon the blunt end of his nose are great and deep'. Maybe another reason for Elizabeth holding off.

9 Many historians see Bjorn Borg's five-year reign at Wimbledon as some kind of revenge for this slight on Sweden's manhood.

10 She *had* been cute:

> *'Her bosom sleek as Paris plaster,*
> *Held two balls of alabaster'.*

Rogering vegetables. The idea of sleeping with a vegetable is not as unusual as might be thought. The Ancient Greeks had a word 'raphanidoo'—meaning 'I thrust a radish up the behind.' This was, however, not an act of love, but is believed to have been a form of torture used to extract information from survivors of the disastrous Athenian expedition against Syracuse in the fifth century BC.

Recent investigations by Cambridge scholar P. Bennett-Jones have cast some doubting light over this 'torture' theory: either radishes must have been a lot larger, or the Greeks were kidding themselves. After conducting practical experiments with radishes under controlled conditions in the Escargot Restaurant, Greek Street, and a villa in Valbonne, South of France, Jones claims to have undergone no lasting pain or damage other than a psychological one. He has, however, been asked not to return to the Escargot, which is, in its way, a form of torture.

ELIZABETH I & THE DUKE OF NORFOLK

Elizabeth's lovers fell into two categories: those who talked and those who didn't talk. Those who talked had their heads cut off. Those who didn't, didn't. Norfolk didn't and so didn't . . .

DUKE OF NORFOLK

Born	**1536, in England.**
Occupation	**Duking.**
Hobbies	**Not duking.**
Romantically Linked With	**Elizabeth I, Mary, Queen of Scots.**
Nickname	**The Duke.**

The Duke of Norfolk must have been a very brave man indeed to roger the two most dangerous sisters in Christendom. Of Elizabeth's lovers, most were executed. Of Mary's all but one were murdered. To roger one might be considered carelessness: to roger two seems the height of foolishness. Perhaps the Duke just wished to commit suicide, and chose a rather peculiar way about it. Suffice it to say, Norfolk can be proud of him, as one of its bravest sons, a bravery which still continues to this day: Lady Carina FitzAllen Howard, daughter of the current Duke, recently married David Frost.

THE DUKE OF NORFOLK & MARY, QUEEN OF SCOTS

Mary was a famous beauty, and a composite princess. She loved dancing (see Princess Diana), hunting (see Princess Anne), and was famous for her red-haired, amber-eyed beauty (see Princess Fergie). As for him, he was pleasingly old-fashioned (see Prince Charles), keen on horses (see Mark Phillips), and was famous for his loud raucous laughter and wide jaw (see Prince Andrew). It is no wonder their relationship developed past the simple Sir–Milady.

MARY, QUEEN OF SCOTS

Born	**1542, in Scotland.**
Occupation	**Queen, almost.**
Hobbies	**Trying to be Queen.**
Romantically Linked With	**Francis of France (m), the Earl of Darnley (m), David Rizzio, Earl of Bothwell (m).**
Nickname	**Scottie.**

Mary was a dangerous woman to love. One of her lovers was killed once, and one of them was actually killed twice. Another died before anyone could get to him.

The problem with Mary's life started because people—mainly Catholics—thought she should be Queen of England instead of Elizabeth. These people encouraged Mary to knock Elizabeth off the throne and she took their advice, and returned to Scotland to set about becoming Queen. Unfortunately for her, by this time Scotland had become Protestant and she didn't get the support she needed. Meanwhile, back in France, her husband, Francis, died, and Mary, disappointed and unhappy, decided she would cheer herself up by marrying someone she loved. The man in question was Henry Stuart, the Earl of Darnley, a 'tall, girlish youth, the properest and best-proportioned man she had ever seen'. Their love, however, did not last for long, and she soon started rogering her secretary, David Rizzio. Rizzio was summarily murdered by Darnley. At a loose end again, Mary began an adulterous affair with James Hepburn, Earl of Bothwell, and many feared for his life. However things turned out unexpectedly. Bothwell survived: and it was Darnley who got murdered. Twice. He was strangled, and then his house was blown up.

After these caperings Mary married Bothwell, but a year later they separated and Mary fled to England. Unwisely. Elizabeth had her captured, and she was imprisoned for eighteen years for attempting a rebellion. Her prison was Kenilworth Castle, home of Robert Dudley, Elizabeth's former lover, and it is said that Elizabeth at one stage wanted Dudley to marry Mary. He, quite rightly, resisted.

PRAYING MANTIS LAY LINE

HENRY VIII

CATHERINE PARR

LORD SEYMOUR

ELIZABETH I

DUKE OF NORFOLK

MARY, QUEEN OF SCOTS

Their Motto: 'Love and Death, What's the Odds?'

THE QUEENS

FROM	**ELIZABETH I**
TO	**JAMES I**
IN	**8 ROGERS**

Rogering in these years seems to go mad: the idea of killing off everyone as soon as you'd rogered them is going slightly out of fashion, but all sorts of craziness is coming in its place. The Queens Line rushes from someone who claimed to roger no one to someone who seemed to roger everyone. Through poison and deprivation, through beheading and voodoo, through tiny willies and huge libidos, through nymphomaniac virgins and utter non-entities, the line sweeps to its decadent conclusion in the court of King James. For fifty years here, rogering is a wild and dangerous toy.

ELIZABETH I

Of Elizabeth, much has been written in the last chapter. Suffice it to say that now we meet her again she is over fifty, bright white, with red hair reddened with every available reddener. But despite a slight lack of lustre she is still the most important and powerful and magnetic woman in the kingdom: she has stopped being Elizabeth Taylor, but she is now Joan Collins: and like Joan Collins, young men keep making passes at her. The most famous of them all is the Earl of Essex.

ELIZABETH & THE EARL OF ESSEX[1,2]

Like all Elizabeth's liaisons, the private details are shrouded in mystery. The public affair was, however, a sensation. Essex catapulted to fame as Elizabeth's favourite of favourites, bearded the Spanish on her behalf, strutted like a peacock through her court, and then just as suddenly went to Ireland, fell from favour, and was beheaded, accused of threatening to overthrow the kingdom. It was said by some that Elizabeth's heart was broken by his death. For all that, the wound was less obvious to the naked eye than the one she inflicted on him.[3]

2nd EARL OF ESSEX

Born	**1567, in England.**
Occupation	**Sea captain, glamour boy, earl.**
Hobbies	**Plotting and rogering and strutting.**
Distinguishing Features	**The Queen's ring on his hand and no head.**
Romantically Linked With	**Elizabeth I, Penelope Devereux.**

The Queen had always had a soft spot for wild sea rovers, and Essex was the most glamorous of them all. His daring exploits at sea excited her, his rudeness and wit at court excited her, his youth excited her, and the fact that he was from Essex was nothing to be sneezed at. Also, she loved the fact he hated the Spanish.[4] Unfortunately, his daring by sea was not reflected in his skill on land. His expedition to Ireland was a disaster, and his march home was construed or misconstrued as a march against Elizabeth herself; she arrested him, imprisoned him and cut off his head. Nothing was heard from him after that.[5,6]

FOOTNOTES

1 There are two Earls of Essex in this line. For a while, here, just to come from Essex was enough to ensure sexual success.*

2 An excellent Hollywood film, called *Elizabeth and Essex*, was made about the relationship between these two: it starred the ever gallant and glamorous Errol Flynn, and the daringly ugly Bette Davis and was directed by the Hungarian Michael Curtiz. For the story of Michael and how he lost his head see Orson Welles.

3 Very few first-hand records survive about the actual measure of pain experienced by those beheaded—for obvious reasons. The only remaining source, left in the diaries of Roger the Liar of Twickenham, can almost certainly be discounted: 'And after that the noble Essex was beheaded, those that pressed near unto the execution did see the head to roll into the appointed basket. But sitting there it closed not its eyes, but seemed still to stare, and left itself open for converse. And Roger the Truthteller, that is to say, I, did ask of it what feeling there was when the head was severed from the body. And the head did reply, "I must be honest with thee, Rog, it hurt like hell . . ." And thereafter conversation made it none'.

4 It is generally held that the British dislike for the Spanish was superseded and replaced by a hatred for the French. This is not true. Cunning plans hatched in the later years of Elizabeth's reign have come firmly to fruition in the reign of Elizabeth II. The seaports of Spain, always Spain's strongest bulwarks, have for ten years now been steadily attacked by some of Britain's most highly trained and cunning military forces. Talking in loud voices, wearing bright red noses and sun cream as their uniform, these shock troops have launched a form of psychological and chemical warfare that is a flagrant violation of all international law. The fumes from beer and regurgitated fish and chips have begun now to break down the physical well-being of the Spaniards: and the psychological wear and tear from having to be polite to these loud, fat monsters is slowly breaking down the morale of the once great Hispanic race. While blaring transistors destroy the Spanish culture to the strains of the 'Chicken Song', England's long overdue revenge for the Armada continues its frightening success. Only recently have the Spaniards seen this invasion for what it is, war, and started planting bombs in hotels in retaliation.

5 Again, presuming that the evidence of Roger the Liar is discounted. Passages such as this one, which immediately follows the section quoted above, prove that it should be: 'After leaving the talking head, I did wend my way homewards, but was soon stopped upon my way by a curious gentleman. Most careless was he of his path, and knocking into men said nought in apology. I challenged him, saying, "Sir, upon my life, apologize or thou diest." The curious fellow said nought, but continued on his path. I pursued him, stopped him once more, and would have looked him in the eye and spoken my mind were it not for the realizing, at that very moment, that he had no eyes, nor indeed any head, but was the very body of Essex himself, wandering around looking for his head, capable of neither speech, nor hearing, nor witty discourse without it. I thought to aid him, and take him to where the head was sat. But then, bethinking me of my wife, Mary, who would most surely be vexed at my not returning, I slipped away, and thought no more about it. I later did tell this tale to a close acquaintance who said he had heard tell of a man with no head who had set himself up as a butcher in Bermondsey, but after cutting off both his hands had retired to less vexing employment.'

6 The beheading of one's loved one does in fact have a gruesome parallel in the animal kingdom. Turkish soldiers, who used to gain their early experiences with chickens, were known to tear off the head of the chicken at the moment of orgasm, as this contracted the chicken and caused extra sensual satisfaction. Slightly alarmingly, a young man known to the editors was recently working in a chicken packing factory, and recounting this story asked, humorously as he took it, whether they had a serious problem in the factory with men rogering the dead chickens. The foreman replied gravely, 'Well, it's not too bad these days.'

*A similar phenomenon occurred with regard to Liverpool in the early 1960s, when just a shade of Merseyside accent meant a week in bed with the girl of your choice.

ESSEX & PENELOPE DEVEREUX

Like Elizabeth, Penelope was noticeably older than Essex, but this did not worry popular opinion.[1] On the other hand, the fact she was his aunt did raise the odd Tudor eyebrow.[2]

PENELOPE DEVEREUX	
Occupation	Aunt.
Distinguishing Features	Important man in her.
Romantically Linked With	The 2nd Earl of Essex, Charles Blount, Duke of Devonshire, Sir Philip Sydney, Lord Rich.
Nickname	Darling, Auntie, and Darling Auntie.

Penelope Devereux is, as so many women of her time, something of a mystery. This is not a coincidence, or chance. Queen Elizabeth's desire for glory, and her desire that all men should desire her, was such that other women were unwise who attempted to attract attention. The cult of Elizabeth reached absurd degrees. It was, for instance, fashionable for ladies to imitate her by dyeing their hair the same colour as their sovereign, and arranging it like hers.[3] No competition with the Queen was allowed, women were not allowed on stage, since the passion of men for actresses was well known,[4] and the Queen wanted all passion herself. Penelope Devereux was one of the wise ones who melted into the background, did a bit of rogering here and there, and then died.

FOOTNOTES

1 Nor does it nowadays: see Ryan O'Neal and Oona Chaplin.

2 This century's great expert on aunts, P.G. Wodehouse, never expressed any particular view about rogering them, the desirability or undesirability thereof. Social scientists and anthropologists, however, observe that it is generally a good idea: finding something to say to one's aunt if one does *not* roger her is so difficult, and places such a strain upon inter-family relationships, that it is best for the structure of society as we know it to roger the aunt and deepen the bond, rather than risk the disillusionment and annoyances of conversation. It is argued that, without a noticeable percentage increase in aunt/nephew rogering, this important relationship will have ceased to exist by the turn of the century—it has recently only survived because of what is known as the Christmas Gift Factor.

3 The fact that everyone in the court looked exactly like Elizabeth was something which made it easier for the Queen to practice her own indiscretions. For a mistaken identity roger—see Warren Beatty and Carol White.

4 See *passim*: from Sarah Bernhardt and Lillie Langtry to Joan Crawford and Britt Ekland.

PENELOPE DEVEREUX & CHARLES BLOUNT

Just as women disguised themselves as Elizabeth, so it was fashionable for men to disguise themselves as Lord Essex. It is therefore the inescapable conclusion that this particular coupling took place under completely false pretences—he thought she was the Queen, she thought he was Lord Essex. Both regretted it deeply, it was all a ghastly mistake.

CHARLES BLOUNT, DUKE OF DEVONSHIRE	
Distinguishing Features	**None.**[1]

Charles Blount forms a strange and interesting link in the peculiar patterns of this lay line by being a man who is not famous and not from Essex, as is clear from his name—'Devonshire'. When it came to lust, in the end, like everyone else, the Elizabethans did not discriminate.[2]

FOOTNOTES

1 See Des O'Connor.
2 See Peter Hamill for rogering non-entities.

THE DUKE OF DEVONSHIRE & ELIZABETH PAULET

Elizabeth Paulet was a very secretive woman who had a real penchant for rogering non-entities. She was very fortunate in finding in the Duke of Devonshire another secretive non-entity, with exactly the same taste. Nothing is known of them or their coupling.

ELIZABETH PAULET	
Romantically Linked With	**Robert Devereux, 3rd Earl of Essex.**
Otherwise Linked With	**Charles Blount, Duke of Devonshire.**
Tragically Linked With	**Robert Devereux, 3rd Earl of Essex.**

ELIZABETH PAULET & ROBERT DEVEREUX, 3rd EARL OF ESSEX

This was a tragic roger. As a result of it, Elizabeth became pregnant. Devereux on hearing said that if the child was born before the 5th of November, it was his. If it was born after the 5th of November, it was not. The child was born on the 5th of November, Elizabeth died and, tragically, Robert never found out whose child it was. If he had known the troubles he was to have in the future, he might well have wished he had died at the same time.

ROBERT DEVEREUX, 3rd EARL OF ESSEX

Born	**1591, in Essex.**
Occupation	**Student, soldier.**
Hobbies	**Drinking, talking with men and not much rogering, but a bit.**
Distinguishing Features	**Large pair of horns emerging from head shortly after marriage.**
Romantically Linked With	**Frances Howard (m), Elizabeth Paulet.**

Robert Devereux, 3rd Earl of Essex, did not have an easy marriage. It did not, for instance, go as well as the relationship that the 2nd Earl had with Elizabeth I, and that one ended with the Earl having his head cut off.

This is the tale. On the day Robert married his wife, Frances Howard, he had to get straight back to Oxford to finish his MA.[1] That was a mistake, because, after finishing at Oxford, he went abroad soldiering, and when he returned two years later, he discovered his beautiful wife enjoying the charms of others at the court of King James. He begged her to come back to Essex with him, but she refused[2] and it took an appeal to her very powerful father to get her home.

At this point the story splits in two, her version, and his version. The reason for the difference is because Frances soon decided that she wanted to divorce Robert, and marry Robert Carr, the Master of the King's Bedchamber: and the only grounds on which she could sue for divorce were that the marriage had never been consummated. So while Essex claimed that they had been home and rogered, Frances claimed that throughout the marriage Robert never laid hands on her, and she was still virgo intacta. It was up to the court to decide who was telling the truth.

And so the trial began. If Frances was to get the divorce, she had to prove that the Earl had not had 'affection, erection, application,[3] penetration, ejaculation and amplification' of his sexual parts during the marriage.

Part one of the proof was to show that Frances was still virgo intacta. This was proved when Frances insisted on wearing a veil to preserve her modesty during inspection, and substituted a real virgin in her place.

Next, however, to add insult to injury, she started to argue that even if she had been willing, her husband had not the wherewithal: in the highest court of the land, she produced her trump card and insisted that Essex had a tiny willy.[4,5] He rebutted this by showing a full erection to 'five or six gents'.[6] The nation waited with bated breath to find out the truth.

But in the end, as so often happens in the law, they never did. The court was rigged. James wanted his favourite Carr to have his desire, his desire was Frances Howard, and so poor Essex found himself condemned for having a tiny willy and never rogering his wife.

While the real truth is that if he hadn't rogered her, this line would stop here: and it doesn't.

FOOTNOTES

1 A most stern rebuttal here of the claim that nothing ever changes. Nowadays, most intelligent students sacrifice good results in university exams in order to get laid. Here is a man who sacrificed getting laid in order to get good results. Such a scoundrel would now be hounded out of university.

2 Even in those days there wasn't anything worth doing in Essex.

3 'Application'—apply for permission to do all the other things.

4 See Edward VIII and Napoleon.

5 Do not see Rasputin, Jimi Hendrix, John Bindon or Frank Sinatra.

6 Proofreader's Note: The original version of this text here reads: "by shoving an erection in 'five or six gents' ". This is surely a misprint.

ROBERT DEVEREUX, 3rd EARL OF ESSEX & FRANCES HOWARD

The truth was that the marriage *had* been consummated,[1] although Frances was spectacularly unkeen that it should be so. After locking herself in her room for weeks to avoid her husband she was at last forced out, and rogered, but was so disgusted that she resorted to witchcraft to reduce her husband's passions. As was later revealed—'No linen came near his body that was not rinsed with camphire compositions and other faint and wasting ingredients and all inward applications were foisted on him by corrupted servants to lessen and debilitate his seminal operation.' When, despite all this, Essex continued to claim his husbandly rites, Frances complained to her witch, asking for her money back—'My lord is lusty and merry and drinketh with his men and all the content he gives me is to abuse me and use me as doggedly as before.'

So Essex, seeing as how his bedclothes and Horlicks were full of poison, turned out to have quite the opposite of a tiny and unimpressive willy. He must have had one of the most resilient swords in history. But even that could do nothing about Frances' final stroke. She went the whole hog and 'got an artifice too immodest to be expressed, to hinder penetration'.[2] So Essex turns out to have been rather hard done by—but Frances appears in the annals of history as one of the first, full-steam-ahead feminists. Good on them both, really.

FRANCES HOWARD, LADY ESSEX	
Occupation	**Trying to roger the man she loved.**
Hobbies	**Doing anything, absolutely anything, to make sure she did.**
Distinguishing Features	**Lies in mouth, poison in hand.**
Romantically Linked With	**Robert Carr, Robert Devereux.**
Nickname	**Fanny.**

Fanny's two uncles were called 'Good Thomas' and 'Bold Willie', suggesting that it was perhaps in the family to be keen on rogering. Certainly she was keen on it—her problem was that she was only keen on it with a man she wasn't married to and she was willing to kill, murder, bewitch and betray in order to get her way.

When Fanny arrived at court, while her husband was away soldiering, she gained a reputation for being 'lustful of appetite, prodigal of expense and light of behaviour'. And since this was the most lustful, prodigal and light English court ever, that means she was *pretty damn* lustful, prodigal and light. She also fell in love with Robert Carr, and after that her life was dedicated to gaining her desire. How she got on once she got it is the story of the next roger.

FOOTNOTES

1 A most curious coincidence raises its head here. The present Managing Director of Virgin Films is also a gentleman called, most strangely, Robert Devereux. Thus, as the ancestor was almost destroyed by someone who claimed to be a virgin, so his descendent, by the curious whirligig of time, is now making a living out of Virgins. The question as to whether Virgin Films is—unlike Frances Howard—really a virgin amongst film companies, innocent, fresh and incapable of deceit, is not one that can be answered here.

2 See Appendix: Great Rogering Excuses.

FRANCES HOWARD & ROBERT CARR[1]

Well, the sad truth is that the course of true love rarely runs smooth and even after Essex had lost his court case and been shunted back to his estate, Robert and Frances had problems.

Robert had a friend named Thomas Overbury, who had written Robert's letter to Frances when first they were a-wooing and became a confidant of the pair. Later, however, he fell out with Frances and to punish him she had him popped in the Tower on trumped up charges. But that wasn't enough for her, because Thomas, being a confidant, had inklings and hints of knowledge about Frances' dabbling with witchcraft and she was keen the story shouldn't get out. So she used a little simple witchcraft. She had him poisoned. Overbury had the distinction of being the first person since the little princes to die in the Tower 'by mistake'.

So it should all have been sorted out, and at last the path should have been clear for the true love of Robert and Frances to blossom: they could now spend the rest of their lives together. Unfortunately, they did, because before you could say 'arsenic', they were found out for the killers that they were and sentenced to house arrest for life.

ROBERT CARR[2]	
Born	**1586, in England.**
Occupation	**Gentleman of the King's Bedchamber and poisoner and prisoner.**
Hobbies	**Rogering his way to the top. And then rogering right back down again.**
Romantically Linked With	**James I, Frances Howard.**

Carr first came to the King's attention by falling off his horse and breaking his bones in front of him. The King was overcome with sympathy,[3] and tended the bones personally. After that, Carr became one of the 'young men that lie in his (James I) chamber and are his minions'. He was very handsome, liked it both ways, and was rewarded with the position of Gentleman of the Bedchamber by the King. James gave him Walter Raleigh's estates, depriving Raleigh's descendants of their birthright[4] and shutting the great sailor up in the Tower.

He then made Carr Viscount Rochester and finally Earl of Somerset. If Carr had played his cards right, heaven knows where he might have ended up. He didn't however, but instead got involved in all the terrible business with Frances Howard and ended up condemned to house arrest for life. It was a sad end to a career which, except for the bore of acting as the King's alarm clock every morning, could have been most glorious. After the house arrest began, the grieving King never saw him again.

FOOTNOTES

1 An incidental and accidental outcome of this relationship was the boost it gave to the popularity of anagrams in the court, when it was discovered that Frances Howard (or Francis Howarde) was, anagramatically, Carr Finds a Whore.
2 Not to be confused with the prominent minister in Edward Heath's cabinet. That Mr Carr never, to our knowledge, slept with a witch or had sex with a King or poisoned a close personal friend who'd written love letters to his mistress. If he had done Mr Heath might not have lost the election in 1974—all the public wanted was for him and his team to be a *little less dull.*
3 See Appendix: Names for Rogering.
4 The descendants did, however, rally as one would expect. Retaining their basic family interest in travel, they developed, from the simplest of workshops, the Raleigh bicycle, which is now, like their great ancestor, a world beater.

ROBERT CARR & JAMES THE FIRST

A contemporary diarist writes: the King 'leaneth on his arm, pinches his cheek, smoothes his ruffled garment'. This roger was presumably what ruffled the garment in the first place.

JAMES I	
Born	**1570, in Scotland.**
Occupation	**King.**
Hobby	**Men.**
Distinguishing Features	**Quite a pretty crown.**
Romantically Linked With	**Robert Carr, George Villiers, Esme Stuart, Patrick Master of Gray, George Gordon, Earl of Huntley, Francis Stuart, Earl of Bothwell, Lord Henry Howard, James Hay, Earl Montgomery and Anne of Denmark (m).[1]**

Before he was James I of England, James was James VI of Scotland, and before he was James VI of Scotland, he was subjected to a peculiarly Scottish training period for kingship[2]—heads rolling all around him, intrigues, religious confusion, men in kilts and occasionally men without them. In fact, confusion was the very key note of James' upbringing. To be both James I and James VI was bad enough, but to have both a mother and an aunt who claimed to be queen of the same place was really confusing. To add to that, his mother had murdered his father, which is always tricky for a lad. And then James was pressed into the company of men as a boy, as a result of which, he was rogered by Esme Stuart, Duke of Lennox and ex-boyfriend of Henry III of France. It really is no wonder James grew up confused.

But having been confused, James was not slow to take advantage of it. When negotiations were proceeding to make him King of England, he rogered the man in charge of them, Lord Henry Howard—and became King. He then married Anne of Denmark, and was sufficiently confused to make passionate love to her for six months and get himself some male heirs. After which, he returned to the male rogers and although he was 'fat, stank of sweat, had spindly legs, a lolling head, rolling eyes, a dirty sense of humour, was pedantic, noisy, maudlin, ill and irritable,' he managed to procure himself most of the most beautiful men in the country as lovers—so perhaps, in fact, he wasn't that confused after all.

FOOTNOTES

1 Competition time: spot the odd one out in this list of rogers*.
2 Prince Charles was educated at Gordonstoun to get just this kind of experience.

*The odd one out is Anne of Denmark, who is the only person not from the British Isles.

THE QUEENS LAY LINE

ELIZABETH I

2nd EARL OF ESSEX

PENELOPE DEVEREUX

CHARLES BLOUNT

ELIZABETH PAULET

ROBERT DEVEREUX

FRANCES HOWARD

ROBERT CARR

JAMES I

It should perhaps be noted that if things look pretty ropey in England, they were no better across the sea. Italy had just been through a century of the Borgias, who make our line look like sweet schoolchildren. And Spain was, apart from its Catholic-spermed King, bound in by the chastity belt of the Church. All said and done, it wasn't bad being English. And the line through the Royal Family continues, strong and sexual . . .

THE MERRY GANG

FROM	**JAMES I**
TO	**CHARLES II**
IN	**5 ROGERS**

And now, at last, rogering starts to be fun. When people talk of it, it is no longer the cause of frightened and fatal rumour, but of bawdy high spirits. Passions are still high, but they have started to take a comic turn. 'Merry' is the word for it, and so we call this group the Merry Gang. Although a Civil War comes and goes in between, it looks like nothing is going to stop the good times, and now, when heads are cut off, it's normally for good old political reasons.

31

JAMES I, KING OF ENGLAND

At the start of this new line, it is time to cast away all James' early traumas, the murdered fathers and imprisoned mothers, and concentrate on the lighter side of life. For James ruled over one of the most licentious and libidinous of English courts. He was centre of all that was scandalous in the land. The modern equivalent might be Prince Philip running the Heaven discotheque and hanging around there having his pick of the boys, while the Queen was merrily indulging in troilism with Vicki Hodge and George Michael.

James was, however, at the same time a man of taste: it was James who commissioned and saw through the Authorised Version of the English Bible, the most perfect book in our language.[1] He also loved and understood his people: it was James who encouraged the Gunpowder Plot by persecuting the Puritans, and thus instituted Guy Fawkes Day, one of the country's most popular holidays.

FOOTNOTE

1 In fact, the Bible had become less perfect by the time Charles was on the throne. The King was forced to fine printers Barker and Lucas £1,000 for leaving a vital word out of their edition. It was one word in Exodus 20.14. The Barker and Lucas version read: 'Thou shalt commit adultery'.

JAMES I & GEORGE VILLIERS

George was the most consistent and most adored of James' favourites, and stayed high in his affections until the King died. So bound together in love were they that when Villiers married Katherine Manners the King was delighted: he just hoped that George could happily carry the burden of the two

marriages, one to Katherine and one to himself. He was also positively pleased, praying that the union of Villiers and his wife would yield 'sweet bedchamber boys to play with me'.[1] There is no doubt that poor Edward II, whose relationship with Piers Gaveston was rewarded by death for Piers and a red hot poker up the bottom for himself, would have been jealous of the ease and open affection allowed in the Merry Court of King James.

GEORGE VILLIERS, DUKE OF BUCKINGHAM

Born	**1592, in England.**
Occupation	**Rogering his way to power.**
Hobby	**Scrubbing his face.**
Distinguishing Features	**Shiny face.**
Romantically Linked With	**James I, Katherine Manners, the Countess of Shrewsbury.**
Nickname	**Steenie.**

When the power brokers of England realized which way the wind was blowing in relation to James' sexual preferences, there was a rush amongst powerful people in the land to put up favourites who the King would fall for, and so represent their interests at court. George Villiers was by far the most successful of these: he stayed in the King's favour longer than any others, and by his efforts gained hereditary peerages for his family and his friends till his death and beyond[2]: in the end his own power was much greater than that of the syndicate, headed by the Archbishop of Canterbury, which put him forward.

George had chestnut hair, was tall, and, most of all, had a brilliant complexion. The importance of this complexion cannot be underestimated.[3] The King thought George resembled Saint Stephen who in the Bible is described as having a face which glowed 'as if it were the face of an angel'.[4] Why the King called him Steenie and not Angelface is a mystery. When rival groups saw the success of the Archbishop's exotic piece of pimping, competition began with renewed vigour. James found himself scarcely able to move down the corridors of power for hundreds of primping pretties parading for his pleasures. Most enthusiastic in competition was Lady Suffolk who was so keen to outdo Villiers that she took her favourites and 'washed their faces with curd posset to make them shine like Villiers'. But it was to no avail. Villiers and his peachy cheeks were there for good.

What was impressive about him, though, was that he was not just a pretty face. He became a useful adviser to James, and when James died, it was Villiers who ushered in the reign of Charles I, to whom he had always been very close. There were even rumours of rogering, but, in the mood of the times, that was really neither here nor there.

FOOTNOTES

1 There might be some who would be somewhat alarmed by the suggestion here, that George and Katherine would bring up sterling sons only to have the living daylights rogered out of them by the King. In fact the idea is not as strange as it sounds. The modern idea of the responsibilities of friends, best summed up in the tradition of godparents, is relatively recent and very Victorian. It was formerly assumed that parents could be trusted to teach their children about God, and bring them up in the ways of virtue: it was the responsibility of good friends of the parents to introduce the children to the seedier sides of life. In the eighteenth century, the first trip to the brothel, the first taste of opium, the first bit of casual killing were all the duty of the best friend of the father. If anyone should want to persevere with this tradition, rather than the more moralistic one now in practice, this revised version of the baptism service may be of some help:

The Priest shall take the child in his arms, and speak unto the Godfathers and Godmothers in this wise:
> *Dearly beloved, after the promise made by Christ, this infant must also faithfully, for his part, promise by you that are his sureties that he will renounce the Devil and all his works, and constantly believe God's Holy Word, and obediently keep his Commandments. I demand therefore, dost thou, in the name of this child, renounce the Devil and all his works, the vain pomp and glory of the world, with all the covetous desires of the same, and the carnal desires of the flesh, so that thou wilt not follow nor be led by them?*

And the Godfather and Godmother shall reply:
> *Thou must be joking.*

And the Priest shall look taken aback and say unto them:
> *No. Why?*

And they shall reply in the sight of God, and of the congregation:
> *Because we have no intention of renouncing the Devil and the lovely carnal desires of the flesh.*

And the priest shall regain his composure and inquire:
> *But the child. Shalt thou not shield and protect him from them?*

And they shall answer, in a loud voice, like unto shouting:
> *Certainly not: we shall introduce him to them.*

And the Priest shall press them, saying:
> *Could you be more specific please.*

And they shall reply in this form, or in a form that close resembles it:
> *Yea. We shall take the child before his maturity to the place where much bawdy is made. And there shall there be much drinking, and spewing and singing of lewd songs that shall take the Lord's name in vain. Then to the cockpit shall we convey the child, as a Lamb to the Slaughter, and there Gamble all the money that has been left unto him, and lose it. Then shall we proceed by way of the Opium Den unto the House of Bawdy, and there Dilly and Dally with Whores and Women of Easy Virtue and Great Skill till early morning, when, covered in Tobacco and Liquor and the Juices of Love we shall return him to the bosom of the family.*

(If that the child be a girl, then shall 'him' be 'her' and 'The House of Bawdy' be 'A Den of Eunuchs'.)

And then shall the Priest bless them saying:
> *May the Lord bless you and preserve you and love you, and grant you peace on Earth, and in Heaven, eternal life.*

And the Godparents shall reply as one:
> *Some hope.*

2 It is perhaps hard for people today to understand how rare a good complexion was in the seventeenth century. Not only were people prey to the normal ravages of time, but washing was not very fashionable, and such make-up as there was was often dangerous and skin-destructive. Life for the face was not easy without the aid of such modern panaceas as Vaseline Intensive Care Cream, Oil of Olay, Clearasil, Phisoderm, Killospot, Stopozit, Pop-o-puss, Acne-axe and other such popular skin preservatives. Not to mention Jojoba Pine-Kernel and Bird-Dropping Dual Action Face Rub, Cucumber and Baby Squid Overnight Mousse, Cod's Roe and Camomile Cleanser, and Maple Syrup and Lamb's Willy Wrinkle Remover.

3 See Mia Farrow.

GEORGE VILLIERS & ANNA MARIA BRUDENELL, COUNTESS OF SHREWSBURY

The Countess of Shrewsbury was trouble, and while George Villiers enjoyed rogering her, he was lucky to get away with so little trouble. George was an enthusiastic bi-sexual and many sexual scientists believe that the modern phenomenon of attraction between beautiful women and homosexuals stems from this era, when they used to roger each other all the time. Other sexual scientists reject this, and say the relationship between beautiful women and homosexuals has grown up just because they don't roger each other. A third grouping of sexual scientists sit on the fence on this issue. These are the people who only became sexual scientists so they could watch couples making love under controlled conditions, and don't actually have an opinion about anything apart from the fact that they like sex a lot. As did George Villiers and the Countess of Shrewsbury.

ANNA MARIA BRUDENELL, COUNTESS OF SHREWSBURY

Occupation	**Rogering.**
Hobby	**Assault and battery.**
Distinguishing Features	**Sex appeal.**
Romantically Linked With	**George Villiers, Harry Killigrew.**

Anna Maria was the most admired and desired beauty at the court of Charles II. Also one of the worst behaved. The King eventually said of her, 'I cannot commend my Lady Shrewsbury's conduct in many things'. The case of dear Harry Killigrew, who follows in the line, may be a good example. Killigrew was her lover but while in exile, he was replaced. On his return he turned up at a theatre,[1] and accused the Countess and her new lover roundly and publicly of immoral behaviour. Killigrew was thrown out of the theatre, but that wasn't quite enough for the Countess. A year later, she drove out in her carriage with four disguised footmen, ambushed Killigrew in Hammersmith in the middle of the night and looked on merrily while the footmen beat him half to death.

There was clearly no man able to accomplish the taming of the Shrewsbury.

FOOTNOTES

1 A great loss to modern culture and society is the loss of the theatre as the official place for public misdemeanour. For years, theatre happened more on the audience side of the footlights than on the stage. Theatres were the place for fighting, shouting, drinking, parading new clothes, new mistresses and new insults. Any really rowdy evening would always climax in a trip to the theatre. Very little of this now remains, except perhaps in a few exceptional cases*. Generally, literary experts think that the respect with which the theatre is now treated has done damage, as playwrights no longer feel they have to be more interesting than what is going on on the other side of the footlights: it is very easy to be more interesting than 400 people sitting in the dark trying hard to eat their chocolates as quietly as possible and to remember where the girl behind the counter said their interval drinks were going to be. The tradition of audience participation and abuse really lives now only in the noisy crowds of American cinemas, who have sex in the back ten rows, throw popcorn and Coca-Cola at the screen and yell 'fast forward' whenever things get either romantic or intelligent.

*The Italians' enthusiastic attitude to opera, always interrupting for praise or abuse, is a pleasing hangover**. Another effort to revive the old sense of excitement was afforded by John Wilkes Booth when he shot Abraham Lincoln in the theatre: Booth was an actor who felt that the sense of danger had gone out of theatre and was trying to bring it back to life: and to some extent he was right: no one ever forgot that night out.

**Even the Italians are now in danger of losing their original expertise in this field. The old distinction between 'bravo!' and 'brava!', bravo for the male singer, brava for the female, is sometimes lost: and the similar distinction, between the 'boo!' of disapproval for the male singer, and the 'baa!' for the female singer has almost completely disappeared. In the nineteenth century, many were the prima donnas whose promising careers were brought to an end by the loud baaing of the 'sound of the sheep', or 'voce d'agnelli'.

ANNA MARIA BRUDENELL & HARRY KILLIGREW

Harry Killigrew was not the kind of man who remembered to be subtle about things. He told friends that he only rogered the Countess 'because he had nothing better to do',[1] and afterwards he 'gave luxurious descriptions of her most secret charms and beauties' to all and sundry. So much so, in fact, that her next lover, 'deafened by descriptions of Lady Shrewsbury's merits' tried her out, was satisfied and stole her from Harry.[2]

HARRY KILLIGREW

Occupation	**Getting drunk, shouting and letting off fire-extinguishers.[3]**
Hobbies	**As above.**
Romantically Linked With	**Barbara Villiers, the Countess of Shrewsbury and the Countless Whores of London Town.**
Nickname	**Lying Killigrew.**

Lying Killigrew was a member of the notorious Merry Gang,[4] which consisted of Charles II, the Earl of Rochester, Lord Buckhurst, Sir Charles Sedley and Killigrew himself. The sole purpose of the club was to have a good time.[5] Rochester was continuously drunk for five years. Buckhurst was put on trial in 1662 for the killing of a tanner for fun. A year after he got out of that, he and Sedley appeared naked on a public balcony and did imitations of buggery.[6] They then abused the Bible and shouted, pointing to Sedley's willy, that 'there he had such powder as should make all cunts run after him'. By this time quite a crowd was gathering: they hadn't had so much fun since Charles I's head was cut off. To further entertain the cheering audience, Sedley and Buckhurst then crapped over the balcony on to the heads of the attentive crowd and a riot ensued.[7]

Mixing with this sort of company didn't do Killigrew much good. 'He will never leave lying as long as his tongue can wag', the King declared to his sister in France to warn her what to expect when Killigrew came to stay. He wasn't the sort of man you'd want to introduce to your mother unless she was already dead. The gang was descended from the Elizabethan gangs: 'The Damned Crew', 'The Roaring Boys', 'The Bravadoes' and 'The Roysters'. A contemporary source notes how they 'incite riots, toss beggars in blankets, throw waiters out of windows, hop around the room with a red hot poker between their teeth and push a blind horse into a china shop'.

Rochester himself killed a landlady by throwing her out of a window after he had thrown her furniture into the street: he then asked for her to be put on the bill along with the price of the furniture.[8] Of course, it was also Rochester, the wittiest poet of the time, who best summed up the lifestyle he and the rest of the Merry Gang strove for:

> *I rise at eleven, I dine about two*
> *I get drunk before seven and the next thing I do*
> *I send for my whore, when for fear of the clap*
> *I dally about her and spew in her lap.*[9]
> *Then we quarrel and scold till I fall asleep*
> *When the jilt, growing bold, to my pockets doth creep,*
> *Then slyly she leaves me and to revenge the affront*
> *At once both my lass and my money I want.*
> *If by chance then I wake hot-headed and drunk*
> *What a coyl do I make for the loss of my punk?*[10]
> *I storm and I roar and I fall in a rage*
> *And missing my lass I fall on my page;*
> *Then crop-sick all morning I rail at my men*
> *And in bed I lie yawning till eleven again.*

With such a philosophy, it was difficult for the members of the Merry Gang to be useful members of society. Harry was eventually banished from the Kingdom, and remembered as a man who 'abhorred all serious discourse and laughed at all sober men'. (Good on him.)

FOOTNOTES

1 See Appendix: Great Rogering Excuses.
2 Who was, fortunately, probably too drunk to notice.
3 Modern parallel: Viscount Althorp.
4 After whom we have named this merry crew of lovers, from James I to Charles II. It is such a relief at last to be in tune with modern times, where beating up ex-lovers or just being rude to them in public places is considered enough, rather than cutting their heads off.
5 See Douglas Fairbanks Jnr and the Cads Club.
6 Which brings us back to the question of fun in the theatre. Many is the literary critic who thinks that Mary Whitehouse's objection to the act of buggery in *The Romans in Britain* actually succeeded in buggering up British theatre for the foreseeable future. So, for once Mrs Whitehouse was in the right: buggery did indeed lead to buggery.
7 Police experts who have studied this incident as an early example of incitement to riot still disagree over the actual cause of the riot. One school of thought argues that the riot was incited because the crapping so infuriated the crowd that they struck out at random. Another school argues that it was in fact the people who had *not* been crapped on who started the riot: in this age of sensory excess the fact that they had missed the chance of being poo-ed on by intimates of the King was enough to drive them to violence. A third viewpoint is

presented by a special inquiry into the incident launched by the Metropolitan Police in the wake of the Tottenham riots in 1985. This report blames the riot on *agents provocateurs* from other parts of London who came with pre-packed poo that had been collected weeks before the incident and slung it on the crowd from nearby buildings. Perhaps the real truth will never be known.

8 In the light of this, the relative tameness of Rod Stewart and The Who should be noted.

9 A curious report has come through of the last time the conference of Prep School English masters took on the vexed question of why Rochester is not taught at Junior level. This poem was read out as an example of the excellence of his work. An English master from Hull, however, objected that this line: 'I dally about her and spew in her lap' was an example of what was most undesirable about Rochester, and that he would not teach boys a poem which encouraged them to vomit. When it was explained to him that in this context 'spew' means 'ejaculate', he withdrew his objection, satisfied that while all his students knew how to vomit, very few were yet capable of ejaculation.

10 'Punk' of course means 'prostitute' and not 'unfashionable hangover from the early 1980s'.

HARRY KILLIGREW & BARBARA VILLIERS

Harry was damn sure as mustard in a daze while this was going on, spewing left, right and centre. The long and short of it was that Barbara, Charles II's mistress, was either such a satisfactory or such an unsatisfactory roger that Harry called her a tart[1] in public, and Charles II banished him from the Kingdom.

BARBARA VILLIERS	
Born	**1641, in England.**
Occupation	**Rogering the King.**
Hobby	**Running the country.**
Romantically Linked With	**Roger Palmer, the Earl of Chesterfield, Charles II, Jacob Hall, Henry Jermyn, the Duke of Marlborough, Beau Fielding, Jacob the Rope Dancer, pages, footmen, etc.**
Nickname	**Curse of the Nation.[2]**

Barbara was the most clinging of Charles' mistresses and was described by Pepys as 'the favourite among the Royal mistresses'. For a time Charles was infatuated by her—he bought a portrait of her and had copies made to send to his friends—and their erotic passion was regularly consummated, regularly enough for her to bear him more than one illegitimate child.

She was, however, not popular with the people: the mob even got together, in a rare moment of strict universal morality, a petition for the King, trying to limit Barbara's power. It was known as the Whore's Petition.[3] And indeed,

Charles did eventually tire of her himself. When she got altogether too power-hungry and too old, he gave her a golden handshake in the shape of the titles of Duchess, Countess and Baroness.

Many thought that the title Whore suited her better. One of these was her poor husband, Roger Palmer, who was given the title Earl of Castlemaine by the King to reward him for his discretion.[4] The thing was, you see, that it wasn't only with the King that Barbara canoodled. She also slept with that monster Killigrew, the playwright Wycherley, Jacob the Rope Dancer,[5] and innumerable other coves including John Churchill, Duke of Marlborough to whom she bore the sixth of her many illegitimate children. She was, in fact, insatiable: if the mob had only waited their turn . . .

FOOTNOTES

1 The derivation of the term 'tart' is still very unclear. The theory that it is because tarts are full of sticky, gooey jam and loose women are full of similar stuff is generally rejected on the grounds of being too disgusting to talk about.

2 Most girls, when they start sleeping with a man, start trying to change him. This is different for kings. When women roger kings, they immediately start trying to change their country. Barbara earned herself the title 'Curse of the Nation' for the havoc that she wreaked upon the country with her economic theories.

3 They were not always puritanical—the tale is told of how a coach carrying Nell Gwyn was stopped by an angry mob, who had heard it contained the King's mistress and took it to be his Catholic French mistress, Louise de Kerouaille. As the situation got dangerous, Nell popped her lovely blonde head out of the window and shouted: 'Pray good people: be civil. I am the Protestant whore'. They cheered her all the way home.

4 The title was hereditary, but only for any of Roger's children by Barbara: which, since she slept with and had children by almost everyone in the Kingdom *except* Roger, wasn't saying much.

5 She wanted to know what went on 'under his tumbling clothes'.

BARBARA VILLIERS & CHARLES II

These were two sexual experts, and coming up with a definitive description of the rogering would be impossible; for instance, there was one time when Charles rogered not only Barbara but also Lord Harry Jermyn at the same time. Whatever, a good time was probably had by all,[1] taking into account Rochester's description of the King's sexual prowess:

> 'Nor are his high desires above his strength.
> His sceptre and his prick are of a length'.[1]

CHARLES II

Born	**1630, in England.**
Occupation	**King.**
Hobby	**Pleasure.**
Romantically Linked With	**Catherine of Braganza(m), Lady Castlemaine, Louise de Kerouaille, Barbara Villiers, Nell Gwyn, Moll Davis, Lady Byron, Duchesse de Chatillon, Hortense Mancini and Lord Henry Jermyn and many more.**
Nickname	**The Merry Monarch.**

'God will never damn a man for allowing himself a little pleasure', Charles said, and proceeded to have fourteen illegitimate children. He wasn't called 'the father of the people' for nothing. Yet, even though his mistresses were the most famous thing about him,[2] Charles did do his best to be nice to his wife. It was generally agreed that she looked like a bat, but he described her more kindly as 'not so exact as to be a beauty'.[3] Her name was Catherine of Braganza, and he married her for financial reasons. (It wasn't a bad deal: Charles got £10,000 cash, with a potential £50,000 bonus, as well as Tangier and Bombay, which sure beats the two ice-cream makers, one silver-set and three 'I'll wait till I find something *just right*' excuse letters that most couples get today.)

But right from the start, though, things were a little tricky. When Catherine first arrived she had had such a difficult sea-journey from Portugal that the marriage could not be consummated. Then, on arriving at court, she found

Barbara Villiers was pregnant by Charles and insisting on having the baby at Hampton Court: a strange thing to deal with on one's honeymoon, the fact that your husband is about to have a son and you've got nothing to do with it.[4] Nevertheless, things did finally settle down, and in the end, Charles found his wife a great source of delight. He only taught her English swear-words, which she employed liberally and unselectively, making her a most delightful and unorthodox conversationalist.

When he wasn't laughing at the Queen's vocabulary, however, Charles was busy rogering. His mistresses included Winifred Wells, who had 'the carriage of a goddess and the physiognomy of a dreamy sheep',[5,6] Mrs Jane Roberts, Mrs Knight, Mary Killigrew, Elizabeth, Countess of Kildare, Moll Davis— 'the most impertinent slut in the world', Duchess of Richmond, Louise de Kerouaille, Catherine Pegge, and, of course, the legendary Nell Gwyn.[7]

Charles died in 1685, 55 years old with enough rogering behind him to fill quite a few books this size. He is the end of this line, when rogering at last started to be taken a little less seriously. Thank the Lord.

FOOTNOTES

1 Not necessarily so. See *Napoleon: Satisfaction and the Small Willy*, Pergamon Press, 1976.
2 See Sir Gordon White.
3 Marvell, less kind, described her as an . . . 'ill-natured goblin . . . designed, for nothing but to dance and vex mankind'.
4 This actually led to a crisis known as Bedchamber Crisis of 1662, when Barbara refused to light a fire outside her room in honour of the new Queen—the only member of the Palace not to do so. The curious thing is that Barbara, though constitutionally incorrect, did turn out to be right about this on safety grounds, and the lighting of real fires outside bedrooms has became very unpopular in England in recent times. A recent attempt to revive it at Hampton Court was a tragic failure.
5 That's a sheep and a bat already. Charles' bedchamber did at times resemble a menagerie.
6 'Dreamy sheep': for people who find sheep dreamy, Greece is generally agreed to be the perfect spot.
7 Nell is now mainly famous for her oranges. In her time, she was also noted for her perfect ankles, her perfect legs, her tiny feet, her second-rate acting and her wit. Charles once complained of his poor finances and she had a ready solution: 'Send the French into France again (meaning Louise de Kerouaille), set me on the stage again and lock up your codpiece'.* Charles didn't take her advice: he never abandoned her. It is said that his last words were, 'Let not poor Nelly starve.'

*The derivation of the word 'codpiece' is one of the great mysteries of English linguistics. The following are the most popular:

  a That it is a sexual metaphor: see *Measure for Measure*, 'fishing for trout in a peculiar river': the codpiece covers that part of man that is most eager to go 'swimming'.
  b That it is a corruption of the term 'God piece', the 'God piece' covering the special piece of his anatomy given to man by God.
  c That it is a corruption not of the word 'cod', but of the word 'piece'. That it was originally a 'cod purse': fishmongers were notably voracious sexually and men would pay for the cod that they wanted by the contents of their 'cod purse'. The only people to disagree with the third theory, which is generally favoured, is the National Union of Fishermen.

THE MERRY GANG LAY LINE

JAMES I

GEORGE VILLIERS

ANNA MARIA BRUDENELL

HARRY KILLIGREW

BARBARA VILLIERS

CHARLES II

And it looks like Happy Days are Here to Stay!

FROM	**LOUIS XIV**
TO	**IVAN THE HORSE**
IN	*7 ROGERS*

From the rampant Merry Gang, the great Lay Line of History moves forward into one of its most extraordinary by-roads. Not satisfied with promiscuity simple, the rogers of history suddenly become increasingly bizarre, strange, decadent. This lay line, with a French king, a Russian empress, a pope, a racehorse and some polite young English girls, shows that suddenly there were no borders, no barriers, no exotic or erotic arrangements too exotic or erotic for the sensual travellers bound together in the universal ronde of rampancy that is the road from Sun King to Ivan the Horse.

(The lay lines in this book will eventually move from Henry VIII right through to the most modern of modern day folk, proving the motto **'If You've Rogered Anyone, You've Rogered Everyone in History'.** The Horseplay line links with 'The Merry Gang' through Louise de Kerouaille, an exotic double agent, mistress at one time of both Louis XIV and Charles II.)

LOUIS XIV

Born	**1638, in France.**
King	**1643.**
Died	**1715.**
Occupation	**Being King for a long time.**
Hobbies	**Rogering.**
Romantically Linked With	**Marie Thérèse of Spain (m), Louise de la Valliere, Marie Mancini, Louise de Kerouaille, Duchesse de Bourgogne, Marquise de Montespan, Henrietta of England, Mme de Maintenon, Mlle des Oeillets, Mme de Thianges, Princesse de Soubise, Mme de Loudres, Mlle de Fantagues.**
Married	**Marie Thérèse of Spain, only.**
Nickname	**The Sun King.**[1]

Louis XIV became King of France at the age of four, master of nineteen million people of whom at least half were women, and any of whom, man or woman, it was his right to roger. At first, he didn't take much advantage of this, but made up for it later by trying to roger as many of them as possible. His reign was considered one of the most glorious in the history of France: during the time he was King, France became the most powerful country in Europe and the cultural centre of the world. That, however, is as nothing beside the achievements of Louis the Rogerer, or *Mr Mistress*.

Louis was a man of few wives, one to be exact, and many mistresses. The wife in question was the patient and long suffering Marie Thérèse of Spain. Throughout her life, she had to put up with a procession of glamorous and totally fabulous mistresses who were installed in suites of rooms close to her husband's bedroom. They made their way to and fro by means of a 'secret' staircase that was about as secret as St Paul's Cathedral. So rampant was Louis indeed, that sometimes two separate mistresses would pass each other on the stairs, one slouching down weary, the other bouncing up.

The first serious mistress was *Mlle de la Valliere*: in fact, she was official. Louis had a daughter by her, and had her immediately legitimized in spite of the existence of the already-and-would-always-have-to-be-patient-and-long-suffering Marie. Indeed, Mlle de la Valliere was so confident about her position that she introduced Louis to a lot of her friends, to show off her boyfriend, the King. It was a mistake.

One of her friends was *Mme de Montespan* and before Valliere could say, 'Monty, this is Louis; Louis, Monty' Montespan was a mistress as well. And soon she was so ambitious that she consulted a witch, praying 'Please let the King love me', 'Please make the Queen sterile' and 'Please make the King hate Mlle de la Valliere'.[2] What she didn't pray was that her husband would behave discreetly, and he didn't. This rather splendid Basil Fawlty of a fellow was furious when he found out about the affair. He boxed his wife round the ears, drove his carriage around town with horns attached to its roof, and then insisted on talking very loudly in Louis' presence about David and Bathsheba.[3] It didn't do much good. Before the end of the affair, Louis and Montespan had had nine illegitimate children. Finally, however, she was caught out by the cruel Catch 22 position into which Louis finally pushed many of his mistresses: to prove his love for them, he made them eat well and hugely. And then when they got fat, he gave them the push. Such was the fate of poor Montespan.[4]

Her true successor was Mme Scarron, soon promoted to *Marquise de Maintenon*. There was one point, when Louis took fright that he would be punished for his infidelity to his wife and went back to her,[5] but in the end he seems, lucky fellow, to have reached a rather charming accommodation between wife and mistress: he rogered his wife twice a month—everyone always knew because she went to Communion the next morning—and yet kept on with Maintenon. When the Queen died, she actually died in Maintenon's arms —not in suspicious circumstances—and Louis kept going with Maintenon until the very end. When she was seventy-five, and Louis seventy, she told her confessor that it exhausted her to roger twice a day. Like solar energy, Louis the Sun King's resources were almost limitless.

FOOTNOTES

1 Or 'Sunshine' to his friends.
2 See also Frances Howard. Nowadays the role of the witch is taken by Claire Rayner or Irma Kurtz.
3 For those who don't remember, David took Bathsheba from a gentleman called Uriah the Hittite, whom he disposed of by putting him in the front line of his army, where Uriah was killed. Uriah's story is surely a parable of the worth of human endeavour: all those Hittites, throughout the history of the race, beating their brains out, working late into the night, fighting and in-fighting to be one of the greatest of the Hittites or at least Hittites of note, and it turns out that the only Hittite of any note at all in the history of the world was a wimp called Uriah who got to be Number One by letting his wife sunbake naked on the roof near the palace.
4 Whom it would, however, be wrong to leave without a mention of her sister, who also had an interesting life. She rogered Louis' brother and then married the Duc de Nevers who was finally jailed for baptizing a pig.*
5 He did not consider the religious implication of his infidelity to his mistress: while dating Maintenon, he was also having flings with *Mme de Thianges*, *Princesse de Soubise* and *Mme de Loudres*.

*There is no need to point out what a curious thing to do this was. An unreliable description of the service claims that a horse and two chickens acted as the godparents, and the baby pig was baptized in a font filled with mud. Nevers also insisted that the pig's religious upbringing should be multi-denominational and had the pig, who was female, circumcised.

LOUIS XIV & MLLE DE FANTAGUES

One important mistress was left out above: the time has come to tell the sad, small tale of Mademoiselle de Fantagues. When she arrived at the court, she was immediately accepted to be the most beautiful woman there, and consequently was immediately rogered by Louis. She was beautiful beyond compare.[1] Her only problem was that she had the intelligence of a little duck, and not a very clever little duck at that. In fact, so silly was she that Louis was ashamed of her; he kept her in a little room next to his and when he wasn't rogering her, pretended not to know her.[2]

Actually, it's too sad. Take a little breath before heading on.

MLLE DE FANTAGUES	
Distinguishing Features	**Utter beauty.**
Romantically Linked With	**Prince Radzini, Louis XIV.**

After first meeting Louis, Fantagues' astonishing beauty had made her a Duchess in record time, but fate was not to be kind to her. First, Montespan took against her badly, and got her witch to send the young girl poisoned gloves, which wasn't nice. Then the Mlle's mind started to go a bit—she started dressing up as Louis—and finally her tiny emotions and her perfect body let her down: she cried and bled too much for the King, who hated people being ill, and he sent her to a convent to be rid of her. A short while later she died there, happy because 'the King has cried on my account'. She was only twenty.

FOOTNOTES

1 So exquisite indeed was Mlle Fantagues' beauty that her slightest action could set a fashion —she once lost her hat while out hunting, and tied her hair up instead with a ribbon. So fetching did it look that by this simple act she set a fashion which outlived her.
2 For pretending not to know someone when actually indulging in sexual activity with them, see Michael Curtiz again, under Orson Welles.

MLLE DE FANTAGUES & PRINCE RADZINI

It was such a little life Mlle de Fantagues had that very little history remains about her other loves. The only name which seems to have slipped through the net of time is that of Prince Radzini. But it sounds such an exotic, Mills and Boon name, that perhaps he never existed, perhaps she just made him up when she was sitting in that little room, waiting for Louis to come in and recognize her again.[1]

PRINCE RADZINI

Distinguishing Features	**An air of utter mystery.**
Romantically Linked With	**Mlle de Fantagues and Miss Chudleigh.**
Nickname	**Zini.[2]**

On the other hand, Radzini must have existed, because it is recorded that he also slept with Miss Chudleigh. He was clearly an attractive guy, but just not someone you wrote home about. Or wrote about at all.

FOOTNOTES

1 See Appendix: Names for Rogering.
2 Or maybe 'Rad'.

PRINCE RADZINI & MISS CHUDLEIGH

When they first met, they were introduced to each other as 'Prince Radzini' and 'Miss Chudleigh'. They exchanged some pleasantries and some time later found themselves in bed with each other. When Miss Chudleigh asked him if he had slept with other women, Radzini said, yes, I once slept with Mlle de Fantagues, the dead nun. When he asked who she'd rogered, it was a slightly longer story . . .

MISS CHUDLEIGH

Born	**1720, in England.**
Occupation	**None.**
Hobby	**Rogering titles.**
Romantically Linked With	**Prince Radzini, the Earl of Bath, the Duke of Hamilton, the Earl of Bristol, George II, Frederick II, the Duke of Kingston, Pope Clement XIV.**
Nickname	**Cuddly Chudleigh.**

Miss Chudleigh was an adventuress who rogered titles. When she realized she had married an earl and actually could have a duke, she got rid of the Earl of Bristol and rogered the Duke of Hamilton instead.[1] When she wasn't rogering either of these two noble fellows, she was busy rogering people a lot more important. Spreading herself across Europe like a cuddly quilt, Miss Chudleigh was one of a new breed of international rogering travellers. As she moved from city to city, she not only took, she gave. She was part of a generation that was starting to learn and enjoy the fact that rogering could get you anywhere and you didn't have to die for it[2]; although clearly, if you were going to be very promiscuous, it did help if you were the kind of girl who *was* dying for it.

Frederick II is said to have loved Miss C. mainly because she could put away two bottles of wine at a sitting.[3] Perhaps Pope Clement tried her out on Communion wine and she passed that test too.

FOOTNOTES

1 For those about to get married, there is always one sure fire way of knowing if you've made a mistake: *watch the fiancée's parents*: if they are really pleased and utterly delighted with you, then you can assume you could have done better, and should get out fast. The thought that they might just like you for yourself is a vain error.

2 Two other extraordinary friends of hers are worth stopping with for a while on this long journey to our times via good times. They are *Miss Gunning*, and *Miss Gunning*. And, believe it, when they were gunning for a man, they got him. Together, they were meant to be the most exquisite sight in Britain—700 people in Yorkshire once sat up all night to see them leave the county, so beautiful were they.[a] When they went walking together in Hyde Park, they had to be protected by an armed guard of soldiers. And through this beauty, these two simple, common girls achieved things beyond their wildest dreams.

The first Miss Gunning married two dukes, one of Hamilton, the other of Argyll, was the mother of two new dukes and was chosen as the official advisor to Queen Charlotte when she came to England to marry George II.

The second Miss Gunning was not to be outdone—she married the boring but wealthy Lord Coventry,[b] and although people weren't as kind about her mind as they were about her beauty,[c] she nevertheless inspired the affection of the public in a completely unprecedented way.[d] It was a terrible shock when her happy story turned out tragically. Lord Coventry used to object to his pretty wife wearing make-up and once chased her round a dinner table, forcing her to wipe it off with a napkin. The terrible thing is that it turned out he was right.[e] Eight years after she married, Miss Gunning the Second died of the lead in her make-up, which poisoned her. At her funeral, 10,000 people passed by the coffin. Such was the respect for beauty at that time.

3 Alcohol still remains the great gamble and calculation in the game of love: it makes it all the more likely that people will decide to sleep with you: but all the more likely that they'll then fall asleep while doing it.

aAnd people in Yorkshire do know something about beauty. Geoff Boycott's stroke play is proof of that.
bHe was described as 'silly in a wise way'.
cLike Samantha Fox.
dLike Samantha Fox again.
eBut perhaps he was 'wise in a silly way'.

MISS CHUDLEIGH & POPE CLEMENT XIV

It is very hard indeed, into such good repute has the position of Pope fallen, to really imagine what it was like scoring with Il Papa, sighing with pleasure at the exertions of God's Chosen leader, resting upon the rocks of the rock upon which God was continuing to build His Church. Miss Chudleigh did not leave a diary behind her, but there is reason to believe that if she had, it might have read like this:

July 3   Rome at last. Think we'll just relax at the pensione today, and really start sightseeing tomorrow.

July 4   Bit of a hangover after last night's two bottles, but got up around nine and started the tour. The fountains are beautiful and the Coliseum quite grand, though a little crumbly. Finally, after a light pasta lunch, we set off for the Vatican. Crept in quietly since there was a service going on. Amazing ritual, thousands of men in robes, and on the way out coming down the aisle, the Pope slipped me a note inviting me to his private residence tomorrow.

July 5   (No entry.)

July 6   What an exciting day. My mother will never believe it. I went to see the Pope yesterday, and he actually took my confession. The head of the whole Catholic Church, the most important man in religion listening to me and my little confessions. Thank God I had a lot to confess: I'd just fucked him stupid. Off to Athens tomorrow. O Athena, Mother of All Culture—how exciting it will be.[1]

POPE CLEMENT XIV	
Born	**1705, in Italy.**
Pope	**1769–74.**
Real Name	**Giovanni Vicenzo Antonio Ganganelli.[2]**
Occupation	**Priest and Pope.**
Hobbies	**Praying, taking communion, taking confession, studying the Holy Scriptures, attending to the administration of the Benediction of the Holy Cross of Jesus of the Flaming Heart, waving about incense cannisters and a teensy weensy bit of rogering.**
Distinguishing Features	**Staff in hand, wise words in mouth and erection under cassock.[3]**
Romantically Linked With	**Miss Chudleigh and Catherine the Great.**

Pope Clement was a Franciscan Monk who was too weak to resist the intimidation and threats of a schism in the Catholic Church—he therefore agreed to suppress the Society of Jesus which later, after great chaos, had to be restored. Fortunately, his lack of success at the job had some personal compensations. He never looked down on the unemployed and was one of the most famous of the Rogering Popes.[4]

FOOTNOTES

1 'P.S. Hope I'm not pregnant. If I am, will it be the Son of God? Rather hope not'.
2 See Marilyn Monroe, La Belle Otero and *passim*. Old Ganganelli would probably have never scored at all if he hadn't changed his name to 'The Pope'.
3 *Proofreader's note*: There was a muddle in the order of words here, but we've sorted it out.
4 The Popes have in many ways been the least religious religious leaders ever. First, blotting the Papal copy book for ever, came *Pope Alexander VI*, the *Borgia Pope*. In 1501, he ordered fifty prostitutes for him, his son and his daughter. Her name was Lucrezia.

   Later the son of *Pope Paul III* actually raped the Bishop of Fano, which must have been bad for church morale, and *Benedict IX* confessed to 'unrestrained licence and shocked the sensibilities of even a dull and barbarous age'. *St Swithin*—a true religious maniac—slept always in the same bed with two virgins: it was to test his virtue to the full. Go tell that to the Borgias.

   However, the most famous of all the real life rogering popes* was *Pope Joan*, the only female Pope. Joanna was a nun who fell in love with a monk called Frumentius. In order to run away together, he gave her a monk's cassock as a disguise, and so she began a life masquerading as a man. As two monks they lived together in the same cell, and Joanna changed her name to John. Their monastic bliss lasted for seven years and then they moved to Athens, where John's fame (and beauty) spread. She tired of Frumentius and went on to roger an abbot, two bishops and the Eparch of Attica. This led her to Rome where she became the private secretary of the pontiff, Pope John VIII. She later rogered the son of Pope Leo and in the end, through a series of events she couldn't put a stop to, became Pope herself. It all ended tragically: she gave birth during a procession on Rogation Sunday, and died.

*For one step up, rogering saints, see Jill St. John.

POPE CLEMENT XIV & CATHERINE THE GREAT[1]

Many historians and health experts attribute the weakness that Pope Clement displayed in his professional capacity as Pope to what probably happened to him the night he spent with Catherine the Great. She'd broken better men.

CATHERINE THE GREAT

Born	**1729, in Germany.**
Died	**(in mysterious circumstances) 1796.**
Occupation	**Empress.**
Hobby	**Rogering and torture.**
Romantically Linked With	**Sergei Saltykov, Gregory Orlov, Vasilichikov, Plato Zubov, Prince Peter, Nikolay Rimski-Korsakov, Alexander Dmitriev Mamonov, Prince Potemkin, Ivan the Horse.**

Whenever anyone is called 'the Great', the immediate reaction is to say 'Ok, but great at what?' In Catherine's case, there isn't much doubt—the full title was Catherine the Great at Rogering.

But whenever anyone is called 'the Great at Rogering', the immediate reaction then is, 'Ok, ok but great at rogering who?' In Catherine's case, there isn't much doubt about that either: she was great at rogering anyone whose name ended in -ov. If you didn't end in -ov, it could be tricky. She would have had Mikael Gorbachov like a shot. Ronald Reagan she would have thought twice. Isaac Asimov—straight into bed. Arthur C. Clarke—a long time on the sofa.

'My heart cannot be happy even for an hour without love', she once said, rather coyly, but although she was a virgin until she was twenty-three, she soon made up for it. Her lovers were first checked for venereal disease, then checked to see if their names really did end in -ov, and finally passed on to a noble woman to test roger. If they came through that, they were taken upstairs to be intimately ruled by Catherine the Great.

And to be fair, she was great at ruling too. Born in Germany, Catherine eventually ruled Russia for thirty-four years—that's thirty-four times as long as Yuri Andropov. At sixteen she married her imbecile cousin, Peter, who apart from being an imbecile and her cousin, was also sterile and impotent —so no great catch there (although he was, of course, Emperor of all Russia). When Peter wanted to divorce her, Catherine led a *coup d'état* which deposed him after six months of rule, and left her on the throne.[2] For the next thirty-four years, she ruled by ruthlessness and rogery. People who didn't approve of her, she either rogered or tortured till they did. She slept with most of the hierarchy of the Horse Guards to keep them sweet. With that power, she enslaved Hungary, broke the clergy, and crushed all rebellion until her death.

And that is where the controversy begins. Most historians *actually do believe* now that Catherine died while rogering a horse: she was Empress: she could *do what she liked*. Others say she didn't, that she died of a stroke. Perhaps the answer lies in finding the Russian for 'horse'. If it ends in -ov, the answer is probably 'yes'.

FOOTNOTES

1 For future reference, an excerpt from *The Nolan Sisters Guide to Correct Forms of Address*. How to Address The Pope in bed

> **Before** *Your Holiness*
> **During** *Big Boy*
> **After** *Your Holiness*

2 She put Peter in gaol and allowed him to keep his monkey and a prostitute there, until she had him killed. Apparently he used to get the prostitute to do tricks and play a barrel organ. There is no record of what he did with the monkey.

CATHERINE THE GREAT & IVAN THE HORSE

Putting anything here might be pre-judging this important historical controversy, did she or did she not die underneath a horse. The only fair thing surely is to let the horse, if he can speak, speak for himself.

IVAN, THE HORSE

Born	**In a field, sometime: typical human behaviour to have no record of it.**
Occupation	**Running about with people on his back. Rogering other horses.**
Hobbies	**Running around without people on his back. Rogering people.**
Distinguishing Features	**Nice coat.**
Romantically Linked With	**A mare. Another mare. Yet another mare. A favourite mare. Ivanovna, a two-year-old mare. And another mare. And another one. And another one. And Catherine the Great of Russia.**
Nickname	**Horsie.**

'I'd been messing around as normal, you know, just running around, eating grass, kicking things, rogering the odd mare, that kind of caper, when the stable boy comes out. As always, I kind of sidled away, trying not to get noticed, holding my breath, trying to look thin, anything to get out of the whole person-on-top, kick-the-hell-out-of-you-with-those-spiky-things routine. Anyway, just my luck, I get picked. As I leave the field, it's the same old story from the guys: "Have a great ride", "Throw the bastard, Karpov",

"Don't give them anything unless they give you sugar", "Poo in front of the Queen, you old bugger".

'Anyway, suffice to say I was at this point led off to the royal stable. Now this is never a bad thing: the noblemen always take it out on us horses: the royals tend to be kind: they're the only people who realize what berks other humans are, I suppose. And when I get there, there's the Empress waiting, but, surprise, surprise, she's still in her nightie.

'Well, you can imagine my surprise at what happens next. The Empress, I mean, we are talking about the Empress here, not some mad peasant girl, takes me through into the house. O my god, I think, this is SICK, SICK, they're going to roast me. Fuck. If only I'd pretended to be lame. Then they would have shot me, which is at least quick.

'But I'm jumping the gun: you could have roasted me: and it wouldn't have been as shocking as what happened next. For far from roasting me, old Empress takes off all her clothes, I mean the lot, nightie and all, and I think, O, this is SICK SICK SICK, she's going to roger the stable boy, and I've been brought in to add authenticity to the whole pallava.

'But no, no, no: that's not it at all. Stable boy stays in the full monty and leads me over. Suddenly I get the message. Hey, wait a bloody minute, mate, I say. This is the Empress. What's the Emperor going to say when he finds out, I tell you, if he challenges me to a duel, I'll never stand a chance. I can't hold a pistol, you see. Hooves are no good for gun-control. And who'd be my second? But, as usual, the stable boy doesn't understand a word, and not one to argue, I do finally what I'm told to do. Won't actually describe it—doesn't seem right—I mean, I do have some respect for royal privacy—but in a word, it's not a very loving experience: and before you can say, "I've just had Catherine, and she wasn't Great", I'm back in the paddock. "How did it go, mate?" they say. "How many kicks did the bastards give you?"

'And I'm just about to tell them, when I think—nah, better not. They'd all just spend their whole time flirting with the Empress, and start giving horses a really bad name—like, you know, humans have got. It happened once again the next week, but that time she was a bit lifeless, no go in her really, at all, you know what I mean.

'And that's vaguely it—all right? Sort of what you're looking for?'

HORSEPLAY LAY LINE

LOUIS XIV

MLLE DE FANTAGUES

PRINCE RADZINI

MISS CHUDLEIGH

POPE CLEMENT XIV

CATHERINE THE GREAT

IVAN, THE HORSE

This line has made it easier for all the rogerers to come. It's no holds barred from now on. Compared to this lot, the moderns will seem *TAME*. Even though God has long given up trying to organize, let's hope He isn't even watching any more.

ENEMIES

FROM	**LOUIS XV**
VIA	**NAPOLEON**
TO	**THE DUKE OF WELLINGTON**
IN	**6 ROGERS**

This line, known as Enemies, is not intended to imply that rogering within it took on a cruel and sado-masochistic streak. Far from it: it runs through an age of relatively relaxed rogering, tamer than the hyper-activity of the lines before. It is a line of enemies be-cause it takes in the major upheavals in Europe during this period, and makes a mockery of them. It shows that regardless of political complexion, rogering binds the world together like a glue. Napoleon rose to power on the back of a revolution that violently overthrew the monarchy represented by Louis XV: and yet they shared the same lover. Napoleon was in turn defeated by Wellington: yet both of them had been led the same merry dance by a certain Mademoiselle George.

It has recently been suggested that photographs be taken of all major world leaders without their clothes on and circulated round every human on Earth: we would be reminded that these people are only hu-mans, the same funny bodies as us beneath their suits, and they shouldn't be making decisions that are al-most certain to kill us all. This friendly lay line makes much the same point.

(Again, the long lay line continues. From Miss Chud-leigh, the purest of English Roses, to The Duke of Hamilton to Miss Gunning to Lord Coventry to Mme Pompadour to Louis XV, 'the Most Licentious of His Race and An Inveterate Hater of the English'.)

LOUIS XV

Born	1709, in France.
Occupation	**Decadence.**
Hobby	**Being a bad king.**
Distinguishing Features	**Hatred in his eye if you're English.**
Romantically Linked With	**Madame Pompadour, Madame du Barry, Madame de Mailly, Madame de Vintimille, Madame de la Tournelle, Queen Marie Leczinska (m).**

The court of King Louis was given over to a good time. The major, serious activities were gambling, hunting, organizing balls and the pursuit of love. Things like ruling, law-making and so on were thought of as trivial and tiresome and unpatriotic. Adultery was viewed with particular seriousness; anyone not involved in it was considered to be welching on his duties: any husband annoyed by it was breaking the law. The houses of the great were actually constructed with adultery in mind, and revolving fireplaces for adulterous liaisons were *de rigueur*.

Yet, the strange thing is that, despite all this opportunity, Louis himself was quite a cautious and restrained rogerer. He was said, for instance, not to enjoy orgies,[1] and actually preferred having one woman at a time. And then he was lazy in his choosing. His first three mistresses were sisters. De Mailly, de Vintimille and de la Tournelle: like the Beverly Sisters, Pointer Sisters and the Windsor sisters they stuck together: but while the Beverlys and the Pointers sang, and the Windsors ruled England, what the 'de' girls did was roger the King.[2]

In the end, however, Louis gave up all three sisters and settled, after one or two flings, for Madame Pompadour. And that is a great big story.[3] A tiny little story is the one of his romance with his wife, Marie Leczinska. Her favourite activity was said to be prayer-reading, and her father, King Stanislas of Poland, said of her and her mother: 'The two dullest Queens in Europe are my wife and my daughter'. It is no wonder Louis strayed a little.

FOOTNOTES

1 This was considered peculiar at the time, but is nowadays quite a popular prejudice: a recent series of orgies in Islington had to be called off after the third of seven for lack of enthusiasm. Girls complained about interrupted orgasms, men complained about rather too much sucking, and everyone complained about a certain John Moreton, who behaved in a quite disgusting manner from beginning to end.

2 Despite their similarities, however, the girls were very different. De Mailly was interested in Louis himself. De Vintimille liked politics and troop movements and apparently stunk, which her sisters didn't. And de la Tournelle was known as the most accomplished liar in the kingdom.

3 It is said that Madame Pompadour singlehandedly destroyed the French monarchy. Louis XIV had been pretty bad for France, but at least he won a few battles. Louis XV, however, advised by Pompadour, entered the Seven Years War and lost France thousands of lives and £80 million. Then while France was busy trying to disentangle itself from this pointless war, Great Britain snatched her American colonies. As a result of all this, not long after Louis XV's death, his successor, XVI, was bucked off the throne and XV's errors were used as an excuse to execute him, his family and most aristocrats who had anything to do with the monarchy and Versailles, which most of them did.

Thank God Pompadour had at least been a good lay.[a]

When she arrived at court, it was said, 'She absolutely extinguished all the other women.' She had been an excellent actress, but all her life had been determined to meet the King. This was not as easy as all that: for a start, her family name was Poisson—'Fish' in English —and it was very rare that anyone with a name like Fish ever got introduced to the Divinely Chosen King[b]—especially after his experience with the aroma of Mme de Vintimille. Nevertheless, Pompadour was determined, and she finally met Louis during a fancy dress ball at which he was disguised as a tree. It had been a difficult evening, full of repeated misunderstandings with dogs and woodcutters, but Pompadour immediately eased Louis' troubled bark, and they were thereafter companions for life.

It was a contentious relationship, however. While Queen Marie liked her—'if there had to be a mistress, better this one than the other'[c]—the rest of the court and the world did not. Eventually, after years of rogering, she lost her strength and the physical passion between her and the King started to wane; she tried a diet of celery, truffles and vanilla to get herself going again, but started getting so weighty that the King told her not to bother, and they settled for friendship instead.

[a]If Louis hadn't rogered Pompadour, there might have been no Revolution, and therefore no Napoleon, no division of Europe, no German nationalism, no Hitler, and consequently no parts for Lawrence Olivier playing ageing Nazis in dreadful movies. This is another Roger That Changed the World, and a leading contender for the Most Expensive Roger.

[b]Of course, the stigma on this name has now been utterly removed by the startling international success of weatherman Michael Fish. With his politely balding hair, his tentative moustache and his curious dress-sense, Michael Fish, who it is thought does not wear underpants during his forecasts, has turned the name Fish from an albatross round the neck, to a big plus point in any romantic or job-applying situation.

[c]The last mistress had been Mme Chateauroux who was so unpopular that she was pelted with eggs whenever she appeared in public.

LOUIS XV & MME DU BARRY

Du Barry was nice, generous, illiterate and very lower class. She became Louis' mistress because he was lonely after Mme Pompadour's death, and she was apparently bright in bed and not terribly bright outside. By this time, Louis was too old to care or notice.

MME DU BARRY

Occupation	**Hairdresser.**
Hobby	**Rogering.**
Romantically Linked With	**Louis XV, Prince de Ligne, Lord March, Duke of Queensbury, Emperor Joseph II of Austria, Duc de Brissac, Henry Seymour, Comte Jean du Barry.**

Not since Delilah had there been such a successful hairdresser as Mme Du Barry.[1] Not since Medusa turned her hair into snakes and then tried to turn Perseus into stone had hair played such an important part in the life of a major international figure. But then sadly this major renaissance in the power of hair-people suddenly came to an abrupt end. Louis died and du Barry was guillotined at the Revolution after a very, to say the least, brutal haircut: the mob took off the lot. Fashion experts always say it was something of a shame that this must have been such an emotional moment for Mme Du Barry, and one where she was probably not thinking about her scissors and brush. She was an imaginative cutter of hair, and the sight of her own shaven head might well have, if she had been more objective, sparked off in her mind the train of thought that has eventually led to the high-fashion hair of such figures as Grace Jones and Annie Lennox.

FOOTNOTE

1 Jon Peters, who did the hair and then tamed the heart of Barbra Streisand, is an interesting modern example of this phenomenon.

MME DU BARRY & COMTE JEAN DU BARRY

Comte Jean was a famous pimp, and ended up setting his wife up with the King. It is very likely that his concentration during the roger was not therefore one hundred per cent. All the time he would have been thinking 'Mmmm, I wonder if he likes it *this* way . . . Mmm, I know he likes it *that* way, so let's give it a try, and see if she does.' It is fortunate that Mme received castles, jewels and titles worth millions of francs in reward for being so cruelly used.

COMTE JEAN DU BARRY	
Born	**France.**
Occupation	**Pimping.**
Hobbies	**Girl-spotting and test-rogering.**
Romantically Linked With	**Desirée Clary, La Belle Dorothée, Mme du Barry and lots of other people's future girlfriends.**
Nickname	**The Roué.**

It was Comte Jean du Barry's function at court to seek out attractive and available girls for lazy courtiers and he saw it as his job personally to test the product before passing it on for full-time use.[1] As they used to say: 'From du Barry, you can get anything except a virgin'. In cases where he thought he had a truly exceptional prize, as in the case of his famous wife, he would marry her first to be sure he was giving his employer a woman who had been comprehensively test-driven.

That he was a scoundrel is eminently witnessed by his survival of the Revolution, and the fact that there he is again, although unwittingly, doing his old-time duty for Napoleon warming up the delightful Desirée Clary.

FOOTNOTE

1 du Barry was the eighteenth century equivalent of the dating service. A recent market study on the comparative efficiency of the two systems, the Computer Dating and the du Barry Dating Services submitted a lengthy report of which this is a résumé:

Availability.
The Computer Dating service is definitely a step forward from the du Barry Dating Service. While Computer Dating makes itself available and accessible to a wide range of consumers through magazines and unsolicited mail, the du Barry Dating Service is only available to members of the elite French aristocracy.

Cost.
It is difficult to assess the comparative costings here. While Computer Dating charges a set amount, du Barry expects favours in return and possibly some kind of reciprocal rogering

situation. On balance it would seem that the Computer Dating is less costly unless the user of the du Barry system has any daughters who can be readily and repeatedly rogered: in this case the du Barry system is, to all intents and purposes, free.

Quality of Product.
This is where the du Barry system wins out hand over fist. While the Computer Dating system doles out endless frustrated and unhappy weirdoes who have slipped through the net of society and are frantically fibbing in the hope that they can snap up someone seriously short-sighted, the du Barry system deals only in perfectly proportioned French gentle-women*, their flesh like peach, their eyes like diamonds and their sexual techniques like nothing on Earth, having been sharpened up by the old Maestro himself.

Conclusion.
Were it not for the fact that du Barry is dead as a doornail and all the women he might have laid his hands on also reduced to dust, he would be a good bet. As it is, Computer Dating is all you've got, Four Eyes.

*'Perfectly proportioned': the breasts of Marie Antoinette were said to be so perfect that cham-pagne glasses were modelled on the shape of them. There is no record upon the breasts of whom brandy glasses were modelled, nor whose interestingly-shaped appendages were the inspiration behind the modern pint beer mug. Any information on this question would be gratefully received by J. K. Larrett, author of *Drinking Receptacles and the Female Breast: A Study in Glass*, whose revelation about the derivation of the word 'jugs' has been of such use to the *New Oxford Dictionary of Slang*, and without whose help this note could never have been written. Thank you, Jerzy.

COMTE JEAN DU BARRY & DESIRÉE CLARY

By the time Comte Jean slept with Desirée, his days of glory were over. The glorious court of Louis XV had been replaced by the slightly grubby court of Louis XVI, which had been overturned in turn by the bloody Revolution. Lucky to escape with his life, unlike his poor, higher-profiled wife, Jean nevertheless continued in his old profession: he is a touching and socially important reminder that, no matter what the grand upheavals of state and changes of government and law, the ordinary working man continues to ply his conscientious trade: the butcher, the baker, the candlestick-maker, the tanner, the blacksmith, the fishmonger and the procurer of high-class pros-titutes.

DÉSIRÉE CLARY

Occupation	**Queen, eventually.**
Hobbies	**Waiting for Napoleon to marry her.**
Distinguishing Features	**Tyrannical father.**
Romantically Linked With	**Captain Napoleon and Count Bernadotte.**

Désirée Clary, first name Eugenie, was young Napoleon's sister-in-law when he first saw her and decided she was the woman he would marry. But Captain Napoleon, as he was then, was not as great a conqueror of women as he was of countries. He left a lot of the romancing in the hands of his brother, and when it came to the crunch, allowed himself to be fobbed off by Désirée's father who firmly asserted that he only wanted one Bonaparte in the family. It is thought that later in life M. Clary regretted which of the Bonaparte brothers he had plumped for.

Désirée never forgave Napoleon for not persevering with his love for her and showed that she would indeed have been a worthy wife for him when, in her determination to do him down, she later met and married Napoleon's single greatest enemy, Count Bernadotte, later King of Sweden. There are those who argue that Napoleon never even got his way with Désirée, but this is unlikely. The sad truth is revealed below.

DÉSIRÉE CLARY & NAPOLEON

Napoleon was in the perfect position to be one of the world's most successful rogerers, and indeed, he did try hard to be. The sad truth, however, is that he was poorly equipped to do so. Severely under-endowed,[1] and always nervous of women, Napoleon was taunted (and this is by the great love of his life, Josephine) with the words 'Bon-a-parte est Bon-à-rien'—'Bonaparte is good at nothing'. When people claim that Désirée is reported to have said that nothing had happened between her and Napoleon, it is a simple journalistic mistake. She actually observed that it was *as though* nothing had happened. Napoleon referred to England as a nation of shopkeepers, but in the bed-chamber, he was all over the shop.[2]

NAPOLEON BONAPARTE

Born	**1769, in Corsica.**
Occupation	**General and Emperor and exile.**
Hobbies	**Writing love letters and rogering.**
Distinguishing Features	**Not tall.**
Romantically Linked With	**Caroline Colombier, Desirée Clary, Josephine 'Not Tonight' Beauharnais (m), Mlle de Montansier, Mme Permon, Pauline Foures, Eleonore Denuelle, Marie Antoinetta Duchatel, Marguerite Weymer, Countess Marie Walewska, Archduchess Marie Louise of Austria(m).**
Nickname	**Bony.**

For all his little troubles, troubles with being little and busy schedule being the greatest general and leader France ever had, Napoleon still found a lot of time for love. He seems to have been a romantic; crying, hugging, protesting passion and getting sentimental Hollywood-style about the children of anyone he loved.[3]

When he saw his first love, Caroline Colombier, in a crowd many years after their liaison, he leapt from his horse and embraced her, bursting into tears. When he was finally exasperated by Josephine's infidelities, he banished her from his sight, but when she sent her children to plead for her, he opened the door and burst into tears. On leaving his second wife and child for exile, he burst into tears again, and people said they had not seen so many tears since when he burst into floods on visiting the room where Josephine died.

But when he wasn't being tearful, Napoleon was being passionate. His love for Josephine was indeed the real thing: she was not a youngster when they married—five years older than him at thirty-two, and no innocent either— she had recently been the mistress of one of his commanders. Yet his letters to her overflow with passion: 'If you hesitate, you will find me ill . . . take wings . . . come . . . come'.[4] And later 'I kiss your breasts, and lower down, and lower down!' Throughout the years, despite her terrible spending of money and her infamous infidelity, he continued to love her.

Even so, love and politics make poor bedfellows and by the end of his time of power Napoleon was having to pay attention to the practicalities rather than the pleasures of sex. He was desperate to produce a male heir, and Josephine, stubborn little Creole devil that she was, wouldn't give him one. He did in the end get one from a Mme Denuelle, and another from Marie Walewska,[5] but these weren't official enough, so finally he had to divorce Josephine and marry Marie Louise of Austria who had 'the kind of womb I want to marry'. Yet even still here, in the context of this calculated child-producing move, Napoleon kept up his passionate flair—he was so keen to see what his new wife was going to look like on the wedding day that he refused to wait for her to arrive, but rode out to meet her half-way and brought her in. She did in fact produce him an heir, though how it came about must have been something of a shock to her.[6]

Unfortunately, by the time the child was just older than a baby, Napoleon's dreams of dynasty were shrinking. He was defeated at Waterloo and forced into exile. By the time of his death, he was scarcely a man at all,[7] and no good for a lover; impotent, without body hair and sporting a polite pair of female breasts. It was all part of the sad end of the century's greatest man.

FOOTNOTES

1 When he died, his willy was measured at under one inch.*
2 Talk of Napoleon reminds the editors of the book of their more serious, educational duties, insisted upon by the publishers. What follows is a short quiz, the answers to which will get the reader through any important political discussion.

The world leader with the smallest willy in history was or is:
   a The Emperor Napoleon.
   b Emperor Hirohito of Japan.
   c Edward VIII of England.
   d Sir Geoffrey Howe.
   e Margaret Thatcher.
   f Ronald Reagan.
Answer **a** but it doesn't really matter, does it?*

The people with the largest willies in the world are:
   a People who drive Ford Escort XR3 GTIs with extra front and rear mud-shields.
   b The tribesmen of Eastern Sudan.
   c Sylvester Stallone, Clint Eastwood and Ronald Reagan.
   d The Central Tanzanian Masai, known locally as the Bigwillis.
   e Lancashire colliery workers.
   f Anyone (except Rod Stewart) who's slept more than three times with Britt Ekland.
   g The residents of the Caribbean Island of Antigua.
   h The visitors to the Caribbean Island of Mustique.
Answer **b**

Which prominent feminist encouraged visiting dignitaries to perform cunnilingus on her on their arrival in order to increase the popularity of the act in her country, and promote female supremacy?
   a Margaret Thatcher.
   b Catherine the Great of Russia.
   c Empress Wu Hu of China.
   d Margaret Trudeau.
   e The Empress Cleopatra.
   f Queen Juliana of the Netherlands.
Answer **c**

3 This romancing was when Napoleon was in love. When out on campaign, it was the job of his aide-de-camp to procure him prostitutes simply to ease the tension and pressures of the day. The girl would be asked to undress and wait in bed. When Napoleon had a moment, between conference and conference, he would pop in and pop in and pop out and pop out again.
4 The repetition of the word 'come' here cannot fail to remind one of an advertisement recently espied in an Austrian newspaper—Austria being one of the countries over which Napoleon

held sway. It was a picture of a pleasant-looking naked girl wearing Tyrolean headgear. Under the picture, for the English tourist, were written the simple words, matching the beckoning look on the face of the girl: 'I'm Heidi! Come with me! Come on me! Come in me!'

5 Some historians believe that Marie was the only woman Napoleon ever truly loved. Other cinema historians claim that this theory is only widespread because she was acted by the divine Garbo in *Conquest*. In that film the part of Napoleon was acted by Charles Boyer. Other actors to aspire to, and usually falter in, the role of the great little man include Marlon Brando, Eli Wallach, Herbert Lom (quite a few times), Rod Steiger, Kenneth Haigh and Ian Holm. Perhaps the finest of all Napoleons was Albert Dieudonne, in Abel Gance's *Napoleon*, a film made so long ago that Napoleon had only just died when it started principal photography.

6 She was twenty-eight and a virgin and her parents were obsessed by her innocence. All her life she had been sheltered from boys, and even male animals. She had never seen anything resembling a male private part, or even heard tell of one until her wedding night. Napoleon no doubt told her that they grew no longer than an inch, and so she was perfectly happy.

7 Doubts about whether Napoleon ever was a man at all began circulating at one time. He caressed his soldiers openly and his personal orderly always referred to him as 'Her Majesty'. See Pope Joan under Pope Clement.

*See Edward VIII and George IV.

NAPOLEON & MARGUERITE WEYMER

Marguerite was another sad interlude in the life of the Emperor. Known as Mademoiselle George, Marguerite Weymer was briefly Napoleon's mistress while he was married to Josephine, and he had hoped to keep her secret. However, scandal broke out when an erotic book was published which showed Marguerite not being mightily quelled by the love-making technique of the Emperor, but engaging in furious erotic combat with another woman, her lover, Raucort. Napoleon's dismay at this was only topped by his discovery that another one of her lovers was none other than . . . the Duke of Wellington himself.

MARGUERITE WEYMER	
Occupation	**Rogering men.**
Hobby	**Rogering women.**
Distinguishing Features	**Weight.**
Romantically Linked With	**Napoleon, the Duke of Wellington and Raucort.**
Nickname	**The Whale.**

Marguerite is exactly the kind of high spirited wench upon whom the lay line of history depends. Not for her a detailed consideration of the political balance of Europe, leading to a scrupulously careful decision about which country and which alliance she should lend her ample charms to. She slept with Wellington and she slept with Napoleon, and she didn't care who knew about it. She was one of the few people who didn't have a strong opinion about who she wanted to win the Battle of Waterloo: she'd already defeated both sides in close combat.

In the end, she was herself only defeated by less personal foes: chocolates, sweets, turkish delights, pasta, cakes and other such tasty treats, which finally earned her the nickname, 'The Whale'.

But then, having slept with the two greatest fighters in the world, she had a right, for a while, to sit back on her truffles.[1]

FOOTNOTES

1 Like many women, Marguerite moved on to chocolate when she had finished with men. There is, however, an increasing feeling that women should move on to chocolate *instead of* men, as being a generally better bet. The arguments are, at their simplest:

  a Chocolates are cheaper and more easily obtainable than men.
  b Chocolates never tell you that you're looking fat.
  c Chocolates never fail to make you feel better—men usually do—and if you find your chocolate unsatisfactory, you can send it back to the manufacturer and get a new one. If you send a man back to his manufacturer, God—by murdering him—you'll get in all sorts of trouble.
  d Once you've actually got a chocolate in your mouth, the worst thing it will ever do there is melt.

MARGUERITE WEYMER & THE DUKE OF WELLINGTON

Only two solid pieces of evidence exist about the Weymer-Napoleon-Wellington rogers, but their importance cannot be underestimated. They are:

1. That Weymer claimed that Wellington was a 'stronger' lover than Napoleon and

2. That the Battle of Waterloo was won on the playing fields of Eton.

In other words, Wellington must have rogered Weymer on the playing fields of Eton, and later, when Weymer rogered Napoleon, she must have told him that he was not as good a lover as Wellington. This revelation clearly broke Napoleon's confidence and led to his defeat when it came to the big day of the Battle of Waterloo. This is another Roger That Changed the World.[1]

THE DUKE OF WELLINGTON

Born	**1769, in England.**
Occupation	**Saving Europe.**
Hobbies	**Rogering and being uppity.**
Distinguishing Features	**Napoleon's scalp.**
Romantically Linked With	**Marguerite Weymer, Catherine Pakenham (m),[2] Lady Frances Shelley, Harriet Arbuthnot, Anna Maria Jenkins,[3] Lady Frances Wedderburn Webster, Lady Charlotte Greville, Marianne Caton Patterson, Mrs John Freese, Angela Burdett-Coutts, Margaret Jones.**
Nickname	**The Iron Duke, Old Nosey.**

Wellington became famous for winning battles in the Peninsular War, then very famous for beating Napoleon at Waterloo, then quite famous for enlightened reforms relating to Catholics, and then infamous for the utter inflexibility which earned him the name the Iron Duke.

But all the time this was going on, he was famous for his iron in another department. Throughout his marriage to Kitty Pakenham, he was unfaithful and yet never allowed it to interfere with his own sense of dignity and importance. It was Wellington who, when threatened with blackmail about his liaison with the famous prostitute Harriette Wilson, said, 'Publish and be damned'. He was so respectable that he made adultery respectable. Husbands were honoured that their wives should have a little metal put in them by the Iron Duke. He is, in the end, pleasant testimony to an age where sex was viewed without hypocrisy, and he did that age proud: when he was eighty rumours were still rife of his affairs with women a quarter of his age.

He was a Tory who did not mind that his private life was made public. It might be said that he was a Tory before, in their zest for returning everything to the private sector, they privatized parts.

FOOTNOTES

1 What remains unanswered still, however, is the vexing question of *where* Weymer rogered Napoleon. The roger with Wellington must presumably, if it was on the playing fields of Eton, have taken place, like all public school rogers, behind the cricket sight screen. Napoleon, however, being French, would have had no sight screen available, so must have rogered Weymer in the open air *without a sight screen*, which would have left them open to the observation and quips of casual passers-by: it is no wonder in these embarrassing circumstances that Napoleon wasn't as 'strong' as he might have been.

2 Of whom he observed, before their marriage—'She has grown ugly, by Jove!'

3 Most of Wellington's relationship with Anna was conducted by post, an enormous number of letters being passed between them over the space of twenty years. This habit of 'making love' by post was to become increasingly popular over the next hundred years, until superseded

by the telephone. Modern lovers find it hard to understand how love-making by letter could have been satisfying. Perhaps the publication of the recently discovered Tessa/Ernest love letters, which some ill-informed scholars think to be genuine, may make clearer the expertise which letter writers of a time gone by eventually gained:

The Oaks, Brighton.

Dearest Tessa,
How I wish I might be with you tonight. Your softest of cheeks, your long, dark hair, and your arms winding round me. Being apart is unbearable. My spirit is heavy with love for you. Please write and tell me you feel the same, and that to make love is your only desire, as, most surely it is mine.
Your ever loving Ernest.

Rose Cottage, Ashford.

Dearest Ernest,
O yes, I am yours, I am yours. I sit here now, in the beautiful satin negligée you bought me when last we were together, and wish that in this mirror I saw you coming towards me, your dark eyes determined, your soft beard rustling in the wind from the window. How it grieves me that all I see is my own sad face, brushing this long sad hair, and missing you.
Love Tessa.

The Oaks, Brighton.

Dearest Tessa,
Take off the negligée. Why leave the negligée on? I want to see you without the negligée, your long hair cascading over your naked breasts.
Your more than affectionate, Ernest, in love.

Rose Cottage, Ashford.

Dear Ernest,
The negligée is off. But now, I feel shy; what of yourself? How are you dressed?
Love Tessa.

The Oaks, Brighton.

Dearest Tessa,
I have on my smoking jacket, black trousers, and a white shirt, one of those loose hanging ones, like an actor about to do a duelling scene.
Love Ernest.

Rose Cottage, Ashford.

Dear Ernest,
Take them off.
Tessa.

The Oaks, Brighton.

Dearest Tessa,
Having trouble with the cufflinks.
Ernest.

Rose Cottage, Ashford.

Dearest Ernest,
I wait for you, but shall have to close the window. It's getting a little chilly.
Love Tessa.

The Oaks, Brighton.

> Dearest Tessa,
> Be cold no more. They are off.
> Love Ernest.

Rose Cottage, Ashford.

> Dear Ernest,
> Look then how I slip under the sheets, naked flesh against satin, ready to drown in your manly arms.
> Love Tessa.

The Oaks, Brighton.

> Dearest Tessa,
> And look how I also slip under the sheets too. O, your firm body, your warm embraces, your tender kisses, the softness of your thighs, the cast of your hips. O, my darling, I love you so.
> Ever your affectionate servant, Ernest.

Rose Cottage, Ashford.

> Dearest Ernest,
> I love you too, so much, so much. O let me kiss you. Let me smother you in kisses. O, O, O. My ears, yes, my ear. O, no, no.
> Love Tessa.

The Oaks, Brighton.

> Dearest Tessa,
> O my sweet, my sweet, you kiss with such passion, o my dearest, my dearest, hold me, love me for ever, the pressure of your breast against my chest, your legs pushed tightly against mine, my hand cupped around your small bottom.
> I am yours Ernest.

Rose Cottage, Ashford.

> Dear Ernest,
> And my hand cupped around your tight . . . Ernest, you haven't left your undergarments on again, have you?
> Tessa.

The Oaks, Brighton.

> Dearest Tessa,
> I am sorry. I was shy.
> Your Ernest.

Rose Cottage, Ashford.

> Ernest,
> Take them off.
> Tessa.

The Oaks, Brighton.

> Dearest, dearest Tessa,
> All right, they're off.
> Ernest.

Rose Cottage, Ashford.

Dearest Ernest,
That's better. I don't know why you're so shy about it. You of all men. But let's forget that. Come on. Come on. O, my neck, my neck. O, come, come, I am here, ready for you, O I love you. I love you so much.
Love Tiny Tessa.

The Oaks, Brighton.

Dearest Tessa,
O, my little darling. I am yours, yours.
Love Ernest.

Rose Cottage, Ashford.

Dear Ernest,
Then prove it to me, now. Now!
Tessa.

The Oaks, Brighton.

Dearest Tessa,
I love you.
Ernest.

Rose Cottage, Ashford.

Dear Ernest,
I know you love me, Ernest. So make love to me. Now.
Tessa.

The Oaks, Brighton.

Dearest Tessa,
Guide me. Sorry. Been a long time,
Ernest.

Rose Cottage, Ashford.

Dearest, Sweet, Loving Ernest,
There you go . . . ,
I'm your Tessa.

The Oaks, Brighton.

DEAREST TESSA,
Ah, ah. O my God this is fabulous.

Rose Cottage, Ashford.

DEAREST, DEAREST ERNEST,
O, that's right, that's right, yes, there, there.

The Oaks, Brighton.

DEAREST, LOVINGEST, EAGEREST TESSA,
No!!! Wait, wait.

Rose Cottage, Ashford.

Dear Ernest,
THERE, THERE, O MY LOVE, MY LOVE, MY OOO!

The Oaks, Brighton.

For God's sake, woman STILL!! Wait.

The Oaks, Brighton.

Dear Tessa,
Too late, I'm afraid. Sorry,
Ernest.

Rose Cottage, Ashford.

Dear Ernest,
O God.
Tessa.

The Oaks, Brighton.

Dearest Tessa,
I said 'Sorry'.
Ernest.

Rose Cottage, Ashford.

Dear Ernest,
No, don't worry.
Love Tessa.

The Oaks, Brighton.

Dearest Tessa,
You are so sweet to me. Surely the time has come for us to meet and do this properly.
Ernest.

Rose Cottage, Ashford.

Dear Ernest,
Yes. Yes. But do give me warning.
Ever Yours,
Miss Tessa Chadwell.
PS. Am moving house. Will inform you when new address comes through. Byeeee!

ENEMIES LAY LINE

LOUIS XV

MME DU BARRY

COMTE JEAN DU BARRY

DESIRÉE CLARY

NAPOLEON BONAPARTE

MARGUERITE WEYMER

THE DUKE OF WELLINGTON

And so across revolution and war, the river of roger flows on, mysteriously binding all in its windy, sinuous, tender, sparkly caresses: never stopping, never ending, always growing, always expanding, almost always fun.

BAD GIRLS

FROM	**CAROLINE OF BRUNSWICK**
TO	**LADY CAROLINE LAMB**
IN	**8 ROGERS**

This line, short on time and long on rogering, shows there's almost no limit to what you can do, or who you can do it to. It's a line of strong women, getting on with the job all over Europe and beyond, and loose men, getting on with the job all over the house, and outside it. But it is also a moral line, a truthful line, bearing a grim warning. For all the merry rogering, page after page after page of it, ends with Caroline Lamb in the most terrible tears.

(Its connection to the previous line, as the great roger of history continues, is as follows: Napoleon Bonaparte—Empress Marie Louise—King Joachim of Naples—Caroline of Brunswick.)

CAROLINE OF BRUNSWICK

Born	**1768, in Brunswick.**
Occupation	**Princess, but not Queen.**
Hobbies	**Annoying her husband, touring Europe and rogering (preferably simultaneously).**
Dislike	**Washing.**
Distinguishing Features	**Visible breasts.**
Romantically Linked With	**George IV (m), Sir Sydney Smith, Major von Tobinge, Prince William Frederick of Gloucester, Duke of Kent, King Joachim of Naples, Sapio, Mr K. Craven, Captain Manby, Sir W. Gell, Captain Hesse, Bartolomeo Pergami, Luigi Pergami.**
Nickname	**The Lion of Brunswick.**

Caroline of Brunswick was the most controversial princess England ever had. Back in Brunswick, people *could not believe it* when the Prince of England said he was going to marry her: anyone who had ever met her knew it was a fatal mistake.[1] And he *could not believe it* the second he met her, but already it was too late. She was the oddest looking plump German girl, in woollen stockings, with a weird sense of humour and an odour problem.

On their first introduction, the future George IV could not even bring himself to talk to her. He simply turned to his best friend and said, 'Harris, I am not well, pray get me a glass of brandy.' Caroline replied loudly: 'I find him very fat and nothing like as handsome as his portraits.'

It was not a good start, but it was like heaven on earth compared to what was to come. Never have two people been more stunningly mismatched. Within months, George had moved into a different wing of the palace to avoid his wife, complaining of her 'personal nastiness'. He then threw her out completely. Which was a mistake. Unfettered in her new home in Blackheath, Caroline went wild: 'I have a bedfellow whenever I like'. Instead of sulking, this extraordinary woman decided to have a devilish good time and do everything she could to annoy the Prince. She threw wild parties every night, lavishly entertaining opposition politicians and sailors, and finally thought it would be amusing to pretend that she'd had an illegitimate child, so borrowed one off a poor woman and paraded him as hers.

Finally, the Prince had had enough. He launched a Delicate Inquiry to find grounds to divorce her. The ruse failed: the inquiry ticked Caroline off for immorality, but, quite ridiculously, cleared her of the charge of adultery. When George made a second attempt to have her ousted, Caroline responded by going abroad on an outrageous rogering tour of the Continent.[2] Gorgeously overweight, wearing a fabulously unsuitable black wig and too much rouge, she slammed round the courts of Europe exposing her breasts to all and sundry and having a public affair with a good-looking Italian stud called Pergami.

While she was away, George III died, and her husband became King. The obese German nymphomaniac with the happy laugh was suddenly prospective Queen of England. But George would have nothing of it. He took the case for divorce to the House of Lords and for forty days the highest court in the land listened to all the evidence about Caroline's misdemeanours, from her fig-leaf love games to the time she was found sleeping naked with her hands nestled over her lover's private parts. By the time the trial was over, Caroline was a national heroine. The public adored her: they followed her through the streets, crying Hail Queen Caroline.[3] Everyone thought the King an absolute skunk for spying on his wife and when the House of Lords vindicated her, the nation exploded into rejoicing not paralleled till VE-Day and Prince Charles' wedding to Lady Diana. Unfortunately, however, the battle was won, but the war was lost. When George was crowned, he simply didn't ask Caroline along. She was turned away from her own coronation for not having a ticket.

After that, it is said that Caroline lost the will to live. This is unlikely. More probable, she just got sick and, getting sick, died, which is perfectly normal. Her last words were: 'I am going to die, Brougham, but it does not signify'. How wrong she was: her happy and outrageous life is an inspiration to happy rogerers throughout the world.

FOOTNOTES

1 Caroline was a difficult child. On one occasion when not invited to a ball, she screamed, fainted, and revealed she was pregnant and just entering labour. After the ball had been cancelled and doctors were literally sprinting around with hot towels, she popped out of bed, perfectly unpregnant and, merrily smiling at her mama, said: 'Will you forbid me to go to a ball again?'

2 This was the eighteenth century equivalent of Club 18-30: although Caroline was over thirty, and *did* get lots of sex.

3 So good was she for public high spirits, that even those against her were witty. They joined in the general celebration, singing this song:

> *Most gracious Queen, we thee implore*
> *To go away and sin no more.*
> *Or if that effort be too great*
> *To go away at any rate.*

CAROLINE OF BRUNSWICK & GEORGE IV

A classic case of role reversal. On the wedding night, it was George who did everything he could to get out of his conjugal duties, while Caroline made no effort to pretend that she was new to the game.[1] First the Prince brought along some friends on the honeymoon to steady his nerves with a game of cards. He then drank more than his due to reinforce himself, but even so was seen fleeing the love-nest pale-faced in the early hours of the morning. And Caroline was so unimpressed by his efforts then and subsequently, that when she learnt she was pregnant, she hooted with disbelief and exclaimed: 'I don't believe it!' The Prince did not forgive her the slight.

GEORGE IV	
Born	1762, in England.
Died	1830.
Occupation	Prince Regent, dandy and King.
Hobbies	Strolling, dressing up, drinking, gambling, being stylish and rogering.
Distinguishing Features	Small but stylish penis.
Romantically Linked With	Mrs Robinson, Mrs Crouch, Mrs Fitzherbert, Harriet Vernon, Lady Hertford, Lady Jersey, Lady Melbourne, Lady Augusta Campbell, Duchess of Devon, and Princess Caroline of Brunswick (m).
Nickname	The First Gentleman of Europe, Prinney.

Both Georges III and IV went mad at some point in their lives. George III at one point insisted on ending all his sentences with the word 'peacock',[2] and tragically his madness was handed down to his son, who by the end of his life spent most of his time under the illusion that he was actually fighting in the Battle of Waterloo, although sitting in his own study.

The most stylish of men, intimate of Beau Brummel, builder of the Brighton Pavilion, George IV was lumbered through life with a crazed summer pudding for a wife, scarcely the thing for a man whose refined sensibilities the incorrect fold of a handkerchief would offend. He only agreed to marry her in return for his father paying off his debts: an act he bitterly regretted.[3] Nevertheless, he had been happy enough to find true love before his marriage in the form of Mrs Fitzherbert.[4] When she left the country, he cried, rolled on the floor, struck his forehead, tore his hair, fell into hysterics and said he'd abandon his country and forego the crown.

FOOTNOTES

1 For those without the amoral courage of Princess Caroline, it was necessary in these days to pretend that one knew nothing of the subject. Mothers, who had suffered the same difficulty, would advise a three-point plan:

    a When the husband removes his trousers, scream in fear: 'O My Lawdy-Milawky, there's a large snake in your purse!'

    b When he asks if you would like to make love, say 'Yes', and begin to shake his hand enthusiastically.

    c When he then begins to make love to you for real, cry out in a loud voice: 'O my God, you've murdered me!' That should convince him.

2 This habit caused George's ministers great alarm. There are few things more likely to imperil public respect for the monarchy than a King who signs off every edict with the words, 'This is the Will of the King Peacock'. The Peacock Crisis was, however, finally solved when the King was cunningly informed that 'peacock' was a magic word, too holy to be allowed into the ears of the common horde. Thereafter, although still peacocking away like a loony in private, the King said the word so quietly on public occasions that no one but his most trusted ministers were privileged to hear it.

3 There are of course many strange reasons for getting married.

Many still marry for money—to pay off debts, to gain tax relief.

Others marry for citizenship, for passports. Before the war, W.H. Auden and a homosexual friend married two German girls to get them out of Germany. When asked about this, he replied: 'What else are buggers for?'

Most, however, marry to plug an embarrassing hole in conversation. A couple are getting on fairly well, when one day, a hole in conversation occurs. Neither party can think of anything to say. Nothing. Stony silence. No anecdotes forthcoming. After a minute this becomes awkward to say the least. After two minutes, something must be done. To cover the pause, the man pretends he has been thinking hard and says, 'Will you marry me?' The woman says 'Yes' and after that, they have something to talk about for the whole of their lives (when to marry, who to ask, where to honeymoon, when to have the child, where to educate it, how to stop it taking drugs, whether to tell it about contraception and finally how to find the money to pay for that wedding) so the silence never happens again.

4 Later rather scandalously re-named Mrs FitzGeorge, after rumours about the King's awkwardly shaped private parts. (See Napoleon and Edward VIII).

GEORGE IV & LADY HERTFORD & LORD HERTFORD

The above title does not mean a complex example of titled troilism is about to be revealed. A man as discriminating as George, who invented the concept of 'strolling', would scarcely have indulged in something so undoubtedly un-relaxing. The truth is that these were discreet rogers: Lady Hertford was one of the King's married mistresses, and Lord Hertford, being the man she was married to, slept with her as well.[1] In the instance of these rogers, unlike those with his wife, George chose not to have the House of Lords look over the details, so they are not as merrily documented as one might have hoped. Although when dealing with Lord Hertford, things were rarely merry . . .

LORD HERTFORD

Occupation	**Miser.**
Hobby	**Counting money, lots of it.**
Distinguishing Features	**No cash in pocket.**
Romantically Linked With	**Lady Hertford, Marchesa di Castiglione, and a large wodge of notes.**

Lord Hertford was in his time the most famously mean man in England. He was the Jack Benny of his generation. In fact, his speciality was being things beginning with 'mis-'. As well as being a miser, he was also a misanthrope: his most famous comment, summing up a life of grim mean-spiritedness, was: 'All men are bad, and when I die, I will at least have the consolation of knowing I have rendered a service to no one'.

And *yet, yet, yet* . . . once in his life, once in his ghastly life, Hertford cast his character aside: once in his life he did something so uncharacteristic that it almost cancels out all his other meanness: a gesture so startling, so grand, so *expensive*, that Lord Hertford, mean, money-grabbing, penny-pinching, debt-collecting, cash-eating, coin-sexing, pocket-picking, wallet-worshipping Lord Hertford is, *startlingly* but *unreservedly*, a prime candidate for the Most Expensive Roger of All Time.

Because when Hertford saw the Marchesa di Castiglione, unquestionably the most beautiful woman of her time, Hertford knew he wanted her. And no matter what it cost him, Hertford was going to have her. And it cost him.

He offered her one million francs for a night of sex. The Marchesa, being flattered and not at all put out, put out.[2]

FOOTNOTES

1 It is generally thought by linguists that the term 'sleeping with' was invented to get people out of duels where obvious and allowed adultery was involved. For instance, in this instance.

 LORD HERTFORD: *Sir, have you been sleeping with my wife?*
 GEORGE, PRINCE REGENT: *No.*
 LORD HERTFORD: *Good.*

 Which is, of course, perfectly true. Although it could be more graphically rephrased:

 LORD HERTFORD: *Sir, have you been sleeping with my wife?*
 GEORGE, PRINCE REGENT: *No. I was far too busy rogering her.*

2 A story is told of one actress who was asked by an admirer if she would sleep with him if he offered her a million pounds. She laughed and replied she would. He smiled and said: 'Good—we have established the principle: now all we have to do is negotiate the price'.

LORD HERTFORD & THE MARCHESA DI CASTIGLIONE

There are no extant drawings of what happened on that million franc night, but in the contract Hertford had made space for all exigencies: 'Give me one night of love, without excluding any erotic refinements, in exchange for one million francs'. What is known, however, is that after it the Marchesa had to spend three days in bed. Recovering. Hertford, old miser that he was, had gone for his money's worth.[1]

MARCHESA DI CASTIGLIONE	
Born	**1837, in Italy.**
Occupation	**Rogering.**
Hobbies	**Collecting jewellery and rogering.**
Romantically Linked With	**Count di Castiglione (m), King Victor Emmanuel II, Napoleon III, Count Anatole Demidoff, Baron James de Rothschild and his three sons, Marquis Ambrogia Doria and his two brothers Andrea and Marcello, Duc de Chartres, Prince Henri de la Tour D'Auvergne, General Estancelin, Duke D'Aumale, Duke of Genoa, Lord Hertford.**
Nickname	**(Others): Her Royal Strangeness.** **(Herself): The Most Beautiful Woman of the Century.**

The Marchesa di Castiglione was one of the legendary lovers of her time. So famous, actually, that she was at one point called up by her country to lie back and think of it officially. Italy was disunited and its great statesman, Cavour, decided that the Marchesa was the negotiating tool to put this right.[2] He explained his plan to King Victor Emmanuel: the Marchesa was to be sent on an official mission to roger Napoleon III until he agreed to help with the union. Emmanuel thought it quite a good plan, as long as the Marchesa was really up to it. He spent a night with her to check. She was up to it. On her first entrance at a ball to meet Napoleon, her beauty (and relative undress) was so startling that the band stopped playing, men stood on tables to look at her, and Napoleon immediately demanded the next dance. Within months, they were lovers.

After such a start, the Marchesa was fated, or perhaps doomed, to a life of rogering. She became the most desired woman in the world, and lovers, always rich, always titled, flooded through the doors of her boudoir, where she would await them in her grey batiste and lace nightgown. Although married, she didn't see her husband at one stage for twelve years, and the day they met, he died a death so bizarre, that she never bothered tying the knot again.[3] Yet his predictions for her came true: he had warned her to beware the day her beauty faded, and, when it did start to fade, her falling off was strange and tragic.

For at the age of forty, the Marchesa di Castiglione locked herself away from the world for ever. She hid in a small apartment in Paris, never venturing out in daylight, mad and obsessive about her past: perhaps not surprising, as a woman who had been given a tiara by the Pope and one by most of the important European heads of state. She grew finally to believe that the spirit of Cleopatra had returned in her body, and lived in a strange and perverse dreamworld, saying she was ill and poor, when she was neither. Twenty-two years after she had last seen daylight, she was found dead, rats gnawing at her feeble frame. And this the woman who, after kissing a friend's child, observed: 'When he grows up you will tell him that the first kiss he ever had was given by the most beautiful woman of the century'.[4]

FOOTNOTES

1 A similar story is told of Napoleon's outrageous sister, Pauline Borghese. She was so exhausted by the attentions of her lover Nicolas Forbin that she had to be carried around in a litter during the daytime. Her nerves were so shattered by her night-time ordeals that any dog that barked within earshot of her was immediately shot.

2 Compare and contrast with Sir Geoffrey Howe's mission to South Africa.

3 Her husband, the Count, died on the most extraordinary wedding day of all time: beyond belief were it not true. She and he were attending the wedding between the Duke D'Acosta and Princess Marie, when, tragically, the Count fell from his horse and was crushed by a carriage. However, this was not the end of the day's misfortunes. Also killed at the wedding were a prince (scalded to death by an exploding boiler), the lady of the robes (who committed suicide), the colonel of the Guard (who contracted sunstroke while performing his duties and fell to his death from a balcony), the station master (crushed by the bride's train), a gateman (suicide again), the best man (he shot himself) and a court official who died of an apoplectic fit.

4 The Marchesa had always known she was beautiful and used her complete charms from an early age. Her diaries are peppered with a code: 'B—a kiss; BX—beyond a kiss; F—everything!!!'

For the regular rogerer, the writing of diaries in code is very important, since many are the love affairs spoiled by the discovery of a lover's over-informative diary. On the whole, the more complex the code, the better: something like 'F—everything' might just be seen through by someone with a real detective's mind. Experience has shown that, while sporting metaphors can be useful ('went to the cricket, where he had a very long innings'), eating metaphors are the most effective.

First, the basic code:

> *Didn't eat*—nothing
> *Ate in*—kissing
> *Just popped out for a bite*—more than kissing
> *Went to an expensive restaurant*—everything

But it is in the *second stage* that the food code really comes into its own, with accurate and graphic descriptions that can be fully garnished without fear of discovery. After going to the expensive restaurant, the diarist might add such observations as:

a lost my appetite when I actually got there;
b took ages for the food to come, but really worth it when it did;
c service was fast, but the food disappointing;
d four great courses: huge portions;
e terribly exotic menu, but very small portions, unfortunately;
e partner absolutely adored the melons, but consumed the rest of the meal with rather less relish;
f had so much wine, fell asleep right in the middle;
g refused to have pudding, 'banana surprise', which rather spoiled the evening.

The possibilities are limitless.

THE MARCHESA DI CASTIGLIONE & NAPOLEON III

This roger, as a piece of diplomacy, was both a success and a failure. When first Napoleon fell to the charms of the Marchesa, he was undecided on the issue of Italian unity, but after a few nights with her, he found out just what fun uniting could be and threw his weight behind the Italian cause. Unfortunately, however, the rest of Europe stepped in and prevented him doing what he wanted to. 'Unfortunately', since, had the mission been more successful, we might now find ourselves with all the fuss and bother of Geneva and its summits disposed of, and Brooke Shields sleeping with Mr Gorbachov, and Olga Korbut sleeping with President Reagan and ironing out the troubles of the world between the four of them.[1,2]

NAPOLEON III	
Born	**1808, in France.**
Died	**1873, in England.**
Occupation	**Emperor.**
Hobby	**Rogering.**
Romantically Linked With	**Maidservant Elisa, Marchesa di Castiglione, Princess Mathilde, Mlle de Padua, Grand Duchess Olga, Countess de Maera, Contessa Baraglini, Lady Blessington, Lady Douglas, Marquise de Belboeuf, Comtesse D'Espel, Mimi la Bouchère, Madame Badinguet, Marguerite Bayeaux, Favart de Longlade, Tagliani, Alice Ozy, Mlle Theric, Jane Digby,[3] Rachel, Mme de Cadave, Mme de la Bedoyere, Julie le Boeuf, Mme Kalergi, Mme de Persigny, Harriet Howard, Eleanora Brault, Jeanne Charlotte Leopoldine Isadora da Cruz Francoise Xavier de Paula Michaella Gabriella Rafaella Louise Gonzague, Eujenie de Montejo (m).**
Nickname	**The Third.**

Napoleon III was a nephew of Napoleon I, and the son of Louis Bonaparte, King of Holland, and Hortense, daughter of Empress Josephine: his political career was chequered but curiously he reigned in France for a lot longer than his famous uncle. He was elected President in 1848 after the revolution that overthrew the Bourbon Louis Phillipe, he appointed himself Emperor in 1852, and remained Emperor till 1870, when he was thrown out by another revolution: in those days the French loved revolting. His politics were better the closer he got to home. Foreign affairs, he made a mess of. Home affairs, he was quite good at. Bedroom affairs, his record is completely staggering.

Napoleon III was, in modern parlance, a *really easy lay*: getting in the sack with Napoleon III was a cinch. Want Nap to wrap his Imperial thighs around you—no problem. Buying a loaf of bread—difficult. His 'love-life' started at the age of thirteen when he rogered a maidservant called Elisa, and from then on he never stopped. That quick game of hide the chipolata in the nursery was the start of fifty years of rogering that was to leave even the normally open-minded French people filled with disgust. Napoleon was completely uncontrollable with women. Anything in a petticoat, he lost his sense of reason.

But, unhappily, as Napoleon humped his way round Europe, French power waned. Occasionally he would claim he was rogering for the national interest, but the one time he did do this seriously, with the Marchesa, it went badly wrong. Eventually, sucked unwillingly into the disastrous Franco-Prussian wars, the French spotted him for a sex-starved scoundrel, and threw him out.

At which point Napoleon, rather charmingly in view of his uncle's attitudes to England, chose to retire to Chislehurst in Kent, where, the word is, he was made to feel welcome and at home. What a strange, and yet pleasant idea it is, the thought of a Napoleon moving next door in England, and no one really minding. Napoleon out doing the shopping. Napoleon chewing over the weather. Napoleon waiting for the Friday fish and chip van. Napoleon opening the fête as guest celebrity because Tennyson dropped out at the last minute. Napoleon winning the rose cup, but coming third in the largest onion competition. How much rogering he did in Chislehurst is unrecorded, but it is known that he died peacefully in 1873.

FOOTNOTES

1 A touching additional note is how the Marchesa's husband put the affairs of his country before his private affairs and parts, and endorsed the whole expedition. He gave his wife a purple and gold bed before her departure on which to do her patriotic deeds—it was her last remaining possession when she died, so she obviously appreciated the gesture.

2 An additional ridiculous note shows what a passionate woman the Marchesa was despite all her calculations. When she was rogering Napoleon, she was so jealous she deliberately wore the same dress and hairstyle as the Empress to a ball to point out how redundant her Highness was.

3 It would be wrong to rush on in this lady's line without a short extra note about Jane Digby. Miss Digby was an Englishwoman 'made for love': she rogered far and wide throughout the nineteenth century, but most especially, she rogered exotic: for having scandalized English society by her divorce, she then rogered Napoleon, then King Otto of Greece and after that

spread her net of love yet further and further: she finally counted among her lovers two sheiks and a man called Medjuel esl Mesrab. She was the founding mother of the great line of oriental passion which leads through Rudolph Valentino and Omar Sharif to some of the more fishy passages of *Lace*. But more, she is proof that in these days, for real passions, you had to get out of England, as Caroline of Brunswick, Byron, and indeed, even as Lord Hertford did.

NAPOLEON III & LADY BLESSINGTON

Napoleon was an easy lay, but not necessarily a pleasant one. He had an affair with Lady Blessington when in England during one of his many exiles before getting a firm grip on power in France. But when she later went to Paris, hounded by debtors and under the cloud of scandal, he was President of the Republic and therefore thought it might be better if he didn't call on her or recognize her.

Fortunately, she was the match for his rudeness. They finally met at a ball and Blessington approached him calmly, having been blatantly ignored. 'Ah, Milady Blessington—are you staying in France for a long time?' he inquired. To which she, remembering the frantic to-ing and fro-ing of his years out of power, calmly replied: 'What about you?'

LADY BLESSINGTON

Born	**1789, in England.**
Occupation	**Hostess.**
Hobbies	**Writing and rogering.**
Romantically Linked With	**Lord Blessington, Lord Byron, Napoleon III.**
Distinguishing Features	**Byron's words in her ear.**

Lady Blessington was another woman of passion and style who had to leave England in the end. The prime confidante of Lord Byron, she lived with Count D'Orsay, the husband of her stepdaughter, at Gore House, and when she was not fulfilling her role as the centre of cultural society, made the money to pay for the canapés and cocktails by writing for cash, something which was considered distinctly *infra dignitate*. Finally, her debts got the better of her, and, as people used to do before international credit cards made it impossible to escape, she fled to France in 1849 to avoid her debtors. Unfortunately, while trying to dodge the debtors she bumped slap bang into Death himself and died the same year. She is much to be blessed for having noted down so much of what Byron had to say.

LADY BLESSINGTON & LORD BYRON

Lady Blessington wrote a book called *Journal of Conversations with Lord Byron*, in which she recorded many of his most intimate *bon mots*. She did not write a book called *Journal of Copulations with Lord Byron*, in which she recorded many of his most intimate bon moves. Whether this is a shame or not is not known.

LORD BYRON

Born	**1788, in England.**
Died	**1824.**
Occupation	**Poet.**
Hobbies	**Being heroic, incest and rogering.**
Distinguishing Features	**Beauty.**
Romantically Linked With	**Lady Caroline Lamb, Frances Ann Kemble, Annabelle Millbanke (m), Lady Oxford, Lady Blessington, Lady Frances Webster, Augusta Leigh, Claire Clairmont, Marianna Segati, Margherita Cogni, Countess Teresa Guiciolli.**
Nickname	**Evil Lord Byron.**

If someone says to you, 'Lord Byron never rogered anyone: he went a virgin to his grave', and then tells you that he/she loves you, it's not a love you can depend on. Because Byron, in his own words, 'tooled in a post chaise, in a hackney coach, in a gondola, against a wall, in a court carriage, on a table, and under it'.[1,2]

He has, in fact, become one of the most famous lovers of all time. His story is too long here to be told, but he ran the gamut of sexual experience and he ran it with style. From boys to girls half his age to women almost twice his age, from his own wife to everyone else's wives,[3] from seducer to seduced,[4] from lover to lovered, from a harem to fidelity, from nameless serving girls to his own sister, Byron, in the words of 'MacArthur Park',[5] 'drank the wine while it was warm, and never let you catch him looking at the sun'. With his fabulous good looks, his romantic poems both atrocious and brilliant, his dark and mysterious mysteriousness, he cast a magic spell over the imaginations of thousands of women in his time and millions of people ever since.[6] He had, in the words of Frank Sinatra, 'a life that's full. He travelled each and every by-way'.

He also, incidentally, bit off more than he could chew quite regularly. Byron's love life is a good one to study, because of its proportion of disasters: most of them we will all come across in one form or another.

They include, realistically:

1. 'Mad person': Caroline Lamb.

2. 'Major mistake': Annabelle Millbanke, his wife.

3. 'High price for worst slip': Augusta Leigh, his sister: pregnant.[7]

4. 'Damnable bad luck': Teresa Guiciolli, love of his life, married three days before he met her.

5. 'Ill-timed sexual experiment': His wife again.[8]

It also includes one big mistake which most of us, however, would hope to avoid. Byron died at the age of thirty-five, halfway through God's appointed time. He left a gap no one's ever been able to fill.

FOOTNOTES

1 'Tool'd'—see Appendix: Names for Rogering.
2 The question to be asked about making love in an exotic place is whether or not the discomfort is worth the excitement; the answer is: when a bout of exotically-placed love-making is on its way, take some advanced precautions.

As always in life, it's in the planning . . .

Thus, if you wish to make mad, spontaneous love on the floor of the living room, try to make sure there are as many cushions as possible around. If there are no cushions, newspapers will do: these also afford an excellent distraction during love-making, and an excellent subject for conversation afterwards.

Likewise, if the love is to occur madly and spontaneously on the kitchen table, make sure that you have just been baking a large amount of bread. The dough from the bread will act as an excellent resting place for bottoms, etc. Other suitable ingredients are cooked pasta and cooked rice. Uncooked pasta or uncooked rice are a mistake, as are nuts, chopped or unchopped.

With careful planning, every room in the house can be turned into *the* spot for love without any real discomfort.
3 Byron to Lady Melbourne: 'I am all for morality and shall confine myself to the strictest adultery'.

4 And to Lady Melbourne again: 'One must make love mechanically, as one swims. I was very fond of both once, but now as I never swim unless I tumble into water, I don't want to make love till almost obliged'.

5 Which he didn't write, although he did write lots of other truly awful poetry*.

6 His effect on people is still astonishing. Recently, he drove the great literary critic George Wilson Knight quite, quite mad. Knight wrote two extraordinary books about Lord Byron. The first showed how Byron's life re-enacted all the plays of Shakespeare. The second set out to prove that Byron was the second Messiah and jolly nearly succeeded. Later in life Wilson Knight, when lecturing about *Timon of Athens*, would suddenly, halfway through the lecture, remove all his clothes and sling on nothing except a torn shred of cloth to replace them, so he could *be* Timon, not just talk about him. If Byron can have this effect on people 150 years after he died, imagine what he must have been like when alive.

7 For those interested, and morally sound enough to ignore it, a clinical study of how to make a pass at your sister reveals this as the best plan:

   a Act natural.
   b Get into conversation, about something that is unsuspicious and equally interesting to both of you: for instance, how your mother and father are.
   c Roger her.

8 The official grounds for divorce, although the rumour was that it was for incest, was for indecent behaviour with his wife. This was perhaps the single moment when women in England held the most power. There was almost no woman in the kingdom who had *not* been indecently behaved with by her husband at some time, and they could have had the lot of them over a barrel. Unfortunately, the moment slipped by.

*And, of course, lots of fabulous poetry as well. Wonderful, wonderful, wonderful, wonderful, wonderful *Don Juan*.

LORD BYRON & LADY CAROLINE LAMB

After much mirth something suddenly goes terribly wrong. This line, following the example of its beginning figure, sloppy Caroline, has been shooting across borders irrespective of class or country from the exotic east to little England, from serving girl to sheik. Everyone's been rogering, and whenever a roger has got them into trouble, another roger seems to set things right. And yet,

somewhere, lurking deep in the dark cave of promiscuity, always lies the great bear . . . of emotion. With poor Caroline Lamb, it *roars out* with a vengeance.

The moment that Caroline first laid eyes on Byron, she knew she was doomed: 'That beautiful, pale face will be my fate'. Never one to refuse a woman, passive blighter that he was, Byron and she slipped swiftly into romance after their first, seductive meeting. Married though she was, for six months their affair was as public as Big Ben, with Caroline being the one who most erred on the side of indiscretion. But when the affair was over, she did not slip on to another, as so many of the heroes of this line have done. She was stuck . . . and there was trouble.

LADY CAROLINE LAMB	
Born	**1784, in England.**
Occupation	**Being mad.**
Hobbies	**Driving Byron mad, writing bad novels.**
Distinguishing Features	**Glint in the eye.**
Romantically Linked With	**Byron, Sir Godfrey Webster, William Lamb (m).**
Nickname	**Caro.**

Caroline Lamb always had a screw loose, but for a good part of her life, she managed to keep her mental furniture fairly together. Married to the dull but earnest William Lamb, she chafed at the bit of their married life in the country, but apart from a brief fling with a rake (type of man, rather than type of gardening implement), behaved quite reasonably. Until, at the age of thirty, always a dangerous time, she met Lord Byron and her cabinet completely fell apart.

The affair was passionate and brief. But the aftermath was madly passionate and horribly drawn out. Caroline was hooked and, like an unhappy salmon, could not let go. It hurts to think how much Caroline hurt. She wrote to Byron every day. She tried to see him everywhere. She tried to kill him and she tried to kill herself. She even took off her top and painted herself black to attract his attention, and sent him clippings of her pubic hair.[1] It was the talk and scandal of English society, as Caroline physically chased poor confused Byron through the streets of London.

Finally, he left her as he left the rest of England, and, although staying quite crazy, she tried to recover. She leapt out of a tureen naked on her husband's birthday, started talking to frogs, and wrote a bad novel called *Glenarvon* about Byron, but basically she was all right. Until Byron died. After that, she left her husband, one day to be Prime Minister, and lived alone for ever.

If the passion that invaded Caroline Lamb after she'd rogered Byron could have been bottled, there would have been no need for nuclear power. The roger bomb would blow everyone clean off the face of the earth. And that roger bomb is why everyone's always got to be a little bit careful before they roger Byron, or anyone else. It is perilous to ignore it.

FOOTNOTES

1 This was a very dangerous move. It is risky enough sending any letter with passion content, so unsure can one be of the circumstances in which it will be received. But to send a letter with pubic hair content is madness. To warn against such things, an effort has been made to recreate the scene when Lord Byron receives the letter, staying, let it be imagined, with his mother's dowager friend, Lady Norfolk:

The scene is a misty Norfolk morning. Byron is late down to breakfast. The atmosphere is not good. Even the butler is a little tetchy. Byron hasn't brushed his hair.

LADY N *How did you sleep, Lord Byron?*
BYRON *Very well, thank you, my lady.*
　　　Long pause.
LADY N *Let us call for the mail.*
BYRON *What a good idea.*
LADY N *James, are there any letters?*
JAMES *Yes, ma'am.*
LADY N *Then fetch them.*
　　　He leaves to go for the mail. There is an awkward pause.
BYRON *I thought perhaps I might go riding later.*
LADY N *You do, sir, as you please. Ah, the mail: thank you, James.*
JAMES *Milady.*
LADY N *And a letter for Lord Byron.*
BYRON *Thank you, James.*
LADY N *While my husband was alive, we used to find it most amusing to read to one another the contents of our mail.*
BYRON *What a charming idea.*
LADY N *My letter is from my dear friend Reverend Pittock. He writes from Bath: 'My dear lady, I have but a short moment to write, for I am in the middle of a most taxing part of my study of the cathedral here at Bath. It is certainly a most exquisite building and I enclose for your inspection a selection of drawings of the northern transepts that I am now studying. I'm sure you will recognize their fine features from the last time you and I were here. Ever Yours, Pittock.'*
BYRON *How charming.*
LADY N *And yours, my Lord Byron, what does your letter read?*
BYRON *Ahm, it's not important.*
LADY N *All the better if not important.*
BYRON *No, but I mean really not important. I mean, incredibly un—*
LADY N *Read it!*
BYRON *Very well . . .*
　　　He opens it; something appears to spill out of it over the table: if one did not know better, one might think it pubic hair.
BYRON *'My darling, I have but a short moment to write, for I am in the middle of a bath.'*
LADY N *What a strange coincidence. The Reverend was in Bath as well.*
BYRON *Yes quite. 'I am thinking about your most exquisite features, and enclose for your*

inspection a selection of the pubic hairs which I am at this moment studying. I'm sure you will recognize them from the last time you were here when you yourself studied them so carefully. I hope they will tempt you to return soon. Love and sex, Caroline.'

Long pause.

LADY N   *How manners change among the young. Reverend Pittock would never think of sending me any of his pubic hair.*

BAD GIRLS LAY LINE

CAROLINE OF BRUNSWICK

GEORGE IV

LORD HERTFORD

MARCHESA DI CASTIGLIONE

NAPOLEON III

LADY BLESSINGTON

LORD BYRON

LADY CAROLINE LAMB

As they always say 'It'll End in Tears.'

ARTISTIC LICENCE

FROM	ONE ARTIST
TO	20 OTHER ARTISTS
IN	30 ARTISTIC ROGERS

This line is a change: a free-flowing, artistic line: not a line at all really, more a series of gentle curves amongst the artists of the nineteenth century. Its intention is not so much to show that this bunch of artists were particularly sensual—although their loose working day did perhaps allow them to oblige at more convenient hours for infidelity—but rather to show how any group of professional people, in any time, might intertwine: we could, we believe, have chosen bootmakers of the sixteenth century, booksellers of the twentieth century, cheese-tasters of the late eighteenth century. The result would have been much the same, and produced, like this does, an astonishing display of how tightly knit we all are together in the net that roger made.

For here, in only thirty rogers, twenty-one of the most famous artists of the century are tied together. They could have been World Cup footballers or medieval crusaders. The line of love goes on . . .

LOLA MONTEZ

Real Name	**Eliza Gilbert.**
Born	**1818, in Ireland.**
Occupation	**Dancer.**
Hobbies	**Horsewhipping and rogering.**
Distinguishing Features	**Black hair and black moods.**
Romantically Linked With	**Henri Dujarier, Captain James, Ned Fallin, George Heald, Patrick Hull, Franz Liszt, Victor Hugo, Prince Jung Bahadoor, Ludwig I of Bavaria, Charles Wellesley, Viscount Peel, Alexandre Dumas.**
Motto	**'What Lola Wants, Lola Gets'.**

Lola Montez is the very glue that ties this line of artists together, although many would say that a lot of people rogered Lola in order to stop her practising her art.[1] She was said to be one of the worst performers of all time. Her tarantella dance, the only act she ever had, was booed off every stage she ever appeared on. But where she was an artist of the very highest rank was in the art of love, a lover whose every movement was greeted with sighs of delight in every country in Europe. She might indeed be thought to be the founding mother of the ideal of the Eurovision Song Contest.

But unlike Eurovision Song Contest performers, Lola did not spread bland consolation and goodwill. She spread utter chaos wherever she went. The Jesuits of Bavaria, whom she persecuted, called her 'an Apocalyptic whore', and certainly every man who ever met her paid a heavy price for the pleasure of her wildly beautiful company. Alexandre Dumas said, 'she is fatal to any man who dares to love her', and the record seems to prove it.

King Ludwig of Bavaria lost his kingdom because of her: he came, saw, was conquered and let this woman, whose only skill was a bad spider dance, decide the policies of his kingdom till his people, wisely, threw him out.

George Heald, a soldier, was utterly bankrupted and then abandoned: 'Learn', said Lola, 'that he who accompanies Lola must always have money at his command'.

Ned Fallin, a theatre manager, was forced into exile, and then mysteriously fell off a ship in the middle of an argument with her.

Much the same treatment was meted out to anyone who casually offended her. In her time she horsewhipped a Melbourne critic and a delegation of Bavarian students, and had her dogs attack a Jesuit priest. Her temper was famous throughout the world. When Liszt left her, secretly sneaking out of a hotel, he gave the proprietor money to pay for the furniture she would throw out of the window on finding out he'd gone. All the money was needed.

Sensible men would lie in bed and pray they never met her: she was the Scylla of her age, a woman so dangerous, so passionate that once in her clutches, you were doomed.

FOOTNOTE

1 This conspiracy theory is probably spurious: it claims that great artists slept with Lola to stop her doing her awful dance. It is the equivalent of the great pop musicians taking it in turns to sleep with the members of Black Lace, just to keep the blonde-haired twerps quiet.

ADAH ISAACS MENCKEN	
Born	1835, in America.
Occupation	(Her) Actress. (Her enemies) Courtesan.
Hobbies	Acting and rogering.
Distinguishing Features	Not many clothes.
Romantically Linked With	Bret Harte, Mark Twain, Baron Frederick von Eberstadt, John C. Heenan, Alexander Isaacs Mencken, W. H. Kneass, Captain Barkley, Jack Hamlin, King Charles of Wurtemberg, Alexandre Dumas.
Nicknames	The Naked Lady, The Bengal Tigress, The Cleopatra in Crinoline.

Adah Isaacs worked in much the same tradition as Lola Montez: preposterous performer, great lay. Her act was more exotic, and as terrible as Lola's tarantella: it was called 'The Naked Lady', and consisted of her, in a flesh-coloured leotard, being tied to the back of a stallion which ran round and round a circus top. But her sexual skills were tremendous, and using them, clad in not even a leotard, she went round and round the world—as she said of her love life, *and* her act: 'No stallion gives Mencken trouble for long'. Her fame as a lover brought her from Havana to Chicago to Europe. She seduced Mark Twain, flagellated Swinburne and rogered the ageing ever-active Dumas.

In fact, it was Adah who performed the first ever recorded striptease on stage, thus raising the very important question: should girls get their Equity cards by taking all their clothes off in a nightclub on the Costa Brava? Apart from the clotheslessness, however, her relationship with the theatre was pretty tenuous. She described herself as 'The Sterling Tragedienne', but on Broadway she forgot *all* her lines as Lady Macbeth. As Mark Twain said, 'she had other charms . . .'[1]

And those charms made Adah one of a group of women in the nineteenth century whose lives are like fabulous fiction, crossing borders of class and race through the simple magnetism of their beauty. She was at one time a whore, at one time a bigamist, at one time married to the US boxing champion and at another time a guest at the court of Emperor Franz Joseph. Unfortunately, she sort of blew it there by doing a trimmed version of her naked lady act, which sent the Emperor out of the room, mortified. But then what do emperors know about having a good time?[2]

FOOTNOTES

1 These were mainly to do with her body, which Adah took every possible opportunity to reveal. She was probably unwise to do so, as curiosity to see the other person's body is one of the major reasons for rogering, and to give the whole game away before the roger may be an error. Clothing throughout the ages has always concealed various and different parts of the body. You knew everything about an Elizabethan's legs, but the codpiece was utterly misleading. On the other hand, you knew nothing about the 1950s American boy's legs, because of the baggy trousers, while, crewcuts the way they were, you were completely *au fait* with the shape of his skull. A Victorian lady's top half was quite well-outlined: her bottom half was a mystery.

In fact, to say, 'Would you like sex?', has always really been a way of saying, 'For God's sake, let me have a proper look at you'.

2 As can be seen from the Napoleons and *passim*, quite a lot.

SARAH BERNHARDT	
Born	**1844, in France.**
Occupation	**Actress.**
Hobbies	**Rogering and not sport.**[1]
Distinguishing Features	**Red hair and intensity.**
Romantically Linked With	**Jean Richepin, Phillipe Garnier, Jean Mounee Sully, Pierre Berton, Gustave Dore, Emile Zola, Edmund Rostand, Count de Keratry, Prince de Ligne, Prince Napoleon, King Alphonso XIII of Spain, King Umberto of Italy, King Christian IX of Denmark, King Edward VII, Napoleon III, Emperor Franz Joseph of Austria, Aristides Jacques Damala (m).**[2]
Possibly Linked With	**Oscar Wilde.**[3]
Nickname	**The Divine Sarah.**

The third of the stage-bound lovers, Sarah is in a league of her own. While the other two were thespianic idiots, Sarah was one of the greatest actresses of all time: the passion in her voice was such that a co-star at a read-through when she was seventy years old could not make his first speech, because he was weeping at the very sound of her voice. She was fêted and adored throughout her life, and courted by the most powerful and wealthy men in the world. Her fame was like the fame of the most famous of film stars, her every performance a sensation. And while she waited for the most glorious men of the era to flock round her, she made it her policy always to have an affair with her leading man, so she always had a good backstop lover to fill in the gaps.

'I have been one of the great lovers of the century,' she said, and it is a claim that seems almost modest in her case. She had over 1000 affairs, she kept a silk-lined coffin at home, purportedly for rogering,[4] and she once attempted to graft a tiger's tail on to her bottom. In other words, she was an unusual and exotic woman. So exotic indeed that when she lost a leg in later life, it seemed only to add to her attraction and her glamour. An American admirer asked her if he could buy her leg for $100,000 and exhibit it: she cabled two words in reply: 'Which leg?'

Like many great rogerers, she had religious leanings at first and when she was sixteen she wanted to be a nun. But once on the rogering road, she never looked back. Her attraction was fabulous, and she seemed able to make anyone do anything for her—an American cowboy rode over 300 miles to see her show, perhaps hoping for a ride for a ride, and in Paris once she persuaded Edward VII to play the part of a corpse in the play *Fédora*. And to repay them, she, like Joan Collins, seemed never to grow old. At the age of seventy, she was playing nineteen-year-olds and knocking them for six. And up until her death in 1925 she still had all the style and panache and wit that characterized her whole life. She lived in a high Paris apartment and when asked why by a friend exhausted by the walk, she replied: 'It is the only way I can still make the hearts of men beat faster'.

FOOTNOTES

1 If acting and rogering were her consummate skills, sport was a blank page. When she had watched a football match in England, she remarked, 'I adore cricket, it's so English'.
2 Most astonishing achievement this: consider its equivalent: David Hockney, John Fowles, Lord Lichfield, Jacques Chirac, King Juan Carlos, Prime Minister of Italy, Prime Minister of Denmark, Prince Charles, François Mitterand and Kurt Waldheim.
3 Wilde was certainly a great admirer of hers, and she appeared in his plays. One tale told of them is when, in the middle of an argument, he asked her if she minded if he smoked. Her reply was: 'I don't care if you burn'. Perhaps they went to bed afterwards to make it up.
4 It was generally thought that the argument behind this was that if one was lucky enough to roger Sarah Bernhardt, one should be perfectly ready to die afterwards.

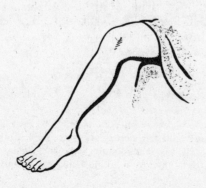

VICTOR HUGO

Born	**1802, in France.**
Occupation	**Writer.**
Hobbies	**Undermining the fabric of French society, and rogering.**
Distinguishing Features	**Girl in arms.**
Romantically Linked With	**Lola Montez, Juliette Drouet, Léonie d'Aunet, Adèle Foucher.**

Victor Hugo is one of the Great Triumvirate of French Rogerers, the Three Musketeers whose 'swordsmanship' was the wonder of the age.[1] Hugo was a great political figure, and an astonishingly powerful and prolific novelist, best remembered for *The Hunchback of Notre Dame* and now revived with the success of the musical of his book, *Les Miserables*.[2] But what is most miraculous about his books is that he had any time to write them with all the rogering he had to fit in.

He was a virgin until he was twenty, but he rogered his bride nine times on the wedding night to make up for lost time. She tired out pretty soon, and left to make way for the great love of Hugo's life, actress Juliette Drouet, who stayed with him for fifty years, and during that time wrote him over 17,000 love letters.

But even this epistolary bonding couldn't keep 'nine times a night' Victor faithful. 'Women find me irresistible', he was justly able to claim and it is known, for instance, that between 1848–50 he slept with over 200 women. He was indefatigable: and his life was scandalously sexually over-active. He often made love to three different women in a day, and often they were other men's wives. He was once caught *in flagrante delicto*, and taken to court for adultery. With typical luck, the woman was imprisoned and Victor let off to roger once more.[3]

A prolific rogerer, he was still rogering at the age of eighty-three, just before he died. In fact, Victor never stopped: at seventy he seduced the daughter of Théophile Gautier, who was twenty-two. At the age of eighty, he was found by his grandson rogering a laundry maid. Delighted at the discovery, he bellowed: 'Look, little Georges, that's what they call genius'.[4] Throughout his life, he lived up to his exhortation: 'Lover . . . seek love . . . give pleasure and take it in loving as fully as you can'.

FOOTNOTES

1 The Honorary Fourth Musketeer is not Zola, as might be expected: for Zola was a rather modest rogerer, who believed in only making love for the purpose of producing children. The D'Artagnan of the French novel is the astonishing Georges Simenon, a good fifty years younger than the others, but a master rogerer. In his life he rogered 10,000 women and said that his

great grief was thinking about all the millions of women that he couldn't get round to. Simenon invented the great detective Maigret: it needs no great detective skill to find out what his favourite activity was.

2 Hugo would have been particularly proud of the production. Outside the theatre, it says, If You Haven't Got a Ticket, Steal One—it was just this kind of revolutionary attack against the moral status quo that was at the very core of Hugo's work.

3 The stigma attached to the unfaithful woman rather than the unfaithful man still remains today. Even worse, it even attaches to the women who just happen to be with an unfaithful man. A man who is cheating on his wife will often be heard described as having been 'seen with some tart' when he should have been with his wife. The woman in question is of course not the tart at all: it is the man who is made of pastry and has jam all over him.

4 Hugo certainly gives the lie to the image of sexless old age, a pose into which most English writers seemed to fall at around their thirtieth birthdays. He even proves England's most sexually aberrant writer, Rochester, quite wrong. Old age, as far as Rochester was concerned, was one of the only two reasons for not being promiscuous:

> Old men and weak, whose idle flame
> Their own defects discovers,
> Since changing can but spread their shame,
> Ought to be constant lovers.

He should have popped into the laundry room and Victor would have taught him a thing or two.

ALEXANDRE DUMAS

Born	**1802, in France.**
Occupation	**Writer.**
Hobbies	**Swordplay and 'swordplay'.**
Romantically Linked With	**Ida Ferrier, Fanny Gordosa, Emilie Cordier, Lola Montez, Adah Isaacs Mencken, Catherine Lebay.**
Nickname	**Père.**

Dumas is most famous for his long novelizations for such great action films as *The Three Musketeers, The Count of Monte Cristo* and *The Man in the Iron Mask*—Richard Chamberlain would hardly have had a career without him. But while he wasn't producing, Alex was busy reproducing—he once claimed he had had 500 illegitimate children, although three seems a more likely figure. Whatever the number, he was a rake of the first order—'Three in a bed' Alexandre would have been his nickname if it wasn't a bit of a mouthful, and the motto of The Three Musketeers: 'All for one and one for all' might have been his motto.

He tried marrying once, but it was no use: Alexandre was not made for monogamy—nor mono-mistressy either. 'I need several mistresses', he once said. 'If I had only one she'd be dead inside eight days'. So Alexandre spread his pleasures far and wide—other men's wives found great happiness with this gutsy rogerer. One Fanny Gordosa was so lustful that her husband made her wear wet towels around her waist to cool her passion—Alexandre took them off and cooled her down another way. His estate, Monte Cristo, became a kind of pleasure park for anybody with as few outmoded morals as Dumas—actresses, prostitutes and artists were free to romp as they chose as Alexandre spent all he earned on pleasure.

And Alexandre, like Victor, seemed to just get wilder with old age: just before his death, he had his fling with the world-famous bad girl Adah Mencken.[1]

FOOTNOTES

1 It is said that men grow more attractive the older they get, but one look at Leo McKern convinces one this is not necessarily so. The truth is that *there must be one moment in one's life when one is at one's most attractive*, and it is, of course, a moment *about which you don't know*. The day you are *your most attractive ever* is probably the day the person you've most wanted to roger *all your life* asks you out and you say you can't come because you're waiting for a man about the new fridge with built-in ice-making compartment. Life is full of such cruelties.

Another one is that you never know the last time you are going to roger someone you love. This is so cruel. You should be warned. You should be allowed to have that extravagant final fling. Instead, one day it just hits you that it's all over, and the last time you rogered was that time you hurried up because there was something interesting on Breakfast TV about penguins.

HONORÉ DE BALZAC

Born	**1799, in France.**
Occupation	**Writer.**
Hobby	**Rogering.**
Distinguishing Features	**Short, fat and ugly, with dirty fingernails, greasy hair and extraordinary sex appeal.**
Romantically Linked With	**Larne de Berny, Duchesse D'Abrantes, Evelina Hansak (m), Marie Louise de Fresnay, Lady Ellenborough, Frances Sarah Lovell, Louise Breugnol.**

And so on to Balzac, the third of the great rogering novelists. So extraordinary is the record of these three, that one is led to think that if F. R. Leavis had written a book about the Great Tradition among authors in France, it would have been a sex manual. While Dickens and George Eliot and Henry James were agonizing over their tiny little love lives, these monster writers were going at it day and night with hammer and tongs. All one can do is stand back and be amazed—and hope that English writers one day learn the lessons. There is no doubting many of them would like to: John Betjeman said before his death that his one regret was that he hadn't had more sex.[1,2]

Despite the most extraordinary physical drawbacks, being 5 foot 2 inches and almost always picking his nose in public, Balzac was a great and popular lover. There was no stopping these guys. In his life he received over 12,000 love letters, and had all the women he desired. Through his great realistic novels, including the enormous *Comédie Humaine*, Balzac convinced ordinary women that he understood them, and they invited and he accepted their invitations to understand them even more deeply. His great attraction was towards the maternal type: most romances were begun by him with the words, 'I never had a mother'.

He was an expert on love and regarded it as a natural appetite, like eating. 'A woman is a well-served meal which one sees through different eyes before and after the meal', he said.[3] He also wisely observed that it was easier being a lover than a husband, and he stuck to his word—only marrying a life-time love a few weeks before he died of drinking too much coffee.[4] His books were full of earthy women and prostitutes—and for sure, Honoré did his research.[5]

FOOTNOTES

1 The American novelist Saul Bellow once said that if you are a writer, anyone will sleep with you. This isn't true, otherwise people like Lawrence and Proust wouldn't have been so wretched all their lives. The truth is probably more that if you think anyone will sleep with you, anyone will sleep with you.

2 There is another literary theory that you can judge a man's sexual prowess by the size of his books: this is backed up by Balzac, but would make Samuel Beckett and J. D. Salinger two

of the most disappointing of literary lovers, of which there is no proof. The truth is that it seems unlikely: a simple time and motion study would reveal that the longer a man's book, the less time he has for developing his love-making skills.

3 This two-fold feeling has been the theme of great artists throughout history. Shakespeare, another one of England's unrelaxed and angry lovers, expressed emotion in a slightly more bitter mood than merry Honoré.

> *The expense of the spirit in a waste of shame*
> *Is lust in action; and till action, lust*
> *Is perjur'd, murd'rous, bloody, full of blame,*
> *Savage, extreme, rude, cruel, not to trust;*
> *Enjoy'd no sooner but despised straight;*
> *Past reason hunted, and no sooner had*
> *Past reason hated, as a swallowed bait,*
> *On purpose laid to make the taker mad;*
> *Mad in pursuit and in possession so;*
> *Had, having, and in quest to have, extreme;*
> *A bliss in proof, and prov'd, a very woe;*
> *Before a joy propos'd, behind a dream,*
> *All this the world well knows yet none knows well;*
> *To shun the heaven that leads men to this hell.*

A more succinct, witty, and generally French outlook on the matter is to be found in the lyric of a great twentieth-century genius, country and western king, Bobby Bare, who observes:

> *I never went to bed with an ugly woman,*
> *But I've sure woken up with a few.*

4 Some social linguists believe that it is as a tribute to this great lover that the phrase, 'Would you like to come in for coffee?' is now the single most used invitation to rogering.
5 In fact, he did so much research, he was lucky to get any books written—he used to believe that ejaculation cost him the vital creative essence that led to his genius at writing. Once he arrived, clearly worn out and scrumpled, at a friend's house at lunch and sighed: 'This morning I lost a novel'. His finest books were, in his opinion, quite literally seminal.

FRANZ LISZT

Born	**1811, in Hungary.**
Occupation	**Composer.**
Hobbies	**Fighting off fans and rogering.**
Distinguishing Features	**Long white hair.**
Romantically Linked With	**Lady Blessington, Caroline de Saint Cricq, Marie D'Agoult, George Sand, Countess Olga Janina, Princess Christine Belgiojoso, Olga von Meyendorff, Lola Montez.**

The only musician who can really compete with the great men above is Liszt, perhaps the first real pop star ever, and suitably promiscuous to go with it.[1] He was a piano virtuoso whose performances literally drove his audiences wild.

Where today girls might kill for George Michael's leather cap, in the nineteenth century they bit and scratched to be the lucky one to steal the cover off the seat of the stool on which Liszt had played.

It was said of him: 'Liszt flung his spear far into the future'[2] and the spear simile is a very useful one. Anyone who has a spear flung into them would, one would imagine, be pretty mad about it, and, indeed, most of the people into whom Liszt flung his spear were mad: Princess Christine kept the mummified body of an ex-lover in the next room.[3] Countess Marie challenged another of his lovers to a duel. Olga Von Meyendorff wore skin-tight black body stockings in a time when thirteen petticoats were considered the decent minimum, and Countess Janina tried to shoot *and* poison Liszt.

Even so, he persevered, and despite all the crazy women had no regrets and said at the end of his life, 'I didn't take a big enough bite of the apple'. Perhaps he would have regretted his life more had he seen 'Lisztomania', the film that it inspired in the mind of Ken Russell.

FOOTNOTES

1 Rossini, the other major musician in this line was slightly put off sex by the fact that he caught gonorrhea off a prostitute at the age of thirteen.*

2 See Appendix: Names for Rogering, although the quote may have referred to his creativity. Liszt was the inventor of the symphonic poem form, a composer whose worth was underestimated, overshadowed by the blinding light of his playing skill.

3 This story cannot fail to remind one of adultery's most terrible tales. A man was committing adultery when he heard his lover's husband enter the house. Sharp as a knife, he popped into the cupboard. The husband entered, smelt a rat, and saw the poor adulterer's shirt-tail peeking out of the corner of the cupboard. However, when he asked his frightened wife what she had been doing in the bedroom in the middle of the afternoon, she denied all funny business. He asked again, she denied again. 'Very well, then,' he said, 'you will not object to me bricking up this cupboard that has been getting on my nerves'. Pause. 'No, I suppose not', said the guilty wife. Before the lover inside could say, 'Now wait a bloody moment', the bricks were got and he remained there, shirt-tail peeking out, amongst the musty harris tweeds, until he died.

   If this book achieves nothing else, we hope that it will discourage readers from making love, in the afternoon, to the wives of bricklayers.

*This did not however put him off doing his share of rogering. Some people with sexual diseases have now taken a very honest approach to the whole thing, and in America it is starting to become the done thing for people with herpes to wear a little badge of the letter 'H'. If the habit catches on, it might grow into a very useful information service, for instance, quite randomly:

H—I've got Herpes.
K—I've got a King-size bed.
N—I've got Nothing on underneath this dress.
P—I've got lots of Pistachio nuts back home.
VAFWVKOSWTPLGR—I've got a Very Attractive Flatmate Who's Very Keen On Sex With Three People: Let's Go Roger.

OSCAR WILDE

Born	**1854, in Dublin.**
Occupation	**Writer and wit.**
Hobby	**The love that dares not speak its name.**
Distinguishing Features	**Velvet coat and tongue.**
Romantically Linked With	**Florrie Balcombe, Lord Alfred Douglas, Sarah Bernhardt, Constance Lloyd (m), Mohammed.**

It still sometimes comes as a surprise to remember that Wilde batted both ways, kicked the ball with both his left and his right foot. When Wilde was a child, his mother dressed him as a girl, but nevertheless, he arrived at maturity heterosexual and had an affair with a girl called Florrie Balcombe, who upped and left him for Bram Stoker, the author of *Dracula*. Surely there can be no grimmer thought than one's own tender embraces being swapped for a man who sleeps all day in a coffin and then bites the hell out of your neck from sundown. Nevertheless, undiscouraged, Wilde continued as an enthusiastic frequenter of prostitutes—'Priapus is calling', he would cry as he entered the brothel—and finally fell in love with and married his wife, Constance Lloyd.

They had two children, before the syphilis that Wilde had contracted in his youth flared up, and he felt he could no longer sleep with her. And so he began to drift into homosexuality, and homosexual prostitution, where he might happily have stayed had he not met Alfred Lord Douglas—Bosie—when he stopped drifting and fell in love. The events that followed, his famous trials and deeply moving defence, established him as the proudest and most famous homosexual of his time.

He was imprisoned, and his life ended mournfully in Paris, where he tried one more time to roger a woman—he said he wanted it reported in England to restore his reputation. Unfortunately, it didn't work out: it was 'like cold mutton' he observed.

He was in his time the wittiest man in the world.

ALGERNON CHARLES SWINBURNE

Born	**1837, in England.**
Occupation	**Poet, dramatist.**
Hobby	**Flagellation.**
Distinguishing Features	**Whip in hand and weals on bottom.**
Romantically Linked With	**Dante Gabriel Rossetti, Adah Isaacs Mencken, George Powell, George Powell's monkey.**

While Oscar Wilde was a wonderful man, Swinburne was a genuinely per-verted basket case. At an early age he had wanted to be a soldier; not long after his father introduced him to the works of the Marquis de Sade; and then, on top of both of those sick influences, he went to Eton. From then on, he was doomed. His entire life, works and all, was utterly obsessed by flagellation, to which he had a glorious introduction at the infamous Eton flogging block.[1] After he left school, he used to write back for news of whippings, and his great wish was to be back there again: 'To assist unseen at the Holy Ceremony . . . I would give any of my poems'.

He thought about very little else, and considered flogging to be the greatest of aristocratic sports. His enthusiasm for the subject was unbounded and would have been most admirable if directed towards stamp collecting, or any such worthy occupation. Others were not so enthusiastic about his chosen interest. 'Swinburne is standing up to his neck in a cesspool and adding to its contents' was a less charitable way of looking at how he spent his life.

His favourite flagellation brothel was 'The Grove of the Evangelist' in St John's Wood, and his notable underground works include: 'The Flogging Block', 'Charlie Collingwood's Flogging', and the 'Whippingham Papers'.

FOOTNOTES

1 Flagellation was at one stage so normal in England that it was known abroad as the English vice. And the main way of catching this was through going to Eton. Consider this list of the nine most famous flagellatory headmasters in English public schools.

16th century
   Dr Colet: Eton.
   Dr Busby: Westminster.
17th century
   Dr Bowyer: Christ's Hospital.
   Dr Gill: St Paul's.
18th and 19th centuries
   Dr Drury: Harrow.
   Dr Vaughan: Harrow.
   Dr Keate: Eton.
   Dr May: Eton.
   Dr Edgeworth: Eton.

Eton fair storms through to the finish, whip flashily flourished, with almost half the leading contenders for the heavy hand crown.

ANDRÉ GIDE	
Born	**1869, in France.**
Occupation	**Writer.**
Hobby	**Angelism.**[1]
Distinguishing Features	**Frankness.**
Romantically Linked With	**Marc Allegret, Meriem, Mohammed, Elizabeth van Rysselberghe.**

Gide was expelled from school for masturbating, threatened by a doctor with castration, banned by the Catholic Church, told to get married to 'cure' his homosexuality, and then awarded a Nobel Prize. 'I am a pederast', he once shouted in public, and was happy to get on with it. He did once marry, but never consummated the marriage, falling for and rogering the son of the best man instead.[2]

After that, he was clear which path he wished to tread: even if it took him to North Africa, where he spent a lot of time rogering in the dunes. On one particularly ecstatic occasion he rogered boys Ali and Mohammed and girl Meriem, a girl prostitute 'black and slim as a female demon' and later 'revived the ecstasy over and over again in my hotel room'.

He wrote 'The Immoralists' and 'The Counterfeiters'—books about homosexuals which gave homosexuality respectability, and by the end of his life hardly needed his creed—'It is better to be hated for what one is than loved for what one is not'—because no one hated him any more.

FOOTNOTES

1 Angelism is the habit of putting girls on a pedestal to such an extent that you don't want to roger them. Unfortunately, in Gide's case, the girl in question was his wife. It is *not* the desire to roger anyone called Angela. That is Angelaism. A similar confusion occurs between Oonaism and onanism. The first is a desire to fall in love with a woman called Oona (see Ryan O'Neal), and the second is horrid.
2 The problem of falling in love with other people at weddings is a very serious one, and a good reason to go for marrying in registry offices where the number of beautifully dressed people is smaller. A completely spurious opinion poll recently revealed that the problem is both wide-ranging and various.

   Bridegrooms.
   24% want to roger the bride.
   11% want to roger the bridesmaids.
   8% want to roger the bride's sister.
   4% want to roger the bride's mother.
   6% want to roger the best man's wife/girlfriend.
   5% want to roger the best man.
   and an astonishing 42% most want to roger the Archbishop of Canterbury's wife.

GOOD OLD TEDDY

FROM	**EDWARD VII**
TO	***THREE LADIES OF LEISURE***
IN	**3 ROGERS**

The lay lines of this book began with Henry VIII, King of England. And now, as our twentieth century approaches, they return to the blood royal to round off the circle of rogering before it spins into the twentieth century.

All the Kings and Queens, cads and coves, tarts and jammy dodgers gather in the benign shadow of Good Old Teddy, who did not have six wives, but had more than six mistresses and cut off none of their heads.

All the artists of the last line tie into him with ease, through Sarah Bernhardt: and through Cora Pearl, the mistress of Napoleon III, the historical lines run strong.

Good Old Teddy, round and plump and promiscuous and popular, leads us on towards the present: and in this, his own, private, merry little line, are some of the ladies who led him on . . .

EDWARD VII

Born	**1841, in England.**
Occupation	**Prince of Wales.**
Hobby	**Rogering.**[1]
Romantically Linked With	**Queen Alexandra (m), Nellie Clifden, Cora Pearl, Guilia Barucci, Hortense Schneider, Louise Weber, La Belle Otero, Countess of Warwick (Daisy Brooke), Lady Harriet Mordaunt, Lillie Langtry, Miss Chamberlain, Alice Keppel, Sarah Bernhardt, La Goulue.**
Nickname	**Good Old Teddy.**

Queen Victoria said of her son: 'I never can, or shall, look at him without a shudder', a sentiment echoed for different reasons by many of the women who came into contact with him.

Edward, having rebelled against the harsh plans and stern ambitions of his mother and father, devoted himself to a life of pleasure. His mother tried to stop him, but failed[2]: her plan to quell him by marrying him off was particularly unsuccessful since his wife, Alexandra of Denmark, was an absolute sweetie who soon saw the limitations of her power and let Edward, within limits, run free.

His wife is indeed the great heroine of the piece: for she took him warts and all and left him as quite the luckiest man in the world: he was allowed to have mistresses, and Alexandra never complained. Indeed, harking back to the wife of Louis XIV, she got to be quite friendly with a couple of them. And for her graciousness, he loved her.[3]

Deprived of serious responsibilities by his quintessentially Victorian mother, Edward, or Albert as he was then, rogered, drank and smoked his life away.[4] Whenever he went away at weekends, tactful hosts would supply rooms for his present mistress. Abroad, he would lead the high life with his specially selected groups of friends, frequenting brothels and all manner of places of pleasure.

All of which seemed to do him remarkably little harm, except in the one case, where he actually appeared in court to deny 'improper familiarity' with one mistress, Harriet Mordaunt. For a while things looked awkward, but fortunately, the court seemed in the end to believe his denial of impropriety, untrue as it was: people liked to think well of Good Old Teddy. When he did finally become King, he was a very popular one, both in England and abroad. His cosmopolitan outlook and familiarity with Europe made him a great ambassador for peace: in fact, he was known in his time as Edward the Peacemaker, a fine tribute to a man whom his mother till her dying day considered completely useless.

In the end, England did well by him and he performed his duties as King nobly, despite great sickness. As Prince, however, he had been taking care of the great Empire of Rogering, while his Mum looked after the great British Empire. Who was doing the better work is a matter of opinion: but one Empire seems to have lasted a lot longer than the other.

The remainder of this line are just three of the pleasant countries that, for a while, Edward colonized, before popping them back into the Commonwealth of Man.

FOOTNOTES

1 The Royal Family have always been keen and enthusiastic pursuers of their hobbies: one only has to look at Princess Anne's riding, and Prince Charles' polo playing to see this strong tradition. Edward was true to it. He stuck to his rogering with a dedication and thoroughness which was an example to all his subjects and makes the formerly publicized canoodles of the now respectable Prince Andrew look like positive dereliction of duty.

2 Quite how she dared be so prim when she was responsible for the most blatantly sexual pairing of buildings in London—the huge breast of the Albert Hall side by side with the elegant little phallus of the Albert Memorial—has never been satisfactorily explained by psychologists.

3 And indeed made love to her, though irregularly. Alexandra was slightly hard of hearing and many sexual historians believe that the reason that Edward was always said to be such a fine lover was because of the experience gained with his wife. He had grown used to being loud in his intimate appreciations of her sexual endeavours, because if he wasn't loud, she wouldn't hear him at all. Edward then continued in his vociferous enthusiasms with other lovers, who thus mistook for extravagant praise what was in fact only a slightly peculiar marital necessity.

4 All three things annoyed his mother. He was addicted to cigars by the age of twenty, and she loathed them. Even more, she would not tolerate his drinking. But Edward, cunning as ever, got round that. When she complained of his drinking brandy at breakfast, he went to Berry Brothers & Rudd of St James' and asked them to concoct a special wine that he could drink at breakfast in the confidence his mother would mistake it for medicine. The resulting King's Ginger Liqueur can still be purchased at Berry Brothers & Rudd to this very day, and is a most delicious beverage.

Edward was lucky in being able to indulge in both vices, women and wine: about which Samuel Johnson spoke, as always, very wisely. The great doctor was asked what he considered to be life's greatest pleasure. He replied, with due frankness—'fucking, and the second is drinking'. He then expressed his surprise that there weren't therefore more drunkards in the world, 'for all can drink, tho' all cannot fuck'.*

*There is, incidentally, no record of the above ever being told to Queen Victoria.

CORA PEARL

Born	**1835, in England.**
Occupation	**Courtesan.**
Hobby	**Gambling.**
Romantically Linked With	**Khalil Bey, Clemenceau, Duc de Rivoli, Duc de Morny, Count de Graumont Caderousse, Count Alonso, Prince Achille Murat, Prince Napoleon, Prince of Orange, King Edward VII.**
Distinguishing Features	**Bankrupt man on his knees beside her.**
Nickname	**Cora Pearl. (Real Name: Eliza Crouch.[1])**

Cora Pearl was one of the great nineteenth-century prostitutes, a one-time mistress of one, maybe even two Napoleons, and Edward was lucky to catch her.

Also lucky to survive her, because, like Lola Montez before her, Cora Pearl, née Crouch, was dangerous to those who loved her. She took a very direct attitude to rogering. It was worth a lot of money. Huge amounts. Amounts that made her lovers commit suicide from debt. They gave her their entire fortunes, and she gambled them away. 'If golden louis were meant to roll and diamonds to glitter, none can accuse me of diverting these noble things from their true channel', she said, and men learnt it to their cost.[2]

'Command me and I will die', said one particularly importunate lover. He received a good, practical working woman's answer—'I'd rather you lived and paid the bills'.

After training as a normal working prostitute, Cora started what she called her 'Golden Chain' of lovers, and slowly worked her way up to the very top of European society, more famous and more desired with every man she took to her expensive bed. At the peak of her career, 'she looked like a jeweller's window', rogering for 19,000 francs a night, spending £80,000 in eight weeks, and eating chocolates wrapped in 100 franc notes.

What her charms were, no one can quite say after all these years. Her face was meant to be quite plain, although her complexion was beautiful. Her body was perfect. But perhaps it was most of all her spirit that appealed. For she was high-spirited, no doubt about that—she once promised guests at dinner that she would serve them up a 'meat nobody can cut'. When dinner came, a huge platter was brought in, the lid lifted, and out popped . . . Cora herself, naked apart from a sprig of parsley.[3] On another occasion, she challenged a competing courtesan to a duel by whip—the pair of them thrashed it out in the early morning mist, and then retired for a month while their scarred faces mended.

In short, Cora lived her life wild, and like many who lived high, she paid high—by the end of her life, she had blown all that she had ever earned, including a million francs in jewellery alone—even her famous gold monogrammed black sheets were gone. She, the great rogerer, had finally rogered herself.

FOOTNOTES

1 Now there *was* a good decision.
2 The most terrible story of all is that of poor Mr Duval—he was a man of enormous wealth, millions and millions of francs, which he then spent on Cora's every whim. And in return, she gave him nothing but hard times. Eventually, utterly bankrupt and wretched, he shot himself in front of her. Her comment—'The dirty pig. He fucked up my beautiful rug!' (See Hedy Lamarr for similar bad behavior.)
3 The connection between sexuality and food has of course always been strong. Men are endlessly finishing the great act of love-making with romantic comments like, 'Are there any of those biscuits left?'

LILLIE LANGTRY

Born	**1853, in Jersey.**
Occupation	**Pin-up model, actress.**
Hobbies	**Keeping fit and rogering and distracting Judge Roy Bean from the proper execution of his duties.[1]**
Romantically Linked With	**Edward Langtry, Edward VII, Freddie Gebhard, George Baird, Louis Alexander of Battenburg, Prince Rudolf of Austria-Hungary.**
Distinguishing Features	**Long red hair.**
Nickname	**Jersey Lillie.**

'Men are born to be slaves', said Lillie Langtry, and was in her time one of the greatest exploiters of their slavishness. The curious thing about the Victorian era is that, while morality was so stiff and strict, those who flouted it most enthusiastically sometimes found themselves fêted and adored. Lillie Langtry was one such. In the space of a few years she went from bored wife to national pin-up girl to mistress of the future king.

It is Lillie's good sense and sense of humour which seems to shine out and distinguish her from the dangerous passions and greed of the likes of Cora Pearl and even La Belle Otero. She laughed when a newspaper said of the death of her parrot: 'We didn't know that the lady possessed such a bird, but we know she has had a cockatoo'. She eventually lost Edward VII when he wasn't amused by her putting ice down his back. Before that problem occurred she did crack one fabulous joke. Edward complained to her that he had 'spent enough on you to buy a battleship'. She replied, 'You've spent enough in me to float one'.

When her time as a mistress was done, she was left with a comfortable amount of money, and a heart still intact. It is good to think of the future King of England spending time with such a sensible girl.

FOOTNOTES

1 Judge Roy Bean, famous ice-cold killing judge, had his heart entirely melted by Lillie. After seeing pictures of her, he renamed his saloon the Jersey Lillie. He then decided that wasn't dedication enough, so upped and moved himself and the saloon to the town of Langtry. When he died, he sent her his pistol, a symbolic act if ever there was one. It had apparently been responsible for more than one death, defending her honour.

LA BELLE OTERO

Real Name	**Augustina Carolina Otero.**
Born	**1863, in Spain.**
Occupation	**Dancer, mistress, courtesan.**
Hobbies	**Wearing jewels and gambling.**
Distinguishing Features	**Extraordinary jewels balanced on extraordinary breasts.**
Romantically Linked With	**King Leopold II of Belgium, Prince Nicholas I of Montenegro, Prince Albert of Monaco, Grand Duke Nicholas of Russia, Baron Lepic, William K. Vanderbilt, Musafar-ed-Din Shah of Persia, The Khedive of Cairo, King Alphonso XIII of Spain, Aristide Briand, Count Luigi Guglielmo, Duc d'Aumale, Kaiser Wilhelm of Germany, Tsar Nicholas II, Baron Ollstreder, Grand Duke Peter and King Edward VII.**

La Belle Otero was the last of the great public prostitutes, 'les grandes horizontales'. She was an astounding looking woman—5 foot 10 inches with black hair, white teeth, and 36-inch breasts that looked 'like elongated lemons, firm and upturned at the tips'.[1] She made a tour of the great beds of Europe that was almost comprehensive: there was time when not having slept with La Belle Otero was almost a sign of political incompetence and inefficiency. The chances of post-conference talk turning to the charms of Otero were so high, that not having slept with her constituted a failure to do proper research and a wanton disregard for the politeness of after dinner conversation.[2]

She started her professional life as a fabulous, wildly erotic dancer, the equivalent of, say, Madonna without the disco backing, but she finally gave it up for the much more profitable prostitution. It is said that during her lifetime she was given $25 million in gifts, and during her lifetime she lost it.[3] In her prime, she was charging $10,000 a night and, whenever she could, she got paid in jewels. She adored them, and on the one occasion when she outfaced a rival by wearing a startlingly bare neck and cleavage, she had a maid carry the jewels she should have been wearing on a tray behind her.

God and the Virgin Mary are the only two who know what tricks she used, but some tricks they must have been, as she was a prostitute from the age of twelve till her late fifties, and for thirty years of that was top of the class in the entire world.[4] Straddling the centuries like a gorgeous colossus, she is the last figure of our history, and the first of modern times.

FOOTNOTES

1 This description is by Colette. There is something about women's breasts which lets the soul of simile free: the breasts of Pauline Borghese, Napoleon's sister, were once described as:

'white as alabaster and seemingly ready to take off from her corsage like birds out of a nest'. Faber and Faber are happy to send the free book of their choice to anyone who can paint a satisfactory rendering of either or both of these strange pairs.

2 The same was at one point almost true in the Kennedy administration with regard to Marilyn Monroe.

3 Most of this money was lost at gambling—she was an obsessive gambler—and great credit it does her; once in her youth, when broke and abandoned by her husband, she won 50,000 francs in a casino, which set her off in life again: the casino table had been her closest and only friend in a crisis. After that, although never faithful to a lover for long, she stayed faithful to the casino table, lavished on it presents and never abandoned it till her dying day.

4 The stories of how much La Belle was paid for her services are many and astonishing. Here, for quick reference, we have tried to sort out a few categories. First, the major title:

Award for He Who Spent Most
Non-starters are folk like Leopold of Belgium, who only managed a villa, or Nicholas of Montenegro, who bid with a diamond bracelet and five gold watches.

3rd: William K. Vanderbilt—he gave her $250,000 of jewels, including one Nap III gave to Eugenie, and the loan of a yacht. Some time later, after she had had a disastrous time in the casino, Willie offered to buy the yacht back for half a million pounds to cover her debts. If he had actually had to honour that offer, he would have been second in front of . . .

2nd: Prince Albert of Monaco, who gave La Belle $300,000 and an apartment for a night of pleasure. The out and out winner however is:

1st: The Shah of Persia, Mussafar-ed-Din. He visited her every afternoon for five years, for three hours. Each time, after he left, a servant would appear with a jewel in gratitude: sometimes the jewels were worth 25,000 francs. Taking half that as an average, the Shah paid out an astonishing $5 \times 365 \times 12,500$ francs $= 22,687,500$ francs for the lovely La Belle. Even taking time off for Christmas, which presumably he would not have celebrated, it is a lot of money.

Apart from these, three more important awards:

The Award for Best Deal must go to Frenchman Aristide Briand, who would one day go on to win the Nobel Prize. Briand was Otero's lover for ten years, and yet got away with only giving her 'cheap jewels and flowers'. Yet some nights, he would make love 'eight times before morning'.

The Award for Worst Deal goes to a figure already familiar in these ceremonies, Albert of Monaco. Albert, who came second in the all time high stakes, got very little in return for his money. Throughout a whole night he was unable to muster an erection, and found he was paying for pleasant conversation. In the early hours of the morning, he did finally rise to the occasion, but not for long—'he was not a very virile man, and I don't think he got his money's worth' said Otero, understating.

The Award for Most Unusual Deal goes to Baron Lepic—the Baron took La Belle up in a hot-air balloon, in which they made passionate love over Paris. There is no recorded payment, but the deal was presumably that by doing what they did, they became joint co-founders of the Mile-High Club.

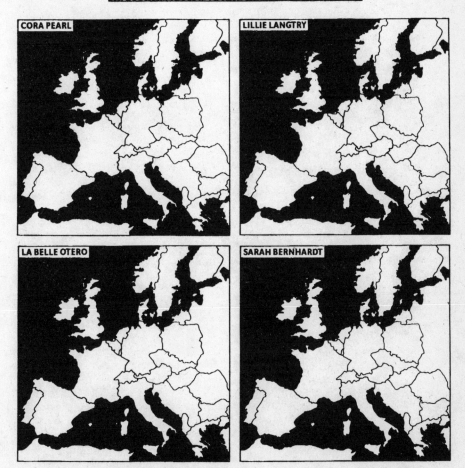

And so, with Edward VII tucked contently between the sheets, cigar in mouth, drink in hand, mistress in a state of undress, and Europe united by rogering, the lines move into the 20th century . . .

MONOLITHIC ENIGMAS

FROM	**GERTRUDE STEIN**
TO	**CLINT EASTWOOD**
IN	**8 ROGERS**

Gertrude Stein and Clint Eastwood have both been, in their time, monolithic enigmas. All 200 pounds of Stein towered monolithically over her generation of experimental artists, as all 6 feet 3 inches of Eastwood towers over his generation of actors. Stein was enigmatic, because no one ever understood a word she said. In his early films, Eastwood never said a word, and no one understood what he meant by his silence. 'Stein' means 'rock' in German and 'Wood' means 'wood' in English and both Clint and Gertrude are elemental forces of nature.

It is terrifying to think what might have been the outcome of a rogering between the two of them: as it is, eight rogers only lie between that cataclysmic union.

GERTRUDE STEIN

Born	**1874, in America.**
Occupation	**Writer.**
Hobbies	**Eating, being monolithically enigmatic and rogering.**
Distinguishing Features	**Mightness.**
Romantically Linked With	**Alice B. Toklas, Picasso, May Bookstaver.**
Nickname	**Lovely.**

Gertrude Stein described herself as 'the greatest creative writer of the century'[1]—and why not? She was certainly one of the great creative lovers of the century. At a time when there weren't any public lesbians, she was a lesbian with a vengeance. Male homosexuality she despised: 'the main thing is that the act male homosexuals commit is ugly and repugnant and afterwards they are disgusted with themselves'. Male heterosexuals she did her best to avoid, except Picasso. Hemingway said of her—'I always wanted to fuck her and she knew it'. Knew it, but didn't do it.

A mighty woman, weighing over 200 pounds with 'pounds and pounds and pounds of flesh piled up on her skeleton', she dominated Parisian intellectual life, and despite the fact that other people found her books impossible to understand and her oxymoronic means of expression nonsensical, she never lost faith in her own genius: quizzing someone about English literature, she asked: 'Apart from Shakespeare[2] and me, who do you think there is?'

Her last words before she went in for the surgery from which she didn't recover were to her lifelong lover, Alice B. Toklas: 'What is the answer?' she inquired. Alice did not reply. 'In which case', said Gertrude finally, 'what is the question?' Quite.

FOOTNOTES

1 A claim now made by Jeffrey Archer—the similarities between the two of them are, in fact, quite extraordinary—both wear male clothes, both are strange looking, and the books of both make only passable television.

2 One of the great glories of English literature is that Shakespeare is so far ahead that no one else ever has to get worried and aspire to being best. Modern lovers can take comfort that very much the same is true of Ryan O'Neal and the rest of us. See Our Mutual Friend Line.

GERTRUDE STEIN & ALICE B. TOKLAS

Along with the love of Bogart and Bacall,[1] this is one of the great stories of true love, passion and romance in this book and so a nice place to start the rogering of this century.[2] Like Bacall and Bogie, Alice nursed Gertrude through illness and was with her at her death and, like Bacall, Alice never found anyone to replace Gertrude. Thirty-eight years after Gertrude's death, she said: 'I miss her: I still miss her very much'.

They met in Paris where Alice had come to find out about lesbianism, and Gertrude was only too happy to show her. On holiday in Tuscany, Gertrude proposed 'marriage'. Alice cried, using thirty handkerchiefs over the next few days, but, in Stein's words, she then 'came, and saw, and seeing cried, "I am your bride" '.[3] They then stayed together till death did them part, in a strange and complex household. Alice did everything practical for Gertrude—cooking, typing and throwing Ernest Hemingway out of the house whenever he made a pass—and Gertrude grew fatter and fatter and Alice didn't mind.

Gertrude said of Alice, 'better than anything Alice likes love', and used to write things for her—her autobiography for one thing. She also wrote lots of poems, many of which, unfortunately, were completely incomprehensible. But then some would say true love is itself incomprehensible.

> *I'll let you kiss me sticky . . .*
> *I say lifting belly and then I say lifting belly and Caesars.*[4]
> *I say lifting belly gently and Caesars gently. I say*
> *lifting belly again and Caesars again . . . I say lifting*
> *belly Caesars and cow come out. I say lifting belly*
> *and Caesars and cow come out.*
> *Can you read my print?*

ALICE B. TOKLAS

Born	1877, in America.
Occupation	Minder.
Hobbies	Manicuring her nails and throwing out Ernest Hemingway.
Distinguishing Features	Stillness.
Romantically Linked With	Gertrude Stein, Mercedes D'Acosta.
Nickname	Pussy.

Lesbianism did not exist when Alice B. was born. She had to discover it herself. Only twenty-five years later, when the *Story of Mary Maclane* was published, which contained the unexpurgated confessions of a lesbian, did American women officially awaken to the possibility of sex with someone other than Buffalo Bill/Abraham Lincoln all-American boys. Alice swiftly discovered that being bonked by frontiersmen with horses on their minds was not the life for her, so she went to Paris, where lesbianism did exist. And it was there that she met Gertrude Stein, and they fell in love.[4] Stein introduced her to Paris and the high literary life, and they lived a life amongst some of the most famous artists of the century, and were famous amongst them.

Picasso once described Alice as having small feet like a Spanish woman and 'earrings like a gypsy and a father who is king of Poland like the ponia-towkiasis'. No one had the faintest idea what he was talking about.

FOOTNOTES

1 See the True Love Line.

2 It was exquisitely portrayed in 1984 by Miriam Margolyes and Natasha Morgan in *Gertrude Stein and Companion*.

3 Taken alongside the comment 'She came, and saw, and seeing cried, "I am your bride" ' it is clear that Alice B. Toklas repeatedly reminded Gertrude Stein of Julius Caesar. Literary scholars have tried to fathom this, but so far only three possible reasons have come to light:

    a Like Alice B. Toklas, Caesar fell in love with the greatest woman of his generation (Caesar with Cleopatra, Toklas with Stein).

    b Like Alice B. Toklas, Caesar came to France and made a mighty conquest (Caesar of Gaul, Toklas of Stein).

    c Like Alice B. Toklas, Caesar tended to wear a skirt.

4 It is said by some that it was originally Alice's vocabulary that made Gertrude fall in love with her. Alice's diction was very quaint and Victorian—'compromise' was her word for 'seduce': 'impure' meant 'bisexual', and a person who was 'inadequate' was dead drunk.

    The whole question of exactly *what* the Victorians were saying is quite a conundrum—their sex lives were clearly as juicy as everyone else's, but they just phrased it differently. It would on the whole be safe to infer that everything in a Victorian novel is a sign for something else. Semanticists generally agree, for instance, that in the novels of Henry James, phrases like 'be introduced to' 'take tea with' and 'walk round the garden in the company of' are all shorthand for complicated sex play.

    A passage such as this from Chapter 5 of *The Europeans* describes an erotic encounter that, if filmed, would certainly be too hot for anything but private clubs and the worst kind of office parties: 'Mr Wentworth, with his cane and his gloves in his hand, went every afternoon to call upon his niece. A couple of hours later she came over to the great house for tea. She had let the proposal that she should regularly dine there fall to the ground; she was in the enjoyment of whatever satisfaction was to be derived from the spectacle of an old negress in a crimson turban shelling peas under the apple trees'. Hot stuff.

ALICE B. TOKLAS & MERCEDES D'ACOSTA

The main point about this roger is that it proves one of the most fundamental tenets of love in the twentieth century, that true love triumphs over weight problems.[1] Mercedes D'Acosta was a gorgeous irresistibly shapely thing, and Gertrude Stein was an enormous lard globule weighing over 200 pounds and yet it was Stein that Toklas loved and lived with.

MERCEDES D'ACOSTA[2]	
Occupation	**Screenwriting.**
Hobby	**Convincing people she was not a car.**
Distinguishing Features	**Three pronged symbol on her bonnet and twinkle in her eyes.**
Romantically Linked With	**Eva la Gallienne, Popoy Kirk, Claire Charles-Roux, Marie Laurencin, Malvina Hoffman, Alice B. Toklas, Marlene Dietrich.**
Nickname	**Benz.**

D'Acosta, unhelpfully described by Tallulah Bankhead as a 'mouse in a teapot',[3] was the most famous lesbian of her day. She was known to be irresistible: when Dietrich first met her, she fell in love with her straightaway. Whenever men got bad, Mercedes was always on hand: she once consoled John Barrymore's wife all night when he upped and ran away. (The whole affair seemed slightly less dramatic when Barrymore was discovered in his own cellar next morning, surrounded by gin bottles.) But Mercedes was no mere love toy: she made a living writing screenplays, where she again put her knowledge of the world of love to good use: one particularly famous script was about the Romanovs and Rasputin, one of the great sexual experimenters of all time.[4] Like him, Mercedes, who was also Russian, lived life in the fast lane, with her top down, her radio blasting, popcorn everywhere, a tank full of juice and an engine full of superlubricating oil: when she died, she was most remembered for her 'passionate and intense devotion to the art of living'.

FOOTNOTES

1 See also Marilyn Monroe, Madonna and Sarah Ferguson: the triumph of stylish plumpness over thinness. Made confident by this, it is strongly suggested that any reader *the slightest bit* concerned about their weight should go out *now, immediately*, and buy and eat in one big scoff a family pack of marshmallows, a huge lump of cherry cheesecake and a whole bag of fun-size Mars Bars.
2 The habit of naming children after cars is not as popular as it once was: the idea of a child called Fiesta, or Montego, or Golf is slightly ridiculous: but it was at one stage very popular. Witness to how many people with such names there must have been all over America is given by the disputed fact that the New York Metropolitan Ballet at one point in the 1940s had three featured artists named Jaguar Evans, Cadillac Yancy and Aston Martin Morrell.
3 For other animal women, see Charles II and Marie Thérèse.

4 Rasputin, along with gangster Ma Baker, and Little Baby Jesus ('Mary's Boy Child'), is one of the few figures of history lucky enough to be immortalized in song by the great pop group Boney M. With their usual lyrical flair, they perfectly summed up the big Russian's life in their Trans-European-Number-One Chart-Busting sound:

> Ra-Ra-Rasputin,
> Russia's Greatest Love Machin(e).

Rasputin was indeed one of the most infamous lovers of all time: big, dirty, bearded and grubby, he began by mass rogering peasant girls in fraudulent ecstatic religious ceremonies, and ended up rogering almost every single aristocratic lady in Russia—often with their husbands' permission. He was not only Russia's Greatest Love Machin(e): he was also Russia's Biggest Love Machin(e): it is said that many of the tall buildings in Leningrad were inspired by Rasputin's wedding tackle, and at one point in 1910, rumour had it that Rasputin's willy constituted half of Imperial Russia's military firepower. (See Elvis Presley's hips and Imelda Marcos' brassieres.)

MERCEDES D'ACOSTA & MARLENE DIETRICH

When Dietrich saw D'Acosta, it was love at first sight, and the next morning she turned up at Mercedes' house carrying an enormous bunch of white roses. One of the most convenient things about a woman falling in love with a woman is that she doesn't have to spend her whole time guessing what a woman really likes because she's a woman herself already. The flowers worked a treat, and Dietrich and D'Acosta stayed faithful friends and true for the rest of D'Acosta's life. At the outbreak of the Second World War it was Marlene who paid to get Mercedes out of the reach of the Nazis. When Marlene went for the white roses treatment, she really meant true love.

MARLENE DIETRICH	
Born	**1904, in Germany.**
Occupation	**Singer and actress.**
Hobbies	**Being languid, falling in love again although never wanting to.**
Distinguishing Features	**Foreign accent, nice legs, smoke.**
Romantically Linked With	**Maurice Chevalier, Fritz Lang, James Stewart, Mike Todd, John Wayne, Yul Brynner, Douglas Fairbanks Jr, Gary Cooper, Mercedes D'Acosta, John Gilbert, Michael Wilding, Joseph von Sternberg, Jean Gabin, Erich Marie Remarque, Burt Bacharach.**

The international cinematic calibre of Dietrich's lovers is absolutely without compare. The lovers of the star of the immortal *Blue Angel* include the major contributors to *Metropolis*, *It's a Wonderful Life*, *Le Jour Se Leve*, *Around the World in 80 Days*, *All Quiet on the Western Front*, *Gigi*, *The King and I*, *The Magnificent Seven*, *High Noon*, *True Grit* and hundreds of other great films. So it should be, for Marlene Dietrich was a goddess placed on earth for the delectation of mankind.

If she is appealing and mystifying on screen, so was she also in real life, where her haze of languid androgynous sexuality added a mystery and depth to life in Hollywood. Transferred from Germany under the wing of Joseph von Sternberg after the sensation of the *Blue Angel*, she rarely was in films as magical as herself, but she was always a goddess, with her indefinable charisma, seducing and yet distancing at the same time.[1] As a summary of her own life she says: 'I have a child and I have made some people happy. That is all'.

FOOTNOTES

1 Speaking of which, the similarities between the great Dietrich and the new goddess Madonna are most extraordinary. The similarity in looks is uncanny: see Dietrich in *Witness for the Prosecution* and Madonna in *Shanghai Surprise*.

   Stranger still (and true), Marlene is in fact an abbreviation of Dietrich's original two names, Mary Magdalene, Mar-lene. And Mary Magdalene was a good friend of the Madonna.

MARLENE DIETRICH & MICHAEL WILDING

The most publicly memorable aspect of this romance was its untimely end brought about by the matrio-maniac, Elizabeth Taylor.

It is easy to see why two such discreet and good-mannered rogerers as Dietrich and Wilding should have been reluctant to go through all the fuss and uproar inevitably involved in trying to thwart Elizabeth Taylor's marriage plans.

Nevertheless, when two such charming and unaffected rogerers part, it must always be a source of great sadness to the world, and ranks here as one of life's Great Rogering Tragedies.

MICHAEL WILDING

Born	**Britain.**
Occupation	**Gentleman.**
Hobby	**Gentleman actor.**
Distinguishing Features	**Gentlemanliness.**
Romantically Linked With	**Margaret Leighton (m), Elizabeth Taylor (m), Susan Neil, Marlene Dietrich, Greta Garbo.**

'Considering I was the worst actor I ever came across . . . I did pretty well', he said. Wilding was the most self-effacing film actor ever, and he was loved by women on and off screen for this unique quality. He couldn't do himself down enough. He turned dignified modesty and self-irony into an art form. When he was told he had a brain tumour, Mr Wilding neither collapsed, nor raved, nor broke down. He merely said: 'That's impossible. I haven't got a brain'.

Wilding was *the* debonair English gentleman of the 1940s cinema, acting light comic roles and behaving throughout them exactly as if he were strolling through his normal habitat of gentleman's clubs and society parties. In fact, a list of his most famous films, all shared leads with the ever gracious and much mourned Dame Anna Neagle, shows that, in fact, he *didn't* have to stray far from his accustomed habitat at all: his big hit films were *Maytime in Mayfair, Spring in Park Lane, Tilly of Bloomsbury, Piccadilly Incident* and *The Curzons of Courtenay Street*. He was not given the great stretching roles of his generation of actors. But while Olivier, Gielgud and Richardson were working their guts out to make Shakespeare interesting to normal people, Wilding was marrying Elizabeth Taylor and relaxing. He often turned down roles because he was too busy sitting by the swimming pool. He was a player who strolled and brought charm, suavity and pleasure to the screen, while off screen he indulged contentedly in his real favourite pastimes—'mucking around, wasting time, and watching tv'. Bravo.

ELIZABETH TAYLOR & MICHAEL WILDING

Elizabeth Taylor quite literally forced Wilding to marry her, despite the fact that he was twice her age and going out with Marlene Dietrich at the time. She bought the engagement ring, and announced the marriage to the press before consulting him. As Kitty Kelley says in her excellent book about Taylor, at the wedding 'She wore a dove grey suit. He wore an air of surprise'. She was 19, and he was 39. Asked how he intended to spend the honeymoon,

the poor sweet stunned man replied, witty as ever: 'Together'. He was then asked if he had the formula for a successful marriage. 'I haven't got a bloody clue' was his reply. Unfortunately he was right, and the five-year marriage sapped and hurt him. He later sighed and said, 'I went to Hollywood for Metro-Goldwyn-Mayer, married Elizabeth Taylor and watched my career turn to ashes'.

ELIZABETH TAYLOR

Born	**1932, in Britain.**
Occupation	**Actress, celebrity.**
Hobbies	**Carrying jewels around.**
Distinguishing Features	**Seven wedding rings on hand.**
Romantically Linked With	**Conrad Nicholas Hilton (m), Michael Wilding (m), Mike Todd (m), Eddie Fisher (m), Richard Burton (m), John Warner (m), Henry Wynberg.**

Always the bride, never the bridesmaid, Elizabeth Taylor is a *massively* important figure in the history of twentieth century rogering, being the single individual most insistent and consistent in keeping faith *in* and committing herself *to* the concept and practice of monogamous marriage. She has been monogamously married[1] seven times.

Her first husband was Hilton (Hotels), her second Wilding (English actor), her third Todd (American producer), her fourth Fisher (American singer), her fifth and sixth Burton (Welsh actor/hellraiser/star of *The Wild Geese*), her seventh Warner (American politician): and the fabulous thing is that each time she has quite believed in what she is doing. Her protestations of faith on each occasion are a deeply moving testament to the indefatigability and gullibility of the human spirit:

'*Your heart knows when you meet the right man. There is no doubt that Nicky is the one I want to spend my life with*'.
Wedding to Conrad Hilton—6 May 1950.

'*I just want to be with Michael, to be his wife. This is, for me, the beginning of a happy end*'.
Wedding to Michael Wilding—21 February 1952.

'*I have given him my eternal love . . . This marriage will last for ever. For me it will be third time lucky*'.
Wedding to Mike Todd—2 February 1957.

'*I have never been happier in my life . . . We will be on our honeymoon for thirty or forty years*'.
Wedding to Eddie Fisher—12 May 1959.

*'I'm so happy you can't believe it . . . I love him enough to stand
by him, no matter what he might do and I would wait'.*
Wedding to Richard Burton—15 March 1964.

*'There will be bloody no more marriage or divorces. We are stuck like
chicken feathers to tar—for lovely always'.*
Second wedding to Richard Burton—10 October 1975.

*'John is the best lover I've ever had . . . I want to spend the rest of
my life with him and I want to be buried with him'.*
Wedding to John Warner—4 December 1976.

She may not numerically be the world record holder in marriage—Zsa Zsa
Gabor has had eight husbands (shared Liz's first, in fact), and a certain American lady called Glynne 'Scotty' Wolfe had twenty-six—but it is in Elizabeth
that the true spirit of marriage has remained the most fresh and everlasting.
In the case of Richard Burton, she loved him so much that she married him
twice, the first her longest running marriage—ten years—and the second one
of her shortest—one year.[2]

She has in her time been the most famous woman in the world, the highest
paid actress in the world, the star of the most expensive film in the world,
the wearer of the most expensive costume in the world and the owner of the
most valuable jewel in the world—it is again a tribute to her magnanimity
and generosity of spirit that she spread the wonder that is Elizabeth Taylor so
widely amongst husbands. As a tribute to her achievements, the editors of this
book, in consultation with high ranking members of the Church of England,
have devised a special wedding service for Elizabeth Taylor, if ever she should
think of doing it all over again.

The Form of Solemnization of Matrimony: Elizabeth Taylor Sup-
plement.

*At the day and time appointed for solemnization of matrimony, or
a bit later, allowing for traffic, the persons to be married shall come
into the body of the church with their friends and neighbours and ex-
husbands even, if they like; and there standing together, the man on
the right hand, and the perfect vision of womanhood on the left, the
priest shall say:*

Dearly Beloved, we are gathered here in the sight of God, and
in the face of this star-studded congregation, to join together this
man and this completely fabulous woman in holy matrimony;
which is an honourable estate, not by anyone to be enterprised
nor taken in hand unadvisedly, lightly, or wantonly; but rever-
ently, discreetly, advisedly, soberly, and again and again, if you
like, Miss Taylor, in fear of God; duly considering the causes for
which matrimony was ordained.

Therefore, if any man can shew any just cause why they may
not be lawfully joined together, let him now speak, or rather let
him not speak now, because if he does, I'll just overrule him.

And also, speaking unto the persons that shall be married, he shall say:

> I require and charge you both, as ye will answer at the dreadful day of judgement, when the secrets of all hearts shall be disclosed and the alimony will be decided, that if one of you knows any impediments, why ye may not be lawfully joined together in matrimony, such as one of you having been married seven times before, I don't mind.

Then shall the showbiz priest say unto the man:

> Bozo, wilt thou have this utterly fabulous superstar to thy wedded wife, to live together after God's ordinance in the holy estate of matrimony? Wilt thou love her, comfort her, honour her, spoil her utterly and keep her in furs, jewels and health farms; and forsaking all others, keep thee only unto her, as long as she's interested in you?[3]

The lucky fella shall answer:

> I will.

Then shall the old family friend, who happens to be a priest, say unto the woman, whom the whole world adores:

> Wilt thou have this incredibly lucky man to thy wedded husband, to live together after God's ordinance in the holy estate of matrimony? Wilt thou love him and spend his money, as long as he's rich and healthy and forsaking all others, keep thee only unto him, so long as ye feel like you're genuinely in love?

And the Goddess shall answer:

> I will.

Then shall the minister say:

> Who giveth this woman to be married to this man?

And some really huge old time Hollywood star shall step forward— and people shall whisper and say, 'My God, is he still alive?'

Then shall they give their troth to each other in this manner. The minister, receiving the woman at Gene Kelly or someone of his stature's hands, shall cause Mr Lucky with his right hand to take the divine Elizabeth by her right hand, and to say after him as followeth:

> I, Bozo, take thee, Elizabeth, to my wedded wife, to have and to hold from this day forward, for better for worse, for richer for poorer, in sickness and in health, to love and to cherish, till you get fed up with me, according to the rewrite of God's holy ordinance; and thereto I plight thee my troth.

Then shall they loose their hands, and the woman, with her right hand taking the man by his right hand, shall likewise say after the minister:

I, Liz, take thee, Bozo, to my wedded husband, to have and to hold from this day forward, for better, for richer and in health, to love and to cherish, till circumstances quite out of our control, such as my falling out of love for the eighth time in a row, do us part, according to the rewrite of God's holy ordinance; and thereto I plight thee my troth.

Then shall they again loose their hands; and the man shall give unto the woman an unbelievably expensive ring, I mean, huge, legendary, no point having gone through with the whole thing if this isn't an absolute stunner, laying the same upon the book: and the priest, taking the ring, if he's fit enough to lift the massive thing, shall deliver it unto the security men standing behind to take it back to the vault, and shall give to the lucky guy who's marrying this legend a paste replica of the multi-million dollar gem, to put it upon the fourth finger of the woman's left hand, if there's any room. And the man, holding the paste replica of the ring, shall say after the priest:

With this incredibly expensive ring, yeah, even more expensive than anyone else who shall be nameless but is in fact Richard Burton ever bought thee, I thee wed; with my body I thee worship, and with all my worldly goods I thee endow: quite frankly, I just cannot believe my luck: is it all right if I say that? In the Name of the Father, and of the Son, and of the Holy Ghost, Amen.

Then, the man leaving the ring upon the fourth finger of the woman's left hand, they shall both kneel down, and the minister shall say:

Let us pray.

O Eternal God, Creator and preserver of all mankind, Giver of all spiritual grace, the Author of everlasting life and inspiration for some very good films as well, things like *Demetrius and the Gladiator* and *The Mission*, send thy blessing upon these thy servants, this man and this completely fabulous woman, whose performances[4] in *National Velvet*,[5] *Ivanhoe*,[6] *Who's Afraid of Virginia Woolf*,[7] and *The Blue Bird*[8] I particularly enjoyed, but I'm sure thou hast thine own favourites. We bless them in thy name; that, as Isaac and Rebecca lived faithfully together, so these persons may surely perform and keep the vow and live according to a lot of thy laws; through Jesus Christ our Lord. Amen.

Then shall the priest join their right hands together and say:

Those whom God hath joined together let no man, who isn't richer, more attractive, or just quite simply more according to Liz's taste at the time in question, put asunder.

Then shall the minister speak unto the people:

> Forasmuch as Liz and Bozo have consented together in holy
> wedlock, and have witnessed the same before God and all you
> fabulous big names, many of whom I have known and admired
> for many years, and thereto have given and pledged their troth,
> either to other, and have declared the same by giving and receiving
> of a seriously expensive ring, and by joining of hands; I pronounce
> that they be man and wife together, In the Name of the Father,
> and of the Son, and of the Holy Ghost. Amen.

And the Minister shall add this Blessing:

> God the Father, God the Son, God the Holy Ghost, bless, preserve
> and keep you; the Lord mercifully with his favours look upon
> you, once he's got over what must be a rather alarming case of
> *déjà vu* here, and so fill you with all spiritual benediction and
> grace that ye may live together in this life and that in the world
> to come the man may be allowed at least a tiny fraction of Liz's
> time, because she's going to have a lot of socializing to do with
> her other husbands in life everlasting. *Amen.*

FOOTNOTES

1 See Appendix: Names for Rogering.
2 Other two-time marriers: see Jane Wyman, Natalie Wood, Elliott Gould.
3 See Hedy Lamarr and the Peul Beurou tribe.
4 It is wise, amidst the marriage ballyhoo, not to forget what a great actress Elizabeth has been.
5 In striving for the part in *National Velvet*, she showed the utter dedication that she always
  felt for marriage. Through exercise and dieting she added three inches to her *height* to fit the
  qualifications for the part of National's young girl rider.
6 In *Ivanhoe* her similarity to singer Kate Bush is quite eerie.
7 Both she and Burton won Oscars for *Virginia Woolf*. It is said that after the release of the
  film very few people ever accepted dinner invitations round to their house again.
8 But perhaps, when all is said and done, *The Blue Bird*, a 1970 George Cukor movie, made
  in co-production with the Russians, is Liz's greatest film achievement—the movie also features
  such great stars as George Cole, Jane Fonda and a very young Patsy Kensit, and is, in the
  view of many, THE WORST FILM EVER MADE IN THE HISTORY OF CINEMA. It
  is wonderful to observe how, working together, the Russians and the Americans can really
  achieve something which apart they could never have come near. It is hoped that the example
  set by this extraordinary picture will be an inspiration to those upon whose combined efforts
  rest the hope of mankind.

ELIZABETH TAYLOR & HENRY WYNBERG

In 1975, when Elizabeth Taylor finally left him to go back to Richard Burton,
Henry Wynberg was unkindly named 'Jiltee of the Year'. It hadn't always been

an easy relationship for Henry: on one rather difficult occasion Burton turned up unexpectedly at the Taylor household in order to discuss the possibility of him and Liz getting back together again. A suitable place had to be found for Henry in this delicate situation. Liz thought long and hard and then shoved him in a cupboard.

This was, unhappily, only one of the indignities suffered by Henry during the affair. Not the least of these was being one of the few men Liz rogered and then *didn't* marry. Henry's wife was heard to remark of Elizabeth Taylor: 'She marries the men she loves', Poor Henry.

HENRY WYNBERG

Born	**In Holland.**
Occupation	**Second-hand car dealer.**
Romantically Linked With	**Carol Wynberg (m), Elizabeth Taylor, Maggie Eastwood (m).**
Nickname	**Clint, oh sorry, Henry, I wasn't concentrating.**

Henry has, by chance or skill, developed a most extraordinary romantic record.[1] His first wife described him as 'a virile young man who smiles a lot',[2] and with those qualifications, he formed the interim period between the two Burton–Taylor weddings. His failure to hold on to Liz, however, did not break this boy's spirit. The next time in the hotseat, he has shown staying power. He is now Mr Mrs Clint Eastwood. In his leisure time, Henry is known to be an enthusiastic reader of *Sports Illustrated*, *National Geographic* and *Hunter's Guide*, in case a man with a beard, a cigar and slits for eyes ever comes hunting him down.

FOOTNOTES

1 Henry is one of a particular breed of men, who, without notable fame or fortune, somehow seem to attract and roger astonishingly famous women: see also Sir Gordon White, and, with an explanation of the phenomenon, Peter Hamill.

2 No bad thing for a young man to be. In the Late Middle Ages, and the Early Late Ages, the only ground for divorce allowed to a woman according to Catholic law was impotence. Long

and complex trials were held where the potency of the accused husband was tested: it even came to judges taking up residence in the house of the poor unfortunate, and rushing into the room if ever or whenever the young man had anything to show them (see Frances Howard and the Earl of Essex). Fortunately for Henry, if ever he gets transported by chance back into those dark times (and you may say that this is pretty unlikely, but who would have thought that the same guy would handle Richard Burton and Clint Eastwood's wives and live to tell the tale), his virility would keep him safe from the worst excesses of a church gone completely bonkers. He would also find, incidentally, that in sixteenth-century France a used motor car would attract quite a lot more attention and respect than it does nowadays.

HENRY WYNBERG & MAGGIE EASTWOOD

Maggie Eastwood gave up the Man With No Name for the Man With not only a Name, but also a Thriving Second-Hand Car Business. She exchanged a Magnum 45 for a glove box with an interior light, a poncho for a Pirelli spare tyre and a sharpshooter for a sharp leatherette interior. And she's probably better off for it. Unlike Clint, Henry was born outside the United States, so he won't be distracted later in life by having to run for president.

MAGGIE EASTWOOD	
Born	1933, in America.
Romantically Linked With	The Man With No Name[1] (m) and Henry Wynberg (m).
Nickname	The Woman with No Name.

Not having a name for so many years finally drove Maggie mad and she left The Man With No Name to get the name of Wynberg—not perfect, no, but better than no name at all. No more for Maggie the harsh life of the spaghetti western hero, all cigar spit and long pauses, or the tough times of the downtown vigilante, all Magnums in your mouth and police cars up your tail: she and Henry now enjoy the quiet life: 'We go for walks and play a lot of tennis'. Nice.

FOOTNOTES

1 People often ask: why was The Man With No Name so angry, why did he spend so much time killing other people? The reason is, of course, that it was very annoying having no name. It's a real conversation killer when someone who is trying to get to know you:

NICE MAN   *Hullo.*

THE MAN WITH NO NAME   *Hullo.*

NICE MAN   *I'm Henry Wynberg.*

THE MAN WITH NO NAME	*Yeah. Hi.*
NICE MAN	*What's your name?*
	Pause.
NICE MAN	*Sorry?*
THE MAN WITH NO NAME	*I didn't say anything.*
NICE MAN	*Ah. Sorry, I didn't catch your name then.*
THE MAN WITH NO NAME	*No.*
NICE MAN	*So—what is it?*
	The Man With No Name pulls his gun and blasts Henry to eternity. And can you blame him?

MAGGIE EASTWOOD AND CLINT EASTWOOD

On her divorce from the Man With No Name, Maggie was awarded a $20 million settlement. Which is a spectacular amount per roger. This is clearly one of the World's Most Expensive Rogers.

CLINT EASTWOOD

Born	**1931, in America.**
Occupation	**Mayor of Carmel.**
Hobbies	**Acting, directing and running a restaurant.**
Distinguishing Features	**Thought by most men to be the most attractive man alive.**
Romantically Linked With	**Maggie Eastwood (m), Sondra Locke.**
Nickname	**The Man With No Nickname.**

Clint Eastwood is one of the greatest film-makers alive. But now, having earned over two billion dollars, deservedly, he has turned his attentions to other matters: the sorting out of planning permission in the small township of Carmel.[1] In other words, he is becoming a politician. While he is denying he has ambitions outside Carmel city limits, there is no doubt that he is now on his way to becoming the President of the United States, unless Bruce Springsteen gets there first. The example of Ronald Reagan presents a role model, not only in that both Eastwood and Reagan were actors, but more eerily, in the fact that they both have acted with apes: Eastwood in *Every Which Way But Loose* and its sequel, Reagan in *Bedtime for Bonzo*. In fact, Johnny Weismuller is the *only* major Ape Actor never to have moved into politics.[2]

Clint's personality has always been shrouded in enigma and secrecy, and very little is known of his private life. Three quotations may be relevant.

1. 'I'm a romantic, I cry easily'.
2. 'I'm a basic person. I like females'.

Ah, well, no, when all is said and done, the chances of getting to the bottom[3] of the Eastwood enigma are no greater than they ever were before. Leave true greatness alone.

FOOTNOTES

1 In electing him, the townsfolk of Carmel wisely ignored the way he treated the townsfolk in *High Plains Drifter*. Within the first ten minutes he had raped the only woman in town and killed three people. He then painted the entire town red, and waited for some visitors to arrive. When they arrived, he killed them.
2 For the purpose of clarity, Ernest Borgnine is not counted as an ape in this context.
3 Curiously, Clint's bottom is not in fact his most admired part. It was his eyes that were voted the sexiest in America. The sexiest bottom award went to his presidential rival, Bruce Springsteen.

MONOLITHIC ENIGMAS LAY LINE

GERTRUDE STEIN

ALICE B. TOKLAS

MERCEDES D'ACOSTA

MARLENE DIETRICH

MICHAEL WILDING

ELIZABETH TAYLOR

HENRY WYNBERG

MAGGIE EASTWOOD

CLINT EASTWOOD

On the evidence of this line, it's more 'Every Which Way You Can', than 'Every Which Way But Loose'. More 'Dirty Harry' than either.

MOTHS AND OLD FLAMES

FROM	**MARLENE DIETRICH**
TO	**DES O'CONNOR**
IN	**9 ROGERS**

Books are forgotten, tales are no longer told, but throughout time, songs live on, handed down from generation to generation. Likewise the gift of song. Here, in a line of nine, the great chanteuse passes her genius down to the great chanteur. This pairing cannot be coincidence: Marlene sung of how men gathered round her like moths around a flame: and eerily, for fear of those same insects of the night, Des is himself kept in mothballs by the light entertainment industry of England, periodically to be hauled out to sing once more and start England falling in love with him . . . all over again.

MARLENE DIETRICH

Although common in nothing else, Marlene is the common denominator between this line and the last. Then, she turned a run of all girl rogers back into hot-blooded heterosexuality. Here she tops an all-heterosexual line. But what a bunch: the relationships of Ava Gardner and Howard Hughes, Stewart Granger and Hedy Lamarr, and Des and Gillian O'Connor make it easy to see why an intelligent woman would think it a good idea to stick to girls.

MARLENE DIETRICH & DOUGLAS FAIRBANKS JNR

Marlene and Douglas had a well-established affair. Marlene rented a London apartment a couple of floors down from Doug's pad near Grosvenor Square. He liked her a lot: 'Marlene was a glamour girl with brains. Amusing and unpretentious. Not at all the mystery character. A gallant, straightforward girl full of ideas'. They used to spend weekends in the country when she'd cook him meals and encourage him in his career, while he heroically killed the insects that kept on buzzing round her.

One of Marlene's favourite fantasies at the time was to imagine all the men in her life attending her funeral. Jean Gabin would be propped up in the corner of the church, smoking and refusing to talk to anyone. Erich Marie Remarque would have gone to the wrong church. Gary Cooper would be yawning and James Stewart would be asking whose funeral it was. But Douglas Fairbanks Junior would always appear at the back in naval uniform, halloo, and deliver a magnificent wreath sent by the Queen of England herself.

DOUGLAS FAIRBANKS JNR.

Born	1909, in America.
Occupation	Son of swashbuckler, then swashbuckler.
Hobbies	Painting, sculpting, collecting toy soldiers, and rogering.
Distinguishing Features	Sword in hand and well-buckled swash.
Romantically Linked With	Mary Lee Epling (m), Joan Crawford (m), Ethel Fairbanks (m), Marlene Dietrich.
Nickname	Jayor, Dodo.

Once upon a time there dwelt in the wood of holly, that is known as Hollywood, two noble kinsmen that hight[1] Douglas Fairbanks and Douglas Fairbanks Junior. And in his youth did Douglas Junior live in the Castle that is known as Pickfair,[2,3] for there did dwell Douglas Fairbanks Senior and his lady wife that was of him much beloved, and she hight Mary Pickford. And Douglas Fairbanks the Elder was a mighty warrior in the land of Celluloid, and there fought he many a noble foe. But then came the day, in the year of our lord nineteen thousand and twenty, when Junior was also desirous to swash his buckle and make his name in the town that is known as Tinsel: and his father did say unto him: 'Do not as I do my son, for the swashing of the buckle, it is no life for a man'. But did ever youth heed unto the words of old age? No, never, and so shall it ever be. For Douglas did go unto the lot that hight Paramount and did make a movie entitled 'Party Girl'—and then for all his life did he serve in the mighty army of dream-makers that doth serve the land of Holly and Wood.

And many noble battles fought he, in many different guises: a Prisoner of Zenda was he, and also hight he Gunga Din: and time was he did don the motley of piracy and Sinbad the Sailor hight he upon the high seas. And in his life did he have many fair companions, noble knights, that hight Sir David of Niven, and Sir Rex, son of Harris, that had a Fair Lady: and many a time and oft did they make merry, and did call themselves the Cads Club. And for their motto had they 'Everything Rampant, Always Couchant', by which they did mean that they should wallop in the todger whensoe'er time was right and fair maiden willing.

And in his loving did the brave Sir Douglas encounter and make merry pantings with the fair Princess Marlene, that came from a land of warriors across the sea. And also came he into the clutches of the cruel witch, Joan, who for an evil sceptre did bear a coat-hanger and with it did bring great fear to her young brood.

And yet, despite this bewitchment, was Sir Douglas always fair, and always merrie, and people did say of him, behold, a gentleman there goes upon his way. And still lives he in the land of England, where rules the fair Elizabeth, and much honour is done to him, for he was always a good sort, and of fair visage: and always he did smile, for the world had been good to him, and he did repay the world in kind.

FOOTNOTES

1 Which signifieth 'named'.
2 And many strange times were there at Pickfair. For thither did come the greatest clown of all, that hight Charlie, and Chaplin hight, and dressed was in garments all of black. And there did he let forth a balloon of air, that did make the noise of merry farting, and he did name it Whoopee Cushion, and much revelry was there, and laughter, for it was the first of its kind, and ever was farting a cause for joy, and ever shall be. And also came there unto the castle a great wizard, whom men did name Albert, and Einstein hight. And upon the table where they did eat did the great wizard display, with aid of only knife and fork, his great magick, that was known as the Theory of Relativity, and all did wonder and were sore amazed.

And thus in its time did the fair castle of Pickfair witness the two greatest of all deeds done in that age.
3 This idea of composite names, here the blending of Fairbanks and Pickford, can be less

fortuitous than the charming Pickfair. In the early seventies, the popular singer Chris Rea was asked if he would like to join Mark Knopfler as lead vocalist of the then unknown Dire Straits. Chris agreed, as long as his name could be incorporated into the band. The experiment was not a success, and after a short while Dire Rea split up in confusion and recriminations.

DOUGLAS FAIRBANKS JNR & JOAN CRAWFORD

The human race is romantic and loves to believe that when a couple meet and fall in love, it is somehow fated, part of a vast cosmic plan, the irresistible drawing together of two souls destined to unite since the dawn of time.

However, a cursory surveillance of life makes it clear that if there ever was such a plan, it's been completely mucked up[1] so either we go on planless, or create one of our own. One of the ones who decided to make a plan of her own was Joan Crawford. Her plan was simple, and it had to do with the number four. She based her life around fourness.

So, she had four husbands, stayed with each of them for four years, and changed the toilet seats in her house four times, once each time a husband left.[2] As a method of organizing one's life, the plan is less ambitious and morally complicated than the plans of, say, Jesus Christ or Muhammad, but just about as realistic: and at least Joan was in control.

The Douglas Fairbanks/Joan Crawford roger thus can be seen not so much as the brief affair of two star crossed lovers, but as a useful statistical interlude facilitating the prompt change of a sedentary toilet device.

JOAN CRAWFORD	
Real Name	**Lucille le Sueur (literally, the Sweater.)**
Born	**1904, in America.**
Occupation	**Actress.**
Hobbies	**Beating up her children and rogering.**
Romantically Linked With	**Douglas Fairbanks Jnr. (m), Franchot Tone (m), Philip Terry (m), Albert Steele (m), Clark Gable, Gary Cooper.**
Nickname	**Queen of the Movies, The Dragon Queen.**

Joan has had a hard time of it recently. *Mommie Dearest* made her look a cruel, strange monster. But what is the truth behind the new myth? If you look really closely, research, probe, question, analyse, will a new, kinder, more understandable Joan Crawford emerge?

S'pose it might. Not bothered really. Wouldn't be much fun if it did. The horrors her adopted children claim to have suffered, as Joan put them through just the kind of trials she had undergone as a child, make much better reading.

Truth is, Joan doesn't sound a real cutey:[3] her career was the only thing that mattered to her, and she was obsessed by it. She loved her fans and is said to have written over 70,000 letters a year to them. Whenever she divorced, she saw it not as a private sorrow, but as an occasion to get a press scoop to benefit her career. When she wasn't divorcing or marrying she was 'very predatory with men', and liked to offer them small roles in return for sex. 'She passed from one love to another with . . . ease'.

And yet, you can't deny it, the dame had something. Gable nearly married her and even in her old age her final husband, Albert Steele, Chairman of Pepsi-Cola, described her as 'a star in every sense of the word'.[4] As long as she lived, she hung on to her strange and perverse standards: as wife of the Chairman of Pepsi-Cola, she became increasingly interested in toilet matters. When they stayed in hotels, she would frequently get down on her hands and knees to scrub clean the floors of the bathroom, presumably making her a star in the 'get down and scrub the bathroom floor' sense of the word.[5]

FOOTNOTES

1 For instance, see: Introduction—The No Bang Theory—and also Appendices: Dogs and Rogering, Marriage, Weddings and Wedding Nights.

2 'Marriage' came to mean to her, 'dirty toilet'. This connection of toilets with marriage is a complex one dating from early childhood when, because of a broken home, Joan had to clean the toilets in boarding houses in Kansas.

3 In fact, sometimes Joan doesn't sound real at all. Of her false breasts, Bette Davis once remarked: 'I keep running into them, like the Hollywood Hills'.

4 Possibly a double-edged compliment if Albert meant a star in the sense of a ball of noxious gas that floats in the cosmos or a *Star*, in its manifestation as a British daily newspaper.

Joni Mitchell was sceptical when she was given the star treatment in 'A Case of You':

> Just before our love got lost you said,
> 'I am as constant as a northern star'.
> And I said, 'Constantly in the darkness:
> Where's that at?
> If you want me, I'll be in the bar'.

5 This is not as strange as it seems in fact. Scientists talk of the phenomenon of the 'garbage star': this is a star that moves around with such heat, that it actually burns up all debris in space, and leaves the area it passes through cleaner than it was before. There has always been a fear that such a garbage star would one day pass through the orbit of our sun, in which case astrophysicists predict all the world would be burnt away in a few seconds, except the *Blue Peter* studio, which is, of course, spotlessly clean.

JOAN CRAWFORD & CLARK GABLE

There is little doubt that Joan Crawford would have had Clark Gable as one of the husbands in her four star plan but for an astonishing interference by the MGM studio. They had decided that having invested in Clark Gable they did not want him involved in any romantic plans, cosmic or otherwise, and set up a trust fund which he would lose if he ever divorced his wife. Money again proved itself, like herpes and a belligerent husband, one of those things which can blight the path of true love. On account of cash, the Crawford and Gable roger, maritally speaking, came to nothing.

CLARK GABLE

Born	**1901, in America.**
Occupation	**Film star[1]**
Hobbies	**Hunting, shooting, fishing, cars and rogering.**
Distinguishing Features	**Enormous ears and no vest.[2]**
Romantically Linked With	**Joan Crawford, Josephine Dillon, Ava Gardner, Paulette Goddard, Virginia Grey, Jean Harlow, Joan Harrison, Rhea Langham, Carole Lombard, Sylvia Ashley, Mrs Kay Williams Spreckels, Nancy Reagan.**
Married[3]	**Dillon,[4] Langham,[5] Lombard,[6] Ashley,[7] and Mrs Kay Williams Spreckels.[8]**
Nickname	**The King.[9]**

Gable was the greatest of the Hollywood heart throbs. Yet, in real life, neither he, nor his women, were over-impressed by the reputation. In his own words: 'I don't believe that I have any of this sex appeal that you hear all the women talk about. As many a disappointed young lady will tell you—I'm a lousy lover'. (See Nancy Reagan and Clark Gable.) His long time mistress said that she never dared close her eyes when she was making love to Gable, because it was only looking at him, and thinking 'This is Clark Gable doing this' that made it a worthwhile experience at all.

And yet Clark Gable was never short of willing women to test out just how rotten a lover he was. At one point, he saw a group shot of all the women on the MGM lot and, laughing, said: 'Aren't they pretty, and I've had everyone of them.' He reigned supreme for nearly thirty years, and looked gorgeous and ironic for every single one of them. He was what people call 'a real man'. He knew how to mend a car, and he knew how to handle a woman. When he slapped Norma Shearer thousands of them wrote in case next time he got slapping,[10] he'd like to practice on them.

FOOTNOTES

1 At Gable's first screen test, Jack Warner, the Hollywood tycoon, said to his son-in-law, Mervyn Leroy: 'Why did you throw away $500 of our money on that big ape? Didn't you see his ears when you talked to him? And those big feet and hands. Not to mention that

ugly face.' For 'ugly face' take a look at Ernest Borgnine, but be sure to put on some dark glasses first.

(See Appendix: Mad Producers.)

2 See Gable in the Great Communicators line.

3 The first woman Gable ever loved was a certain *Franz Dorfier*, the daughter of an Oregon farmer: he is said to have told her that 'he loved her as no man had ever loved a woman from the beginning of time'.* He did not marry her, but Franz remembered, and sixty years later was still single, despite twelve proposals of marriage.

4 *Josephine Dillon*: he married her in 1924: she was a drama teacher eleven years his senior who tutored him and helped turn him into a star. They divorced in 1930 and she blamed it on his 'overwhelming ambition'. She is said to have felt particularly bitter about the hours wasted each night sitting on his face, trying to squash his ears with her thighs.

5 *Rhea Langham*: Texan widow: it lasted eight years.

6 *Gable and Lombard* was another of Hollywood's true romances, and, like Bacall and Bogart, ended tragically. Gable described her as 'the most lovable scatterbrain in the world' and loved her more than any other woman, ever. Her death in an aeroplane crash in 1942 broke his heart. He was buried next to her when he died. Marvell said:

> *The grave's a fine and private place,*
> *But none, I think, do there embrace'.*

For the sake of Gable and Lombard, let's hope that isn't true, and that in fact graves are nice and cuddly and quite sexy.

7 *Sylvia Ashley*: The worst of them: he left her after seven months.

8 *Kay Williams Spreckels*: when they married, Kay said she was thirty-seven. Other of her documents hinted it might have been more like forty-two. Never mind that: the Justice who performed the ceremony said, 'I suggested that Gable kiss the bride, and, man, it lasted all the time I was taking down the witnesses'. It was a happy marriage: Gable said, 'I've raised my share of hell in my time, now I'm more interested in raising kids'. (See Appendix: Age Differences and Rogering.)

9 *vis-à-vis* Prince Charles, this is an extraordinary coincidence. It is quite clear that any man who wants to be king must have generous ears.**

10 See Names for Rogering.

*See Appendix: Pulling Techniques.
**Howard Hughes said of him: 'His ears made him look like a taxi cab with both doors open'— but then Howard was probably jealous. Clark didn't have to lock women in hotels in order to sleep with them, and he wasn't scared of toilets either. In the end, it is now thought that Gable was a star *because* of his ears. Proof for this lies in the success of *Playboy*, with its large ears for women, but, more startlingly, in the similarity between Clark Gable's ears and the hermaphrodite snail when in its shell. (See King Size Pair line.)

CLARK GABLE & AVA GARDNER

It could be that under other circumstances, Gable and Gardner might have just had a platonic relationship, talking, conversing, chewing the cud. But the lines in the movies in which they were paired were so ridiculous, that they clearly lost faith in the value of verbal communication and went for the roger instead. It was lines like these that forced them between the sheets:

'You're a lot of woman . . . you're a strange woman . . . but still a lot of woman'. (Gable)

'You're a strange man . . . but quite a lot of man'. (Gardner) The fact that Gardner had always fancied Gable might have been another contributory factor: when she married Mickey Rooney, she said: 'He wasn't my type at all. I really wanted someone who looked like Clark Gable'. And in the end she did get someone who looked almost exactly like Clark Gable.

AVA GARDNER	
Born	**1922, on Christmas Eve.**[1]
Occupation	**Actress.**
Hobbies	**Drinking, eating and rogering.**
Distinguishing Features	**Perfect face, perfect green eyes.**
Romantically Linked With	**Mickey Rooney (m), Frank Sinatra (m), Howard Hughes, Artie Shaw (m), Porfirio Rubirosa, Luis Miguel Dominguan,[2] Clark Gable, Robert Walker, Peter Lawford.**
Married	**Frank Sinatra, Mickey Rooney,[3] Artie Shaw.**
Divorced	**The lot of them.**
Non Romantic Links With	**Robert Mitchum,[4] George C. Scott.[5]**
Nickname	**The World's Most Beautiful Animal,[6] The Cheetah with the Roar.**

When she arrived in Hollywood, Gardner was a virgin farmer's daughter from Grabtown, Carolina.[7] Within a few months she was dating Mickey Rooney, at that time Hollywood's highest paid box-office star. When she first met him, he was dressed as Carmen Miranda and throughout their relationship he remained five-and-a-half inches shorter than her, but she still married him.[8] It was the start of quite a love life.

Second she married Artie Shaw,[9] the bandleader, but left him when he turned out to be an intellectual snob and went out with Howard Hughes instead, who in one physical set-to dislocated her jaw before she knocked him out with a brass bell. After that came Frank Sinatra, who was the worst of the lot; after Sinatra Ava took up with a bullfighter for a rest.

All said and done Ava was one hell of a woman[10]—and one who triumphantly broke many of the unspoken rules of Hollywood—she drank like a fish, ate steak for breakfast, lunch and dinner and, most of all, she broke the great rule that if you've been a star you've got to go tragically down the drain. She lives now as an elegant retired woman in Kensington with a Welsh Corgi—content and self-sufficient—'There comes a point when every woman has to face up to being an old broad', she says. 'Most evenings I have supper alone on a tray in front of the television. It's just the way I always wanted to live, but never could in the old days'.

FOOTNOTES

1 Similarity between Ava Gardner and the little baby Jesus: both touched Frank Sinatra—one with genius, the other with her body.
2 He was a bullfighter, and Ava had a go at it herself—she got gored in the cheek—'After that I never felt the same again about Spain or those goddamn bullfighters'.
3 Mickey Rooney was always very short, and always one for the ladies. He once rather bluntly told a chorus girl that he wanted to roger her. Her reply: 'If you do, and I get to hear about it, there'll be trouble'.
4 Mitchum fell for Ava, but knew that she was a Hughes girl—he therefore rang Hughes to find out if it would be okay for him to step in. Next day on the set Gardner put it bluntly —'Well, do we have an affair or don't we?' They didn't. (See Appendix: Pulling Techniques.)
5 During the filming of *The Bible* George C. Scott fell desperately in love with Ava—said director John Huston—'He was out of his mind over her—literally. At one stage he had to be put into a nursing home'.
6 There are a lot of shepherds who would disagree with this, of course—according to the Hite report, a frightening number of Americans have their first sexual experiences with sheep*.
7 *Grabtown*—it is interesting to think how places like these get their names: there is a street in the East End of London that has recently had its name changed from 'Gropecuntlane'.
8 Mickey is up there in the Gruesome Wedding Night stakes. He brought along his golf clubs on the honeymoon, and apparently during the wedding night got up to write letters: perhaps it was meant to be a rather literal compliment—rogering Ava Gardner was certainly something to write home about. (See Appendix: Marriage, Weddings and Wedding Nights).
9 Artie is actually up with Zsa Zsa Gabor on marriages—he married eight times, his wives including Lana Turner and Jean Harlow. (See Appendix: Marriage, Weddings and Wedding Nights.)
10 Although not necessarily one hell of an actress: Louis B. Mayer said of her—'She can't act, she can't talk, but she's terrific'—but then, what did Louis B. Mayer know about anything? (See Appendix: Marriage, Weddings and Wedding Nights.)

*Which puts a rather strange gloss on the Biblical assertion: 'The Lord is My Shepherd'.**
**Although, on reflection, not so strange: if you look at the world, God does fuck a lot of us around.

AVA GARDNER & HOWARD HUGHES

'I was never really in love with Howard. To be honest, I never really even liked him, but he stuck to me like molasses'. Noah Dietrich, Howard Hughes' right hand man, describes Hughes as the most boring man in the world: 'He only had two topics of conversation—business and women's breasts. That's how he was first attracted to Ava. He was obsessed by big boobies and she had big boobies'.

In the end, she made Hughes look like a big booby himself—ten years after they had split up, Hughes was still having Ava followed.

HOWARD HUGHES

Born	**1905, in America.**
Occupations	**Producer, airplane designer, test pilot, entrepreneur, tool-maker, will-maker, prisoner.**
Hobbies	**Avoiding germs and rogering.**[1]
Romantically Linked With	**Lana Turner, Ava Gardner, Ida Lupino, Billie Dove, Jean Harlow, Olivia de Havilland, Marion Marsh, Ginger Rogers, Katherine Hepburn, Terry Moore, Jean Peters (m), Ella Rice (m).**

Howard Hughes was one of the most dedicated rogerers of all time. He devoted fortunes to rogering. He kept a harem in Hollywood, buying several houses to store his girls in and hiring hotel suites which were guarded by his own bodyguards to make sure they didn't roger anyone else.[2] He was one of the most ruthless ever casting couchers.[3] Rare were the occasions when he made love without first promising to make the poor girl a star once the deed was done. However, he was not always successful in the ways of love: many are the instances of quite how ridiculous Howard could be in the pursuit of rogering: for example . . .

He bought a whole ballet company in order to roger Zizi Jean-Marie—and failed to roger her.

He flew in seven Miss Universe finalists in order to roger them, but they escaped from the hotels he was keeping them in.

He had his detectives call him every forty-five minutes when they were tailing Elizabeth Taylor: but in the end she married almost everyone in Hollywood except him.

He had Stewart Granger followed to London, Paris, Rome, Palermo and Tunis, watched every moment to see if he was cheating on his wife, Jean Simmons, so Howard could tell on him, and get Brownie points. But Stewart stayed faithful.

What was so particularly grim about Howard is that apparently on the occasions when he *did* get the sex he was spending so much money on, he didn't enjoy it particularly: he was so obsessed by the cleanliness thing that eventually led him to lock himself away in a germ-free penthouse,[4] that he tried to get the whole thing over as quickly as possible. To Howard, sex was a quick one. When he did eventually marry, Howard was already descending into madness.[5] God alone knows why Jean Peters agreed to marry him—by that time he stayed in bed all day and night watching tv. She had to put Kleenex between his toes to stop the noise of his permanently clicking toenails. He used to write long memos about tiny subjects: three pages on how to open a can of fruit, for instance.[6]

When all is said and done, Howard probably had some fun, but not enough of it. Eventually he spent all his time in bed, but chose to watch tv rather than roger. Perhaps the real tragedy is that a man who spent all his time watching tv had to watch American tv.

FOOTNOTES

1 The two eventually proved to be mutually exclusive and avoiding germs won. Most intelligent people give up on the idea of hygiene completely the first time they ever French kiss. The definition of hypocrisy is complaining to a waiter about a fork that needs an extra polish after you've just been passed every germ in your companion's mouth in a quick pre-dinner kiss. (For more on sex and hygiene, see Farrah Fawcett.)

2 Jealousy: *big subject*: Shakespeare said in *Othello*, rather unhelpfully, that jealousy is a green-eyed monster. Unfortunately, this is just wishful thinking. It would of course be completely fabulous if jealousy was a green-eyed monster, because then at least we'd be able to spot the little bugger. The worst thing about jealousy is that it is so often festering, secret, concealed, bitter. If every time someone was jealous they strolled around with this bloody great green bug-eyed monster on their shoulder, barfing up nastiness left, right and centre-field, there'd be a lot less suffering around. But alas, that's only a dream. If jealousy is a monster at all, it's a monster that lives in people's stomachs, tearing them apart, waiting to explode like the Alien through John Hurt's tummy, spreading destruction and poison through the whole spaceship of our lives.

3 There was a time when the use of the casting couch became so widespread that there was a shortage of couches in California. Actresses were eventually advised to carry their couches around with them. A girl without a couch really couldn't think about getting a part. A well-sprung couch, or, at the very worst, a fairly sturdy li-lo was the Hollywood equivalent of an Equity card.

4 Our sociological advisor points out that Howard Hughes is quite a good example of how urban myths are established. The image of him, alone in his penthouse, with telephones, power and a white beard is so potent that it has now become a generalized image. People believe when they look to the top of high buildings that there's probably an old miser up there, going mad in the company of Mormons.

5 People did try to marry him before. When he told Lana Turner that marriage was out of the question, she said, 'But, Howie, I've had all the sheets monogrammed HH'. He replied, 'Then you'll just have to marry Huntingdon Hartford'.

6 One of the funniest pieces of English prose ever is about the opening of a can of pineapple by three men and a dog in *Three Men in A Boat*, but it is unlikely that Howard would have seen the funny side of it. Hughes hated animals. A dog once bit him on the penis*, leaving him to have six stitches. A girlfriend once brought a hamster to his house: Hughes was frightened by it, accused it of being an anteater and had it forcibly removed by a bodyguard.

However, when Jean Peters brought a cat with her, Hughes was gracious enough to have it put in a special home, where each cat had a house of its own, and he actually assigned one of his employees to write to the animal once a month.

*Don't ask how he got into the situation for this to happen. Just don't.

HOWARD HUGHES & HEDY LAMARR

Hedy Lamarr was so unimpressed by Howard Hughes as a rogerer that she didn't mention him once in her extended two week newspaper feature on

Rogers of Her Life. Despite this fact, he is still having her followed, even though they are both now dead.

	HEDY LAMARR
Born	**1915, in America.**
Occupation	**Actress.[1]**
Romantically Linked With	**Howard Hughes, Stewart Granger and 'countless other men'.**
Married and Divorced	**Fritz Mandl (millionaire arms dealer),[2] Gene Markey (producer), John Lode (actor), Ernest Stauffer (Mexican hotel owner),[3] Howard Lee (Texan oil tycoon) and Lewis Boles (Hollywood lawyer).[4]**

As with many famous sex symbols, Hedy's rogering career did not get off to a good start. On the set of *Ecstasy*, her enjoyment in the sex scenes was so transparently fake that it had to be stimulated by the director jabbing her in the bottom with a safety pin.[5] She didn't enjoy rogering her husband Fritz much either, and claimed that she didn't like sex at all. Her cover was slightly blown when he discovered her about to roger a stranger in a brothel. She claimed to have 'wandered in by mistake'.[6]

In fact, sexually, hers was a strange life. She had one lover, Sid, who was so jealous he tried to get her to wear a chastity belt. When she locked herself in a friend's house, he shinned up to the window, waving a second chastity belt which he had bought for himself 'to make things fair'.

Another man's love for her left him in hospital. Get some Kleenex. This is a sad tale indeed . . .

The man in question, Peter by name, met Hedy in France. He fell in love with her, but they decided an affair would ruin his marriage, and so refrained from rogering.

Imagine her surprise when six months later, Peter turned up in Hollywood announcing that his wife—for a large sum of money—had allowed him a four week divorce to roger Hedy, after which they would be married again.[7] Hedy was not really very enthusiastic about him, as always happens with holiday romances, but, as she put it, 'How could I turn him down?'

In her own words, this is what then happened:

'I showed him a guest room where he could prepare and I went into my room. When I was ready, I called him and then I heard a terrible crash. Peter appeared in pyjamas, covered in blood. The glass door in his room looked just like a passage way to him, and he walked through it. He was cut badly on his neck, head, one arm and chest. I quickly called the police. After two weeks in hospital, he went back to France. We never did have an affair'.

The moral of the tale is quite clear: if you want to roger Hedy Lamarr, for

God's sake don't go next door and put on pyjamas. Women hate pyjamas. Willies look so silly popping out of them.

FOOTNOTES

1 There is a curious link between Hedy's two most famous roles. In the first, *Ecstasy*, she caused a sensation by showing her breasts: whereas of her other great film, *Samson and Delilah*, Groucho Marx said: 'You can't expect the public to get excited about a film where the leading man's bust is bigger than the leading lady's.

2 Fritz married her when she was seventeen, and gave her seventeen dogs as a present. (See Appendix: Love Tokens.) Then he introduced her to two friends of his, called Hitler and Mussolini. She was, it seems, well shot of him.

3 She divorced him because he fell asleep all the time.

4 She divorced him because he wouldn't fall asleep and kept on and on talking in bed.

5 This did, however, seem to have the required effect (don't try it): during the premiere her parents walked out, taking her with them. Her first husband, Fritz, the dog-obsessed fascist, tried to buy all the prints and negatives.

6 See Appendix: Great Rogering Excuses for other suggestions.

7 Scholars note that this brilliant ruse of the four week divorce is actually very similar to that used by the Peul Beurou tribe of Niger. In this tribe, as in many parts of America and Yorkshire, the wives are in charge. If they take a fancy to a new man, their husband has to wait quietly and sensibly outside their tent while she rogers him*. If the woman wants to continue the rogering she disappears into the desert for five weeks** to really give it a good going over. If she's still keen on the new roger when she comes back, then he is accepted as the new husband, and the old one has to go away without making a fuss.

*It will come as no surprise to pop *aficionados* that the Jimi Hendrix song, 'Hey Joe', was not a chart hit amongst the Peul Beurou tribe. Its opening lyric,

> *Hey Joe, what you doing with that gun in your hand?*
> *I'm going to shoot my old lady,*
> *Caught her messing around with another man.*

was considered socially unrealistic.

However, a member of the Peul Beurou did send Jimi Hendrix what he thought was a more realistic framework for a song about the situation of infidelity:

First Tribesman is standing outside a darkened hut, carving a wooden object. Enter Second Tribesman.

SECOND TRIBESMAN	*Hello, Joe. What are you doing with that camel in your hand?*
FIRST TRIBESMAN	*Nothing much* (Loud noise of rogering from inside hut.)
SECOND TRIBESMAN	*Wow!!! What was that noise?*
FIRST TRIBESMAN	*Noise, what noise?*
SECOND TRIBESMAN	*That noise: sounds like someone is shagging someone else absolutely stupid in there.*
FIRST TRIBESMAN	*Oh.*
SECOND TRIBESMAN	*Yes. Whoo-weee!!! Listen to that: that is serious sexual madness in there. Why don't we take a peek?*
FIRST TRIBESMAN	*Ah, no thanks.*
SECOND TRIBESMAN	*Come on, your wife would never know.*
FIRST TRIBESMAN	*No, really. It's fine. Got to finish this camel.* (He starts to cry.) (More loud noises from inside: 'Yes, baby, yes, give it to me, Jimi!' etc.)
SECOND TRIBESMAN	*Listen to that!!!! That is fantastic!!!! My God, the building is going to fall down!!!! We are in serious danger of an earthquake here!!!!*

FIRST TRIBESMAN *Yes. (Enter First Tribesman's Wife, exiting naked and worn out from hut.)*
WIFE *Hullo.*
SECOND TRIBESMAN *Oh, hullo.*
WIFE *Have you finished the camel?*
FIRST TRIBESMAN *Nearly.*
WIFE *Good, let's get on then. (Exit Wife and First Tribesman.)*

**See Viviane Ventura for Advantages of Rogering in Deserts. Also, The Gospel According to St Mark, for alternative ways to spend time in desert.

HEDY LAMARR & STEWART GRANGER

'If only she had shut up and stopped giving me orders the ordeal might have been consummated with pleasure'.[1]

STEWART GRANGER	
Born	**1913, in Britain.**
Occupation	**Acting,[2] with particular stress on buckling his swash.**
Distinguishing Features	**Thick hair.**
Married	**Elspeth Marsh, Jean Simmons, Caroline Laceri, Belgian Beauty Queen.**
Divorced	**Elspeth Marsh, Jean Simmons, Caroline Laceri, Belgian Beauty Queen.**
Romantically Linked With	**Sandra (wife of Tony Bennett), Gillian (future wife of Des O'Connor), Deborah Kerr, Hedy Lamarr.**
Nickname	**Stewart Granger.[4]**

Stewart Granger was one of Hollywood's most glamorous swashbucklers,[5] although he perhaps never got quite as close to the hearts of the public as Errol Flynn, the greatest of all. His English accent and smooth brow graced many a glamorous and historically incorrect costume in the midst of many a historically incorrect plot. He is now, after his three marriages, single again, and claims to be searching for his perfect woman, who will be a thirty-five-year-old virgin. What is unclear is whether, having found her, he would want her to stay a virgin. The suspicion is, yes, he would. He recently announced: 'I adore women, but I'm a bit old for that sort of thing now. Now I just like to look at them'.

When not hunting virgins, the still glamorous Stewart spends a lot of time complaining that he doesn't get parts anymore, because 'A lot of people don't know I'm still alive'.

FOOTNOTES

1 For an equally unfriendly résumé: Walter, an eighteenth-century sex writer, records his wife saying: 'Get off. You've done it and your language is most revolting'.
2 Stewart described acting as 'A complex form of whoring'. See Lola Montez, Sarah Bernhardt, La Belle Otero and many others.
3 He was born James Stewart, but that space in the History of Movies had already been most beautifully filled.
4 What is a swash, and what design feature was so faulty that it had so repeatedly to be buckled?

STEWART GRANGER & GILLIAN O'CONNOR

When Gillian met Des O'Connor, she was going out with Stewart Granger. Granger had told his mother that this was the girl he was going to marry, and yet, Gillian married Des: the question to be pondered, a Great Rogering Mystery, is . . . why?

GILLIAN O'CONNOR	
Occupation	Actress,[1] ballet dancer, housewife.
Hobbies	Rogering, until she married Des O'Connor.
Distinguishing Features	Tall, blonde, and posh with perverse desire to marry Des O'Connor.

Experts on human behavior agree that the possible reasons for Gillian marrying Des instead of Stewart are as follows:

1 Gillian is very short-sighted, so couldn't see Stewart.

2 Gillian is deaf, so couldn't hear Des.

3 Gillian is stark staring mad.

4 Love, love, that young blind imp that has no rhyme nor reason in his dealings with us poor humans, invaded her heart.

Career evidence certainly did not bode well for Des as a rational choice.[2] However, what becomes clear from closer investigation is that Gillian never actually made the choice. She was in her flat with Des one day when Stewart rang. Des picked up the phone, clocked who it was, and shouted down it before hanging up, 'I'd appreciate it if you never rang my fiancée again'. Whatever else you think of Des, this surely does rank as one of the Great Lines For Getting Out of Trouble When Caught Sleeping With Someone's Girlfriend.

FOOTNOTES

1 Gillian played opposite Alec Guinness in *The Horse's Mouth*, as one of *Alfie's* girlfriends and nearly took over from Diana Rigg in *The Avengers*.
2 Des O'Connor and Stewart Granger:

COMPARATIVE ACTING AND ROMANTIC ACHIEVEMENTS.

Stewart Granger, Star in	Des O'Connor, Buttons in
King Solomon's Mines	*Cinderella*.
The Prisoner of Zenda	
The Man in Grey	
Scaramouche	
The Madonna of the 7 Moons	
Queen Bess	
Any Second Now	
Captain Boycott	

OTHER CONQUESTS

Jean Simmons	Phyllis—'Miss Wolverhampton'
Hedy Lamarr	
Deborah Kerr	

GILLIAN O'CONNOR & DES O'CONNOR

The tone of the whole marriage was set by the honeymoon night, spent, according to Gillian, 'Chatting to friends and sipping cocoa'.[1] It was the shape of things to come—Des wanted their marriage 'to be like a scene from *The Sound of Music*'.[2]

Des was so scared of Gillian running off with other men that he stopped her making herself look attractive—yet in the end it was he who left her, announcing his engagement on the day of his daughter's birthday party, to which he failed to turn up. An example, some might say, of the comic timing that has made Des a legend in his lifetime.

DES O'CONNOR

Born	**1932, in Stepney, East London.**
Occupation	**Entertainer.**
Distinguishing Features	**None.**
Romantically Linked With	**Gillian, Phyllis and Jay Rufer.**[3]
Nicknames	**Desdemona, Desperate, 'The Stepney Nightingale'.**
Hobbies	**Trying to persuade people to call him the Stepney Nightingale, instead of Desperate or Desdemona.**

One of the great tv entertainers of our era, Des originally took to the screen sporting a pair of glasses, but the station in question received so many letters complaining that he looked like a sex maniac, that he had to take them off. Nowadays, Mr O'Connor is an accepted master of the easy light entertainment show, but he was not always so highly regarded as he now is. Once in Glasgow he had to pretend to faint in order to get off the stage safely, and in normally polite Chiswick, an audience rioted when Des attempted to do an encore, throwing lightbulbs on to the stage. For a while these kind of incidents gave him a reputation as a below par entertainer—Morecambe and Wise referred to his four minute long 'Greatest Hits' album, and taxi drivers[5] have been known to give him lifts 'Only if you promise not to sing'. Des gamely claims not to be offended by this, but rather flattered. 'I take it as a compliment', he says. Good old Des.

FOOTNOTES

1 See Caroline of Brunswick, and Alexandre Dumas' wife (and Appendix: Marriage, Weddings and Wedding Nights).
2 Great Rogering Mysteries: which scene from *The Sound of Music*? If it is the one where all those children gather in the bedroom and talk about their favourite things, then Des is sick, sick, sick.
3 She is half his age: See Appendix: Age and Rogering.

MOTHS & OLD FLAMES LAY LINE

MARLENE DIETRICH

DOUGLAS FAIRBANKS JNR

JOAN CRAWFORD

CLARK GABLE

AVA GARDNER

HOWARD HUGHES

HEDY LAMARR

STEWART GRANGER

GILLIAN O'CONNOR

DES O'CONNOR

Rarely has there been a line of such catastrophic rogers: the only consolation can be that great art never came easy, and perhaps, just perhaps, it took all that catastrophe to produce the passion and the wisdom that cries out in every note that our Des sings. Take a listen to 'Careless Hands', and you'll know what we mean.

FROM	EVA PERON
TO	BRITT EKLAND
IN	8 ROGERS

EVA PERON

Born	**1919, in Argentina.**
Occupation	**Actress, radio columnist, dictator's wife, dictator, West End star.**
Hobbies	**Being popular and rogering.**
Distinguishing Features	**Looked quite like Elaine Paige.**
Romantically Linked With	**Aristotle Onassis, Porfirio Rubirosa, Colonel Juan Peron.**
Nickname	**Evita,[1] La Flaca (the skinny one).**

As a radio actress, Eva Peron (née Duarte) began her career playing Queen Elizabeth I and Napoleon's wife, Josephine, and it gave her a taste for the kind of heroine she would like to play in her own life.[2] But more importantly, the radio gave her the opportunity to listen to much of the popular music of the day, and gave her the idea of living a life that could one day be turned into a major West End musical by Andrew Lloyd Webber and Timothy Rice.

Since the most successful Rice–Webber musical was about Jesus, Eva did her best to be like him. She had the initial advantage of also being of humble origins, but then she imitated him by hanging around with prostitutes[3] and surrounding herself with unmarried men. She also succeeded in earning the tremendous love of the poor, or the 'shirtless ones', just as Jesus had. Eva ostentatiously aided the poor, and, while she was alive, the peasants believed her to be 'the closest thing to the Virgin Mary this side of Heaven'—which was true of Jesus too.

However, looking at the other Webber–Rice musical, *Joseph and His Amazing Technicolour Dreamcoat*, Eva quickly realized she would also have to have some amazing clothes, so she kept a lot of the money she was meant to be spending on the poor in a private bank account in Switzerland. Also, observing the show-stopping success of Herod in *Superstar*, she thought she should have a bit of a nasty side as well. Her attitude to those who opposed her is very Herodian: 'If you hear anyone speaking ill of me, break his head open'.

Nevertheless Jesus was always her major role model (*Superstar* was a much bigger hit than *Joseph*, and had yielded more hit singles) and Eva's fidelity to imitating Jesus' life story became, by the end, distinctly eerie. She too, like him, died tragically young. And like him, her dead body became a symbol: when her husband returned to power in Argentina he had to bring it with him. Then, of course, most extraordinarily, just like him she did finally achieve that greatest of honours, as she had always dreamed: Tim and Andrew sat down one weekend and wrote a bloody great musical about her.

FOOTNOTES

1 Evita

Born	**1977, in London.**
Occupation	**Making money.**
Hobby	**Entertaining foreigners.**
Distinguishing Features	**Political realism.**
Nickname	**The Greatest of Musicals.**

2 Eva went on to become nearly as powerful as Elizabeth, and as famous for marrying a dictator as Josephine. Although, there are, of course, differences between them: Elizabeth was more obviously virginal than Eva, and Josephine never had a number one record blasting its way right to the top of the hit-parade, and occupying that big number one position, like Eva did with 'Don't Cry For Me Argentina'.

3 Once, when Eva was travelling in Italy with a retired admiral, she complained—'They called me "whore".' The Admiral replied tactfully: 'I'm still called admiral, yet I haven't been to sea for fifteen years'.

EVA PERON & PORFIRIO RUBIROSA

While working for the Dominican foreign office under President Trujillo, Rubirosa was sent to Argentina. When he presented himself to Eva, her striking opening line was: 'I believe you divorce rather frequently, your Excellency'. Porfirio replied seductively, showing a deep understanding of relationships and life: 'When things no longer go according to plan, when quarrels are frequent, when life together is a trial rather than a pleasure, it is better to separate'. In other words, 'Why don't you get rid of that tiny-willied fascist dictator you're dragging around with, baby, and come shag yourself stupid at my diplomatic residence'. And he pulled it off—soon he began to 'see a lot' of Eva.[1]

Unfortunately his employer Trujillo soon got worried that instead of exercising diplomacy by rogering, Porfirio was just rogering full stop, and recalled him. Musicologists point out what a tragedy this was: for had Peron found out and beheaded the pair of them, Rice and Lloyd Webber would have had the *greatest plot of all time* to work on in *Evita*.

PORFIRIO RUBIROSA

Born	**1909, in Dominica.**
Occupation	**Soldier, diplomat.**
Hobby	**Rogering.**
Romantically Linked With	**Ava Gardner, Kim Novak, Flor de Trujillo (m), Danielle Darieux (m), Doris Duke (m), Eva Peron, Zsa Zsa Gabor,[2] Barbara Hutton (m), Odile Rodin (m).**
Nickname	**Rubi (pretty unimaginative, these Dominicans).**

Rubirosa's rogering achievements stretched the imaginations, credibility and patience of his contemporaries. He was in many respects the luckiest man alive—and certainly the luckiest man to be alive. The luckiest alive for reasons that are obvious. The luckiest to be alive, because anyone who rogers the daughter of the most feared South American dictator (Rafael de Trujillo) has to be mad. But the man who rogers, marries and then dumps her must be utterly and completely stark staring every single screw entirely loose *mad*. He must feel like he's stepped into Harrods—he has entered a different world. Marrying Trujillo's daughter, shafting her, and then shifting her on is like offering your private parts to the Marquis de Sade, and then handing him a scalpel just in case he hasn't got one of his own. But somehow Rubirosa got over his risk, and by the time he axed Flor, he was a firm friend of Trujillo's.

And so began Rubi's career as a rogering diplomat. From Berlin to London to Rio—all over the world Rubirosa rogered for Dominica. In far flung corners of the globe where people could hardly spell Dominica (or is it Domeinhicka?), Rubirosa ran up the flag and thought of home. He was cited in so many divorce cases that he came to be affectionately known as the 'foreign co-respondent'.

Porfirio started life poor, but after Trujillo gave him 50,000 dollars, he began a steady career of rogering money. He loved heiresses. After the war (during which he was imprisoned for slugging a German officer in a nightclub) he headed west for Doris Duke—a 300 million dollar heiress, possibly the richest woman in the world. For the wedding she gave him an aeroplane, but pretty soon after he gave her the push. Stated reason was because he hated jazz and Doris loved it. He then moved on to Barbara Hutton, the Woolworth's heiress—one of America's many 'poor little rich girls'. She too gave him an aeroplane[3] for *their* wedding—and a string of polo ponies and £300,000 when they divorced seventy-two days later. She made old Doris Duke look like a positive miser.

At forty-seven Rubi married Odile Rodin and like all good playboys in the sixties, died, tragically, in a car crash.

FOOTNOTES

1 See Appendix: Names for Rogering.
2 What is so utterly fabulous about young Zsa Zsa is that even though married those eight times, she still had time and inclination to roger men she wasn't married to. When asked what was the first thing she noticed about a woman, she replied 'her husband'. * (See Appendix: Marriage, Weddings and Wedding Nights.)
3 See Appendix: Love Tokens.

* And indeed, when asked how many husbands she had had, she replied—'You mean apart from my own?'

PORFIRIO RUBIROSA & AVA GARDNER

Porfirio Rubirosa and Ava Gardner hung around together between great loves in their lives, and had an all right time. Which just goes to show that rich and famous people aren't that different from anyone else: in exactly the same way, at Hunslet Grammar School, the outrageously sexy rugby captain and the unbelievably good looking cookery teacher will just have a quick roger between grand amours, not because it'll ever work or anything, but just so they can say they've done it.

AVA GARDNER

(For full biography, see the Moths and Old Flames line.)

Since the delightful Ava is the single female rogerer who appears most frequently in these lay lines, it would be both boring and dishonest to the book-buying public to keep repeating the same biography every time she appears sandwiched between another pair of divine men. (See also The Great Communicators.) The regularity with which she appears is not an indication that the sensible and well-balanced Ava was a rampant rogerer, but rather that she could have her pick of absolutely anyone and she chose the best of the bunch. The editors are very grateful to her for the connections she has made possible.

AVA GARDNER & SIR GORDON WHITE

Gordon White is a lucky and cunning old devil: his name has been linked with Ava Gardner, Rita Hayworth, Susan Hayward and Marilyn Monroe. No details of what he actually does when he's rogering have ever been revealed, but the directness and daring of his method of getting going is worth noting. As a not particularly rich, famous or successful young cove in his twenties, Gordon realized that he wanted to roger all the most beautiful women in the world and that all the most beautiful women in the world were actresses. So he simply founded a theatrical agency, went to Hollywood and represented (see Appendix: Names for Rogering) them.

SIR GORDON WHITE	
Born	**1923, in England.**
Occupation	**Transatlantic businessman.**
Hobbies	**Rogering, definitely.**
Distinguishing Features	**Utter incredulity in the faces of people he's talking to when he tells them who he's rogered.**
Romantically Linked With	**Ava Gardner, Rita Hayworth, Susan Hayward, Marilyn Monroe, Mary Tyler Moore, Cheryl Tiegs, Vanessa Llewellyn, Jane Russell, Shelley Smith and Joan Collins.**
Married	**Elizabeth Kalen,[1] Virginia North.[2]**
Divorced	**Both of them.**
Nickname	**The White Knight.**

Sir Gordon is a rather dashing James Bond type figure. He's a self-made millionaire who started the Hanson Trust[3] with Jimmy Hanson when they were both Yorkshire lads with not much money, who lived in cardboard boxes, etc. Sir Gordon was brave and rocky in the war, going on parachuting and submarining missions, and he continues to do equally rock-like things now, being a pilot and setting transatlantic records—he once got from his Knightsbridge to his New York office in 4 hours and 23 minutes.

He has in his time known most of the world's most beautiful women, and even had the pleasure of meeting Princess Grace, of whom he said: 'She makes you feel like the only person in the world'.[4] Now he lives in America most of the time, and likes it apart from the habit of breakfast meetings: 'It is the most uncivilized idea I've ever heard of. If you're going to have a breakfast meeting, it should be in bed with a beautiful woman'.[5]

FOOTNOTES

1 Elizabeth was a Venezuelan, and 'Venezuelans breed very quickly' (Sir Gordon). She had two daughters very quickly, talked constantly in a very dramatic way and then got homesick and went back to Venezuela.

2 Virginia North was a long term lover and a short term wife. Gordon says of her: 'All the guests wore white, Virginia, who was seven months pregnant, wore bright red'. * (See Appendix: Marriage, Weddings and Wedding Nights.)

3 Presumably a deal was struck *vis-à-vis* the name early on. 'You get to have your name on the company, I get to sleep with Marilyn Monroe'.

4 He later pointed out that this might have been literally true since Grace was so short-sighted that when he was talking to her, he *was* the only person in her world of vision at the time.

5 Breakfast features large in pick-up lines of today:

    a *Should we have a breakfast meeting tomorrow?*
    b *That sounds lovely.*
    a *Good—shall I phone you or nudge you?*
    Alternatively
    a *Would you like to come to breakfast tomorrow?*
    b *Yes, what time should I come round?*
    a *How about 8.30 this evening.*

*And good on her. The failure of symbolic imagination on the part of modern brides is a source of shame to our century. Wedding gowns were white because they symbolised the virginity of the bride: brides aren't virgins any longer, so a huge new range of colours is technically available and should be employed. Here is a short key, but any number of combinations can be employed:
    Yellow: Frightened of making love.
    Black: Shy; likes making love in the dark without lights on.
    Black with White Polka-Dots: Likes making love with just a few candles *or* likes sleeping with black people, although has slept with some whites.
    White with Black Polka-Dots: Likes sleeping with white people, although has slept with some blacks.
    Red: Wild and passionate lover.
    Peach: Pleasant, mellow lover with particularly nice breasts.
    Blue: Victim of deep post-coital depression.
    Blue & Orange: Victim of deep post-coital depression, eased by eating oranges afterwards.
    Green: Inexperienced lover *or* jealous lover *or* has just been making love on the grass outside and was going to come as a virgin.
    Grey: Cold, clinical lover.
    Grey with Banana Motif: Cold, clinical lover, but gives terrific blow-jobs.

SIR GORDON WHITE & VANESSA LLEWELLYN

After his tremendous beginning, it is now easy for Sir Gordon to have his way with girls, because 1 who would dare turn down someone Marilyn Monroe thought just fine and 2 his daughters introduce him to all their friends. His new companions, such as the delightful Vanessa Llewellyn, are always photographed next to Sir Gordon, who is usually wearing a top hat, with a quote from a friend (i.e. the journalist writing the article who's never met either of them) saying that the woman has been criss-crossing the Atlantic in pursuit of the White Knight, and that marriage is imminent.

The truth is, however, that Sir Gordon never marries anyone these days. It would clearly be mad to do so, as it would stop him rogering his daughters' friends. On the other hand, it might give him a whole new generation of daughters.

VANESSA LLEWELLYN	
Born	**1959, in England.**
Occupation	**Model, wife, mother.**
Married	**Dai Llewellyn.**
Romantically Linked With	**Sir Gordon White.**

Vanessa is the niece of the Duke of Norfolk, has two sons and obviously likes the company of older men. Her husband Dai (thirteen years her senior) was obviously not nearly old enough for her. In fact, she was so repulsed by his extreme youth (39 years old) that she left him and moved out to a small cottage. Sir Gordon, thirty-seven years her senior,[1] is clearly a much more suitable rogering companion.

FOOTNOTES

1 This ranks as one of the highest rogering age differences in the book: other enthusiasts for rogering older men include Lauren Bacall and Margaret Trudeau, although Margaret went off it pretty quickly. The danger of this sort of preference comes as the woman grows older: at the age of fifty, it is both difficult and dangerous for a girl to do too much, too energetically with a man thirty-seven years her senior. (See Appendix: Age Differences and Rogering.)

VANESSA & DAI LLEWELLYN

For the while that she was married to him, Vanessa was touchingly described as Dai's 'anchor'. Unfortunately, as happens to so many anchors in the stormy waters of our modern times, the huge shark of discontent came and bit her free.

DAI LLEWELLYN

Born	**1946, in Britain.**
Occupation	**Welsh baronet to be, night club consultant, travel agent, male model.**
Hobbies	**Rogering.**
Romantically Linked With	**Vanessa (m), Isabel Richli, Beatrice Welles, Tessa Dahl, Lady Charlotte Curzon, Princess Aila Ausberg, Lady Jacqueline Rufus Isaacs.**

Dai Llewellyn is one of those people who is famous and well known by everybody, but at the same time nobody can quite remember what he is famous for. In Dai's case, the actual answer is—rogering. And having a brother who rogered Princess Margaret.

For a time, while married to Vanessa and fathering his two children, Dai declared that he had given up widespread rogering, but happily he is now back living the life for which he was intended and fulfilling the purpose for which, it may well be, he was placed by some merry God upon this lovely green and brown planet of ours.

DAI LLEWELLYN & TESSA DAHL

Before his engagement to Vanessa, Dai had previously been engaged many, many times. In the early 1970s, for example, he was engaged to Tessa Dahl, daughter of Roald Dahl, the tall short scary story writer. Unfortunately for Tessa, in the same year he was also engaged to two other women—Isabel Richli and Beatrice Welles.[1] All of the engagements were finally called off— including Tessa's, which is a particular shame because she'd already bought the wedding dress.[2]

TESSA DAHL

Born	**1937.**
Occupation	**Actress, nanny and writer.**
Hobbies	**Rogering.**
Distinguishing Features	**Big girl.**
Distinguished Parents	**Roald Dahl and Patricia Neal.**
Romantically Linked With	**Dai Llewellyn, Peter Sellers, James Kelly (m).**

Tessa was expelled from Roedean at the age of eleven for 'persistent naughtiness'. She has been persistently naughty ever since. Some of this must be put down to the kind of bedtime stories she was read as a child. Presumably if you have been brought up on tales of landladies killing their tenants and stuffing them, and wives murdering their husbands with frozen legs of lamb, then letting off the odd stink bomb and rogering the odd completely unsuitable *roué* must seem pretty tame by comparison.

FOOTNOTES

1 This is a very effective way of dealing with the over hasty engagement. The moment that you realize what you've done, simply pop out and propose to four or five other women, preferably close friends of the first one. Then, when the news gets out, break down and claim that your behavior was brought around by nervous exhaustion, exacerbated by dietary imbalance. You can then get a lot of sympathy from all five of them and rush off to a health farm and roger the receptionist.

2 See Lana Turner and Howard Hughes and the monogrammed sheets. The question of what to do with an unused wedding dress is a vexing one. It can be worn to balls as a ball gown, but the train makes it difficult to dance in. It can be used as a table cloth, but will tend to be a little bumpy. On the whole the best idea is to cut it up into sheet-shaped sizes and then sleep on it with all the groom's best friends and break their hearts one by one.

TESSA DAHL & PETER SELLERS

The story goes that Tessa 'loved him and left Peter'. Presumably if you do get the chance to love[1] a famous rogerer—who doesn't make a habit of sticking around unless you're Britt Ekland in her prime and then not for long—leaving him is a pretty smart thing to do. Instead of being another of his discarded beauties, you become the ice-maiden he couldn't melt, the impenetrable fortress he couldn't penetrate, or rather could a couple of times, but then wasn't allowed to any more.

The only trouble with this approach is that, unless you're actually chucked, you can never be sure you wouldn't have been 'the one', and you may well spend the rest of your life saying 'damn and blast'.[2]

PETER SELLERS

Born	**1925, in England.**
Occupation	**Goon, French policeman, actor.**
Distinguishing Features	**Ability to hide his distinguishing features.**
Romantically Linked With	**Anne Howe (m), Britt Ekland (m), Miranda Quarry, Janette Scott, Liza Minnelli, Trudi Pacter, Tessa Dahl, Christina 'Titti' Wachmeister, Carol White, Carole Mallory, Lynne Frederick (m).**

Any study of the life of Peter Sellers cannot but make one sad, that a man who made everyone so happy should so often have been so gloomy himself. It is thus profoundly to be hoped that he had a good time rogering whenever he did. And he often did. When young, like so many members of his generation, he enlisted the aid of Frank Sinatra in his seductions: he possessed a coin-operated record player that played eight records in a row. He would put on eight Sinatra records, and claimed that if he hadn't scored by the fifth, he would pack it in—the sixth song was 'The Lady is a Tramp'.

In his later years, he had his own comic genius to rely on. The question of comedy and sex is a taxing one. Michael Caine in *Alfie* may have come the closest to defining it. Make a married woman laugh, and you're there. But get a single woman to laugh, and that's all you get.

Whatever, Sellers spent time with, or married, many of the most glamorous women of his time: Sophia Loren and Princess Margaret were numbered among his friends, and such glorious stars as Britt Ekland and Lynne Frederick, and almost the fabulous Liza Minnelli,[3] were his for the marrying.

One of Peter's pick-up lines was to claim that he was directly descended from Lord Nelson. Had he been, he would, we are glad to say, have won many more important victories than the admiral himself.

FOOTNOTES

1 See Appendix: Names for Rogering.
2 See Carol White and Frank Sinatra.
3 This was a most tantalizing affair for the public. Liza and Peter met in the Dorchester Hotel and barricaded themselves up for a week and then announced they were getting married. It was enormous sorrow to the world as a whole when reality reared its ugly head once more, and they decided to call it off.

There are many political and psychological theorists who believe that if the marriage *had* gone ahead, it would have had a profound effect on the social and psychological state of the world, extending the bounds of what we take to be possible, keeping us away from the cynicism which has characterized the eighties, and leading us into an era of light and enlightenment and hope.

There are other political and psychological theorists who think the effect might not have been so profound.

PETER SELLERS & BRITT EKLAND

Britt's marriage with Peter was a happy and then a sad affair; it started, as things always did with Peter Sellers, in a rush of enthusiastic passion: the funniest man in the world, the prettiest starlet in the business. She liked to describe herself as 'the little Swedish mouse Sellers got to marry'. But in the end, Sellers was too difficult to deal with and the relationship fell apart with rancour. Britt always remembered him with a kind of hurt affection, and perhaps too keen an eye for detail—'his hairy cladded chest did much to perpetuate the argument of mankind's evolution from the gorilla'.

BRITT EKLAND	
Born	**1942, in Sweden.**
Occupation	**Actress, author.**
Hobbies	**Staying beautiful and rogering.**
Romantically Linked With	**Kjell,[1] Boris,[2] Igi Polidori, Gio,[3] Peter Sellers (m), Count Ascanio Cicogna,[4] Anon 1,[5] Patrick Lichfield,[6] Warren Beatty,[7] George Hamilton,[8] Lou Adler, Anon 2,[9] Ryan O'Neal,[10] Rod Stewart,[11,12] Les McKeown, James McDonnell—alias Slim Jim Phantom, drummer of the Stray Cats (m).**
Not Linked With	**Roger Moore,[13] Lee Majors,[14] Ron 'Tarzan' Ely.[15]**

'Think of me as the girl you saw in the holiday brochure', says Britt at the end of her masterpiece of candour, *True Britt*. Some holidays we all would have if that were so, for Britt has lived a life so full of physical love that with her around holidays would be a sexual paradise, rather than those disappointing fortnights in the sun with sore skin, bad food, Nivea and Diocalm. From her loss of virginity to crew-cut Kjell in Stockholm through to her present marriage to a rock-star half her age, Britt has dedicated herself to love. She is, of all the women in these modern lines, the most notable: the prime female rogerer.

It is a position she holds with great dignity. In Patrick Lichfield's book of *The World's Most Beautiful Women*, there is a picture of Britt, and below it these words: 'She has lately enjoyed additional success as a writer of "fiction".' Yet at that time Britt's only published work (unless Iris Murdoch is Britt Ekland working under pseudonym) was her autobiography, *True Britt*. Lichfield is clearly implying that the book should be taken with a pinch of salt (as should his claim that those are the World's Most Beautiful Women): but even with that pinch of salt, what emerges from *True Britt* is a sweet, rather trusting young Swede, dead keen on sex and not letting her search for true love stop her getting lots of it.

Britt is not yet one of the world's great actresses—she was unlucky that her Bond film, *The Man with the Golden Gun,* was not one of the best; but she hopes one day to match her romantic achievements with her dramatic ones. She writes, passionately: 'My whole ambition for the future still revolves around my deeply cherished ambition to gain absolute recognition as one of the world's leading actresses'. If she could only put all the passion she has expended on love into her acting, she damn well one day just might be. Watch out Vanessa, take care Glenda, have an eye to your laurels, young Meryl Streep. Here comes Britt.

FOOTNOTES

Let Britt speak in her own well-chosen words:

1 *Kjell*: 'It was strange'.
2 *Boris*: 'We made love on the hard wooden benches in the ballet school changing rooms'.
3 *Gio*: 'Cufflinks, medallions, bracelets, buckles gleamed on that bronzed frame—there were no preliminaries'.
4 *Count Cicogna*: 'Those were precious days'.
5 *Anon I*: 'I suddenly had this compulsive urge to become a hippy—in our spare time, we smoked dope'.
6 *Patrick Lichfield*: 'Patrick was a bit hung up that we should have slept together on our first night'. (Possibly fictional.)
7 *Warren Beatty*: 'The most divine lover of all'. (See Warren Beatty for further details.)
8 *George Hamilton*: 'George did a marvellous imitation of Warren'.
9 *Anon 2*: 'A cheap and ghastly mistake that jarred my emotions'. He can't have enjoyed his reading of *True Britt* much.
10 *Ryan O'Neal*: 'Comfort and consolation'. Ryan emerges, along with Lou Adler, as the good guy in Britt's tale.
11 *Rod Stewart*: 1975: 'With Rod I found total unison . . . Rod regarded every orgasm as a testimony of his love for me. Greater love hath no man'.
12 *Rod Stewart*: 1977: 'Obediently accepting my lawyer's advice, I filed a $12,500,000 lawsuit against Rod'.
13 *Roger Moore*: 'Intelligent, witty, brimming with dry humour—I didn't fancy him'.

14 *Lee Majors*: 'I must have blunted his ego'. (She got to him anyway, through Ryan and Farrah.)

15 *Ron Ely*: 'He was a typical male chauvinist'. But then who wouldn't be, having played Tarzan all your life. And the one time you don't they make you play Doc Savage.

MUSICAL GREATS LAY LINE

EVA PERON

PORFIRIO RUBIROSA

AVA GARDNER

SIR GORDON WHITE

VANESSA LLEWELLYN

DAI LLEWELLYN

TESSA DAHL

PETER SELLERS

BRITT EKLAND

As time passes, it will be interesting to see just how many of the other members of this line are immortalised in the form of musicals. It surely cannot be long before *Britt!* follows in the footsteps of such current hits as *Marilyn* and *Judy*, and *Peter!* will be a musical subject hard to resist after the success of *Lennon!* and *Les Miserables!* It may be a while before *Sir Gordon!* takes the stage, but when it does, it will have been well worth the waiting for, with Elaine Paige as Ava Gardner, Barbara Dickson as Vanessa Llewellyn, and the old inimitable Rex Harrison at last returning to play the part of game Sir Gordon. If Rex is busy, then David Essex will probably do.

BEAUTY AND THE BEAST

FROM	**PRESIDENT MARCOS**
TO	**PRINCESS DIANA**
IN	**7 ROGERS**

It is hard to imagine two figures less like each other than ex-President Marcos and Princess Diana. The one was a dictator full of darkness and cruelty. The other is a confirmed democrat who brings nothing but joy and laughter and light everywhere she goes. The one was thrown out of his country on his ear for being a complete rotter. The other is her country's most be-loved possession. The one didn't think twice before killing people. The other loves children and animals and would probably think twice before killing a flower, and then decide not to do it after all.

For once, the lay line goes disastrously wrong, un-willingly yoking together two people who would have nothing in common, because one is a beauty, and the other a beast.

PRESIDENT MARCOS

Born	**1918, in the Philippines.**
Occupation	**Ex-president.**
Hobbies	**Talking to his wife about shoes, trying to work out how to be president again.**
Distinguishing Features	**Tyranny.**
Romantically Linked With	**Imelda.**
Married	**Imelda.**
Nickname	**(To 1986) Mr President. (From 1986) Mr Ex-President.**

President Marcos seems to be nearly as mad as his wife. While people lived in desperate poverty in the Philippines, he used to go on diplomatic visits taking whole planeloads of furniture with him to put in his hotel room. This sort of behaviour raises two crucial questions:

1 Are world leaders mad before they become world leaders?[1]

2 What colour was the furniture and how could Marcos be sure it wouldn't clash with the hotel wallpaper?

On the whole, Marcos seems to be in the Ronald 'politics, not rogering' Reagan mould. One has only to give a moment's thought to how extraordinarily cross the mighty Imelda would have been if Marcos *had been* found rogering out of wedlock to see why he gave up the whole caper and started shooting people in airports instead.

FOOTNOTES

1 The answer is 'yes'. You've got to be mad to want to rule a world like ours. No one who isn't mad would be mad enough to think they knew the answers to its problems. And if by any chance someone who isn't mad slips through the net and becomes a world leader, then, because they spend so much time with other world leaders, who are already mad, they swiftly lose their sense of reality and go mad anyway.

PRESIDENT & IMELDA MARCOS

This is one of those classic rogerings where at the outset it looks as though one partner is getting all the luck, but in the end, it turns out that the exact opposite is true.

At the point of their wedding it looked as though President Marcos was the lucky one, allowed to roger a beautiful and exotic young singer who looked as though she would surely know all sorts of ancient oriental rogering tricks. She, on the other hand, was stuck having to roger a tiny weird-looking fascist who'd like as not get his head blown off while they were at it.

However, as it turned out, it was President Marcos who ended up with the sharp end of the stick, having to fight his way through layer after layer of black Marks and Spencer girdles to roger an overweight lunatic spendthrift.[1] Whereas Imelda was just fine, since she was so powerful she could start film festivals whenever she wanted, spend as much money as she liked, and also have 'platonic relationships'[2] with whomsoever she pleased.

As to the question, why couldn't President Marcos also have 'platonic relationships' with whomsoever he pleased, the answers are:

1 Look at him.

2 Well, if you don't think that's an answer, why didn't he then?

IMELDA MARCOS

Born	**In the Philippines.**
Occupation	**Buying shoes and underwear, ruling the Philippines.**
Hobbies	**Shoes, underwear and rogering.**
Distinguishing Features	**Big black hair and cross look now she's out of power.**
Married	**President Marcos.**
Romantic Links With	**President Marcos.**
Probable Links With[3]	**George Hamilton.**
Nickname	**The Beautiful Imelda.**

Imelda Marcos is probably completely stark staring mad. When President Aquino opened up the Marcos' palace, there for all to see (as well as 3,000 pairs of shoes, 35 racks of furs and 1,200 dresses) were a thousand pairs of knickers, a thousand unopened packets of stockings, 500 black bras and 200 Marks and Spencer girdles.

When interviewed afterwards Imelda claimed these were presents: 'I would keep a whole big inventory of presents. I was too busy thinking about electrical power, education, roads, bridges and transportation to shop'. She was obviously also too busy thinking about electrical power, education, roads, bridges and transportation to think what is an appropriate present for a president's wife to give. It is hard to imagine an item less suitable for a diplomatic gift than a Marks and Spencer black nylon brassiere.[4] As for the shoes, Imelda says: 'Shoes are one of our biggest exports. As first lady, it was one of my duties and responsibilities to promote Philippine products, to act as a model for them'. Other mad things she has done include building a whole palace out of coconuts for the Pope to stay in (the Pope refused to stay, because it was too extravagant) and giving Prince Charles a speedboat with no engine in it.

Although popularly known as 'The Beautiful Imelda', certain beauty and fashion experts have described Imelda as 'a hideous fat old gran'. Even so it does seem likely that she must have been quite interested in rogering—otherwise what are all those clean knickers for—and anyone with more than a passing interest in rogering is not going to be satisfied with the weird midget President Marcos for a partner. In view of this, starting the Manila Film Festival was a good idea,[5] even though it seems like a strange idea for a very poor country.

But then strangeness was the name of the game for 'Beautiful', as became clear to officials who broke into the Marcos' holiday home near the Santo Nino Shrine on Leyte Island. Apart from a hundred or so missing Russian icons, and most of the contents of the National Museum, they found that the place was more a shrine to Imelda than to Santo Nino.[6] The corridors were full of photographs and portraits of Imelda with various world leaders, some of whom she had never met. The person she appeared with most—interestingly—was Colonel Gadaffi, and one particularly good portrait, subtitled The Two Crazies, now has pride of place in the National Gallery of Manila's broom cupboard.

FOOTNOTES

1 See Appendix: Great Rogering Excuses.
2 When asked if he believed in platonic relationships, a wit replied: 'Yes—afterwards'.
3 It is the policy of this book to beware of tyrants (see Nancy Reagan—The Alternative Route). All we would assert is that it is as likely that this isn't true as it is likely that President Marcos had nothing to do with Mr Aquino's assassination.
4 Unless the recipients were either George Hamilton's mother* or Colonel Gadaffi.**
5 See Appendix: Love Tokens.
6 The second mention of Santo Nino compels an inquiring book such as this to look into the history of this obviously quite important saint. We quote from the Vatican's Third Addendum to Neophilus' Official Book of Saints: 'Saint Nino is known as the patron saint of patience. He was born in Germany in 1944, the twin brother of Nina Van Pallendt. Brought up in a musical household, Nino was always the more talented of the two and hoped one day to play in the local orchestra. However, in 1962, Nina met a man called Frederick and together they formed a folk duet called Nina and Frederick, which shot to international fame on the back of a surprise Christmas hit, 'Little Donkey'.

It then became Nino's lot to defend his sister patiently every time she was attacked for releasing one of the most pathetic songs ever to ride high in the international pop charts. Nino, who was at university at the time, began by casually saying that the song had a hidden meaning; but gradually he found himself forced to curtail and then give up his education in order to dedicate his life full time to defending his sister by researching the subtext of the song, which detailed the adventures of a little donkey who had to plod along a dusty road carrying a precious load. Nino was eventually murdered by an irate Bob Dylan fan when he claimed that 'Little Donkey' had been a major influence on 'Blowin' in the Wind'.

His book, *Little Donkey, T.S. Eliot and Modern Religious Poetry* did not sell any copies and yet, throughout his life, Nino never complained and never begrudged his sister her success. This is particularly noble in view of the deep, homosexual passion he felt for Frederick right from their very first meeting when, Nino's diary records, 'Frederick was wearing skin tight lederhosen, and had an enormous yodelling horn'. The miracle which finally confirmed Nino for sainthood was when Rolf Harris, who had prayed fervently to Nino at his shrine outside Munich, reached number one with 'Two Little Boys', a song many think as frightful and sentimental as 'Little Donkey' itself.

*See under George Hamilton.
**The brassieres *might* in fact have been useful to Gadaffi: it has been mooted by military experts that 500 such bras, with their new tight-fitting elastication, might be, if properly deployed, a cheap and effective way of catching any bombs that Ronald Reagan might wish, in the future, to dispatch against Libya.

IMELDA MARCOS & GEORGE HAMILTON

This is a roger which the protagonists deny, but everyone else thinks happened. George and Imelda met at the Manila Film Festival, and became 'close friends'. They had a lot of things in common—films, festivals and the problems of how to organize their extensive wardrobes. George has a computer coded wardrobe, with different matchings for every day of the year, and Imelda had, for example, 3,000 pairs of shoes.

When Marcos was deposed, a storm of scandal hung over George's head. There was talk of the parties he and Imelda had held at his Beverly Hills mansion, where Imelda handed out gems from a basket to the guests as though they were Easter eggs.[1] On top of this, word even spread that love letters between the two of them had been discovered in the abandoned palace.

Nevertheless, Imelda insists that the relationship was purely platonic— which relates interestingly to George's own definition of 'platonic'—'play for me, and a tonic for the women'.

GEORGE HAMILTON

Born	**1939, in America.**
Occupation	**Actor,[2] escort.**
Hobbies	**Rogering and improving his body.**
Romantically Linked With	**Britt Ekland, Imelda Marcos, Catherine Oxenburg, Sylvia Kristel (Emmanuelle),[3] Françoise Pascale, Vanessa Redgrave.[3]**
Married	**Alana Stewart.**
Distinguishing Features	**Orangy colour.[4]**
Nickname	**Gorgeous George, The Man With the All Year Tan, The Ultimate Escort.**

George's devotion to rogering and related crafts is exemplary. He takes 120 vitamin pills a day, has injections of cells from unborn lambs, drinks a mixture of cayenne pepper, maple syrup, Evian water and lemon juice to keep his system free of toxins, and, when he sunbathes, puts matchsticks between his toes to make sure that he isn't left with unsightly white marks[5] should he spread them in public. His wardrobe is computer coded so he can wear a different, perfectly blended outfit every day of the year.[6]

'The age of chivalry is not dead, but it's on the critical list', quips Gorgeous—'I like to make my women feel like ladies'. Sadly, with some girls, feeling like a lady is obviously not quite hot and raunchy enough these days: why else would Alana have left him for Rod Stewart? (Although come to think of it, the idea of having children by someone endlessly injected with lamb cells can't be *that* attractive either: only the most heartless of mothers could view with equanimity the idea that her child might grow up to be nothing more than a tasty Sunday roast.)

Even so, more women have loved him than left him, and George is a lighthouse of glamour and style and charm in a stormy world where too often the smart tuxedo has been swapped for the dirty vest, and the glass of champagne for the snort of cocaine. Suave and debonair, he puts his arm gracefully through ours and glides with us back to the charmed chateau where chandeliers are hung with real candles and the melody of a waltz wafts through the scented air. With Gorgeous George, romance lives on.

FOOTNOTES

1 This was a cruel trick typical of a tyrant's wife. Imagine greedily taking a lovely chocolate Easter egg and being just about to pop it into your mouth only to realize it's just a valuable gem, and not a gorgeous choccy at all.
2 After years of slightly serious roles, George has really come into his own (see Oedipus) with the villainy of *Dynasty*, and the camp humour of the excellent *Love At First Bite*.

3 It is extraordinary that one list should contain two of the finest screen actresses of this generation.
4 See Sarah Ferguson and the Orange People.
5 'Unsightly white marks'. Other examples are Mark Hamill, Marc Almond and Mark Cox.
6 Some of this care about appearance must be inherited from George's mother. She recently had a hugely expensive operation to have her breasts lifted. 'I have told George', she said, 'that if anything happens to me, I want to be buried topless'. Mrs Hamilton is seventy-three and one of the Great Mums. (See Appendix: Mothers' Page.)

GEORGE HAMILTON & ALANA HAMILTON STEWART

George and Alana were married for several years and during that time had a small child. Eventually, however, for the good of her looks, Alana was obliged to leave him. 'I always look better when a marriage ends', she said, and she sure looked good enough to attract Rod Stewart pretty swiftly afterwards.

George unhappily did not find the separation made him lovelier, and soon resorted to the baby lamb injections and curious potions described above. Apart from turning him orange, and there's not much wrong with that, they have proved reasonably effective, and he and Alana are now, once again, the best of friends.

ALANA STEWART

Born	**1947.**
Occupation	**Model, actress.**
Hobbies	**Talking to journalists about her relationship with Rod Stewart and rogering.**
Distinguishing Features	**Someone like George Hamilton or Rod Stewart hanging round.**
Romantically Linked With	**George Hamilton, Rod Stewart.**
Married	**George Hamilton, Rod Stewart.**
Divorced	**George Hamilton, Rod Stewart.**
Children By	**George Hamilton (one), Rod Stewart (two).**
Nickname	**Alana the Piranha.**

Alana is wonderful and she knows it and says it: 'I'm having a wonderful time. Men think I'm beautiful and terrific—they take me to dinner and tell me how wonderful I am—it's fun'. But she is also a character of strong principles and strong passion. Strong principles: when Britt Ekland published her confessions about life with Rod, Alana said: 'I wouldn't read such garbage'. Strong passions: when Alana herself split up with Rod, her passions were so strong, that she also went to the papers to tell the world the details about her relationship.

Fortunately, as details, they're not too gruesome. Alana and Rod married in a 'haze of euphoria', had two children and only then started to start to think about marriage, children and the responsibility of them both. And that was too late. Rod wasn't for changing, and Alana wasn't for waiting for him to change. Perhaps Rod should have listened to his mum, who was worried that there was 'always an atmosphere when Alana was around'.[1] Rod was made for singing, not listening.

Alana now talks about the difficulty of bringing up her children alone: fortunately, her staff includes a butler, governess, gardener, cook and more than one maid, so she's got some help. And Rod rings every day.

FOOTNOTES

1 To understand what modest and constructive criticism this is, see Sylvester Stallone's mum: Mothers' Page. Rod's mother said: 'I wished Rod had married a Scottish girl. He'd have been a lot better off'. Sheena Easton has made no comment.

ALANA & ROD STEWART

Sometimes you pick up a newspaper and cannot believe that you are reading yet another story about Rod Stewart. You just wish you could go back and listen to a Rod Stewart song, and remember how and why he got so famous in the first place. If this is one of those moments, why not have a listen to . . .
'Hot Legs' from *Footloose and Fancy Free*
'Maggie May' from *Every Picture Tells a Story*
'Sailing' from *Atlantic Crossing* and
'I Don't Want to Talk About It' from *Greatest Hits I*.
They'll put you right.

ROD STEWART

Born	**1944, in England.**
Occupation	**Footballer, gravedigger, rock star, rock superstar.**
Hobbies	**Football, rogering and sailing.**
Distinguishing Features	**Blonde in bed.**
Romantically Linked With	**Dee Harrington (model), Bebe Bluebell (model), Britt Ekland, Alana Hamilton (model), Kelly Emburg (model), Joanna Lumley, Sabrina Guinness.[1]**
Nickname	**Roderick.**

Rod is said to have been discovered by Long John Baldry,[2] sitting on a Scottish train station, singing to himself and playing the harmonica. Since that romantic beginning he has done two very important things. He has become a pop legend, and he has rogered a phenomenal number of blondes.[3]

In fact, Rod is so fond of blondes, that he actually became one himself in case there wasn't one around at any time. When they are around, 'the most memorable is always the current one—the rest just merge into a sea of blondes'. His present blonde is the very memorable and very pretty Kelly Emburg, and it is to be hoped that, like Canute, she can stem the tide of that platinum sea. Kelly has spoken of her high hopes for a romantic proposal from Rod, which might once have seemed unlikely from the old hellraiser himself. But Rod claims that recently he has calmed down and says the thing he most likes now is going to bed with a good book. As long as Kelly doesn't mind being referred to as a good book, they should both be very happy.

FOOTNOTES

1 There is absolutely no question that this liaison never took place, but for the sake of true love and potential rogers the world over, we wish it had.
2 Long John himself has drifted out of view since his chart-topping, 'Let The Heartaches Begin'. He is, however, still believed to be the tallest man ever to have a number one hit.
3 When asked if he's a good lover, Rod replied: 'I should think so—I've had enough practice'. Which should be a good argument, were it not for the frightening evidence to the contrary supplied by Tony Blackburn's 250.

ROD STEWART & SABRINA GUINNESS

Rod has a tendency to write songs about those he loves. 'Tonight's The Night' was written for Britt Ekland, his 'virgin child', and there was a strong rumour that 'Maggie May' was inspired by Princess Margaret. Unfortunately, it is not known which of his songs Rod wrote for Sabrina—all that is known for sure is that Sabrina is a brunette, which on its own makes her totally unique in the bright blonde line-up of loves that is the private life of Rod the God. She is, you see, very special.

SABRINA GUINNESS	
Born	1955, in England.
Occupation	Heiress.
Hobbies	Being discreet.
Distinguishing Feature	Satisfied smile on face.
Romantically Linked With	Prince Charles, Mick Jagger, Rod Stewart, David Bowie, Jack Nicolson, Dai Llewellyn, Jonathan Aitken.

What has this girl got? Sabrina has been linked with the most eligible man in the world and three of the most attractive. Many girls would be willing to sacrifice lives for the chance to shake hands with Bowie, Jagger or Nicolson, and yet Sabrina has loved them all and lived to tell the tale.

There may also be even more to her glory. She once went out to Hollywood to be Tatum O'Neal's nanny, and yet there is a rumour, vicious or no, that she never actually slept with Ryan O'Neal. Now Ryan (see *passim*) is the World's Greatest Living Rogerer, and if, alongside all her other achievements, Sabrina managed *not* to be tempted by the auburn bombshell, then she is a woman destined for great, great things. There is no doubt that if Mrs Thatcher is to have a successor, no one would earn the love and admiration of that country quicker than Sabrina, this generation's great romantic over-achiever, and national treasure.

And word does indeed have it that Sabrina may be looking for new challenges. She has been quoted recently as complaining about the shortage of 'decent men'—a complaint, interestingly, that Mrs Thatcher herself has also echoed, although of course with reference to a completely different area of activity.

SABRINA GUINNESS & PRINCE CHARLES[1]

Ironically, this royal pair were first seen together at a musical called *Ain't Misbehavin* in 1978 when Sabrina returned from Hollywood. Their friendship then continued for about nine months—during which Sabrina went through the usual routine of polo matches and secret rendezvous in Charles' private

Buckingham Palace rooms, where even his mother wasn't allowed to enter without telephoning first.

Like all of Charles' friends, Sabrina never 'kissed and told': but rumours are that it was because of her 'past', with such folk as Bowie and Jagger, that she was never considered a suitable match. Most people would probably agree that a past like that was worth the price of a crown.[2]

PRINCE CHARLES

Born	**1948, in England.**
Occupation	**Prince.**
Hobbies	**Taking interest in literally thousands of worthwhile things.**
Distinguishing Features	**Ears like Clark Gable.**
Romantically Linked With	**(Owing to the laws of high treason and the fact that the death penalty hasn't been completely abolished[3] and you can still be beheaded for certain things, the editors of this book wish to make clear that the term 'romantically linked with' does not, in this instance, allow for the slightest possibility of anything untoward, but rather can be accurately translated as 'shared a harmless joke or two with' . . .) Lucia Santa Cruz, Davina Sheffield, Sabrina Guinness, Lady Jane Wellesley, Anna Wallace.**
Married	**Princess Diana.**
Nickname	**Brian.**

Prince Charles is a massively popular prince and rightly so. As for his sex appeal, you only have to look at the facts: Princess Diana is one of the most attractive women in the world, and certainly the most difficult to pull: and yet, Charles pulls her almost every night. Admittedly they are married, but it is well known that even before they were married Diana thought him to be 'pretty amazing', and slept with a picture of him on her wall.

Clearly Charles, or 'Chuck' as he likes to be called amongst his intimates, is not *immediately* an obvious sex symbol. His body does not cry out 'this is it, baby, take it, it's hot, it's yours, it's amazing, it will kill you but it'll be worth every minute' like his brother Andrew's does, nor do Charles' eyes have that 'I wouldn't mind giving you a seeing-to, young lady' twinkle that has often been noted in the eyes of his father during long ceremonial dances in far flung isles where ladies don't seem to realize there is anything wrong with leaving their tops off in front of royalty. But what Charles lacks in outer glamour, he gains in inner charm, and he is one of the very few men who really know how to make a woman feel like a princess.

May God bless him and Diana and William and Harry for ever.

FOOTNOTES

1 It is often asked: what is it like rogering someone terribly famous? The general feeling is that it is distinctly odd: the head is terribly familiar, but the rest of the body comes as a complete surprise.
2 Sabrina's predicament does, however, suggest a great excuse (see Appendix: Great Rogering Excuses) for not rogering: 'I'm sorry, I can't. I might have to be Queen of England one day'.
3 One of the great mysteries of English law is why the death penalty has been retained specifically for the offence of arson in the Queen's Dockyards. Many eminent lawyers and maritime experts believe that the deterioration of Britain as a great shipping nation has been almost entirely due to the nervousness bred in dockyard workers by the fact that they may accidentally drop a cigarette, start a fire and be summarily executed for the aforementioned offence. Anyone who has recently visited the Queen's Dockyards and seen the enormous no smoking signs, the giant ashtrays in every corner, and the fire hydrants attached to the backs of all working members of staff will appreciate just how sapping on morale this law has been.

Some eminent historians claim, however, that the law has been completely misunderstood and that 'arson in the Queen's Dockyards' was originally simply a euphemism for rogering Queen Elizabeth, which, as mentioned earlier in this book, led to almost immediate beheading.

CHARLES & DIANA

Historically speaking, what is important about this roger is that it is probably the only time since the war that a bridegroom has married a virgin.

Until comparatively recently, to marry a king while not a virgin was a treasonable offence and the question of how to make sure a woman was a virgin on her wedding night was one which perplexed bridegrooms for centuries. In ancient Rome it was believed that when a woman rogered for the first time her breasts actually grew and it was the habit of bridegrooms to measure their wives' breasts before and after the first rogering to find out the truth of their virtue. This was a distinctly bad method, since after a day of wedding festivities followed by a night of enthusiastic rogering the young bride was more likely to have lost weight than gained it. For instance, Prince Charles, had he been a Roman, would have been alarmed by the fact that Diana's breasts, rather than growing, clearly shrunk dramatically—and quite honestly, *can you blame them?* If one thinks back to how it felt the first time one had sex—and then imagine having to go through the Royal Wedding beforehand, marrying the future King of England in front of half the world and getting his name wrong—it is no wonder her bosoms shrunk at the ordeal. In fact, it is surely surprising and to their great and everlasting credit that they didn't leave permanently in fright.

PRINCESS DIANA

Born	**1961, in England.**
Occupations	**Nursery school teacher, princess and mother.**
Future Occupation	**Queen.**
Hobbies	**Lovely dresses and outfits, lovely children, lovely pop music and lots of seriously worthy causes.**
Distinguishing Features	**Prince with Clark Gable ears and understanding eyes on arm.[1]**
Future Distinguishing Features	**King with Clark Gable ears and understanding eyes on arm.[2]**
Romantically Linked With	**Prince Charles and wash your mouth out with soap.**
Married	**Prince Charles.**
Nickname	**Di, La Didi (in France).**

The very interesting thing about Princess Diana in the context of a book such as this is the unique nature of her position as rogerer. She could now have, quite literally, anyone in the whole world. Nobody is seriously going to say 'no thanks' to Diana. *And yet*, she can't roger anyone. The world is her sexual oyster and she can't even have a nibble. It is hard to imagine how frustrating this must be. Diana loves pop music. She used to love Simon le Bon and, in the nursery days, she must have been dying to roger him, but didn't have a hope in hell. Now suddenly she meets him all the time and just *knows* that she only need drop her eyes in just the right way,[3] and every inch of his plump, sunburned little body would be hers. But she can't do it. Everyone would be furious. It is the ultimate sexual Catch 22 and it's rotten.

FOOTNOTES

1 See Wallis Simpson: Prince with tiny willy on arm.*
2 Don't see Wallis Simpson.
3 For how, see Lauren Bacall.

*i.e. Prince, who has tiny willy, on her arm. Full apologies for horrid mental picture conjured up by possible misunderstanding.

BEAUTY & THE BEAST LAY LINE

PRESIDENT MARCOS

IMELDA MARCOS

GEORGE HAMILTON

ALANA STEWART

ROD STEWART

SABRINA GUINNESS

PRINCE CHARLES

PRINCESS DIANA

This line represents the journey from darkness into light, from evil to goodness, from someone no one wants to sleep with to someone everyone adores. If every seven rogers produced such a startling improvement in quality within a generation we'd have heaven on earth.

FROM	**BERNARD LEVIN**
TO	**JIMI HENDRIX**
IN	**6 ROGERS**

It is not known whether Jimi Hendrix and Bernard Levin ever actually met each other, but there can be little doubt that, had they done so, they would have got on like a house on fire. Both were great music lovers. Jimi could have learnt from Bernard about subtlety in the use of punctuation, something he rather let drift in his later songs, and Jimi in turn could have taught Bernard how to make a bloody great racket on an electric guitar. Later on, when they'd grooved down a little and were getting into a slightly heavier and more personal scene, Bernard might have begun to confide in Jimi about the difficulty of being a little on the short side and having trouble getting on with girls, and Jimi might have confided in Bernard about the problems of having a whopping great todger and never a moment's rest with so many girls wanting to play hide the broomstick with it. And later on they probably would have jammed. Jimi might well have chosen 'All Along the Watchtower.' Bernard would almost certainly have chosen raspberry.

BERNARD LEVIN

Born	**1929, in Britain.**
Occupation	**Journalist and author.**
Hobbies	**Climbing mountains,[1] writing long sentences and wearing big glasses.**
Romantically Linked With	**Arianna Stassinopoulos.**
Nickname	**Mr Levin.**

Bernard Levin is a man of strong opinions. He likes lots of things. He hates lots of things. He always tells us about these things. He lets us know. Then he lets us know again. Sometimes this is great. Sometimes this is grim. In other words, sometimes we hate him. And sometimes we love him. In that way he reflects his audience—we also, like him, love and hate. Some of the things he loves are good food and opera. Some of the things he hates are red tape and red communism. He also hates short sentences. He actually wrote the longest sentence ever. It had 1,672 words in it. It was sodding long. One of the other things he has loved is Arianna Stassinopoulos.

In a way it was easy for him to love her. Her name makes sentences long. For instance take the sentence: 'She saw her name was on her book'. It is a short sentence now. But put Arianna in it. Now it is a long sentence. 'Arianna Stassinopoulos saw that Arianna Stassinopoulos' name, Arianna Stassinopoulos, was on Arianna Stassinopoulos' book'.

In another way it was hard for him to love her. Arianna is tall. Bernard is short. He once said, 'There's nothing worse than spending two and a half hours addressing someone's fly buttons'.[2] They used to be called Little and Large. This was not because they were funny, like the other Little and Large are meant to be. It was more because they *looked* funny. Nevertheless, true love prevailed. They stayed together for five years. After that little is known of Bernard's love life. He is 'the only bachelor in London who has invited girls back to see his etchings, and then actually done so'. It is known he likes the look of Anna Ford. He recently said to her, 'I always said you were the most beautiful woman in Europe. Now I must extend it to the world'. Which actually, come to think of it, are two short sentences. So that thing about the long sentences isn't true. Damn.

FOOTNOTES

1 Arianna also liked climbing. But society, not mountains.
2 Sometimes Bernard exaggerates. There are lots of things worse than this. For instance, spending two and a half hours talking to someone who then takes out a saw and cuts your head off is worse, surely.

BERNARD LEVIN & ARIANNA STASSINOPOULOS

Everything we wanted to say about Bernard and Arianna was said above. If we were Bernard, this would not stop us saying it again. But we are not Bernard.

ARIANNA STASSINOPOULOS	
Born	**Greece.**
Occupation	**Writing.**
Hobbies	**Climbing and rogering and explaining to people about the number of 'nn's and 'ss's in her name.**
Romantically Linked With	**Bernard Levin, Mort Zuckerman, Jerry Brown, Michael Huffington (m).**
Nickname	**The Gigantic Greek Pudding.**[1]

Arianna has been described as 'the most upwardly mobile Greek since Icarus'. But, unlike Icarus, she has not fallen into the sea. If she had, her fall would surely have been broken by the swimming pool of a very expensive yacht, full of happy folk with champagne bottles and interesting opinions on lots of different subjects. That's very much Arianna's milieu.[2]

She started life as president of the Cambridge Union, where champagne bottles are very much the order of the day, although the interesting opinions are rather harder to come by. However, she soon compensated by taking up with Bernard, who's got more interesting opinions than he needs. She herself then formed some interesting opinions about Maria Callas, wrote them down in a book, and earned a million pounds for it, which is an interesting amount of money. With this money she went to New York, met more interesting people, like Nancy Reagan, and finally met someone fantastically interesting, Mr Huffington, a 300 million interesting dollars heir, whose grandfather died in South America from a poisoned arrow. He, in obedience to the family tradition, was in turn struck by an arrow, Cupid's arrow, at the sight of Arianna and they are now married and, we trust, very happy. She now 'lies in bed propped up against an abundance of satin pillows, writing letters, making phone calls and plans'. Details of those plans the world expectantly awaits. Whatever they may be, on their announcement, we hope to open a bottle of bubbly.

FOOTNOTES

1 It is unlikely this name caught on amongst her friends for everyday use. It is much too long for a nickname.
2 So one hears: Arianna is another one of those people everyone seems to know about but no one actually knows why they know about them. Sean Hardie, in his excellent book *Prince Harry's First Quiz Book,* has identified many people like this. He posits the existence of a mysterious lost decade, when people like Kenny Lynch and Joanna Lumley and Arianna actually did the things they are now famous for.

ARIANNA STASSINOPOULOS & JERRY BROWN

Arianna was an extremely unusual girlfriend for Jerry, being neither a singer, nor an actress. He was able to perceive in her some special something, some hidden talent yet to blossom that made him love her. She loved him because he was so perceptive.

JERRY BROWN	
Born	**1947, in America.**
Occupation	**Politician.**
Romantically Linked With	**Linda Ronstadt, Stevie Nicks, Arianna Stassinopoulos, Liv Ullmann, Candice Bergen, Natalie Wood.**
Nickname	**Ghandi in pinstripe.**

Jerry Brown, like Ronald Reagan, has been governor of California and has stood for presidential nomination. But that is where the similarity between them ends. Because if Reagan had slept with the girls Jerry has, he would be worn out and in bed *all* day, instead of most of it. And, as for Jerry, well it looks as though he'll never be president—he has, unhappily, the political subtlety of Enoch Powell on a very bad day. When going for the presidential nomination on a ticket of caring politics, big on concern and sympathy for the under-privileged, Jerry decided to whizz off to Africa for a safari with Linda Ronstadt, an image-raising exercise that misfired massively. The under-privileged back home felt that anyone who had time to go gazing at elephants and had Linda Ronstadt in his tent once the gazing was done, didn't share their problems and sure as hell didn't need anything, let alone a vote.[1]

The one time Jerry was elected, he didn't do too well either. His popularity rating was the worst rating of any governor for two decades and his judgement seemed really to let him down: out of four judges picked by Brown, one was busted for marijuana, one for making obscene telephone calls, one for being involved with the so-called 'Mexican Mafia' and one for passing bad cheques. In 1981 an opponent said, 'If Jerry ran for re-election against Rin Tin Tin, he'd lose'.[2]

Nevertheless, an aura and glow still hangs around the man, and in an America of Reagan and madmen on television preaching right-wing fervour, there's no harm in the odd woolly idealist. And Jerry Brown certainly has been linked with some ideal women.

FOOTNOTES

1 Jerry paid a heavy price for his nights of African love with Linda Ronstadt. It would be nice to think that he did it because of a deep and profound love and understanding of popular music, and Linda's position in it. Unfortunately, nothing could be further from the truth. Says Linda: 'His kind of music is the kind you hear in elevators'.
2 The election of Rin Tin Tin is not as ridiculous as it sounds. Members of Parliament in Britain still receive more letters about subjects to do with animals than with people. In other words, such is the popularity of dogs that were quite a lot of them to stand for Parliament as independents, it would, under proportional representation, be highly likely that at least a couple of dogs would finally take their place in the House of Commons. The advantage of this might be that at least they, unlike many current Members of Parliament, would be properly house-trained.

JERRY BROWN & LINDA RONSTADT

The explanation for the attraction here may lie with the fact that Jerry started out his adult life as a Jesuit seminar trainee and went on to become a Zen convert. This ties in intriguingly with Linda's comment during an interview: 'My big fantasy has been to seduce a priest'.[1,2]

It is hard to believe that any questionnaire in American monasteries and seminaries would not also conclude that the big fantasy of most priests was to seduce Linda Ronstadt.[2]

LINDA RONSTADT

Born	**1946, in America.**
Occupation	**Singer.**
Distinguishing Features	**Rosy cheeks.**
Romantically Linked With	**George (Star Wars) Lucas, Jerry Brown, Peter Hamill, Mick Jagger.**

Linda Ronstadt's magical transformations from chubby country music girl to great pop singer, and then to Queen of Soft Rock, finally culminated in her starring role in *The Pirates of Penzance* on Broadway, merrily slamming away at Gilbert and Sullivan in the shadow of the Jolly Roger. Her own rogers have been many and merry, as expressed in her records and press statements. On *Heart Like A Wheel*, she asks the poignant question: 'I've been cheated, been mistreated, when will I be loved?' The answer is, of course, as soon as she stops saying things like, 'I thought meeting a man was like shopping for shoes'.

Ever since she was at school Linda has been 'boy crazy' and nowadays a lot of boys are crazy about her. She was once offered a clean million to take off her clothes for a magazine and, even without doing that sort of thing, she earns six million a year for her dreamy voice. She is a great and sensitive singer and meanwhile she also says that 'I can't be expected to fall in love with every man I sleep with' and 'I love sex as much as I love music'. And that's a lot.

FOOTNOTES

1 It is interesting to note that, although now priests are assumed to be innocent, in medieval times the church was the only place where details of sexual knowledge were documented and investigated. The church was the very centre of in-depth sexual research. The equivalent of Masters + Johnson in medieval times would have been Friar Benjamin of Putney + the Bishop of Sienna.

2 Such a questionnaire *was*, rumour has it, conducted in seminaries on the West Coast of America recently. The question asked was: *What is the thing you most desire on this earth?* The answers were:

> 5% 'I have no desires on this Earth. All my desires are directed to Heaven and the life everlasting'.
> 11% 'I desire to serve the Lord and achieve a state of grace'.
> 18% 'I desire to serve the Lord, and relieve the suffering of the needy'.
> 23% 'I desire to resist the Devil and all his temptations'.
> 43% 'I desire not to resist the Devil and to have a night of utter ecstasy in the arms of the completely fabulous Linda Ronstadt. Forgive me, Lord, for I have sinned in my heart and in my word'.

LINDA RONSTADT & MICK JAGGER

Linda Ronstadt here takes her desire to seduce a priest to its logical pinnacle by seducing the High Priest of Rock 'n' Roll himself. After the experience, she sounded suitably satisfied: 'He's as bad as people say, and as good'.

MICK JAGGER

Born	**1939, in England.**
Occupation	**Greatest living rock 'n' roll star.**
Hobbies	**Rogering, acting and not writing an autobiography.**
Distinguishing Features	**His lips.[1]**
Romantically Linked With	**Bianca Jagger, Jerry Hall, Marianne Faithful, Anita Pallenburg, Astrid Lundstrom, Carly Simon, Linda Ronstadt, Marsha Hunt, Margaret Trudeau, and at a conservative estimate 1000 other women.**
Nickname	**Butterfly.**

While the Beatles were busy pretending to be good, Mick Jagger was busy being bad.[2] It was always part of his job as greatest living rock 'n' roll star to roger people, a responsibility that weighed even heavier after Elvis' death, and not to have rogered would have been a dereliction of duty that his generation would have found it hard to forgive. This has nevertheless never stopped Mick getting on with his job of writing hot raunchy lyrics for Keith 'Dead Man' Richard, and in the end, after all the tossing and heaving and one false start, he seems to have displayed fabulous good taste and settled for Jerry Hall. His face is one of the accepted seven new wonders of the world[3]—Raquel Welch once said: 'It's very lucky to look as ugly as him'. Which, *vis-à-vis* rogering, must make almost every other man in the world wish he was a hell of a lot uglier.

Anyone wanting more details about Mick's life should wait to find them in his autobiography, which is apparently a little slow in coming because he has forgotten everything.

FOOTNOTES

1 Mick Jagger was voted to have the sexiest lips in the business even after a vicious challenge had been thrown down by Tina Turner. His lips have been likened to 'raw giblets' and have never failed to excite women of all ages and countries.
   This does not, however, mean that waving raw giblets in front of women is certain to drive them wild with desire. Although it might be worth a try.
2 For instance, Mick once rogered Keith Richard's girlfriend *and* Bill Wyman's girlfriend in the back of the same bus. (See Appendix: Unusual Places to Roger.)
3 Other wonders include: John Bindon's willy, W. H. Auden's wrinkles, Prince's moustache, Arthur Scargill's hair, Karl Malden's nose and the fact that Keith Richard is still alive.

MICK JAGGER & DEVON WILSON

Mick Jagger has unfortunately forgotten all the details about this. Anyone wanting more should ask Bill Wyman if there's anything in his computer about it.

DEVON WILSON[1]	
Occupation	**Good time girl.**
Hobbies	**Not rogering once in a while.**
Romantically Linked With	**Jimi Hendrix and Mick Jagger—when you've rogered them, why bother with anyone else?**

Jimi Hendrix wrote the song 'Dolly Dagger' for Wilson, a reference to her affair with Mick Jagger. Unfortunately for Jimi, when he tried to ease in on Mick's patch in return and made a pass at Marianne Faithful, Marianne lived up to her surname and turned him down.

Wilson was a completely gorgeous girl whose love-making skills were such that even Hendrix felt forced to write of her:

'*Her love's so heavy,*
Gonna make you stagger'.

She was a girl of whom her county could be proud.

FOOTNOTES

1 At first, there weren't any obvious notes about Devon Wilson—the editors' only thought when faced by this vacuum was to point out that one of us knows someone else called Devon, but our second thought was that that was of no interest whatsoever.

The third thought was to point out that Devon Wilson is a sister of the Beach Boys, Carl and Brian and Dennis, and that it was about her that *Good Vibrations* was written. However, this isn't true, so it was also decided against.

Finally, since Devon is a pretty gorgeous name, it seemed a good moment to alert parents to the importance of the naming of children if you wish them to grow up promiscuous. This is an important subject, and could be crucial to their futures. Unless the child is already showing signs of being fat and ugly, in which case the sex name would be a cruel and unwarranted joke, you would be well advised to give her names such as the following, which will increase her chances of pulling immeasurably:

Suki
Koo
Conchita

Devon
&
Tallulah.

If you want to be even more sure, a slightly more direct approach encourages names like:

Paradise
Beauty
Heaven
&
Divine.

The utterly committed parent will, however, go for a real sure-fire label, such as:

Fukme
Fablay
&
Shithouse Doreen A. Gale.

It cannot be denied that these will at least bring the subject of sex up, whereas anyone called Fiona, Karen or Caroline is going to have to spend the whole evening just getting round to the subject.

On the other hand, careful welding of Christian name with surname can be equally effective, without resorting to very unusual names. For instance Honour is a dull name, but if this child's father's name is Mr Back, then the daughter can hope to spend most of her life Honour Back, if she plays her cards right. Also names can very effectively refer to particular practices at which it is hoped that a girl will be particularly adept: Hedy Lamarr is the perfect example.

DEVON WILSON & JIMI HENDRIX

If Mick Jagger can't remember anything about rogering Devon, how much less chance there is that Jimi Hendrix, who has been dead for ten years now, can. The details of this affair must rest, like so many other things in Jimi's life, in a purple haze of unknowing.

JIMI HENDRIX

Born	**1942, in America.**
Occupation	**Rock guitarist.**
Hobbies	**Rogering and, tragically, taking drugs.**
Distinguishing Features	**Guitar in groin, playing sweet music.**
Romantically Linked With	**His guitar (m), Devon Wilson and hundreds of groupies.**

Jimi was said to have children in Sweden, Germany and the US as a result of his almost constant rogering. He chain-rogered, 'using girls like some people use cigarettes',[1] and was said to be well-equipped for the purpose.[2] When he wasn't rogering, he was producing rock music far ahead of his time—'Hey Joe', 'Purple Haze', *Electric Ladyland* and *Are You Experienced?* are classics all. Although nobody ever really understood the meaning of any of Hendrix's lyrics, everyone agrees he was the greatest rock guitarist of them all. When he wasn't rogering or musicing, he was, unfortunately, taking the drugs and drinking the drink that led to his death in 1970.

After his death, the mayor of Seattle,[3] his birthplace, put up a monument to Hendrix in the shape of an electrically heated boulder to symbolize 'hot rock'. The idea of a proper statue had been rejected after long discussion and consultation.

FOOTNOTES

1 Jimi was certainly lucky to find people to go along with this chain-rogering: few and far between are the girls who like to be put in people's mouths and then lit.
2 The Jimi Hendrix experience was apparently quite a frightening one—lovers speak of 'the biggest rig I have ever seen'—'damn near as big as his guitar'.
3 Seattle was also, coincidentally, the birthplace of Bruce Lee: both made a fortune out of being loud, violent and brilliant. Both died too young.

MUSIC LOVERS LAY LINE

BERNARD LEVIN

ARIANNA STASSINOPOULOS

JERRY BROWN

LINDA RONSTADT

MICK JAGGER

DEVON WILSON

JIMI HENDRIX

So, faster than you would ever have imagined, two great music lovers have been joined by the music of limbs uniting. Jimi and Bernard—the names sing, like a sixties group: Peter and Gordon, Simon and Garfunkel, Jimi and Bernard. It brings a tear to the eye to think that this unique musical pairing is now never to be, that we will never hear the unique sound of Jimi on lead guitar and Bernard on comb and paper. But at the same time, let us smile to think that, if not musically, sexually at least Bernard and Jimi are now, at last, united.

THE ONCE AND FUTURE KINGS

FROM	**ELVIS PRESLEY**
TO	**PRINCE CHARLES**
IN	**14 ROGERS**

Elvis and Charles, the once and future kings, find themselves unexpectedly tied together by fate. Placed next door to each other they are not obvious soulmates. One in a sensible dark suit, the other in something that looks like a sequined space suit. One talking good sense about urban architecture, the other hollering about a hound dog and a pair of blue suede shoes. And yet, inspected more closely, there is a great affinity between the two. Both of them were born to be king, both of them married young brides, and neither of them ever appeared in a good movie. Perhaps it was the spirit of Elvis, moving in mysterious ways, that drew the Prince of Wales to the Live Aid concert: and perhaps it will, in time, encourage Charles to lay down his sceptre and pick up a microphone, lay down his mitre and pick up a guitar, and give rock 'n' roll the new hero it's been looking for since that awful day in 1977 when time ran out at Graceland.

ELVIS PRESLEY

Born	**1935, in America.**
Occupation	**Ruling rock 'n' roll.**
Hobbies	**Motorbikes, guns, uniforms and rogering.**
Romantically Linked With	**Jayne Mansfield, Priscilla Presley (Beaulieu) (m), Ann Margret, Juliet Prowse and Tuesday Weld.**
Nickname	**The King, The Pelvis, Swivel Hips.**

Elvis didn't like girls who had big breasts, big feet, or children. Otherwise he was relaxed enough to roger two or three women every day between the ages of twenty and thirty. By the time he met Priscilla Beaulieu when she was fourteen he could say, 'I've been to bed with 1000 women in my life'.

Such flagrant sexuality terrified the American establishment, who were thrown into blind panic by Elvis and the effect he was having on young girls throughout the nation. Indeed there was a time in the early 1950s when Elvis' hips were thought to be the gravest moral problem to have attacked America since the Salem witches.[1] In 1955 he was forced, by law, to perform without moving his hips. He was only allowed to be filmed for television above the waist. His hips had become a 'menace to young girls' even though Elvis, a good Southern boy, always insisted, 'I don't feel sexy when I sing'.

The moral fervour finally subsided, and Elvis joined the army and became almost an establishment figure in comparison to the drug-takers and Englishmen who followed him. Unfortunately, this respectability wasn't reflected in his own life. After his pleasant five year marriage to Priscilla, things got worse and worse. By 1965 Elvis was the highest paid performer in the history of music, having grossed over a billion dollars in his lifetime—but the strain had made him mad. He would fly 1000 miles for a sandwich, and strange tales are told of him and hookers and hamburgers and two-way mirrors.

Fortunately the voice never faltered, and, despite all the torrid tales, he always was and always will be the King of Rock 'n' Roll.

FOOTNOTES

1 In a poll conducted at the time, Elvis' hips just pipped the threat of international communism as the most serious danger facing the United States. Such was their destructive power that secret efforts were made by the military to harness that power into weapon form. Enormous Elvis-shaped air balloons were tested over the desert in Nevada which, by the use of simple turbines, would swivel their hips in the direction of the enemy. Initial early successes (five deaths among some local Indians) were later discovered to be attributable to alcohol poisoning, not 'sex-shock' (the technical word used at the time) and the experiments were dropped in favour of the invention of an antidote, lest the enemy ever used an Elvis-style weapon on the Americans. This experiment, called The Carpenters, was not altogether successful either, although 'Goodbye To Love' did almost reach number one.

ELVIS PRESLEY & JAYNE MANSFIELD

After this roger, Elvis came up with one of the gentlest and most considerate methods of getting out of a relationship ever devised. He presented Jayne with a substitute for his most private self in the shape of a giant pink motorbike. By the sweetness of this gift, the relationship ended without a trace of acrimony.

Elvis busily started back on his diet of three girls a day and Jayne happily experimented with all the things the motorbike could do that Elvis couldn't. It is worth noting that, even if you can't run to a motorbike, the gift of some suitably sized replacement is a far better way of giving someone the axe than others to be encountered in this book, such as locking them out of the house, or pretending to have been run over by a train.[1] (See Appendix: Great Rogering Excuses.)

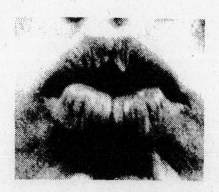

JAYNE MANSFIELD

Born	**1932, in America.**
Occupation	**Actress.**
Hobbies	**Rogering and pretending to be dumb.**
Distinguishing Features	**Nice pair of brains.**
Romantically Linked With	**Sam Brody, Elvis Presley, Robert Kennedy, Paul Mansfield (m), Matt Cimber (m), Mickey Hargitay (m).**

Jayne Mansfield is famous for acting in *The Girl Can't Help It* in 1957 and for having a 43-inch bust all the time. She also had a 163 IQ, four times the size of the bust, but as she said, 'Who wants a brainy dumb blonde?' So, she dedicated her life to pretending to be dumb, and also to rogering. She had a voracious appetite for men: 'Every man was a challenge to her': and she was never short of them, as these large breasts of hers dazzled men and photographers wherever she went.[2] Unfortunately all this breast business did eventually damage what there was of her career. She wasn't really allowed to act: that wasn't why they'd hired her.

Her other voracious appetite was for the colour pink. Elvis and the motorbike is just one example. She was once noticed walking down Sunset Boulevard wearing nothing but a pink ribbon. Her house was pink, and in it there was a pink bathroom, which contained a heart-shaped pool that was pink. She bathed in it using pink champagne instead of water, and while bathing used pink soap to soap her pubic hair—which was heart-shaped and dyed, well, yes, all right, pink. Nice touch for the Kennedy brothers that—something they could talk about when they got tired of the Missile Crisis.[3]

FOOTNOTES

1 There is one other remarkable thing about this relationship: Elvis, with three girls a day, was not the most discriminating of rogerers. There were, however, four things that he couldn't stand in a woman—big feet and big bosoms. Yet Jayne Mansfield did not only have big bosoms—she had enormous ones. The contradiction here qualifies this as one of the Great Rogering Mysteries: did Elvis go out with Jayne in order to overcome his fear of large breasts: or was it Jayne's breasts that gave him the fear in the first place? It is a perplexing question, which now, since all four of the major protagonists are no more, may never be answered.
2 Once when Jane Russell was having a photocall, Jayne arrived and fell into the swimming pool (dumb, you see). As she screamed that she couldn't swim, her top floated away from her and one of the photographers called out, 'Come and drown over here please!'
3 After her death, Engelbert Humperdinck, always a man of exquisite taste, bought Jayne's pink house and claimed he often saw her ghost wandering around it. It is the only pink ghost ever recorded.

JAYNE MANSFIELD & ROBERT KENNEDY

The difference between the Kennedy and the Thatcher Administrations cannot be stressed often enough. Robert and Jayne's affair is the equivalent of Sir Geoffrey Howe rogering Samantha Fox, which is difficult to imagine. Even when Cecil Parkinson slept with an extremely respectable young lady with very moderately sized breasts there was no end of hell to pay.

The reasons for this moral tightening are hard to perceive, but one man, John Fosby, has perhaps come closer to an explanation than any other. Fosby, an anthropologist at Ashford University, claims that the new moral tone in politics is simply a re-emergence of the old 'survival' instinct. Politicians no longer *dare* to admit they like sex. They fear if they so much as admitted they liked the idea of rogering in general they might be forced, at some time or other, to roger Margaret Thatcher herself.

ROBERT KENNEDY

Born	**1925, in America.**
Occupation	**Politician.**
Distinguishing Features	**Youth, charisma, wit, charm, power and big teeth.**
Romantically Linked With	**Ethel Kennedy, Marilyn Monroe, Jayne Mansfield, Mariella Novotny.**[1]
Nickname	**Bobby.**

Like his brother Jack, Bobby was keen on girls. Often on the same girls as his brother Jack. They passed them between each other without a thought. And perhaps without much consideration. In his time he was a brilliant and controversial politician, hated by many powerful men (the Mafia, the Unions, Jimmy Hoffa, J. Edgar Hoover, Lyndon Johnson and Eisenhower among others), most of them twice his age. Many hated him for his determined efforts to clean up the corruption throughout American society. If there is hatred towards him now, it is from people who wish he'd cleaned up his act with regard to Marilyn Monroe at the same time.

Nevertheless, Mariella Novotny described Bobby as 'very boyish and cheerful in bed', and it is nice to think that Bobby had a pleasant time when he was rogering, since he got so fair and squarely rogered in the end.

FOOTNOTES

1 Mariella, such a pretty name, and Bobby made love in the UN Headquarters in New York —many political historians think this to have been the most decisive single act ever performed in the building.

ROBERT KENNEDY & MARILYN MONROE

A grim tale, perhaps even grimmer than was originally thought. Time may reveal the truth.

MARILYN MONROE[1]

Born	1926, in America.
Occupation	Actress.[2]
Distinguishing Features	All of them.
Romantically Linked With	Jim Dougherty (m),[3] Joe DiMaggio (m),[4] Arthur Miller (m),[5] Orson Welles, John F. Kennedy, Robert Kennedy, Yves Montand, Andre de Dienes, Joe Schenk, Johnny Hyde, Frank Sinatra, Fred Karger, David Canover.
Nicknames	The Woo Woo Girl, The Divine Monroe.

In any book about sexuality, Marilyn Monroe is the uncontested star. She is not Marilyn Monroe, but

MARILYN MONROE

Out there on her own, exquisite, beautiful, 'fed on sexual candy', the most desired woman in the world, and pleasantly plump to boot.[6] Her perfection is an undeniable fact of life. Rose are red,[7] violets are blue, books are square, sea water is salty, mountains are high, grass is green, night is dark, water is liquid, Alistair Burnett is a creep, Russia is big, Clint is God, life is a bitch, bananas are yellow, oranges are orange, McDonalds are addictive, circles are round, coffee is brown, chocolate is nice, the Great Wall of China is long, the Queen is very nice, and Marilyn Monroe is perfect.

All details of her life are mere footnotes to that.

FOOTNOTES

1 Not, of course, her real name, which was Norma Jean Baker. The choice of the name Marilyn was a strange coincidence, since it was inspired by Marilyn Miller, whose husband, Arthur, Marilyn later married.*

2 It is now generally accepted that, for all the chaos of how her performances came to be,** Marilyn was one of the great film actresses: *Bus Stop, Gentlemen Prefer Blondes, All About Eve, Some Like It Hot, How To Marry A Millionaire* all bear witness to an extraordinary talent:

'I have never met anyone . . . as utterly fabulous on the screen, and that includes Garbo'—Billy Wilder.

'As near genius as any actress I ever knew'—Joshua Logan.

3 Jim married her when she was sixteen, and said of her: 'She had the cleanest beauty I have ever seen'.

4 This marriage was the equivalent of Meryl Streep marrying Carl Lewis or Madonna marrying Kenny Dalglish.

5 One of the great marriages. As one newspaper announced it: 'Egghead Weds Hourglass'.

Miller later showed great tenderness and sadness about Marilyn: 'If she was simple, it would have been easy to help her. She could have made it with a little luck'.***

6 Any man having trouble with a girlfriend being ridiculous about her weight, should make her sit through *Let's Make Love*—Marilyn is genuinely overweight, and, as ever, divine.

7 Actually, of course, they are not, or not all of them: roses are white, orange, pink, yellow, all sorts of other colours as well. Two particularly beautiful varieties are 'Peace', which can be white with candy coloured pink, and 'Masquerade', which starts yellow before it does indeed turn to red.

*Many other strange coincidences occurred in Monroe's life. In her youth, having no father, she kept a picture of Clark Gable in her room. And in the end her last picture, *The Misfits*, was made with Clark Gable. It was also a strangely coincidental movie, being the last film of all its three stars. Clark Gable, Marilyn, and Montgomery Clift.
**'Directing her was like directing Lassie'—Otto Preminger. 'Extracting a performance from her is like pulling teeth'—Billy Wilder.
***Since Miller is the man of words, let him have the last one—'Her beauty shines because the spirit is forever showing through'.

MARILYN MONROE & JOHN KENNEDY

Same story as with Bobby, alas.

JOHN KENNEDY	
Born	1917,[1] in America.
Occupation	President of the United States.[2]
Hobby	Rogering.
Distinguishing Features	Youth, charm and good looks. Money too. And power. And wit, and nerve.[3] Everything basically.
Romantically Linked With	Jacqueline Bouvier (m), Marilyn Monroe, Inga Arvad, Blaze Starr, Mary Pinchot, Judith Campbell Exner, Gene Tierney.

'I'm not the tragic lover type'. Thank God. So clouded by tragedy is the story of the Kennedys that it's a relief to be able to take a breather.

Kennedy had what many people would call a healthy attitude to sex: and many others (the rest) would call an unhealthy interest in it. He was famously keen: 'I'm never through with a girl until I've had her three ways', and in fact remarkably frank: he complained once to Harold Macmillan that if he went too long without sex he got headaches.[4]

When Kennedy took over as President, an aide observed: 'This administration is going to do for sex what the last one did for golf'.[5] Certainly sex was built into Kennedy's routine. As sleeping is to Ronald Reagan, so was rogering to Jack Kennedy, with and without Jackie. This can be seen as either the behaviour of a cad, or of a hero. A cad for obvious reasons. A hero because lots of things were against Kennedy and the random roger. To distract him, he had a bad back, a heavy schedule, a finger on the button and Khrushchev on the hotline most of the time, ranting on endlessly about Cuba. Yet still he blasted on—'he went in more for quantity than quality'—and appears to have shown the cavalier attitude of politicians of an earlier era, rather than the sour-faced fear of many of our time.[6]

In the end it could be that his promiscuity might have caught up with him—the scandal of Judith Exner's connections with the Mafia, and the everlasting question mark over Monroe's death might have done their share of damage. If it had got really bad, he could presumably have given it all up and become an actor—swapping careers with Ronald; it is hard to believe that such a charismatic character as JFK would not now be slugging away with the best of them in *Wild Geese* 2, playing Russian generals in *Rambo 3*, putting in guest appearances as Miss Ellie's old lover in *Dallas*, and of course, with a little Grecian 2000 borrowed from Ronald, perhaps playing the brilliant young senator from Massachusetts in the brilliant mini-series, *Kennedy*.[7]

FOOTNOTES

1 This makes him six years younger than Ronald Reagan.
2 After he failed to win the vice-presidential nomination in 1956, someone asked Kennedy why he still wanted to be President. Kennedy's reply: 'I guess it's the only thing I can do'.
3 'Nerve'—when JFK appointed Bobby as attorney general there was an uproar of charges of nepotism. Kennedy's reply: 'I can't see that it's wrong to give him a little legal experience before he goes out to practice law'.
4 Rumour would suggest Macmillan had the opposite trouble. Any sex at all gave him a headache.
5 By which he did not mean that they would turn sex into a sport for old people in ridiculous trousers where you have to hit a ball into eighteen different holes in the course of a morning.
6 Certainly, apart from a heroic lapse by Sir Harold Wilson, which he did his best to make public on every opportunity, British politicians of recent times have quite shamed the great tradition of the rogerer politician.* It is only the brave actions of certain minor Cabinet ministers and Jeremy Thorpe that have kept things going at all.
7 This would not be as bizarre as it seems: in *Jolson Sings Again*, Larry Parks, playing Jolson, attends an audition for a young actor to play the part of Jolson in *The Jolson Story*. The young actor is Larry Parks, played, of course, by Larry Parks. Larry Parks, as Jolson, is amazed how like himself, i.e. Jolson, he, Larry Parks, as Larry Parks, is, and he, Jolson (i.e. Larry Parks), trains Larry Parks, till he, Larry Parks, looks almost exactly like Jolson, acted by Larry Parks. Actually, it's a very good film.

Rogering politicians. The great years of rogering politicians reached their climax with the career of Metternich, the famous Austro-Hungarian chancellor. At the Congress of Vienna, which lasted a year, the efforts to untangle the problems of Europe were minor in comparison to the efforts of the leaders of Europe to tangle their limbs with the ladies who flocked into the city to join them. A newspaper report on the recent Tokyo summit should have read like this, had these fine ways continued, and not been replaced by the grim drudgery of serious negotiation.

Tokyo A Go-Go.
Ronald Reagan arrived in Tokyo on Tuesday full of the joys of spring. Met by the wife of the American Ambassador, luscious blonde Mrs Cartwright, the President was swiftly whipped away to a reception where his eye was met by the Cartwright's young daughter, already in eager conversation with the elegant President Mitterand. Mr Nakasone made a welcoming speech outlining the grave economic and political issues at stake, and also praising the beauty of his hostess, the elegant Mrs Nagamuchi who was unfortunately not in the room at the moment of the tribute. Helmut Kohl, who was also missing, soon returned and pledged his commitment to the war against terrorism, and to Mrs Nagamuchi.
   The conference proper began on Thursday with only two days to run till the issue of the final statement and resolution. A late start, occasioned by the fall out from the French Embassy Ball, was swiftly turned into decisive action as the leaders decided to cancel the rest of the day's proceedings in order to pursue more important personal matters. President Mitterand and President Reagan were seen locked in deep discussion, at the end of which a compromise seemed to have been reached, based on the Cartwright's youngest daughter, Jane.
   Friday saw the final day of the conference, and the long awaited discussion on terrorism and international violence. As a graphic demonstration of it, the early morning coffee broke up in a flurry of fists, as Reagan accused Mitterand, a late arrival, of being a slimy double crossing frog, and Mr Kohl and Mr Nakasone slugged it out over Mrs Nagamuchi. Finally, a statement was issued pledging the world leaders' deep commitment to international terrorism in all shapes and forms, particularly that instigated by Mr Gadaffi. Fortunately, the drafting error was spotted by a

translator, and the world leaders went to the ball on Friday able to concentrate on the more important matter of saying farewell to their belles and beloveds at the end of this hugely successful summit. No one is as yet willing to predict exactly what will come of it, but high hopes are being held out for two grandchildren for the Cartwrights, a divorce for Mr Nagamuchi, and a new hairstyle for Mrs Thatcher, who was genuinely hurt that no one made a pass at her all week.

JOHN KENNEDY & JACKIE KENNEDY ONASSIS

Jackie emerges very well from all the stories told—she both did her duty, and kept her cool. Dutifully, every afternoon, White House business would stop as the President and First Lady retired to their bedroom—not, as in the case of the Reagans, to watch repeats of *Rawhide* and *The Flintstones*. As for keeping her cool, when once Jackie found a pair of alien knickers in their bedroom, she merely commented: 'You'd better find out who these belong to. They're not my size'.

JACKIE ONASSIS

Born	**1929, in America.**
Occupation	**President's wife, millionaire's wife, publisher.**
Hobbies	**Sailing, hunting, reading proofs.**
Distinguishing Features	**Dark glasses.**
Romantically Linked With	**John Kennedy (m), Aristotle Onassis (m), Peter Hamill.**
Nickname	**Banjo legs.**

When Jackie was a little girl, her father's advice was 'Be mysterious'. Since then, neither she nor anyone else has known what is going on. Her personality has been kept studiously hidden. Nothing gives her away. She doesn't sweat. She never loses her temper. She likes total darkness in the bedroom and she chain-smokes to keep her in a permanent soft-focus haze. Another mysterious aspect of Jackie O. is her penchant for flushing toilets with hot water. Her father's advice certainly whammed home.

In the Kennedy years she had to put up with Jack's indiscretions, including the Bay of Pigs and Bobby's appointment, and yet she always kept her subtle dignity. There were times she was more famous than her President—JFK introduced himself to an audience in France as 'The man who accompanied Jacqueline Kennedy to Paris'—and Jackie's bearing at the time of his death was an example and a wonder to the world.

When she married Onassis she was the most famous woman in the world, and drew up a legal document as a wedding agreement asking for 20 million dollars up front. The Kennedy/Onassis wedding was 'more like an acquisition instead of a marriage'. She was like 'a show horse, or an oil tanker'.[1] Onassis complained, 'All she does is spend, spend, spend' and on one occasion, she did spend $500,000 to stop a photographer bothering her. Indeed, her marriage with Onassis must vie for the accolade of Most Expensive Roger in History.

After Onassis, things stabilized, and Jackie could be found back in her New York flat, claiming a rate rebate of 2 dollars and 79 cents, and publishing, where she is both mysterious and successful, and has concentrated on biographies.[2]

When someone suggested that it was really Frank Sinatra who wanted to marry Jackie, Sinatra replied, 'I never wished to marry Jackie Kennedy, but when I find the author of that rumour, I shall happily arrange for his or her parents to be wed'. It is, of course, very unlikely that the rumour-monger will ever be found because, like everything else with Jackie, he, or she, is so mysterious.

FOOTNOTES

1 Whoever said this was obviously not referring to the look of Jackie Onassis: although she does look like a fabulous horse, she bears no resemblance whatsoever to an oil tanker, but rather to a slender and beautiful sloop, wearing dark glasses.
2 She failed to get Prince, Princess Diana and Diana Dors, but has produced the definitive Michael Jackson. The father of one of the editors of this book actually dated Diana Dors three times. On all three occasions he took her to do the single thing he most liked doing. After three nights out watching her own films, she axed him.

___

JACKIE ONASSIS & PETER HAMILL

Peter first met Jackie in the sixties when he was writing speeches for her brother-in-law, Bobby. Years later they fell out over an article he wrote attacking Jackie for marrying Aristotle Onassis for money. It was a strange thing to 'attack' her for—what other possible reason could she be expected to have for marrying Ari, with his thick glasses and Brylcreem hair? Of course, it finally emerged that what had blinded the seasoned journalist in Hamill to this obvious fact was, obviously . . . love. For a time the two were at daggers drawn, but as often happens, hate turned out to be nothing more than an elaborate form of foreplay.

Hamill now says, 'I would never write about Jackie. It would be like writing about my own brother'. God knows, and He alone, what Hamill and his brother get up to.

PETER HAMILL

Born	**1934, in America.**
Occupation	**Journalist.**
Hobbies	**Rogering.**
Distinguishing Features	**List of Romantic Links.**
Romantically Linked With	**Jackie Onassis, Mary Tyler Moore, Linda Ronstadt, Shirley MacLaine.**

Peter Hamill is a sharp New York journalist who has slept with quite a few famous women. Indeed, his extraordinary list pushes one to ask how he has done it, what secret quality, what magic ingredient he has that has brought him into contact with such a bunch of intelligent and attractive women. It leads one to muse for a second about the whole question of *What Makes a Woman Want to Roger a Man?*

What Makes a Woman Want to Roger a Man is far too potentially a rude subject to be gone into in detail in anything but a large medical encyclopaedia where it can be comfortably concealed between articles on chicken pox and water on the knee. However, what we do know for certain is that, medically, there is no connection between being good in bed and being famous, powerful, or rich. The Rod Stewart theory,[1] which says that rich, famous and powerful people are good at sex because they get more practice, seems sensible enough; however, the corresponding Joan Collins theory provides an antidote to this advantage. It says (based on Joan's relationship with Maxwell Reid) that the rich, famous and powerful women that the rich, famous and powerful men meet may well actually like sex *less* than ordinary women, because:

1 They don't want their hair messed up.

2 They can't stand being naked when they're not properly lit.

3 They miss the audience,
  and
4 They're always shocked when they have to do it for real, having got used to just wriggling around with their pants on under the covers and making a lot of 'oo-oo' noises.

Thus, in the end, there's no reason why the President of the Batley Rotary Club—a charming and good looking man, rather well known by the women of Batley and with slightly more power, money, good looks, humour and charm than most of the other men they could reasonably expect to roger in Batley—shouldn't have just as much 'practice' as Rod Stewart, or Napoleon, and be just as good at sex. In fact, the chances are—since famous, rich and powerful people are likely to be a little self-obsessed and short of time—that there are loads and loads of perfectly ordinary chaps wandering around who are much better lovers than everyone mentioned in this book.[2] This is the explanation behind the astonishing phenomenon of the utter non-entity roger:

if ever one of these ordinary fellows gets mixed up with a film star or famous person, the film star or famous person will be so bowled over by his gentle unselfish loving ways, and so delighted at only having to think how she matched up to the Batley Rotary Club secretary's wife, rather than Elizabeth Taylor, or Marie-Thérèse of Austria, that she cannot help but go on and on about it to her girlfriends. The word spreads like wildfire and so as soon as one celebrity has finished with him, another will be queueing up waiting to have a go.

This is the reason why, in the midst of all this famous rogering, when it starts to look as though you've got to have either been in *Gone With the Wind*, *or* slept with Marilyn Monroe, *or* married Frank Sinatra to sleep with anyone, no one should give up hope. Peter Hamill, and Henry Wynberg in the Monolithic Enigmas line, should be an inspiration to all men.

FOOTNOTES

1 See Rod Stewart in the Musical Giants line.
2 Except, of course, the super-rogerers: see Ryan O'Neal, Sir Gordon White, Warren Beatty.

PETER HAMILL & SHIRLEY MACLAINE

The first time that Peter Hamill met Shirley MacLaine, they talked about whether dogs have souls. This is curiously reminiscent of Humphrey Bogart and his first wife, who talked about whether dogs should be allowed to eat caviar.[1] It also goes to show that it doesn't matter what you talk about—if it's going to happen, it's going to happen.[2]

SHIRLEY MACLAINE

Born	**1934, in America.**
Occupation	**Actress and dancer.**
Hobbies	**Contacting the dead and writing autobiographies.**
Romantically Linked With	**Andrei Konchalovsky, Steve Parker, Lewis van Bergan, a Labour Party politician in the Cabinet, Peter Hamill, Andrew Peacock.**
Nickname	**My Sunshine, Nif Nif.[3]**

The Oscar for 'Terms of Endearment'[4] duly rewarded Shirley MacLaine for what has been a beautiful career in the movies, comprising some lovely performances in some lovely films, including 'The Apartment', 'Irma la Douce' and 'Being There'. As far as her private life is concerned, Shirley could never hope to match her brother Warren, and so has been pleasantly discreet and secretive. Two mysteries dominate any study of her:

1 When Shirley admitted having rogered a Labour Party politician 'in the Cabinet', who was he? And did she mean she rogered him while he was a member of the Cabinet, or actually in the Cabinet Rooms while he was aspiring to be a Cabinet member? Speculation as to who this politician was has been rife for five years. It is generally thought, and hoped, that it was not Eric Heffer.

2 How did Shirley find anyone to roger at all, given her strange announcements on sex and 'life'? The great American word 'kookie' springs to mind in reaction to statements like these:

> 'I was a man in my previous lives'.
> 'I was in Atlantis when it sank'.
> 'Three minutes after Peter Sellers died he was in the same room as me'.

It would need a man with nerves of steel to live with this—it is a measure of the greatness of Fidel Castro that he sustained a nine hour long conversation with her—let alone to co-exist with Shirley's stranger habits. When she has a bath she sniffs a glass of sea-water, sings Hindu mantras, gives her chest a salt rub down and finishes up with yoga.

The truth is, Shirley has never led a promiscuous life. She says: 'I know women who have four lovers at once. If I had all that going on, I wouldn't be able to figure out when to jog and when to make love'. She has, however, and no wonder in view of her general loveliness, had at least ten men who adored her. She wears a Lover's Necklace, with ten diamonds from ten engagement rings. The reason is simple: 'Marriage is obsolete', says Shirley. At exactly what point she tells that to the men who give her the diamonds is another Rogering Mystery.

FOOTNOTES

1 See Appendix: Dogs and Rogering.
2 Although, whether or not dogs have souls *is* in fact quite an interesting topic. If they do, it both explains and complicates matters.

 It explains why it is that so often people trip over for no reason whatsoever: clearly we are just tripping over ghost dogs. *It complicates* things because if dogs do have souls then they must presumably go to Heaven: and things in Heaven are everlasting, which means that the roads of Heaven, far from being paved with gold, must by now be piled deep with eternal dog-poo. Which is complicated, because it makes you think twice about going to Heaven in the first place.
3 Shirley was called this by Andrei: in Russian it means—My Little Pig.*

---

*It is always slightly perplexing why people call their lovers 'pig'. Presumably it is because pigs are sweet and small and soft and cuddly when they are little, and not because they are big and fat and dirty and unshaven with horrid hard hoofs and giant snouts covered with mud.

4 There are carnal movie enthusiasts who believe that this film starred the two most attractive women, and the single most attractive man now working on celluloid.

SHIRLEY MACLAINE & ANDREW PEACOCK

These two giants from different worlds, the glamour of Hollywood and the hard politics of Canberra, spent a loving weekend together by the Australian sea, where what most profoundly impressed Shirley was that Andrew was 'the only man I know with a Gucci toothbrush'. There is, of course, always the possibility with Shirley that they spent the entire weekend discussing re-incarnation, rather than incarnating their friendship, and just happened to share a bathroom. For the sake of the honour of Australian politics, so be-smirched by Bob Hawke's drunken behavior when they won the Americas Cup, let us pray it ain't so.

ANDREW PEACOCK

Born	In Australia.
Occupation	Australian politician (former Leader of the Opposition).
Distinguishing Features	Tan.
Romantically Linked With	Shirley MacLaine, Susan Peacock (m), Margaret St George, Jacqueline Getty.
Nicknames	The Sunlamp Kid, Gucci Boots.

Australia's most glamorous politician is one of the few who can mix that tricky cocktail of being glamorous and a politician (even more, an Australian politician) at the same time. In the morning he can be photographed walking along a beach in (Gucci) swimming trunks with a beautiful girl: in the afternoon he can be standing in Parliament saying things like, 'Australia is very interested in the economic resonances of the power balances and imbalances in the Indian Ocean.'

It should be pointed out that, sadly, in trying to manage this high-wire act, Andrew has sometimes lost out on both counts. His wife Susan left him for Sangster, and Shirley left in search of more fascinating conversations. And then Bob Hawke[1] became Prime Minister without the aid of a single Gucci accessory, not that he doesn't need one. For heaven's sake, Bob, smarten up a little.

FOOTNOTE

1 The mention of Bob Hawke highlights the strange 'bird' factor in Australian politics which has so puzzled sociologists and psephologists alike. It would appear that only people named after birds can succeed in Australian politics at the moment. Thus the leaders of the two opposing parties at the last election were a Hawke and a Peacock, and high hopes are being held out for two young politicians in Queensland, John Humming-Bird and Bruce Lesser-Spotted-Thrush. If the same situation applied in England, not Mrs Thatcher, but the delicious and scandalous Mynah Bird would now be ruling the country, contesting daily business in Parliament with Leader of the Opposition Sir 'Robin' Day.

ANDREW PEACOCK & SUSAN SANGSTER

Susan Sangster was married to Andrew Peacock before she married Robert Sangster. The fact that Andrew has been divorced should not, however, count against him in his bid for power in Australia. Ronald Reagan has been divorced, and Denis Thatcher, who cunningly rules Great Britain with his poor homely wife taking all the flack and doing all the interviews, is also the veteran of a previous marriage.

SUSAN SANGSTER

Born	**In Australia.**
Occupation	**Travel and meeting interesting people.**
Hobbies	**Politics, cricket and horseracing.**
Romantically Linked With	**Dennis Lillee, Andrew Peacock (m), Frank Renouf, Robert Sangster.**

Susan, unlike so many tunnel-visioned lovers of both sexes, has made a particular feature of choosing men from varied careers, covering the very best in horse-breeding, politics and cricket. This whole aspect of the educational value of rogering is one which is greatly underplayed in schools and sex-education. A relationship which does not reach the rogering stage can be sustained on the most trivial levels of conversation—'Who slept with who?', 'How's the weather?' and 'Did you hear about that particularly brutal murder?' can easily fill up the available time. But if the relationship progresses to rogering, it is highly likely that *out of simple politeness* the subject of the other person's career will have to come up and all sorts of interesting facts and the benefits of all sorts of experience can be picked up. Love-making need not be all: 'Was it good for you?', 'Have you done this before?' and 'Are you all right down there?' It can also be 'Exactly what is a Eurobond and how much influence does it have on the money markets?' and 'I'm sorry, I got a little lost around the stopcock—is it clockwise or anti-clockwise to turn the gas off?' In the current climate of pressure for vocational education, it is profoundly to be hoped that the question of sleeping around with the professional people will not be entirely overlooked.

SUSAN SANGSTER & ROBERT SANGSTER

The Robert Sangster love-life is a hard one to get to grips with. This is because both his wives have been called Susan. So, when he recently had a little fling with Jerry Hall, one Susan Sangster was presumably furious, and another Susan Sangster was probably quite delighted.[1]

ROBERT SANGSTER	
Born	In Britain.
Occupation	Heir, horse owner.
Hobbies	Breeding and rogering (with no particular connection between the two).
Distinguishing Features	Balding a bit.
Romantically Linked With	Christine Street, Susan Peacock (m), Jerry Hall, and Susan Lilley (m).

Robert Sangster has spent his married life satisfactorily seeking Susans, marrying both Susan Sangster (formerly Peacock) and Susan Lilley.[2] He does, however, spend a considerable amount of time breeding horses for money, and it is perhaps worth considering how much this affects his attitude to his own love-making. For the sake of Susan, we hope not much. For a start, it's

[6] **The Flying Opossum of New South Wales**

bloody cold and wet and uncomfortable doing all the tender, naked business in a field.

FOOTNOTES

1 There are both advantages and disadvantages to always rogering girls with the same name:

Advantages:
 a You won't get their name wrong.
 b It makes it a lot easier to choose which girl to roger.
 c After a while, you can pretty much lay claim to a certain number of girls within your immediate circle. Since your friends know you are going to limit yourself to these few girls, it is only reasonable for them to leave them alone, for your sake. Also, if you are a bit of a rogerer, it would be only prudent for friends to avoid having one of the Susans as their regular girlfriends since they know that, sooner or later, you are going to 'get round' to her.

Disadvantages:
 a If the first girl you roger is called something like Mhairi or Kosimosho, you're in real trouble.
 b You may find there are a lot of girls with other names who are much prettier and nicer than the girls of the name of your choice.
 c If you continue only to pick girls called Susan, people will think you are mad.
 d If you continue only to pick girls called Susan, you will be mad.

2 Susan Lilley was previously married to Peter Lilley, the shoe heir to Lilley & Skinner: she has now married three millionaires, the first being the founder of Kwik Save. Her most famous remark was the beautifully condensed: 'Reports calling me heartless were heartbreaking'. She is also famous for drinking beer—once consuming a pint in four seconds. This implies that, if the whirligig keeps going round, she might do well to end up in the arms of that other Australian politician, old Bob Hawke, who is also quite fond of a spot of the amber from time to time.*

*All right, often. He loves the stuff. Loves it. Can't get enough of it. 'Yummy, yummy, glug, glug, glug—give us another one, mate, whoops it's down me trousers'.

ROBERT SANGSTER & JERRY HALL

This well-publicized affair was a brilliantly transparent trick by Jerry to make Mick jealous, stop him rogering teenage girls and persuade him to fill her with babies.

It is easy to see why Sangster should have co-operated with the scheme—who would, or could, say no to Jerry Hall? But why Jerry Hall should have lighted on this rather kindly, balding old gent is rather hard to say. In the end, it must have been because no one could compare sexually with Mick, and at least Jerry and Robert could talk about horses when it was all rather disappointingly over.

Whatever, it did in the end achieve the required result. Mick got his girl back, Jerry got her baby and Robert sure as hell wasn't complaining. The only people who really lost out were a bunch of genuinely disappointed teenage girls.

JERRY HALL	
Born	**1958, in Texas.**[1]
Occupation	**Model.**
Hobbies	**Horses and rogering.**
Distinguishing Features	**Height and elegance.**
Romantically Linked With	**Bryan Ferry, Mick Jagger, Robert Sangster.**
Nickname	**La Grande Horizontale.**

Jerry Hall is one of five daughters from a poorish Texan family, who has risen to the very top of the modelling profession, become fabulously rich as a person in her own right, and gone out with Mick Jagger for years and years. She has produced two children by him and presumably will before long persuade him to marry her.

In other words—she's done well.

In this country, however, she is primarily famous for being the first person to break the great barrier of silence about sex in the *Sunday Times* 'Life in the Day of . . .' series. For years and years, celebrity after celebrity went through interminable nonsense about eggs and newspapers and offices and faithful old secretaries and faithful old dogs, and pleasant suppers and children and 'Marilyn and I usually watch *News at Ten*, then she goes to bed and I read through some incredibly boring documents before climbing into my four pairs of safety underpants and pyjamas and get in beside her, not touching'.

But Jerry threw all that aside once and for all. Out of the blue, one glorious Sunday, Jerry finished her 'Life in the Day' with these unforgettable words: 'At the end of the day, I climb into my black suspenders and get into bed with Mick'. There is no record of how many people died of shock when they got to that sentence, but as a killer in its year the article put hypothermia into the shade.

Ever since then, Jerry has been to the British public what she's always looked like. A sex goddess.[2]

FOOTNOTES

1 Jerry is Texan through and through: she lost her virginity 'with her boots on', and is skilled in the art of leg-wrestling.
2 And a witty one at that: when asked on TV how she felt at the end of a day's modelling, she answered: 'rich'.

JERRY HALL & MICK JAGGER

Mick effectively pinched Jerry from Bryan Ferry, thus saving her from the comic fate of being Mrs Jerry Ferry. Jerry in fact wasn't all that nuts about Bryan anyway—she found him 'squeaky clean' and left him because he was frightened of a cockroach.

Now Jerry keeps Mick by sticking to the advice of her Texan Mama—be a cook in the kitchen, a maid in the living room, and a whore in the bed. Which doesn't sound too much fun—but if you've actually got a cook, and a maid to help you out with the dull bits, then it begins to look more like a recipe for a good time.

MICK JAGGER & SABRINA GUINNESS

(See The Music Lover's line for the full story on Mick.)

It is almost inconceivable that Mick Jagger should not appear in this line. It goes from King to King, and Mick Jagger is surely England's King of Rock 'n' Roll. No one has said that Mick *never* makes fashion mistakes—there was a time he kept *on and on* wearing white frocks no self-respecting girl would be seen dead in—but he has been the sexiest man in England for decades now, and if this line was King of Sex to King of Sex, then, as sure as eggs is eggs and Oil of Olay is good for the skin, it would stop here.

And since Sabrina couldn't be queen for real, let her then be our Queen of Love with her lovely eyes and all those Hollywood tricks that made Prince Charles the man he is today.

SABRINA GUINNESS & PRINCE CHARLES

(See the Beauty and the Beast line for Sabrina's biography.)

It is one of the great sadnesses of our age that the lovely Sabrina missed out on her chance to form the noble physical link between Prince Charles and the next King of England. It is deeply gratifying, therefore, to see Sabrina here forming, still through rogering, a different, but no less noble link between King and king. Hurrah!

PRINCE CHARLES

Since the start of this line, even deeper bonds have been discovered between Charles and Elvis. Elvis joined the army: Charles is going, one day, to be head of the Army. At the start of his career, Elvis wasn't the King: Charles wasn't either (and, of course, still isn't—when he is, all his subjects fervently hope that he will be given a proper crown, and not just the little furry one he wore when he got to be Prince of Wales). Elvis was used to performing in front of huge audiences: 400 million watched Charles' wedding. Both Elvis and Charles could have their choice of experienced girls: both settled for an image of perfect innocent womanhood, Priscilla and Diana.

In fact, the similarities are so astonishing that it puts one in fear of Charles' future. Will our King one day be found dead of a drug overdose, stuffed full of junk food, an underage groupie in the next door room, sideburns down to his jaw and not a friend in the world to save him from himself? The answer is . . .

No. The Queen Mother wouldn't let him.

ONCE & FUTURE KINGS LAY LINE

ELVIS PRESLEY

JAYNE MANSFIELD

ROBERT KENNEDY

MARILYN MONROE

JOHN KENNEDY

JACKIE ONASSIS

PETER HAMILL

SHIRLEY MACLAINE

ANDREW PEACOCK

SUSAN SANGSTER

ROBERT SANGSTER

JERRY HALL

MICK JAGGER

SABRINA GUINNESS

PRINCE CHARLES

'God save our gracious Kings,
Long live our noble Kings,
God save our Kings'.

COMEDIANS

FROM	**ZEPPO MARX**
TO	**WOODY ALLEN**
IN	**4 ROGERS**

This is the shortest of all the modern lines, and reveals an important link between comedy and sex. No, it doesn't—just joking.

ZEPPO MARX

Born	1901, in America.
Occupation	Brother.
Hobby	Agent.
Distinguishing Features	Didn't look like Groucho, Chico or Harpo.
Romantically Linked With	Barbara Marx/Sinatra.
Nickname	The Other One.

In the movies, Zeppo benefitted from being the least funny[1] and most attractive of the brothers, so he always got the girl. (See Woody Allen for being funny *and* getting the girl.) Let us hope this was also so in real life, since he was otherwise the most insulted man in Hollywood. To be butt and fall-guy to his wise-cracking brothers meant a history of constant scorn, insult and humiliation. In *Horse Feathers*, Groucho, playing Zeppo's father, says, 'I married your mother because I wanted children. Imagine how I felt when you turned up'. This was par for the course for poor Zeppo, and as soon as he could, he got out of the movies and became an agent—a job where you do all the insulting.

It would, however, be completely wrong and a travesty of all that Zeppo strived for and achieved if we were to allow his entry to be as long as the footnote we are about to write about his brothers. That's the way it was, that's the way it always should be. 'No lines for Zeppy' was their motto.

FOOTNOTE

1 Controversy rages still over the question of just how funny the Marx Brothers were, but what cannot be doubted is that they said, or had written for them and pretended they said, some cracking funny lines.

A major contender for best excuse ever offered when caught in a compromising situation was said by *Chico Marx*. When caught by his wife kissing a chorus girl, Chico proudly declared: 'I wasn't kissing her, I was whispering in her mouth'. (See Appendix: Great Rogering Excuses.)

As for *Groucho*, he was responsible for perhaps the rudest joke ever not cracked on television. It was filmed live in his programme, *You Bet Your Life*, but tragically cut before transmission. Groucho was talking to a Mrs Story, mother of twenty-two children. 'I love my husband', she said in enthusiastic explanation of her brood. 'I like my cigar, too', observed Groucho, 'but I take it out once in a while'.

And as for *Harpo*, well, he didn't say anything. His name, before he changed it to Harpo, was Adolf Marx: the confusion of being named after the most important communist *and* the most important fascist leader of all time, whose words were responsible for millions of deaths apiece, would have reduced any man to silence.

ZEPPO MARX & BARBARA SINATRA

Barbara was a Las Vegas showgirl, and she showed herself all girl to Zeppo and married him in 1959, a long, long time after the Marx Brothers had stopped making their movies. Zeppo was no youngster when they married, he was old enough to be her dad: by the time they divorced in 1972, he was old enough to be her grandfather. Their divorce settlement asked Zeppo to pay £750 a month for ten years: which all things considered is a pleasantly fair amount. Life, at last was being fair to Zeppo (*née* Herbert).[1]

BARBARA SINATRA

Born	**1931, in America.**
Occupation	**Showgirl and wife.**
Distinguishing Features	**Increasingly talented husbands.**
Romantically Linked With	**Zeppo Marx, Frank Sinatra.**
Unbelievable Link With	**Spiro Agnew.**

It has been said that Barbara Sinatra is like a combination of Sinatra's other wives: which does not mean she has six breasts and a strange elfin haircut. Rather, in the words of one Hollywood columnist, she has 'Looks to equal Ava Gardner, the quiet charm of Mia Farrow and is just enough of a homebody to remind Frank of the early days with Nancy before he became famous'. She is a gloriously sensible choice—a sensible age, fifty-five to Frank's seventy, already used to marriage to a famous man, and apparently tolerant of Frank's occasional benders, as a former showgirl who knows what the showboys occasionally get up to would be.

> *Perhaps she is 'that mate,*
> *that fate*
> *had him create*
> *-ed for'.*

Let's hope so—Frank's getting a bit old to be changing love-and-marriage carriages again.

FOOTNOTE

1 On the other hand, life was spectacularly fair to Zeppo in comparison to the way it treated
  Gummo. Gummo was the fifth Marx Brother, and never got into any of the films at all. His

real name was Milton and perhaps the contrast between sharing a name with the most humourless of English poets and being a comedian was too much for him. Not, of course, that Milton was completely without humour. Writing a poem to the glory of God in which the Devil comes out as being a really neat guy and God as an utter bore is a pretty good joke for starters.

BARBARA & FRANK SINATRA

Despite all her obvious charms and virtues, who knows whether even Barbara would have been able to tame Frank in his old wild days. She is really the living proof of the adage almost proved in this book that if you want a peaceful and happy marriage with a famous sex object, *catch him when he's old*. Right from the very beginning, and Henry VIII with solid old Catherine Parr, through to Clark Gable's final wife, Kay Spreckels, and old Humphrey lighting upon young Lauren, that's the way it's been. As Gable said: 'I've raised my share of hell in my time. Now I'm more interested in raising children'.[1]

Frankie and Barbara had a pleasant and dignified courtship, dating for three years before they married, and now they have been married for ten happy years. The only slight cross that Barbara has to bear is that every birthday Frank will insist on sitting in the living room and singing 'True Love', even though his voice ain't quite what it used to be. But then, every birthday each of us ain't what we used to be, so why should Frank be different?

FRANK SINATRA	
Born	**1915, in America.**
Occupation	**Singer (greatest living), actor.**
Hobbies	**Toy trains, rogering, and consorting with . . . no, doesn't matter.**
Distinguishing Features	**Blue Eyes.**
Romantically Linked With[2]	**Angie Dickinson, Dorothy Provine, Juliet Prowse, Jill St John, Natalie Wood, Marilyn Maxwell, Lana Turner, Judy Garland, Anita Ekberg, Donna Reed, Marilyn Monroe, Kim Novak, Lauren Bacall, Carol White, Nancy Sinatra (m), Ava Gardner (m), Mia Farrow (m), Barbara Marx (m).**

When we see the old sweet man with soft hair and a tuxedo that's clearly the only piece of clothing he now possesses, it is sometimes easy to forget that Sinatra was the first great pop star, the one the girls in bobby socks mobbed, the great sex symbol of his time.[3] Thus it was his duty to date around, and as can be seen from the list, he did as he oughta have done. Exactly how much is a controversial question, but the controversy is only about degree: Frank once said: 'I like broads, but if I did half the things they say, I'd be in a jar in Harvard University'. On the other hand, Dean Martin observed: 'When he dies, they are giving his zipper to the Smithsonian Institute'.

One thing is for certain, Frank has always been startlingly desirable—'I shiver up and down my spine when I hear you sing', said one fan, 'just like when I had scarlet fever'. But he has also been pretty difficult: an anonymous lover said: 'He's the kind of man every woman desires, but can't stand for more than five minutes'. The much less anonymous Ava Gardner has already observed: 'It was always great in bed. But the quarrelling always started on the way to the bidet'. Which must have been very disappointing, as presumably one of the main reasons for sleeping with Frank Sinatra is to hear him sing in the shower afterwards: and if he's in a grump, little hope there.

But bad side or no, Frank is one of the great rogerers, an invaluable contributor to this book, spanning the generations as he has, and slugging it out with Clark Gable for the Ryan O'Neal Award for the Rogerer of His Generation. A legend himself, he has been linked with more legends than anyone else in this book. Since he has always been the greatest of all the bedroom singers, he has surely deserved it if, over the years, a fair share of dames have said to themselves, in the words of Lorenz Hart,

> *I'll sing to him*
> *Each spring to him,*
> *Worship the trousers that cling to him.*

Or to put it even more graphically, it could be that Frank's motto was summed up years ago in the startlingly frank opening lines of the great Van Heusen–Kahn song, 'All the Way', which make Frankie Goes to Hollywood seem tame . . .

> *When somebody loves you,*
> *It's no good unless he loves you,*
> *All the Way.*
> *Happy to be near you*
> *When you need someone to cheer you*
> *All the Way.*

(wait for it . . .)

> *Taller than the tallest tree is,*
> *That's how it's got to feel.*
> *Deeper than the deep blue sea is,*
> *That how deep it goes, if it's real.*

Phew.

FOOTNOTES

1 See Appendix: Age Differences and Rogering.
2 It's quite a list, but obviously we wouldn't stick by any of them if Frank wanted to argue: it's a good idea to be polite to Frank: 'If people are polite to me, I am. They shouldn't try to get away with not being polite'.
3 There was once a nine-year theory; 1945, Frank Sinatra; 1954, Elvis Presley; 1963, the Beatles: this broke down, tragically, when 1972 came and went and it was the Bay City Rollers and Gary Glitter to choose between.

FRANK SINATRA & MIA FARROW

The most notable thing about this relationship was its end. Nothing so ill became Frank as the leaving of it.[1] Mia was sitting on the set of *Rosemary's Baby* one day (bad enough having to be the Devil's Mum without extra hassle) when her husband's lawyer appeared with some papers to sign. Mia was just about to oblige, assuming they were stocks, or shares, or something to do with garbage disposal, when she noticed that they were divorce papers. A few minutes later Roman Polanski found her 'sobbing like a two-year-old' and no longer Frank Sinatra's wife.

Frank, that wasn't nice, and you would do well to have a quick sing through 'Tell Me On A Sunday' for some idea of how it should have been done.[2]

MIA FARROW	
Born	**1945, in England.**
Occupation	**Actress.**
Hobby	**Hiding.**
Romantically Linked With	**Frank Sinatra (m), Woody Allen, Leslie Briscusse, Andre Previn (m), Ryan O'Neal.**
Nickname	**Mama Mia.**

Mia Farrow first started acting with the Royal Shakespeare Company, and perhaps it was there that she first heard the line 'If music be the food of love, play on' that was so profoundly to influence her life. Because throughout her life, Mia sure has been inclined to 'play'[3] when music was on. In Andre Previn, Frank Sinatra and Leslie Briscusse (who wrote the musicals *Charly Girl* and *Dr Doolittle*), she covered a huge range of modern popular music. And now she lives with Woody Allen, one of the best two hundred clarinettists in New York.

After those early RSC days, Mia went to America and, like Ryan O'Neal, became famous in *Peyton Place*. This was followed by some pretty rocky movies, with the exception of *Rosemary's Baby*,[4] before she started to work with Woody Allen. Those who admire her wonder at the translucent innocence and radiance of her face: what was once said of Nicol Williamson is even more true of her: when she acts it is as though she has one layer of skin missing, so much do her emotions and vulnerability shine out.

In real life, though, the word on the street is that she may not be all that vulnerable: she says her favourite occupation today is 'sneaking around and following people, bugging people and being a witness to crimes'.

When she isn't watching Woody committing crimes round the back of the house, Mia spends much of her time taking care of her seven children—four of them adopted: hence her nickname, Mama Mia.

FOOTNOTES

1 See Appendix: Great Rogering Excuses.
2 There has been some alarm about the amount of rogering of apes in this book: see Eastwood and Clive—'he's a sloppy kisser', Stewart Granger and Deborah Kerr—'We should never have come down out of that tree' and Ekland and Sellers—'His hairy cladded chest did much to perpetuate the arguments of mankind's evolution from the gorilla'. The otherwise sensitive 'Tell Me on a Sunday'—a lovely song about parting that Frank should have heeded—provides yet another frightening and unexpected example of this widespread perversion. It starts beautifully . . .

> Don't write a letter when you want to leave
> Don't call me at 3 a.m. from a friend's apartment,
> I'd like to choose
> How I hear the news.
> Take me to a park that's covered with trees,
> Tell me on a Sunday, please.

(continues well . . .)

> Let me down easy,
> No big song and dance,
> No long faces, no long looks,
> No deep conversation.
> I know the way we should spend that day . . .

(then suddenly . . . quite inexplicably, we're back with rogering apes . . .)

> Take me to a zoo that's got chimpanzees,
> Tell me on a Sunday, please.

What have these apes got?
3 See Appendix: Names for Rogering.
4 The mention of *Rosemary's Baby* brings up another subject that is very important: *rogering the Devil*. Unfortunately, none of the people in this book admit to having officially rogered the Devil, so there is a lack of first-hand experience, but there are some accepted guidelines about what to do should you ever be put in a position where you might have to service the Lord of Darkness.

First, it seems most likely that when the Devil rogers you, he is not the Devil at all, but some dreadful creep from Cornwall pretending to be the Devil in order to get more sex. This normally occurs at the climax of a frantic sex orgy, when more people from Cornwall, and perhaps one or two people with weekend houses in Cornwall, all dance around, worship the

Devil and take their clothes off. You will normally be able to spot this situation because everyone except you has horrible bodies: that is the reason why they go through all this ridiculous mumbo-jumbo: it's the only way they can get sex with anyone with a half-decent figure. You will normally be able to spot the 'Devil' because he is the most disgusting and has the horriblest figure. He is usually the local darts champion. When the time comes for the rogering, therefore, you must be unafraid and simply think up a good excuse for getting out of it and leave: 'Sorry, I must get home before the babysitter goes' is not a bad excuse.

You may *on the other hand* find that you are actually being rogered by the Devil himself. Because he is unpopular on Earth, and therefore shy, the Devil normally tries to roger you while you are asleep. In this instance, you will wake up thinking, 'O God, I've got a tummy ache', and find that you are *in coitu Beelzeebubbi*. You will be able to recognize the Devil because he is red, and has two large horns. What you must not do at this point is get into any kind of religious discussion, which is obviously one's natural reaction on meeting the Devil. ('What's God really like?' 'Is Hell as bad as it's made out?', 'Was Eve good in the sack?', 'All right, so I know what happened in Sodom, but Gomorrah: what was that all about?') This kind of time-wasting can only lead to impregnation by the Satanic seed and that leads to all kind of hassle. The thing to do, therefore, is to say, 'O God, it must be a bad dream: I thought I was being rogered by the Devil, but surely the Lord of All Sinful Doings would be better in bed than this horny little red guy'. Nobody, least of all the Master of All Vanity can take this kind of pressure *in coitu*, and you can be positive he'll make a quick withdrawal and zip off to Hell and torture some Nazis a bit to restore his pride.

Thirdly, however, we must consider what to do if you don't wake up during the Satanic rogering, and find three months later that you are bearing the Devil's child. There is, unfortunately, no easy answer to this dilemma, which has been disgracefully ignored in most maternity literature. The truth is, if you bear Satan's baby, you must face the fact that you are bound to have special troubles with your little boy. He will undoubtedly be a bully at school and will probably eat or torture your other children when he gets home. The only thing you can do is bring him up with all the love in the world—(while trying not to ram Christianity down his throat—it would only give him an inferiority complex)—and hope that he finally finds a job suiting his particular talents. It might be worth considering tag-wrestling.

MIA FARROW & WOODY ALLEN

Nearing the end of the comedy line, which, faster than the speed of laughter, has moved from one of the least to one of the greatest of comedians, we come slap bang against the question: Will rogering a comedian make me funny? The answer, as supplied by this notable roger is: Yes. Before meeting Woody, Mia was not famed for her comic skill—now in *Zelig*, *Broadway Danny Rose* and *The Purple Rose of Cairo*, she is, comically speaking, the real McCoy. If you are at a dinner party, therefore, and depressed by your lack of anecdotes, you would be well advised to make a pass at the most amusing person at the table.

If you are a woman and you haven't been listening enough to find out who is funny, then it is safest to sleep with anyone who is:

1 Called Norman Wisdom.

2 Small, short and Jewish—this takes in Woody Allen, Mel Brooks and Groucho Marx.

3 6 foot 5 inches tall—most English comedians are 6 foot 5 inches tall—Douglas Adams, Galton and Simpson (authors of *Steptoe* and *Hancock*), Muir and Norden, Peter Cook and John Cleese are all this height.

WOODY ALLEN

Real Name	**Allen Stewart Konigsberg.**
Born	**1935, in Brooklyn, America.**
Occupation	**Stand-up comedian, screen writer, actor, director.**
Hobby	**Psychoanalysis.**
Distinguishing Features	**'I'm a short skinny red-haired Jewish guy from Brooklyn with lousy eyesight'.**
Romantically Linked With	**Diane Keaton, Mia Farrow.**
Nickname	**Woody Allen.**

Every possible amusing extrapolation from the life of Woody Allen has been made by Woody Allen himself, and most of the amusing comments about sex have been made by him too, for sex—'the most fun I've had without laughing'—and himself have been the central subjects of this films. Death has also been a big subject—'I don't want to achieve immortality through my work—I want to achieve it through not dying', he once said, and the many people who believe him the finest film-maker alive hope that his wish comes true.

In case it doesn't, though, people have recently been keen to catch a glimpse of Woody before he dies, and a legend has grown up that if you want to see him, you have only to go to Michael's Pub in New York and there he will be, playing his clarinet. So, many people go, and sure enough, he isn't there. They are naturally a little angry, but should not be. There could be no more important lesson that one could learn from actually talking to Woody Allen

than the lesson that you learn when you go all the way to New York, pay for an expensive meal in a restaurant and then after waiting all night for the music to come on, discover he isn't there.

The lesson is: real life is full of disappointments. Stay home and have sex instead.

THE COMEDIANS LAY LINE

ZEPPO MARX

BARBARA SINATRA

FRANK SINATRA

MIA FARROW

WOODY ALLEN

Let Woody Allen have the final helpful word. 'Sex between two people is a wonderful thing. If you manage to get between the right two people'.

AMERICA RAMPANT

FROM	**WALLIS SIMPSON, DUCHESS**
	OF WINDSOR
TO	**SYLVESTER STALLONE**
IN	**15 ROGERS**

Though not at first apparent because of a difference in physique and chest size, the similarities between Mrs Simpson and Mr Stallone are immense. Mrs Simpson came from America to liberate Edward VIII from his English strait-jacket. Stallone as Rambo was also in the business of liberating—and both, in doing the job they came for, wreaked untold havoc upon the victim countries. And again, Mrs Simpson knocked out the top guy in Britain, and took his title away: *exactly* what Rocky has been doing throughout his illustrious career.

They are both classic examples of *America Rampant*, and a lot of rampant Americans, including perhaps the three greatest lovers of our time, help bring them together in the rogering bout of the century.

WALLIS SIMPSON

Born	**1897, in America.**
Occupation	**Wife/mistress. i.e. Official Rogerer.**
Romantically Linked With	**Earl Spencer, Ernest Simpson, Edward VIII.**
Married	**Earl Spencer, Ernest Simpson, Edward VIII.**
Divorced	**Earl Spencer. *Reason*: He was an alcoholic sadistic wife beater. Ernest Simpson. *Reason*: (1) He was very boring. (2) His first name was Mr rather than King.**
Distinguishing Features	**Crown on head (just around the house, when no one was looking).**
Nickname	**The woman I love.**

Wallis Simpson was at the very centre of one of the great love stories and love mysteries of our time. At first glance, she is a strange figure to occupy that position. At second glance she is too. This strange stick insect of a woman looks more like a harsh aunt with some horrid medicine concealed behind her back, than a glamorous doll worth chucking in a kingdom for.

It was perhaps this unprepossessing look which led the British public not to rally around her, as had been their wont in that earlier case of constitutional promiscuity, the trial of Caroline of Brunswick.

So where did Wallis go wrong?

1 *Her breasts*: Wallis' breasts were definitely not large enough. Nothing puts the British in a better mood than a nice large pair of breasts. They find them friendly. A large pair of breasts is what they expect of a good time girl, happy bubbly things, always poking their noses out of the low cut dresses. Wallis Simpson, in contrast, had breasts that were always a good five inches below her high buttoned frocks, and one always had the suspicion that even if they were to put in a public appearance, they might have been rather disappointing and unfriendly.

2 *Her name*: 'Mrs Simpson' as a name is again completely against the spirit of what the public want out of a royal mistress. If the king is going to have a mistress, the public want a pretty cheeky one with suspenders and bloomers and a name made for headlines: *Koo Stark* (Koo Starkers!—Koo-er!, etc.) and *Nell Gwyn* (Not on Your Nelly!—Gwyn Flagrante Delicto!!!!) had the right idea. There is no doubt that had Mrs Simpson been Nellie Naked she would have been queen.

3 *Her swimming costume*: There was always a chance everyone would change their minds, and invite Wallis and Edward back, perhaps to rule in turns with George and Mary. This chance was unfortunately blown by the famous swimming costume episode, when Wallis, in the very thick of the Second World

War, contacted the American Ambassador in Paris to send her a swimming suit because she found herself in the South of France without the nile green one she wanted. What was so rash about this was not the tactlessness of it— it *is* annoying when you set off on holiday and forget your favourite swimsuit, and you never *can* find anything half-decent in those resort shops. No, Wallis's big mistake here was the missed opportunity—why didn't she just throw caution to the winds and take the plunge in an obviously ill-fitting swimming top? There is no doubt that within seconds she could have been photographed with her playful little cherries popping out to taste the breeze—and within days she would have been back on the throne where she belonged.

The second crucial question with Wallis Simpson is therefore:

Where did she go right with Edward? Taking into account all the above negatives, what was it that attracted the King of England to this strange American lady enough to make him give up his kingdom for her?

And the answer is: no one knows. Two major theories have been put forward:

1 It was Something Mysterious to Do with Sex.

2 It was Love, in all its strange and mysterious and wondrous blindness.

It is up to every reader to choose which theory he/she believes. The answer may reveal something to him/her about him/her that he/she didn't know.

EDWARD VIII & MRS SIMPSON

Obviously any close inquiry into this roger, which is one of the Rogers That Changed the World, will tend to prejudice the crucial question asked above,

whether it was love or sex which was at the heart of this affair. Therefore let discretion be the better part of book-writing, and no comment be made about the roger at all.[1,2,3,4,5]

EDWARD VIII	
Born	**1894, in England.**
Occupation	**Being Prince, being King, being Duke of Windsor.**
Hobbies	**Gadding about, rogering, and wondering if he did the right thing.**
Distinguishing Features	**Head that looked as though it ought to have a crown on it.**
Romantically Linked With	**Thelma Furness, Wallis Simpson (m).**
Nickname	**A Boy.**

Edward, called David, was a man who was a prince and then was a king and then wasn't a king any longer, but a duke instead. His story was made into a lovely television series starring Edward Fox and Cynthia Harris, which was directed by Waris Hussein and won a lot of awards quite rightly.

What he did, he did for love. Or thought he did, which is much the same thing.

FOOTNOTES

1 On the other hand, just in case you're one of the ones who *did* think it was Something Mysterious to Do with Sex, and not Love at all, here are a few signs of what could certainly be construed to be a *most peculiar rogering situation*.

2 The Wallis/Edward letters are full of the most extraordinary love-talk: most interesting is the word 'drowsel', that seems to refer to something halfway between a roger and a nice afternoon rest—which does not bode well for a good sex life. On the other hand, after referring to themselves as a boy and a girl, Wallis and Edward refer to parts of themselves as 'him' and 'her'. 'He will be missing her as much as we will each other'—which bodes a little better.

3 It is absolutely none of anyone's business, and that's why it's in a footnote, but one of Edward's friends referred to him as having 'the smallest pecker I have ever seen'.*

4 Also, it has been claimed from reliable sources, that Edward was impotent and a homosexual. None of these things are either of great interest, or provable.** The only point is that, if Edward did have some problems, Wallis seems to have solved them.

5 In short, the unromantic version of their story says that he was infatuated with her and gave up the throne for her, and had no choice, because of his sexual peculiarities. She, on the other hand, would dearly have liked him to hold on as king and would have preferred a crown, or at least a small tiara, to a roger any time. Certainly her letters don't reveal her as being at all passionate about him, but then she didn't need to be cured of homosexuality,

impotence and fear of the letter 'p'. Whatever, when all is said and done, Wallis and Edward stuck together, faithful till the last, bound together by fate and whatever that other thing was.

*As with Wallis' breasts, it is a point of principle here at Faber and Faber that size is not important. This principle was originally developed to defend small but perfectly formed books of poetry which would otherwise be condemned as being 'a little slight' but it also applies to private parts.
**The *Daily Mail* handwriting expert has claimed that proof of Edward's homosexuality can be found in the way he formed the letter 'p'—a tell-tale phallic symbol which speaks about a person's sex-life. There may be something in this—in writing his own name, Edward, Duke of Windsor, it is noticeable that he *leaves out the letter 'p' entirely.*

EDWARD VIII & THELMA FURNESS

Thelma Furness was one of the convenient and well-picked happily married girls who kept Edward happy before he met Wallis. They went to Africa together, and made happy love in various tents in various Commonwealth territories. Those who think that Edward should have stuck with that type would, however, do well to pay some attention to the small print of this relationship. The two kept teddy bears, which they exchanged whenever they were apart, and he called her Toodles and she called his willy (after a cartoon) The Tower of London. Another cartoon in France describing the 'fairy like Venetian nights' was lifted by a British newspaper who associated the remark with Edward—'our Prince of Wales is even more so'.[1]

THELMA FURNESS	
Occupation	**Social butterfly and tracer of inheritances.**
Hobby	**Spending inheritances and rogering.**
Romantically Linked With	**Lord Marmaduke Furness (m), Aly Khan, The Prince of Wales (later Edward VIII).**
Nickname	**Toodles.**

Thelma Furness was called Vanderbilt but then she tracked down Marmaduke and his £20 million inheritance, and promptly changed her name. She did, however, not really change her behaviour, as she and Marmy both took a casual attitude to their marriage, leaving her free to begin a famous affair with the Prince of Wales. Had it continued, Edward might never have fallen into the arms of Wallis Simpson, but while away from him, Thelma had another famous affair, this time with Aly Khan. Hearing of it, Edward dropped her like a brick. We should, however, not blame Thelma too much: had they married, Queen Thelma would have been quite as ridiculous as Queen Wallis.

FOOTNOTE

1 Apologies: this sentence is a complex transpositional misprint, and makes no sense whatsoever.

THELMA FURNESS & ALY KHAN

Aly met Thelma Furness on the night before she was due to sail back to London from America. Aly begged her to stay. She, good girl, refused and left, but found her cabin on board ship filled with red roses and a note pleading undying love. Two days later, she received a phone call asking her to come to dinner. It was Aly, who had secretly boarded the liner to be with her.

ALY KHAN	
Occupation	**Playboy.**
Hobby	**Rogering.**
Distinguishing Features	**Another guy's gal on his arm.**
Romantically Linked With	**Gene Tierney, Yvonne de Carlo, Kim Novak, Joan Fontaine, Rita Hayworth (m), Thelma Furness, Joan Guinness (m), Simone Bodin (m), the Duchess of Argyll.**

Aly Khan was the son of the Aga Khan, the spiritual leader of the world's twelve million Ismaelis, and should himself have been Aga Khan in turn. But when his father hired an Indian mystic to educate his young son, the man's job was not to tutor him in the details of Ismaeli law with particular reference to the Aga Khan's duties, but rather in the details of love-making with particular reference to how to hold back orgasms. Aly was a good and conscientious student, and when he later found that he also possessed limitless charm, he launched into a life of making love.

Aly was a classic, oriental chauvinist, and appealed to that streak in women that wants to roger mysterious desert princes (see Jane Digby and Viviane Ventura). But unlike many a real desert prince, all camels and kaftans and perplexing odours, he also had a smooth veneer of Western education that made him the perfect guest for the drawing rooms, and bedrooms, of high society girls.

His style and romantic success were legendary. He was named as a co-respondent in the divorce case of Mrs Joel Guinness, who he then married. After that he convinced Rita Hayworth to divorce Orson Welles and marry him instead. He then left Rita and rogered Joan Fontaine, before finally finding the 'wife of his heart' Simone Bodin.

However, by now, fate had struck its second cruellest blow. It transpired that Aly's father was not a believer in vocational education and all the stuff with the orgasm at the beginning was not meant to be career-training at all. Aly was passed over in the succession, and his brother became Aga Khan— it was thought that expending so much time on the physical needs of attractive women, Aly might not have enough left to dedicate to the spiritual needs of the twelve million Ismaelis.[1]

The cruellest blow fate struck him was killing him in a car crash in 1960.

FOOTNOTE

1 Quite what useful function the training of racehorses and Derby winners, a major duty of the present Aga, has to do with the Ismaelis' welfare is, however, also a bit perplexing. Presumably it is something symbolic: breeding Derby winners is a symbol for the Aga's efforts to lead his people to the front of the spiritual field, to make them first across the line in the great race to heaven, hardly sweating at all when they reach the paddock.

ALY KHAN & RITA HAYWORTH

Aly and Rita were introduced by mutual friends in the south of France, and such was the success of the ensuing rogering that Rita, in a fit of optimism about things lasting for ever,[1] divorced Orson Welles and married Aly instead. The marriage also got off to a big bang: at the wedding, a thousand turtles were dispatched across a swimming pool with lighted candles on their backs.[2] However, when the relationship got past the preliminary scalded-turtle stage, it started to fall apart fast. Rita wanted to settle down and live a family life, which was not at all what Aly had expected—as Rita's first husband had said: 'Who'd marry Rita for her cooking?' Eventually Aly got so bored by Rita's refusal to join him on his gallivanting that he went off and rogered someone else. And that was it. Rita, sweet-hearted thing, was very sad: 'Leaving Aly was almost unbearable'.

RITA HAYWORTH

Real Name	**Margarita Carmen Cansino[3].**
Born	**1918, in America.**
Occupation	**Actress.**
Hobbies	**Cooking and rogering.**
Distinguishing Features	**Divine Red Hair.**
Romantically Linked With	**Dick Haymes (m), Aly Khan (m), Orson Welles (m), Ed Judson (m), James Hill (m),[4] Victor Mature, David Niven, Howard Hughes.**
Nickname	**The Love Goddess.**

Love Goddess of the forties, Rita Hayworth, 5 feet 6 inches, 36-inch bust and 35-inch hips, love-bombed her way through gorgeous roles in movies like *Pal Joey, Cover Girl, Gilda* and *The Lady From Shanghai*. Her time as a star was the epitome of glamour: in one year she had her face, the one that launched a thousand turtles, on the cover of twenty-three leading magazines.

And yet, Rita Hayworth was a classic example of just how like the shallow end of a swimming pool all Hollywood glamour is. When she first arrived at the studio, she was judged imperfect: her hair-line was raised with electrolysis, and her slightly less divine hair was actually dyed that final divine red. Whenever people got to know her, she thought they were disappointed. 'Men would go to bed with Gilda, and wake to find they were only with me'.

Even so, there is no need to get too gloomy here: people pretended Rita was a dumb redhead, but she wasn't that dumb. When an unfriendly interviewer asked her what it was like to wake up every morning and face herself in the mirror, she replied: 'That's a problem I don't have, honey. I never get up till the afternoon'. And later on, with a quip that is almost the motto of this book, she observed, *'Why have an impulse if you can't act on it?'*

FOOTNOTES

1 See Appendix: Marriage, Weddings and Wedding Nights.
2 Candles often seem to pop up in questions of sex. Candlelight is supposed to be the ideal light for love-making, and one noted female singer is known to have carried one round in her handbag, to be taken out and lit when necessary.
3 This is a strange example of the reverse of changing your name to something exotic: what could be more glamorous than Margarita Carmen Cansino? See Appendix: Mad Producers.
4 Rita in the end married five times and once starred in the interestingly titled film: *Fire Down Below*. (See Appendix: Marriage, Weddings and Wedding Nights.)

RITA HAYWORTH & ORSON WELLES

One of Hollywood's most glamorous matches while it lasted, Rita finally broke it all off with the immortal words: 'I adore enormous men . . . but I just can't take his genius any more'.

ORSON WELLES	
Born	**1915, in America.**
Occupation	**Actor/Writer/Director/Raconteur/Genius/ Producer/Voice-over artiste extraordinaire.**
Hobby	**Talking in a deep voice about Carlsberg.**[1]
Distinguishing Features	**Made the most distinguished features in the history of the movies.**
Romantically Linked With	**Rita Hayworth (m), Virginia Welles (m), Marilyn Monroe, Judy Garland, Eartha Kitt, Paola Welles (m).**
Nickname	**Awesome.**

Orson Welles frightened nearly everyone throughout his life either by his physical size, or by the size of his genius. He started doing it at the age of eighteen months: a doctor came in to look at him in his cot, and Orson, baby teeth not even pushed through, observed in casual conversational tone, 'The desire to take up medicine is one of the greatest features which distinguishes men from the animals'. The doctor fled.

Orson continued as precociously as he had begun—his theatre company, with its all black *Othello*, was a startling success—his radio broadcast of *The War of the Worlds* spread panic throughout the nation—and when he came to Hollywood to make a film, he made the greatest film ever, *Citizen Kane*: it was epic, exquisite, satirical, and cheeky as hell: Rosebud, the name of the most famous sleigh in history, also happened to be the name Randolph Hearst reserved for the pudenda of his mistress, Marion Davies.

This is not the place to survey is what happened to Welles and his movies throughout the rest of his life.[2] What it is is the place to survey is whether or not the sex in his life was as grand, daring and magnificent as everything else he did; whether, since Orson spent all his life being merrily fucked around by movie-makers, he merrily fucked around a bit in turn. And the answer is, yes. He was big, but he was lovely—he was *that* fat, because he needed *that much* space to do all that living in. His energy was enormous: a secretary once said—'You didn't get one night stands with Orson: you got afternoon stands, before dinner stands, after dinner stands'.

And he could be pretty flash as well. Once, he invited a girl outside to show her a card trick. She chose a card, looked at it, and then put it back in the pack. Orson then told her to look up in the sky. At which moment, a plane shot by: flying behind it was an enormous flag carrying the design of the chosen card. Pretty awesome.[3]

FOOTNOTES

1 Orson also talked in a deep voice about other things and his most famous unconsummated sexual experience occurred during a recording of a radio advert for peas. In the course of the recording, an increasingly testy Orson was asked by the director whether he could put a little more feeling into the word 'June'. Orson exploded and offered to come up into the control box and give the director a blow-job if he could demonstrate just how you do put more expression into the word 'June'. The visual image of Orson up in that production box on his knees is quite mind-boggling—but no sound on the tape implies that it actually took place.

2 The place to survey that is in front of a television playing a cassette of the BBC's magnificent *Omnibus* interview with Orson Welles—a huge, grand work of art in itself—Welles summing up with consummate wit and seriousness the progress of his life through some of the finest films, and some of the most chaotic, ever made.

3 See Appendix: Pulling Techniques and Pick-up Lines.

ORSON WELLES & MARILYN MONROE

This romantic linking is notable for uniting two of the century's most famous plumpies. It also raises the question of whether there are certain experiences which, once experienced, leave you with no right to complain about anything else for the rest of your life. Certainly Orson Welles' bearing during the later years of his life, merry, witty and uncomplaining—despite the fact that he, greatest living director, somehow never directed any films—seems to confirm that there *are* such perfect experiences and sleeping with Marilyn Monroe is one of them.

MARILYN MONROE

(Marilyn's full biography is in the Once and Future Kings line.)

It is meet and right that Marilyn should appear in this line as well, sandwiched between two great symbols of America, Simpson and Stallone, and in the company of the greatest singing rogerer, Sinatra, and the greatest acting rogerer, Ryan O'Neal. In a line with so much vintage Americana, the editors only regret that they were unable to find a niche for Uncle Sam, Mickey Mouse and E.T. If anyone does know of any sexual details of the lives of these three great honorary American citizens, we would be most grateful to hear. Confidentiality will, as always, be respected.

MARILYN MONROE & FRANK SINATRA

Marilyn is said to have had a short affair with Frank Sinatra and to have been 'delighted' by his sexual techniques. It is nice to think of Marilyn having a happy time with men—the last time she featured in a lay line, between Robert and John Kennedy, she was anything but happy.

It is curious to think of such a major sex symbol being otherwise than totally happy and successful with men. If plain, divorced, unpopular Wallis Simpson could get the King of England against everyone's wishes *and keep him*, why did gorgeous adored Marilyn Monroe have so much trouble holding on to men? Perhaps it is a question of determination and self-confidence, something which Wallis had, and poor Marilyn did not.

Fortunately, our present sex-queen, Madonna, is happily married to Sean Penn, the 'coolest guy in the universe'—but it is interesting to think what she could have done with all her determination and self-confidence had she really put her mind to it. Prince Andrew and Madonna is a lovely idea, and would have done no end of good for Anglo-Puerto Rican relations, to mention nothing of the boost it would have given to church unity: the son of the Head of the Church of England marrying one of the three top people in the Catholic hierarchy.

FRANK SINATRA

(For full biography, see the Comedians line.)

As a lay line rogerer, Frank Sinatra is the male equivalent of Ava Gardner, whom, of course, he had his fair share of dealings with. Not even Ryan O'Neal, the Greatest Living Rogerer, is responsible for forming so many links in so many lines. Frank's secret is partly, of course, that he is older than Ryan and his rogering therefore spans the generations with more ease. No doubt when Ryan is Frank's age, he will be spawning thousands upon thousands of new lines—that is, if he doesn't continue in the rather alarming current trend of abandoning wide range random rogering altogether in favour of spawning babies with Farrah Fawcett.

FRANK SINATRA & JILL ST JOHN

Jill is one of the many of Frank's women who have complained that part of his sexual technique is the insistence on singing his own songs to prospective rogerees. This used to be a charming and romantic habit. But recently it has become more difficult: the truth is that nowadays the Nelson Riddle recordings of Frank's songs are so much finer than his own voice. This is difficult. He is left with three lines of attack:

1 He can sit holding the woman's hand and looking into her eyes, nodding in agreement with the record whenever it expresses a particularly worthy sentiment.

2 He can leave the room, and put the record player on in the next room, thus pretending that it is actually him singing.

3 Worst of all, he can mime to the record, pretending it is one of those ones, like in the back of Japanese taxis, with just the backing track.

Any which way, it works out all right—in the old days, it was the singing that got the girls to bed. Nowadays, the singing is so technically difficult to orchestrate, that the girls just go to bed to avoid all the hassle.

JILL ST JOHN

Born	**1941, in England.**
Occupation	**Actress.**
Hobby	**Chess.**
Distinguishing Features	**Red hair.**
Romantically Linked With	**Robert Wagner, Lance Reventlow (m), Neil Dubin (m), Jack Jones (m), Henry Kissinger, Frank Sinatra.**

Jill's most famous statement on the subject of her love life is one of the most dangerous statements a woman could have made: 'Give me an ugly man with a fabulous mind'. It makes things very difficult for everyone. If you're good looking and she goes out with you, it means that you're stupid. And if you're clever and she goes out with you, it means that you're ugly. It is no wonder that all the men in her life have run into hard times. Jack Jones hasn't sung a note in tune for years, Robert Wagner's *Hart to Hart* has been slipping in the ratings, and if anyone ever knew who Lance Reventlow was in the first place, they sure don't now.

The only person who would have been at ease with the comment is Henry Kissinger, who knows he's ugly and does have a fabulous mind. Certainly Jill was sweet about him: 'I enjoyed playing chess with Henry Kissinger more than with Sean Connery.[1] I don't know why. He's just more fun to play with'.[2] So much for Connery: great chest, terrible chess.

It is, however, for her performance with Connery in *Diamonds Are Forever* that Jill St John is most remembered.[3] Many experts believe she was the most intelligent and ballsiest of all the Bond heroines.[4]

FOOTNOTES

1 See Appendix: Names for Rogering.
2 See Appendix: Names for Rogering.
3 In the context of Jill St John and the James Bond films, it is high time to look at an important category.
Rogering Saints
   Apart from Jill St John the clearest modern example of the Rogering Saint is Roger Moore. He played the Saint for seven years, and certainly at least his wives, Doorn Van Steyn, Dorothy Squires, and Louisa Mattioli have all been rogered by Roger.* However, such achievements pall in the face of famous rogering saints of the past. Most notable of all was Pope John Paul XII, who died in 963 AD. At his trial before his death, he—and remember, this guy is Pope—was accused of 'sacrilege, simony, perjury, adultery and incest'. His sister, sister-in-law, two abbesses and countless religious sisters had fallen to his libido. *Nevertheless*, soon after his death he was canonized and became St John Lutheran, patron saint of little sick children.**

4 See Andrew Rissik's excellent *The James Bond Man* for a startlingly intelligent view of the Bond films—he points out that Jill is particularly good in the petrol station scene.

*Along with Roger Moore, see other Orange People—Sarah Ferguson and George Hamilton.
This very end bit isn't true, although the rest is. St John Lutheran is in fact patron Saint of Sacrilege, Simony, Perjury, Adultery and Incest. If you ever, for instance, want to commit adultery, or sleep with an aunt, or roger someone called Simon, you pray to St John, and he will help you achieve your desires. Then he'll send you to Hell for your pains.*
***A lot of people ask: 'Hell sounds a pretty sexy place—why shouldn't we all aim for there instead of Heaven?'

Well, this is a tricky question. Certainly all the greatest rogerers are in Hell and it's pretty hot and steamy so no one wears any clothes. Added to which, there's no sick, sordid vice that someone isn't an expert on.

On the other hand, there are drawbacks:

a Once you roger someone you're stuck with them not just for a week, or until your wife or husband finds out, but *for eternity*.
b After sex you have to spend years and years with your partner moaning on and on and on about his/her problems: 'I'm in Hell for ever, you see, and all I did was get my sister to . . .'
c You have to wait years to get your turn on the bidet.

So, on balance, it is better to go to Heaven, where there isn't much sex, but on the other hand, the sheets are clean, there's lots of pretty music, and Marilyn Monroe walks around topless because she's been told no one there has impure thoughts.

JILL ST JOHN & ROBERT WAGNER

This is an on-going romance, but has had all sorts of troubles since Jill described Robert as 'the handsomest man I've ever seen'. Read on . . .

ROBERT WAGNER

Born	1930, in America.
Occupation	Actor.
Hobbies	Marrying Natalie Wood.
Distinguishing Features	The Handsomest Man in the World, *or* The Third Handsomest Man in the World.
Romantically Linked With	Jill St John.
Married	Marion Marshall,[1] Natalie Wood, Natalie Wood again.

It was bad enough for Robert Wagner when Jill St John described him as 'the handsomest man in the world', having just announced that she liked men who were ugly and clever. But what made things for him truly unbearable was that shortly afterwards a tv poll voted Wagner only the Third Most Handsome Man in the World. The inevitable uncertainty and confusion that this caused would have disturbed the mind of the most solid of gents, let alone a sensitive actor who has delighted tv audiences for years with his performances in *It Takes a Thief, Colditz* and *Hart to Hart*. Every morning he would wake up, look in the mirror and say to himself: 'Is this the face of the Most Handsome Man in the World, or of just the Third Most Handsome Man in the World?'

The pressure eventually got the better of Robert: a newspaper recently reported that he turned up one day and gave a piglet to Jill St John telling her, slightly illogically, to go out and buy herself a ring. She did. It cost a quarter of a million pounds. Robert is now said to be in a state of shock.[2,3]

FOOTNOTES

1 Marion Marshall must not be confused with Marion Morrison, better known as John Wayne. This unfortunately happened in one recent biography of Robert Wagner. The biography in question: *Robert and John, the Whole Sordid Truth* foundered badly on the misunderstanding, and its argument, that Robert Wagner was the second most famous homosexual of the century, the first being John Wayne himself, didn't really hold up, once the mistake had been spotted. Wagner and Wayne *did* meet, and they did get on well, but the whole idea of them thinking about settling down and starting a family, either through adoption, or Robert having an operation, never came up.

2 Which either made him more good looking because more rugged, or less good looking because more haggard. The vicious circle of indecision thus continued.

3 Robert Wagner's uncertainty raises the question, reader, of How Decisive Are You? A decisiveness quiz.

You want to know how attractive you are. Jill St John tells you you are the Most Attractive Man in the World, yet, in a tv poll you are voted only the Third Most Handsome Man on Television. You want to believe Jill St John but the thought of the poll keeps nagging on your mind. Do you:

a Decide Jill St John is right—after all, she should know better than a load of old housewives.

b Decide the poll is right—why should Jill St John know better than a million sensitive viewers?

c Feel undecided—Jill St John certainly ought to know better than a load of old housewives, but the thought of the poll just nags at your mind.

d Buy a little piglet.

ROBERT WAGNER & NATALIE WOOD

Seldom has the pressure of the lay line been more terrifyingly apparent than in the case of Natalie Wood and Robert Wagner. When first she saw him, Natalie reported that she said to herself 'That's the man I'm going to marry'. And sure enough, she did—well almost—she should in fact have said: 'That's the man I'm going to marry twice'.

Theirs was a long and loving marriage interrupted only by the intervention of Warren Beatty, a starred lay line rogerer and therefore technically irresistible, so no blame attaches to any party. Natalie left Robert for Warren, but then Warren left Natalie for someone else, leaving her free, twelve years later, to marry Robert again.

She attributed their union of spirit to something called 'sanpaku', a state where you can't see the lower white part of a person's eye.

NATALIE WOOD	
Real Name	Natasha Zacherenko.[1]
Born	1938, in America.
Occupation	Actress.[2]
Distinguishing Features	Prettiness.
Romantically Linked With	Warren Beatty, Elvis Presley, Robert Wagner (m), Frank Sinatra, Richard Gregson (m).

Natalie attributed the secret of beauty to 'smelling beautiful'.[3] This may be true in some instances: in her case, though, the secret of beauty was being beautiful. Her grim death in 1981 is a reminder that things on Earth are grim indeed: as the saying goes: 'Life's a bitch, and then you die'.

While alive, Natalie Wood was a surprisingly good actress: she was also a surprisingly civilized one, and knowing how much all her male fans would love to see her without her clothes on, made every effort to oblige them. While with most actresses, nude photographs or movies usually take the form of early indiscretions when short of cash, to be hidden and bought out when the actress is Taken Seriously,[4] Natalie's case is the exact opposite. Having established herself as a serious actress, try as hard as she might she just couldn't get her gear off. It is a strange tale indeed, revealing yet again the dark underbelly of the beast that is called Hollywood.

First in *Splendour*[5] *in the Grass* Natalie ran naked along a corridor: but the enraged producer, Jack Warner, ordered the scene to be cut.[6]

Next, Natalie took the lead in *Gypsy*, the film about the famous stripper, Gypsy Rose Lee: surely her naked moment had arrived? But no—in a film that stretched credibility to its outer limits and way, way beyond, the nomadic striptease artist never once took her clothes off.

In the permissive climate of the seventies, things looked more optimistic and when Natalie landed the starring role in the tv remake of *From Here To Eternity* it looked like at last she'd cracked it. Few movie enthusiasts will ever forget the utter frustration of the scene where Burt Lancaster and Deborah Kerr make love in the Atlantic surf *both wearing their swimming costumes.*[7] Natalie was apparently prepared to move with the times and take off her costume, and indeed did so: but *once again*, good sense was thwarted and the producer insisted that the costume-less scenes in the surf ended up, as the saying goes amongst the Hollywood big-wigs,[8] 'on the cutting room floor'.

Happily, however, in the end the day was saved by *Playboy* magazine, who were also on the cutting room floor at the time and preserved Natalie's ex-quisitely perfumed nakedness for eternity.

FOOTNOTES

1 Another example, like Rita Hayworth, of Hollywood fooling with a perfectly fabulous name. See Appendix: Mad Producers.
2 Try to see *Splendour in the Grass, West Side Story, The Great Race.*
3 Rasputin, another great rogerer, attributed his success to the opposite: smelling terrible. This may well be a trait that is attractive to Russian aristocrats—see Catherine the Great and Ivan the Horse.
4 Another of the Great Mysteries of the World is: why does everyone want to be *taken seriously*, when everyone else knows what a drag serious people are and how much nicer it is to be silly?
5 See Appendix: Names for Rogering.
6 See Appendix: Mad Producers.
7 Wearing swimsuits during sex is a popular method of contraception in Australia, but elsewhere is really one of those Things That Just Don't Happen—anyone who's been on a beach with a man with intentions will know that the costume is off before you can say 'O my God, Spiros, stop doing that, I said *stop it*, you great Greek git, yes, yes, now, push it in now!'
8 The term 'big-wig' comes from a time when the importance of a person at court was judged by the size of their wig. Marie Antoinette once wore a wig that weighed four times as much as she did, and had to be held in place by seven servants. The term, though more generally used to mean 'important people', is still sometimes used of public figures in its original sense, as in the case of Paul Daniels and Molly Sugden.

NATALIE WOOD & WARREN BEATTY

Natalie Wood was not the first person to fall prey to the charms of Warren Beatty. He has over the years proved himself an irresistible force of nature, like an earthquake, a tidal wave, a sexual atom bomb, and sweeping Natalie away from the arms of the man she truly loved was small fry for Warren. He made her happy for a while, and then moved on. He's done that before too . . .

**FASTEN YOUR SEAT BELTS, AND HOLD YOUR HATS—
THIS IS THE BIG ONE!!!**
(well, almost—Ryan O'Neal is bigger, but only just.)

WARREN BEATTY

Born	**1938, in America, the brother of Shirley MacLaine.[1]**
Occupation	**Actor, director, producer.**
Hobbies	**Politics and rogering, then more rogering.**
Distinguishing Features	**Charm, intelligence, looks, and a telephone attached to his ear.**
Romantically Linked With	**Mynah Bird,[2] Leslie Caron,[3] Joan Collins, Julie Christie,[4] Britt Ekland,[5] Goldie Hawn, Kate Jackson,[6] Diane Keaton, Carole Moore,[7] Michelle Phillips,[8] Natalie Wood, Brigitte Bardot, Diana Ross, Liv Ullmann, Candice Bergen, Carly Simon.**
Rumoured Links With	**Elizabeth Taylor, Maria Callas, Odile Rodin, Vivien Leigh.**
Cuckolded	**Richard Wagner.[9]**
Tried Links With	**Jane Seymour, Jaclyn Smith.[10]**
Married	**No one.**

Warren Beatty is known in Hollywood as an extremely talented, though slightly maverick film-maker; as a charming and intelligent and politically astute companion; and as an easy lay. His film career has not been as full as one might think, but its peaks—*Bonnie and Clyde*, *Heaven Can Wait* and *Reds*—have been magnificent: his romantic career has been more full than one can believe, and its peaks have been both magnificent and very frequent indeed.

As with most great lovers, he is also willing to go to any ends to get what he wants. He's been said to write, produce and star in huge multi-million dollar pictures simply in order to get the woman he desires. This was the plan with *Heaven Can Wait*, to win back Julie Christie. It failed. At the other, cheaper end, of the market, as a young man Warren was once seen standing on a New York street corner handing out his phone number to every pretty girl who passed by. If he were a woman, Warren might well be described as a nymphomaniac: which is, naturally, a completely fabulous thing to be.

FOOTNOTES

1 Shirley herself said: 'I would like to do a film with him with a love scene. Then I could see what all the shouting was about'. See Lord Byron.

2 *Mynah Bird*: she was rogered in Roman Polanski's bed and charmed by Warren's absent mindedness—'When it was over I was amused to find that Warren had forgotten to tell me that there was another girl there with us—in the excitement and the dark, I hadn't noticed'. This story reveals that Warren's sexual reputation is so extraordinary that a girl can go to bed with him *and another woman* and assume that all the extra attention being paid to her is simply a manifestation of Warren's skill.

3 *Leslie Caron*: of whom Warren said: 'I remember the first painting that ever made a really emotional impact on me was Renoir's 'A Girl With a Watering Can'. Leslie's very like the girl in the picture. And I feel about Leslie as I feel about that picture'. The incident gives a new and worrying gloss to the phrase 'mounting a picture'.

4 *Julie Christie*: Warren described her as 'an unmade bed' and she was for a long while 'The Only Woman He Ever Loved' (as was Diane Keaton). Warren's father wanted him to marry her, but Julie's mother didn't comment. Eventually, however, Warren was outrageously unfaithful to her (see Britt Ekland, Carol White, Goldie Hawn, and various waitresses), and she gave up on him, despite his efforts to win her back by giving her whopping great parts in films.

5 *Britt Ekland*: she has two interesting things to say about Warren.

   a 'It was like a dream. We were so much in love we never stopped laughing'.
   b 'He could handle a woman like a lift. He knew exactly where to locate the top button. One flick and we were on our way'.*

6 *Kate Jackson*: the intelligent one in *Charlie's Angels*, not that they weren't all quite clever.

7 *Carole Moore*: 'I wouldn't give him ten out of ten—let's say nine and a half. He was pretty good, but he wasn't the best. Rod Stewart was'.

8 *Michelle Phillips*: Michelle lived with Warren for three years, and, like other members of the Mamas and the Papas, was often depressed on Mondays.

*This lift metaphor is the single most specific description of Warren's love-making techniques ever offered, and may well repay careful study for those interested in emulating his achievements. Important facets of lift operation are that you get out almost as soon as you get in, and there are normally quite a lot of other people in there with you.

9 *Richard Wagner*: this is a mistake: should be Robert Wagner, the actor not Richard Wagner, the composer. Cosima Wagner is one of the few women Warren Beatty hasn't slept with.
10 *Jaclyn Smith*: She refused: 'I'd just lost my grandfather'. (See Appendix: Great Rogering Excuses.)

WARREN BEATTY & JOAN COLLINS

This was a sweet and early rogering in two great rogering careers, and, for a while, it was very serious. Joan and Warren were actually engaged, even though the fact that Warren presented Joan with the ring in a carton of chopped liver did not perhaps bode well for the good sense and permanence of the relationship.

At first it was all excitement and coloured lights, but in the end, Joan just could not take the pressure of Warren's astonishing demands: 'four times a day, every day' was the minimum requirement, and eventually she began to feel like a 'sex machine'. She was also irritated by Warren's habit of talking on the telephone during sex. At the end, they split up, and both moved on to their present glorious careers. Joan felt that Warren had, under her tutelage, 'become a man'.

JOAN COLLINS

Born	**1933, in England.**
Occupation	**Actress.**
Distinguishing Features	**Age and beauty.**
Romantically Linked With	**Maxwell Reid (m),[1] Arthur Loew Jnr, Harry Belafonte, Sydney Chaplin, Raphael Trujillo, Warren Beatty, Ryan O'Neal, a blonde young camera assistant, a married man called 'The General', Anthony Newley (m), Ron Cass (m), Peter Holm (m) and a sadist called Barry.**
Refused Links With	**Richard Burton.[2]**
Married	**Maxwell Reid, Anthony Newley, Ron Cass and Peter Holm.**
Divorced	**The first three, thank God, otherwise the fourth one would be in a tricky situation.**

Joan Collins is not only one of the most famous women in the world. She is also undoubtedly one of the most important. Because she is so fabulous, *and so old*. She has entirely changed the way a whole generation of women think about themselves, and the attitude of a whole generation of men to that whole generation of women. At the age of fifty-three she is a sex symbol supreme and all those guys who thought that women went off the boil at around eighteen are bright red with shame and kicking themselves about all the gorgeous women they've missed. Throughout the world, boys are looking at their mothers through newly-coloured spectacles. Nephews are asking their aunts round for cocktails instead of tea. Husbands have stopped buying their mother-in-laws tea-towels and started buying them contraceptive shields. Headmistresses on the point of retirement are being French kissed by students at farewell ceremonies and women with white hair are starting to dye it mouse-brown to keep free from sexual advances. Joan Collins has made the over fifty an object of sex instead of an object of pity. She has refused to grow old with dignity: she has grown old with lace underwear and let the world know it. Clerks working in ministries have started sneaking names of pensioners in their private diaries, and there is a lord in Scotland who has made a quantum leap of the imagination and started fancying Margaret Thatcher.

Joan Collins' new fame looks like a fairy story: but she's not the sweet princess—she's the evil godmother and she's going to roger the living daylights out of Prince Charming herself. Britain is proud of her.

FOOTNOTES

1 It is surprising and to her eternal credit that Joan ever rogered again after her early experiences with Maxwell. The first time he made love to her 'I had a vague idea that something was put somewhere but no idea where and how'. Eventually Joan started watching television while Max got on with the job.

2 Joan turned Richard down when he appeared on her raft while on location in the Caribbean,* saying she was actually in love with Anthony Newley, whom she did soon marry. Richard replied, in that divine voice which made *Where Eagles Dare* the cinema classic that it is: 'My dear, what the eye doesn't see, the heart doesn't grieve for'. Joan takes up the tale: 'I gritted my teeth and let him kiss me—there is nothing more off-putting to a man than to kiss a girl who is a block of stone'. Poor Welsh Dick gave up straightaway and, tail between his legs, went back to Liz. (See Appendix: Unusual Places to Roger.)

*This tale is ever more remarkable, since Joan professes to belong to the New Etiquette school of DCOL—Doesn't Count On Location. She has the sweetest of phrases for lying about infidelity: she calls it 'Oscar time'—may she win many more Oscars before her time is up.

JOAN COLLINS & RYAN O'NEAL

Of all the sandwiches in this long book, this is the most exotic: this is the caviar and lobster sandwich, the quail's eggs and venison torpedo, Joan Collins sandwiched in between the two greatest lovers of our time. When Joan first met Ryan, she knew of his reputation, but decided she was 'not going to open up this can of beans'. (See Appendix: Names for Rogering.) However, temptation soon got the better of her, and arriving at a nightclub on her birthday, she spied Ryan and 'suddenly decided what I wanted for my birthday'. And she got it.

RYAN O'NEAL

The question has often been asked during the preparation of this book: 'Is there one person who is the greatest rogerer of our time?' The answer is 'Yes. Yes. Yes. He is Ryan O'Neal'.

To write about him here would be to steal the thunder from all the other conscientious rogerers in this rich lay line, so please refer to the Our Mutual Friend lay line.

RYAN O'NEAL & FARRAH FAWCETT MAJORS

This is a phenomenally important roger, because there is a chance it may bring to an end the most extraordinary rogering career of our time. How Farrah managed it, nobody knows, and Ryan isn't saying anything. The scale of the achievement can only be appreciated by full reference to the Our Mutual Friend line, but suffice it to say that pinning down Ryan O'Neal would be a deed in the same league as drinking the Atlantic Ocean, eating Mount Everest, and getting Sir Geoffrey Howe to say something funny. It immediately puts Farrah up alongside the Queen, Mother Theresa, and Billy Jean King as one of the great women achievers of the century.

FARRAH FAWCETT MAJORS[1]

Born	1947, in America.
Occupation	Model, angel, serious actress.
Hobbies	Jogging and jogging.[2]
Distinguishing Features	Hair and teeth.
Romantically Linked With	Burt Reynolds,[3] Lee Majors (m), Sylvester Stallone, and Ryan O'Neal.
Nickname	Teeth and hair.

The loveliest thing about Farrah Fawcett is how *clean* she is. Her couturière once said of her, 'She so beautiful, so sexy, and so *hygienic*'. When she was in *Charlie's Angels* she used to wash her hair *fifty times a day*. When she left Lee Majors, he said to the world: 'I used to be the only one who could shower[4] Farrah, now anyone can do it who buys her shampoo'. As you will see by the annotation, 'showering' is another of the many words used for rogering, and the thought does occur that if Farrah was washing her hair fifty times a day, the shower could well have been *the only* place that the Majors were able to consummate their legendary marriage.[5] It is surely no coincidence that Farrah's second name, Fawcett, is phonetically the same as the American word for tap. The inevitable conclusion is that to turn on Fawcett, you have to turn on the faucet.

Farrah is now with Ryan O'Neal and it is presumed that when she bore him a child, it was also done in the bath, as recommended by the best theorists of natural childbirth. She is gaining increasing respect these days as a serious actress, particularly after her performance in *Extremities* in New York, and she certainly has to be taken incredibly seriously as a rogerer if she has Ryan, king of them all, under her thumb. If she keeps him, she certainly has, more than ever in her life, cleaned up.

FOOTNOTES

1 Farrah named a range of cosmetics after her own name, 'Farrah', but was once heard to complain: 'I have been so tied up with promoting the Farrah cosmetic range that I don't feel I've had any time for world affairs'. She clearly had no conception of how important cosmetics, and particularly perfumes, are to almost all the affairs in the world. More adulterous men are caught out by lingering perfume than by any other form of revelation. Because this is so, extra-marital sexual counsellors in America have recently started to advise men to wear perfume themselves, in the normal course of affairs. An exotic after-shave will normally cut out the tell-tale smell of the other woman's perfume.

    The same theory, in fact, applies to all the other major reasons for the discovery of adultery: drink, cigarette smoke, and garlic. The presence of these on the breath is a certain give-away for the adulterer, male or female. It is therefore advised that anyone who wants to be seriously sinful *and safe* should take up all three, smoking, heavy drinking, and chewing garlic, as soon and as dedicatedly as possible. *This way they will never be discovered.* *

2 See Appendix: Names for Rogering.

3 Burt very nearly married Farrah, but chickened out just before the wedding. He has been heard to muse: 'I must have been mad. Today she'd be Farrah Fawcett Reynolds and I could sit by the pool all day'. He still is mad if he thinks that Fitness Farrah would allow him to sit at all, let alone all day: she almost jogged her first husband Lee into an early grave.

4 See Appendix: Names for Rogering.

5 It is also possible that they tried to consummate the marriage elsewhere, but the number of unclean odours and emissions caused by the rogering forced them to take to the shower almost the moment the rogering started. The whole question of hygiene and sex is certainly a testing one and in Europe love-making in baths is becoming increasingly popular, as the lovers are able to consummate and clean up simultaneously. (For more on sex and hygiene, see Howard Hughes.)

*This effort to prepare for discovery can be taken too far: as seen in the experience of the American company who, in 1924 in Indiana, tried to patent a shirt with lipstick already on the collar. Since at that stage wives still bought the shirts for most American males, the pre-stained shirts were a commercial failure: anyone found buying the shirt was immediately assumed to be involved in an adulterous connection, and ejected from the haberdashery department.

FARRAH FAWCETT MAJORS & SYLVESTER STALLONE

At the time when Farrah had recently parted from Lee, New York gossip columns were abuzz with stories of a romance between these two. Stallone was reported to have made visits to her hotel room and to have 'clip-clopped' around Central Park with her in a hansom cab for two hours. This was at the time when Ryan O'Neal was trying to woo Farrah too and, as a close friend[1] of Farrah's said, it was a good job the hotel she was staying in had a revolving door 'otherwise he (Ryan) would have bumped into Stallone coming out as he was coming in'.

SYLVESTER STALLONE	
Born	1946, in America.
Occupation	Actor, writer, director, producer.
Hobbies	Polo and blowing/beating people's brains out on film.
Distinguishing Features	Big chest, little to say.
Romantically Linked With	Farrah Fawcett, Red Sonja.[2]
Married	Susan Szack, Brigitte Neilson (Red Sonja).
Nickname	Sly, Rocky, Rambo, Titch.

There are those who think that Sylvester Stallone is a kind of natural genius, and those who think he isn't.[3] The two will probably have to go on slugging it out for ever. What is true is that he is an utter clot if he doesn't one day make a film about his own rise to fame, which has been as dramatic as that of Rocky Balboa. At twenty-nine Stallone was broke, married to a cinema usherette and living in a one room hovel—'you don't know what poor is until you've had to suckle a radiator'.[4] He then had the idea for *Rocky*, wrote it in three weeks, and became the most successful film-maker in the world after Steven Spielberg. *Rocky* won the Oscar for Best Film, and *Rocky 2*, *Rocky 3*, *Rocky 4* and *Rambo* are four of the most profitable films of all time.[5]

As you might expect, a private price was paid. Sly left wife Susan, 'ran around'[6] for a while, and then finally married Danish-born giant, Brigitte Neilson. The price was a rumoured $22 million dollar alimony for the abandoned usherette.

Things are never easy between young marrieds and their respective families. Things with Brigitte and the Stallones have been particularly uneasy: first the family nicknamed her 'The Great Dane', which seemed harsh until Sly's mother starting calling her 'That Big Pig'.[7] In the end an armed guard had to be hired for the wedding to keep Mrs Stallone, whom Sly lovingly describes as half French and half Martian, away.

Meanwhile Sly and Brigitte, who played the cool Russian in *Rocky 4* and the girl in *Cobra*, drew up an extraordinary contract to protect their marriage. She, the Dane, agreed to settle for a salary of $360,000 a year (plus various other handouts) in return for promising not to sue him, the Rock, when or if they divorced.

The Dane apparently spent the first year's salary almost immediately, and had to ask for an advance on the next one. Sly now faced a difficult choice: either he could:

1 punch her to death;

2 blow her brains out;

3 cut her head off with a big knife; or

4 laugh and give her more cash.

As yet another demonstration of the glorious power of true love, Sly laughed, and gave her more cash.

FOOTNOTES

1 For 'close friend' read 'bitter enemy'.
2 For a man nicknamed the Italian Stallion, Sly is remarkably discreet about his private life. He refuses to do any sex scenes in his films—a moral scruple much admired by those of his fans who want him to hurry up and get on with the massacring.
3 Those who think he is a genius point out how he has improved the art of action in movies: the boxing in his films is far more exciting than boxing in real life, and the last forty minutes of *Rambo* is almost unparalleled in movie history for the escalation and skill of destruction. They claim that the character of Rocky is an intriguing mixture of gentleness and aggression, of violence and good conscience and that you *haven't lived* till you've seen all four *Rockys* in one day.
4 The editors of this book are among those who *don't* know what poor is, because they have never had to suckle a radiator. On the other hand, it sounds like just the kind of perversion which, if you were poor, would act as a charming distraction from the grimness of everyday life.

5 A witty studio executive, when asked what *Rocky* 3 was like, replied 'Well, it's no *Rocky 2*'. In fact he was wrong, and many consider *Rocky 3*, with the triumphant Mr T. and the 'Eye of the Tiger' theme tune, to be the finest of the *Rocky* movies.

6 See Appendix: Names for Rogering

7 See Appendix: Mothers' Page.

AMERICA RAMPANT LAY LINE

WALLIS SIMPSON

EDWARD VIII

THELMA FURNESS

ALY KHAN

RITA HAYWORTH

ORSON WELLES

MARILYN MONROE

FRANK SINATRA

JILL ST JOHN

ROBERT WAGNER

NATALIE WOOD

WARREN BEATTY

JOAN COLLINS

RYAN O'NEAL

FARRAH FAWCETT-MAJORS

SYLVESTER STALLONE

'No man, no law, no war could stop them'—when a lay line gets going, nothing stands in its way.

FROM	**RONALD REAGAN**
TO	**TONY BLACKBURN**
IN	**8 ROGERS**

Ronnie & Tony: the Great Communicators, their deep spiritual tie reflected in their nearly rhyming names. Every morning when Tony 'gets out his twelve-incher' on Radio London, he brightly begins a day which is certain to end with his communicating counterpart, Ronnie, also talking happy nonsense on our tv screens, also a man with a great big gun in his pocket. Ronnie and Tony never fail to get their message across: but that's not all they have in common: both love simple things, both grin a lot, both have thick dark hair and both are in danger of being assassinated.

277

RONALD REAGAN

Born	**1911, in America.**
Occupation	**Acting and being President of the United States.**
Hobbies	**Trying to get out of rogering, and rogering on the few occasions he couldn't.**
Distinguishing Features	**Button on finger.**
Married	**Jane Wyman, Nancy Davis.**
Divorced	**Jane Wyman.**

All evidence seems to suggest that Ronald Reagan is not a rogerer as such, and even actively dislikes it. In fact, it could be argued that his whole political career has been an attempt to escape finally from the rogering demands placed on him by being a film star. Although, of course, as a politician he is not entirely free of that pressure—taking the precedent of the Kennedys and Monroe, Caspar Weinburger and Ronnie should at this moment be rogering the living daylights out of Madonna.

Ronnie's first wife, Jane Wyman, showed some of the marks of a rogerer, but it is unlikely that she got much mileage out of young Ronnie. Certainly his marriage with Nancy has shown a lot of kissing, but there's damn little rogering in the public view.

The truth is that Ronald Reagan, along with Margaret Thatcher[1] and the Ayatollah Khomeini, is part of the grand conspiracy to rob the profession of politics of its birthright as one of *the* great launch pads for rogering achievement, and the sooner he gracefully steps down and hands over to some sexy Southerner with a lot of skeletons in his cupboard the better.

FOOTNOTES

1 Now, there's been a lot of loose talk going round about some kind of hanky panky between Reagan and Thatcher, which has been given as the reason for the strange level of co-operation

at the moment between the two countries. There is absolutely no truth in this whatsoever. The incident normally stated as evidence, when Reagan and Thatcher came out of Downing Street, him doing up his flies, and her with petticoat round her ankles, brassiere over her ears and a half-squeezed tube of raspberry flavoured spermicidal jelly in her right hand can, according to sources close to the Government, be easily explained.

ALTERNATIVES

It is the policy of this book, as stated before, to beware of tyrants, so we must tread with great care around the subject of the present President of the United States. He has a large fleet of aeroplanes and would find Faber and Faber an easy and inviting target, being, as it is, in close proximity to three important London hospitals.

This lay line, therefore, will take two alternative routes. The first, which we will treat speedily, takes us from Jane Wyman, Reagan's first wife, to Frank Sinatra. And then on.

The second, which is distinctly more dangerous, takes us the official route, through Nancy Reagan and Clark Gable. It is the Nancy–Clark roger that might well make this section of London a military target, and therefore, here, officially, right at the beginning, we deny it ever happened.

RONALD REAGAN & JANE WYMAN

The affair which led to Jane and Ronnie becoming the 'perfect marriage', 'Hollywood's ideal couple' and 'the constant honeymooners' started off pretty slowly. Ronnie, or 'Dutch' as he was called,[1] just didn't seem to have the drive you'd expect of a hot-blooded youth—when he was filming *Love in the Air*, he invited Jane to sit at his table, but made no attempt to date her. She rang up later and asked him over to her place. His reaction was, 'What for?'

When Ronnie did finally propose, Jane describes it as 'about as unromantic as anything that ever happened on set'. But then they weren't a very romantic couple: so far, Jane's most notable line in the movies had been 'My name is Bessie Fufnick. I swim, I dive, I imitate wild birds and play the trombone'— she was known as the 'Queen of the Subplots'. Ronnie was training to be the glamorous successor to Flynn—but Flynn had taken against him and used to encourage other actors to stand in front of Ronnie during takes.

In the end, the marriage didn't last, mainly because of Ronnie's obsession with politics. Says Jane: 'Ronnie went around blindly joining every organization he could find that would guarantee to save the world'.[2]

However, it had not all been entirely unproductive: by the time the marriage was over, a child and a monster had been born. The child became Reagan's daughter, Maureen,[3] the monster became President of the United States.

JANE WYMAN

Born	**1914, in America.**
Occupation	**Actress.**
Distinguishing Features	**Expression of relief on face.**
Romantically Linked With	**Ronald Reagan(m), Myron Futterman, Fred Karger(m. twice).**
Nickname	**Button Nose.**

Jane Wyman started her career as a dumb blonde, and ended up as a serious actress: an extraordinary parallel with her ex-husband, Ronald Reagan: he started off as a dumb brunette, and ended up as a seriously dumb politician.

Before she married Ronnie, Jane's legs had been voted 'The Best Legs in New York', and she held the record for the longest ever screen kiss—in *You're In the Army Now* she remained joined at the lips to Regis Toomey for 3 minutes and 5 seconds—4 per cent of the total length of the movie.[4] After she left him, she became an increasingly serious actress,[5] and is now a charming and well respected older woman, who, when asked if she has any regrets about leaving Ronnie, politely says that the White House was not for her. She is obviously, forty years on, just hugely relieved to have got the hell out when she did. Reminiscing about the President, all she could think of was that, 'He was such a sunny person. I never felt free to talk to anyone until I met Ronnie'.

Sadly, the only thing you *could* do with Ronnie was talk to him: when they separated Jane said, disappointed, 'There was nothing between us', and Ronnie entirely missed the point, as usual, commenting, 'Perhaps my seriousness about public affairs has bored Jane'.

Many would say, 'Lucky Jane; it just bored her—it looks like killing the rest of us'.

FOOTNOTES

1 Now why *is* Ronnie called Dutch? Suggestions most popular are:

    a His brain is like Holland—it has no distinguishing characteristics.
    b People thought that by calling him Dutch, he might grow to believe that he was actually a Dutch citizen, and therefore never get to be President of the United States.
    c He once had an affair with Gertrude Stein.

2 Except the Communist Party, of course.
3 Of whom Jane rather touchingly said: 'Oh Ronnie, it took so long, and it's still only a girl'.
4 If this kiss had been in Bertolucci's film *1900*, it would have had to last 9 minutes and 36 seconds—try it at home, for fun.
5 And when not serious, seriously rich: Jane now earns £100,000 per episode of *Falcon Crest*.

The route from Jane into the line, our insurance to protect against the military might of America, goes *Ronald Reagan–Jane Wyman–Fred Karger–Marilyn Monroe–Frank Sinatra* and then on. But meanwhile, back to Nancy.

RONALD & NANCY REAGAN

On their first date, Ronnie was on crutches. Clearly this was yet another sad example of Reagan desperately trying to avoid the always frightening possibility of having to do any rogering at all. He was President of the Screen Actors Guild at the time, and Nancy came to him aghast because she had received some unsolicited communist propaganda through her mail box. They were obviously soulmates: the romance blossomed and they were married a year later.

But to what extent they were more than just soulmates must be the focus of this article. The lack of signs of rogering in their relationship is obviously of concern to everyone. There is a lot of hand-holding and gazing, but not a lot of raw animal passion on show. Occasionally Nancy's memoirs and interviews lead one to hope that a raunchy passage is on its way, but it always ends disappointingly:

'After dinner, it's straight upstairs when we get undressed as quickly as possible' . . . (looking good) . . . 'We share a king-size bed which we brought from California, but we rarely go straight to sleep' . . . (looking grrrrrreat!!!) . . . 'Ronnie usually has stacks of reading, so I'll read a book or *Time* or *Newsweek* or something'. DAMN!!!!

Thus, an image of the platonic marriage is presented and sustained. An image which, leading sociologists agree, is doing inestimable damage to American married life. The inevitable conclusion observers draw from this rogerless

relationship is that all really satisfactory sexual activity must take place outside marriage, which isn't true.

With examples like that, it's no wonder Ryan and Warren are having such a good time.

NANCY REAGAN	
Born	**12 A.R.**[1]
Occupation	**Ronnie's wife.**
Hobbies	**Ronnie.**
Distinguishing Features	**Ronnie reflected in eyes.**
Romantically Linked With	**Ronnie.**[2]

Nancy has always been more a wife and mother than a rogerer. While still an actress she was noted by casting directors as suitable for 'devoted wife/ devoted mother' parts. And now she has become wife and mother to the whole of America.

Before meeting Ronnie, Nancy had not been lucky in love. She had been twice engaged, but never wed, and on one sad occasion an early boyfriend had been run over by a train on his way to meet her.[3] Nevertheless she persevered and finally got her man of men, and has since then created an ideal marriage for all the world to see. This is a far cry from her own youth: her parents split up when she was a baby and her mother then went on tour as an actress for five years, leaving Nancy to be brought up by an aged aunt.

There are people who claim that Nancy is actually more interesting than Ronnie: 'Nancy is the astute one'—but this does not stop her getting confused sometimes in the glare of the political arena. She was once asked to address a gathering and began by saying, 'I wish Ronnie could be here to see all these beautiful white people'. Unhappily, half the audience was black. Nancy, in panic, quickly amended her opening to 'black and white people' but this didn't improve things. Later aides explained that Nancy had been referring to the snow on people's coats, and had just got rather mixed up. Which should come as no surprise. She must be confused. She married a bad actor, and, confusingly, he ended up as President of the United States. And even now he's so confused that he calls her Mommy in private. Perhaps this also explains the lack of public rogering: while kissing your Mommy is all right, rogering her is a less popular pastime.[4]

FOOTNOTES

1 After Ronnie.
2 Maybe Clarkie too (see below).

3 See Appendix: Great Rogering Excuses.

4 Except with Oedipus of course: see *The Faber Book of Unpublishable Jokes*, p. 36. 'It was only when he married his mother that Oedipus really came into his own'.

NANCY REAGAN & CLARK GABLE

It would take the files of the CIA to find out *exactly* what happened here. Clark Gable and Nancy Davies, as she was then, did definitely date and Clark was definitely irresistible. *But*, there is no doubt that whereas 'going out together' nowadays actually *means* 'rogering' (see *New Edition Oxford Dict.* —'go out with'), there was a slim chance, a positively anorexic chance if the date is Clark 'I've had 'em all' Gable, that dating did not necessarily lead to rogering. And, because of Ronald Reagan's superior fire-power, that possibility must be respected here.

Counter-arguments centre around the fact that anyone who will spend thirty years with Ronald Reagan would scarcely be choosy enough to turn down Clark Gable. The only hard evidence is that Nancy has said she has a horror of pre-marital sex. The question is: did that horror *stop* her from rogering Clark, or was it because of what happened *when* she rogered Clark that the horror came to be? (See Clark Gable: 'I'm a lousy lover'.) Only Nancy knows the truth.

CLARK GABLE

This is Clark's second appearance in the lay lines, and his contentious one. It is hard to believe that Old Rabbit Ears would not have tempted Nancy into his burrow, but in these lines stranger things have happened: so many people rogering Sir Gordon White, so few people rogering Princess Diana, and anyone at all rogering Tony Blackburn.

The truth is, though, that in his time there was almost no limit to the power of Mr Gable. When Clark was seen undressing in *It Happened One Night* and revealed to be wearing no vest, sales of vests throughout America plummetted: vest manufacturers actually went to Hollywood to plead with the producers of the film to remove the offending scene. The producers refused —a matter of high principle—and vests did not really come back into fashion until Marlon Brando's startling piece of vest acting in *A Streetcar Named Desire*. Even this only partially helped the industry, because Marlon was wearing a dirty greasy vest, rather than the spruce new clean one that manufacturers would have preferred.[1]

What there is no doubt about is Clark's rogering with Ava, which can be found in the Moths and Old Flames line. Ava also puts in an appearance in the Musical Giants line—it is profoundly to be hoped that this central position she holds in the history of twentieth century rogering is some kind of compensation for all the trouble she had with Frank. Although she did give as good as she got . . .

FOOTNOTE

1 Of course the commercial power of cinema has become much greater and much more obvious in recent years. Apart from obvious direct merchandising, movies can create important commercial fashions. The bicycle scene in *E.T.* almost doubled American sales of bikes, and recently the skateboarding scenes in *Back to the Future* brought skateboards back into fashion. On a slightly more adult level, Sylvester Stallone's characterisation of *Rambo* has caused such a demand for major frontal lobotomies that the neuro-surgical departments of American hospitals are only now, over a year after the film's release, starting to get back to normal.

AVA GARDNER & FRANK SINATRA

Ava married Frank with the observation: 'How would I look if I didn't?' She had stolen him from his wife, and thought she ought to round off the episode neatly. Not that she thought that much of him: 'All Frank Sinatra will ever be remembered for is that he was one of my husbands', she observed incorrectly, and later added: 'I didn't like him at all. In fact, we couldn't stand each other. It was always great in bed, but the quarrelling always started on the way to the bidet'.

Careful study seems to point out that what they really enjoyed *was* fighting, and as such it was a very successful marriage: they fought so much that at one point concerned neighbours called in the police to have a care to their safety. Finally it all proved too much and they split up, but the bravado continued: the wedding ring 'went back and forwards between us for years— even after we were divorced'. Apparently, the two of them are still the best of friends, which just goes to show that a little fighting never did anyone any harm.

Or rather, a little fighting and a lot of rogering: once, on a film set in Africa, Ava was asked what it was like being married to a '120 pound runt like Sinatra'. She replied: 'There's only ten pounds of Frank, but 110 pounds of cock'. Ava Maria!

FRANK SINATRA

(For the full Frank biography, see the Comedians line.)

The editors of this book can only be grateful that Ava and Frank did find so much to fight about. Had they not done, they might have settled down quietly and failed to fulfil their crucial task of linking the rogers of the century together with their spectacular and carefully chosen wide-ranging rogering.

FRANK SINATRA & CAROL WHITE

When *Carol* met *Frank*, she was going out with a certain *Paul* Burke. She used to arrive back at her hotel room, with *Paul*, and find it filled with flowers and champagne from *Frank*. Finally, *Frank* flew her to Las Vegas to see his show—inviting *Paul* along as well—and put them in a luxury suite together. After the show, during which *Frank* sang 'Fly Me To The Moon' and glanced romantically up at *Carol* a few times, the three of them, *Frank* and *Carol* and *Paul* gathered together for a drink. You can imagine *Carol*'s surprise then, when after a few moments *Frank*'s personal assistant turned up with two glamorous 'hostesses' on his arm, and *Paul* disappeared, leaving *Carol* and *Frank* together.[1] You can imagine her even deeper surprise when *Paul* never turned up again, and *Carol* found herself spending three romantic weeks together with *Frank* in Palm Beach.

But you cannot, we would venture, imagine *Carol*'s state of mind when after the three weeks, she upped and returned to none other than . . . *Paul*. *Carol* describes it, and this is no surprise, as—'the biggest mistake of my life'.[2]

CAROL WHITE	
Born	**1941, in Britain.**
Occupation	**Actress.**
Hobby	**Rogering.**
Romantically Linked With	**Frank Sinatra, Adam Faith, Peter Sellers, Richard O'Sullivan, Warren Beatty, Oliver Reed, John Barry, Michael Arnold (m).**
Nickname	**The Battersea Bardot.**

Carol White began life as a fruitshop owner's daughter, shy about the size of her breasts, but as she later learnt, 'Life isn't just a twenty-two inch waist and big boobs'.[3] She shot to stardom in the sixties in *Cathy Come Home*, Ken Loach's study of a runaway girl but, unfortunately, Carol seems to have been runawaying and lost ever since. Her next film, *Poor Cow*, was less successful, and when she moved to Hollywood, she made the mistake of getting involved with too many private and not enough film parts. In a film entitled *The Squeeze* she acted in a nude scene, about which a man called Michael Arnold said, 'I heard all about her nude scene and I hope not to see any of that garbage'. Unfortunately, Michael Arnold was Carol's husband at the time, so their relationship then went through a slightly cool patch. So cool indeed that soon after Michael left her, prompting a deliciously mercenary response from his wife: 'I'm broke without him and I want him back'.

Carol has not had a glorious film career since then, but has, as the list above implies, not entirely wasted her time.

FOOTNOTES

1 See Appendix: How to Get Rid of Your Partner's Partner.
2 Although it might *not* have been: see Loving and Leaving: Tessa Dahl and Peter Sellers.
3 Although not so deliciously phrased, this has been very much the attitude of another great high-street good-food purveyor, Margaret Thatcher, whose sexuality it was inevitable this book would sometime have to come to grips with. Margaret provides an interesting contrast with Carol White; not for Margaret Thatcher the sinewy charms of Warren Beatty, not for Margaret Thatcher the sexual serenading of Frank Sinatra, not for Margaret Thatcher the explosive hard-core rogering, no holds barred, time and time again and then again before you've had time to rest, let's go, go, go, baby: I love your hair, gives me something to *hang* on to as we squeeze our love juices as dry as a lemon, O God I love your peaches want to shake your tree after you've shaken mine of course sex sessions with Oliver *I am absolutely huge* Reed. Rather, she has chosen the love of a good man (Denis Thatcher) and God has smiled upon their union with two lovely children, Carol and Mark. God alone knows what would have happened if Margaret had taken a different route in life, and instead of entering Parliament for Finchley had acted in a nude scene in a movie called *The Squeeze*, like Carol did, and found herself in the Hollywood sex circuit, where a blonde is a blonde is an object you want in bed, day or night. Margaret has been fortunate that the only Hollywood film star she has ever been in close contact with is Ronald Reagan and his rogering days are really over now.

What is certain though is that, with the independence of spirit that she has so magnificently displayed time and time again throughout her great career, Margaret Thatcher would have made a huge success of it *had* she chosen to go the rogering 'my body is my tool' way of life. There cannot be a reader of this book who is sufficiently blinded by political prejudice not to agree that, had sex, not politics, been Margaret's chosen profession, she would have gone like a bloody train, given blow jobs that tore the knobs off men and experimented with revolutionary positions that would quite have altered our way of looking at love and sex and our bodies. As it is, she chose politics, and rogering has tragically missed one of its great twentieth century opportunities.

CAROL WHITE & RICHARD O'SULLIVAN

Carol and Richard were childhood and not-quite-childhood sweethearts. They met at the Corona Stage School, where Carol was particularly enchanted by the green leotard and tights that Richard wore in ballet classes: when he actually began to move and 'dance around like a little Irish leprechaun', her heart was quite lost.

The affair progressed the way these things do when you're twelve and growing older every day: eyes met across classrooms, cider was nervously shared, and finally snogging parties at Carol's parents' house made firm that which had for so long been only filled with yearning. Carol wrote: 'With Richard, I discovered what it felt like to be a woman[1]—until my parents came home'.

As in *Romeo & Juliet*, Shakespeare's play, the first blush of love did not last: the two star-crossed leotard-clad lovers soon drifted apart, Carol to a date with Frank Sinatra and Richard to the cultivation of two of the most startling sideburns ever known to man.

RICHARD O'SULLIVAN

Born	1943, in England.
Occupation	Comic actor.
Distinguishing Features	Terrifying sideburns.[2]
Romantically Linked With	Carol White, Tessa Wyatt, Francesca Annis.
Nickname	Dick.

Richard O'Sullivan, star of such classic happy-making tv caperings as *Doctor in the House*, *Man About the House* and *Robin's Nest*, is a merry and un-expected visitor in this line. Like some of the finest acting coves—see Michael Wilding—Dick doesn't take his acting very seriously. Perhaps he has learnt that there is no point trying to imitate life as it's almost always utterly unrealistic and unlife-like: he certainly must have some cause for reflection after being involved in two of the most bizarre relationships of the century: the Wyatt/Blackburn connection, and the Taylor/Burton love-affair: it is not a well known fact, but O'Sullivan had a very small part in *Cleopatra*.[3]

FOOTNOTES

1 See Appendix: Names for Rogering.
2 Sideburns, like flares, are out of fashion, and there are lots of people working day and night throughout England to make sure they don't come back. The recent repeats of *Man About*

the House are part of this important and well-orchestrated campaign. Every time O'Sullivan enters—his sideburns resembling nothing so much as two large, furry rats—hundreds of people reach for their electric shavers.

3 'Small part in *Cleopatra*': see *Great Theatrical Jokes, vol. 3*, published by Samuel French and Mother-in-Law Ltd.

RICHARD O'SULLIVAN & TESSA WYATT

Richard swept Tessa up at the end of her relationship with Tony Blackburn, of whom more later. It is not hard to imagine what a haven of normality, what a rock of good sense and good taste, what a mid-ocean refuelling station of sanity Richard must have seemed after the stormy seas of Tessa's wild marital fling with someone whom Shakespeare described as 'one of the strangest men in England'.[1] Seven years later, however, the itch got itching, and Richard and Tessa are no longer a nice pair.

TESSA WYATT

Occupation	**Actress.**
Hobbies	**Rogering and trying to forget about one specific rogering.**
Distinguishing Features	**Tendency to mutter 'The horror, the horror'.**
Romantically Linked With	**Richard O'Sullivan, Tony Blackburn.**
Married	**Tony Blackburn.**[2,3,4,5,6,7,8]

Tessa will go down in history as the woman who did the unthinkable.

FOOTNOTES

1 The only other people as strange as Tony are, for some strange reason, also disc jockeys: Kid Jensen and Simon Bates leap to mind. No social scientist has yet satisfactorily explained what it is that makes disc jockeys mad, but the time-warp theory is gaining in strength and support. This posits that, for some strange psychological reason not yet explained, disc jockeys are frozen into the fashions and phraseology of the *exact moment* they first pick up a microphone, and can never, try as hard as they may, escape from it. They are thus often ten, fifteen and, in Jimmy Young's case, sixty-four years out of date.

2 See Appendix: Disastrous Marriages.

3 See Appendix: Mad Irrational Acts.

4 See Appendix: Beyond Human Endurance.

5 See Appendix: Utterly Crazy and Inexplicable Human Behaviour.

6 See Appendix: Rogers Which Completely Defy Reason in Every Possible Way.

7 See Appendix: The Most Astonishing Thing a Human Being Has Ever, Ever Done, No Exceptions *AT ALL*.
8 Don't bother seeing these. They don't exist.

TESSA WYATT & TONY BLACKBURN

Blackburn's marriage proposal to Tessa went as follows: 'In my life I wanted to be the top disc jockey, and I am. I wanted an E-type Jaguar, and I have one. And I want you, and, of course, I'll get you'.

It was downhill from there on. By the end of this earth-shattering relationship, Tony confesses—'She liked to sleep alone in the afternoon'.[1,2]

When the marriage broke up, Tony surprisingly transformed from a shallow figure of light entertainment into a character of true tragic depth. He felt true grief and 'shared his sorrow' with his listeners, playing moving records and mourning that the divorce laws made it too easy for people to leave their husbands. He then tried to commit suicide by taking an overdose whilst watching *Fawlty Towers*—'I wanted to die laughing'.

TONY BLACKBURN	
Born	**1943, in England.**
Occupation	**Disc jockey.[3]**
Distinguishing Features	**Nonsense coming out of mouth at great speed.**
Romantically Linked With	**None.**
Unromantically Linked With	**250.**
Married	**Tessa Wyatt.**
Divorced	**Much against his will by Tessa Wyatt.**
Nickname	**King of Corn.**
Describes Himself As	**The Country's Number One Heart-Throb.**

Tony's autobiography is entitled *The Living Legend*, and there can be no doubt that he is indeed one of the Legendary Figures of our time—no one can really believe that someone like Tony quite exists. But he does, and we should, therefore, take advantage of some of his wisdom:

Great Rogering Quotations of Tony Blackburn

'I see myself as a cross between an amateur sex-therapist and a self-ordained priest'.

'Actually I've had more than 250 lovers, but I don't want to appear flash'.
'O Gladys, I'd love to caress your naughty parts'.[4]

How to Seduce a Girl—by Tony Blackburn

'I invite all the ladies in my life into the same Italian restaurant in London,
where the waiters understand how to create the mood of love. I have a
special table and as I take the girl's hand in mine or look deeply into her
eyes, the lighting is lowered by an attentive waiter to cast a seductive glow.
I tell each girl that life is a journey and it is up to each one of us to fill
our time on earth with as many wonderful events as possible'.

Truth is that Tony, though numerically an impressive performer, has not
really shown great discrimination or staying power as a rogerer. He admits
that most of his loves have been one-night stands: and the nearest he has got
to a major sex symbol was Frank Sinatra's agent's assistant, whom he rogered
in Sinatra's flat. He did once nearly roger 'a bubbly blonde', who was, in his
words, 'the major sex symbol in England at the time' but when it came to it,
'to my horror I was not able to perform'.

Nowadays Tony is a strange and rather lonely figure: 'If someone stays, I
find it intensely annoying. It interrupts my routine', he has said, and also
mused: 'I never entertain partly because of the cooking and partly because I
don't have any actual friends'.

Let us hope then, as he sits alone at home, he can gain some solace from
the fact that he is a public figure who has never done anyone any harm, who
has given us all more laughter and amusement that he might think he has.
His taste in music isn't bad either. Living legend or no, the world's a better
place for him.

FOOTNOTES

1 A strange and rather eerie parallel is to be found here with Ronald Reagan, who started this
line and *also likes to sleep in the afternoon*. The difference of course lies in the fact that Tessa
has a rather tighter grasp on the world political situation.

2 This is a useful entry in the category of How Subtly to Suggest to Your Partner That You've
Gone off Him. See Appendix: Great Rogering Excuses.

Other alternatives:
before love-making

a *'God—do we have to do this again?'*
b *'Yucch.'*

during love-making

a *'God—I wish Steve was here.'*
b *'Yucch.'*

and after love-making

a *'That was absolutely horrid, I'm never doing that again.'*
b *'Yucch, yucch, yucch,—YUCCHY YUCCH!!!!!'*.

Another alternative was that taken by Howard Hughes' dog.
3 At the height of his fame, Tony's school, Millfield, hung a photograph of him in the school hall—underneath it was a notice saying 'Before you leave, consult your careers master. This boy didn't'.
4 This was said, on air, to a phone-in caller. Gladys never recovered.

GREAT COMMUNICATORS LAY LINE

RONALD REAGAN

JANE WYMAN

RONALD REAGAN

NANCY REAGAN

CLARK GABLE

AVA GARDNER

FRANK SINATRA

CAROL WHITE

RICHARD O'SULLIVAN

TESSA WYATT

TONY BLACKBURN

A question to engage the mind is this: if Ronald Reagan were to take over the Radio London Soul Spot, and Tony Blackburn were to start running America ... would it make any difference?

OUR MUTUAL FRIEND

FROM	**JOAN COLLINS**
TO	**FARRAH FAWCETT (AT ONE TIME . . .) MAJORS**
IN	**19 ROGERS**

This is a most unusual line.

JOAN COLLINS

Joan Collins put in her official appearance in the America Rampant line. There she was joined to Farrah Fawcett by one man. Now, nineteen rogers separate them, but things are not so different from that first time as the number might suggest.

This line is a tribute to a man whom Joan described as a 'terrific and imaginative lover'. And she really ought to know.

JOAN COLLINS & RYAN O'NEAL

Joan Collins' husband, Anthony Newley, described Ryan O'Neal as an 'Irish poof'. As will become clear, this was not a technically accurate description.

RYAN O'NEAL

Born	1941, in America.

RYAN O'NEAL & URSULA ANDRESS

Born in Switzerland, Ursula Andress was the girl who came out of the waves in *Dr No*, the girl to whom no sensible man in the sixties would say 'no'. She ended up in the eighties playing a goddess in *The Clash of the Titans*. Ryan and Ursula are known to have romped naked[1] in 12-foot waves—perhaps an effort to recreate her most famous film appearance, or perhaps just a damn dangerous thing to do when you could be back on the beach making love.

RYAN O'NEAL

Born	1941, in America.
Occupation	Acting.

RYAN O'NEAL & MARISA BERENSON

Ryan seems to have found acting a charming way for getting round to rogering. Marisa and he acted together in Stanley Kubrick's beautiful film 'Barry Lyndon'. It was not a success in America or England, but achieved huge popularity in Europe, particularly France—a subtle tribute from the country of lovers to the great lover himself.

RYAN O'NEAL	
Born	**1941, in America.**
Occupation	**Acting.**
Hobbies	**Weightlifting, jogging, sunbathing, hitting people, listening to music and rogering.**

RYAN O'NEAL & JONI MITCHELL

When asked about his daughter's husband, John McEnroe, Ryan says that one of the things he likes about him is that John can sit for hours in front of a fire, just strumming on his guitar. If he likes this in McEnroe, imagine how much Ryan must have enjoyed having Joni Mitchell around, a genius with a guitar and a fire. Joni described Ryan as 'warm and sensitive', making her one of the many women who have found Ryan, despite his enthusiasm for punching people, a kind and pleasant haven in life's stormy seas.

And, according to Tatum, Joni was all right too.

RYAN O'NEAL & CAROLE KING

While on great songwriters, Carole King pops in here, too. Living next door to Ryan, Carole wrote a song about a sexy neighbour, whom she was just dying to meet—as soon as Ryan realized she meant him, he came round and met her.[1] (See Appendix: Pulling Techniques and Pick-up Lines.)

RYAN O'NEAL

Born	**1941, in America.**
Occupation	**Acting.**
Hobbies	**Weightlifting, jogging, sunbathing, hitting people, listening to music and rogering.**
Trod On Toes Of	**Albert Finney.**

RYAN O'NEAL & ANOUK AIMEE

Ryan's never had that much concern about the established romantic status of his lovers. Ryan and Anouk got together at the time when she was officially with Albert Finney, a great actor who might have expected better treatment. Albert was apparently rather annoyed.

RYAN O'NEAL

Born	**1941, in America.**
Occupation	**Acting.**
Hobbies	**Weightlifting, jogging, sunbathing, hitting people, listening to music and rogering.**
Trod On Toes Of	**Albert Finney, Jack Nicolson.**

RYAN O'NEAL & ANJELICA HUSTON

Ryan and the beautiful Anjelica had their rendezvous with fate at the time she was the girlfriend of Jack Nicolson. Jack was apparently *very, very* annoyed.

RYAN O'NEAL

Born	**1941, in America.**
Occupation	**Acting.**
Hobbies	**Weightlifting, jogging, sunbathing, hitting people, listening to music and rogering.**
Trod On Toes Of	**Albert Finney, Jack Nicolson, Mick Jagger.**

RYAN O'NEAL & BIANCA JAGGER

Ryan and Bianca made beautiful music at the time she was the wife of Mick Jagger: she confessed to Mick and said it was the only time she had been unfaithful to him. And Mick wasn't at all annoyed, apparently.

RYAN O'NEAL

Born	**1941, in America.**
Occupation	**Acting.**
Hobbies	**Weightlifting, jogging, sunbathing, hitting people, listening to music and rogering.**
Trod On Toes Of	**Albert Finney, Jack Nicolson, Mick Jagger.**
Married	**Joanna Moore.**

RYAN O'NEAL & JOANNA MOORE

Joanna Moore was Ryan's first wife, and someone from whom it might be hoped to glean exactly what *is* the magic of the man. Unfortunately, her official comment is that 'Ryan is all man' which doesn't help all that much. What was she expecting? Half-man, half-frying-pan?

They divorced when Ryan started 'running around with'[1] Leigh Taylor Hunt. Joanna was another one Tatum thought was all right—but then that's right and proper—Joanna is her mum.

RYAN O'NEAL

Born	1941, in America.
Occupation	Acting.
Hobbies	Weightlifting, jogging, sunbathing, hitting people, listening to music and rogering.
Trod On Toes Of	Albert Finney, Jack Nicolson, Mick Jagger.
Married	Joanna Moore, Leigh Taylor Hunt.
Divorced	Joanna Moore.

RYAN O'NEAL & LEIGH TAYLOR HUNT

Leigh Taylor Hunt was Ryan's second wife. Unfortunately she is no better an analyser of the essence of Ryan than her predecessor: she said of him: 'He has the ability to make a woman feel like a woman'. Again, this raises more questions than answers. What does Leigh expect to feel like? A woman as opposed to what? A man? A gnu? A little piggy?

They divorced when Ryan started 'seeing'[1] Barbra Streisand. He said with some surprise: 'Leigh didn't like me "playing around"[1] with other women'. In the end, the truth is that Ryan was not at that time a wise choice for a husband: 'I have an insatiable appetite for girls. I am incapable of being faithful to one woman'.

RYAN O'NEAL

Born	1941, in America.
Occupation	Acting.
Hobbies	Weightlifting, jogging, sunbathing, hitting people, listening to music and rogering.
Trod On Toes Of	Albert Finney, Jack Nicolson, Mick Jagger.
Married	Joanna Moore, Leigh Taylor Hunt.
Divorced	Joanna Moore, Leigh Taylor Hunt.

RYAN O'NEAL & BRITT EKLAND

But just in case it is starting to look as though Ryan is just a bounder and a cad, let Britt come to his rescue. At a time when she was under strain, and having trouble bringing up her children alone, Ryan came along and treated her fine—it was 'comfort and consolation'.[1] He made her feel a little happier again. And when they saw each other later, 'we abstained, rather than spoil anything we had valued before'. Divorce as many times as he likes, Ryan clearly has a real nice side.

RYAN O'NEAL

Born	**1941, in America.**
Occupation	**Acting.**
Hobbies	**Weightlifting, jogging, sunbathing, hitting people, listening to music and rogering.**
Trod On Toes Of	**Albert Finney, Jack Nicolson, Mick Jagger.**
Married	**Joanna Moore, Leigh Taylor Hunt.**
Divorced	**Joanna Moore, Leigh Taylor Hunt.**
Children	**Tatum, Redmond, Griffin and Patrick.**

RYAN O'NEAL & OONA CHAPLIN

Ryan's four children are possibly the major influence on his life—they take up a lot of his thinking time, and once in a while he finds he has to punch one of them to put them in their place. They in turn make sure they make their feelings known to him pretty clearly as well. When Ryan decided that Oona Chaplin was the woman for him for a while, Tatum observed, 'Someone's gotta put a stop to this. She's too old'.

RYAN O'NEAL

Born	**1941, in America.**
Occupation	**Acting.**
Hobbies	**Weightlifting, jogging, sunbathing, hitting people, listening to music and rogering.**
Trod On Toes Of	**Albert Finney, Jack Nicolson, Mick Jagger.**
Married	**Joanna Moore, Leigh Taylor Hunt.**
Divorced	**Joanna Moore, Leigh Taylor Hunt.**
Children	**Tatum, Redmond, Griffin and Patrick.**
	And that's enough of his vital statistics. Now on to:
Ryan's Career	**Ryan first became famous in the early dramatic soap opera, *Peyton Place*, of which he did 530 episodes.**

RYAN O'NEAL & MIA FARROW

Mia was also in *Peyton Place*.

RYAN O'NEAL

Career Continued	**But his greatest hit ever was in the classic sentimental weepie, *Love Story*, in which he starred opposite Ali MacGraw.**

RYAN O'NEAL & ALI MACGRAW

When Ryan and Ali were riding on the crest of the *Love Story* wave, there was a certain undertow of criticism about the quality of the product. But this has now been fairly and squarely stilled by people who go back to Erich Segal's original book and find it to be an American masterpiece, sharp, witty, clear, and impossible to read past page 73 without crying.

RYAN O'NEAL	
Career Continued	**Other criticisms of *Love Story* centred round the fact that, in view of everything above and below, it might be that 'Rogering Story' would have been a more truthful title. And there is some truth in that.**

RYAN O'NEAL & LIZA MINNELLI

For instance, Ryan and Liza made it clear that Ryan didn't have to star in a movie with a girl before he could roger her.

RYAN O'NEAL & JACQUELINE BISSET

And Jacqueline proved the point once and for all.

RYAN O'NEAL	
Career Continued	**But, such things set aside after *Love Story*, Ryan was suddenly a major international celebrity, fêted and desired throughout the world.**

RYAN O'NEAL & MARGARET TRUDEAU

Margaret, one-time wife of the Canadian Prime Minister, was one of those who fell for Ryan's international charms. Fell heavily. She had a one-week stand with him in his Hollywood home but, unfortunately, at the end of the week, he refused to let her in when she came round. Massively unhappy, she climbed over the wall to argue about the decision, but made no head-way. She was later seen wreaking terrible revenge by throwing a Japanese meal at a poster of Ryan.

RYAN O'NEAL

Career Continued	**But this didn't stop things for Ryan getting better. In his next films, unexpectedly, he proved that he had a delicious comic touch. He was funny in *Paper Moon* with Tatum, and even more so in *What's Up, Doc?*, wearing glasses and chasing rocks with the great comedienne, Barbra Streisand.**

RYAN O'NEAL & BARBRA STREISAND

Not that there's necessarily anything funny about rogering Streisand. Jon Peters, who ought to know, has said: 'She's a maneater. A ballbreaker. If you want Streisand, you have to bite the bullet'. Ryan's second film with Streisand was *The Main Event*: perhaps, in view of all this man-eating, it should have been 'The Main Course'.

RYAN O'NEAL

The End	**Whatever, Ryan has since then been having trouble getting the public interested again, and has had a bit of time to take stock. And the outcome of this stock-taking has been one of the greatest international shocks since the Russian Revolution.**
	For in the last few years, Ryan, the man of a thousand gals, has . . . settled down.
	The leopard is changing his spots. The King is standing down. And the girl he's doing it for is . . .
	Farrah Fawcett (at one time) Majors.

RYAN O'NEAL & FARRAH FAWCETT

'I have made a lot of mistakes, but at last I have found the right woman, and I am not going to let her go. I ask Farrah to marry me every day. I would get married tomorrow'. When Farrah left her husband, Lee Majors, for Ryan,

Lee was none too pleased, but no one thought it was going to last. Yet, lo and behold, years later, there's a son and a commitment that seems, well, really real.

We wish her and them all the joy in the world. That's some man she's got her hands on.

FOOTNOTE

1 See Appendix: Names for Rogering.

OUR MUTUAL FRIEND LAY LINE

JOAN COLLINS

RYAN O'NEAL

URSULA ANDRESS

RYAN O'NEAL

MARISA BERENSON

RYAN O'NEAL

JONI MITCHELL

RYAN O'NEAL

CAROLE KING

RYAN O'NEAL

ANOUK AIMEE

RYAN O'NEAL

ANJELICA HUSTON

RYAN O'NEAL

BIANCA JAGGER

RYAN O'NEAL

JOANNA MOORE

RYAN O'NEAL

LEIGH TAYLOR HUNT

RYAN O'NEAL

BRITT EKLAND

RYAN O'NEAL

OONA CHAPLIN

RYAN O'NEAL

CONTINUED

MIA FARROW

RYAN O'NEAL

ALI MACGRAW

RYAN O'NEAL

LIZA MINNELLI

RYAN O'NEAL

JACQUELINE BISSET

RYAN O'NEAL

MARGARET TRUDEAU

RYAN O'NEAL

BARBRA STREISAND

RYAN O'NEAL

FARRAH FAWCETT MAJORS

And so the line finally comes out, binding Joan and Farrah, by, to say the least, a roundabout route. And what have we learned *en route*? Is there any hint as to what has been Ryan's secret as he journeyed time and time again into the realms of paradise? Was it, as Joni Mitchell said all those women ago, that he was 'warm and sensitive'? Perhaps, but then Ryan himself once admitted, 'When I'm depressed or disappointed, I drink or run after girls' which doesn't sound particularly warm or sensitive.

No, the painful truth for all other travellers on the road to sexual success, is that, as has been proved time and time again, there is no map on this journey. All we can do is hear the tales of where Ryan has been and sit back and wonder.

TRUE LOVE

FROM	**HUMPHREY BOGART**
TO	**SARAH FERGUSON**
IN	**11 ROGERS**

This is the True Love line—from Hollywood to Windsor Castle, from Lauren and Bogie to Andy and Fergie, four lovers like they used to make them. Unfortunately, in between their grand passions, there are one or two slightly dodgy rogers, but then the course of true love did never run smooth.

HUMPHREY BOGART[1]

Born	**Christmas Day, 1898,[2] in America.**
Occupation	**Acting.**
Hobbies	**Whistling, drinking, rogering, and being tough —by drinking a lot and rogering.**
Distinguishing Features	**Cigarette in corner of mouth, raincoat,[3] and saying 'sh' instead of 's'.**
Romantically Linked With	**His four wives and a lot of chorus girls.**
Married	**Helen Menken, Mary Philips, Helen Mayo, Lauren Bacall.**
Nickname	**Bogey.[4]**

It is sometimes hard to believe that Humphrey Bogart was a real person, so heavy hangs the legend. Apparently Bogey himself had trouble sorting out life from legend: a barman once said: 'Bogart's a helluva nice guy until 11.30. After that he thinks he's Bogart'. There is also something very difficult about getting to grips with the life of a man when you have seen him hanged or electrocuted eight times, and shot to death twelve times. And then, Bogey's real life does indeed have a legendary flavour, comprising two of the grisliest,[5,6] and one of the finest marriages ever.

In the end, however, he is and ever will be remembered for making a remarkable number of great movies, and for forgetting to say 'Play it again, Sam', the most famous line he was ever given to deliver.

FOOTNOTES

1 Humphrey Bogart—a really weird name if you think about it for a second. *

2 Similarities between Christ and Bogart—both died too young and drank too much—see 'The Wedding at Cana'.

3 *What is sexy about raincoats?*

    a The same thing that is sexy about any garment which isn't meant to be sexy when someone terribly attractive wears it in a film—other notable examples are Julie Andrews' habit and Cary Grant's pyjamas.

    b The idea that someone might not be wearing anything underneath it.

    c The idea that someone might not be wearing anything underneath it, and might also *be wet.*

4 Many sociologists attribute the ill-discipline of the post-war years to the change in meaning of the sentence 'If you don't stop doing that, the bogey man will come and get you'. Mothers would threaten their daughters with the arrival of the bogey man, and the daughters would just go on doing as they damn well pleased, because there was nothing they'd like more than for Bogey to come and 'get them'. (See Appendix: Names for Rogering.)

5 Bogart's first wife had hysterics after their wedding—her parents were deaf mutes and the

entire service had taken place in sign language, accompanied by a strange humming sing-song. (See Appendix: Marriage, Weddings and Wedding Nights.) They finally broke up eighteen months later over a quarrel as to whether it was wrong to give their dog caviar when there were people starving in the world.

6 Bogart's third wife, Helen Mayo, was called 'Sluggy' and could and should have been a professional fighter. They fought on their wedding night and spent it separately. Thereafter her favourite household activity was throwing things at Bogey while he sat peacefully by saying 'Sluggy's a lousy shot'. She only actually damaged him once when she stabbed him with a butcher's knife for going to a Turkish bath, although she nearly got him on the occasion she burnt their house down. After the divorce she said, 'Bogey and I are still the best of friends. It was a very pleasant marriage'. (See Appendix: Marriage, Weddings and Wedding Nights.)

*Think about it for another second, and you'll realize that the word 'weird' is pretty weird as well.

BOGART & BACALL

This is one of the moments in the book when you can just sit back, take a deep breath, and sigh a sigh of relief, because there is such a thing as true love after all. When Lauren and Bogart met she was only nineteen, making her film debut in the film *To Have and Have Not*. She was so shy she shook when she was acting, and had to hold her chin down to stop it shaking—which was where her famous 'Look' came from. Bogart was married and twenty-five years older than her, but he remembered saying to himself, 'What the hell, the girl's got class'—and he was right. Defying his wife, her mother and the studio manager, Bogart pursued Bacall and true love prevailed. The tough guy cried at their wedding. She gave up acting for him—he was fed up with actresses—and though he didn't exactly give up drinking for her, he gave up being *completely* drunk *all the time*. They lived together for eleven years, and she nursed him through cancer to his death. He was fifty-nine. She was thirty-three.

The first sentence she had ever said to him was in the screen test for *To Have and Have Not*. 'You know how to whistle, don't you? Just put your lips together and blow'. When they married his first present to her was a cigarette box. It was inscribed: 'For Mrs Me, who need never whistle for Bogie'.

LAUREN BACALL

Born	**1924, in America.**
Occupation	**Actress.**
Hobbies	**Teaching Bogey how to whistle.**
Distinguishing Features	**Class.**
Romantically Linked With	**Humphrey Bogart (m), Jason Robards (m), Frank Sinatra and James Garner.**
Nicknames	**Kid, Baby, Lauren (real name—Betty), and Slim.**

All the men in Lauren's life seem to have been difficult and most of them have drunk like fishes. Her private life has been an aquarium—'My nature is to be in trouble again'. In the end, no one ever seems to have matched up to Bogey, but then that's no surprise. She now claims that 'men are getting fewer and fewer' and the truth is there are probably few men who deserve her.

Bacall started in Hollywood at nineteen after being spotted on a magazine cover, and her debut, with Bogart in *To Have and Have Not*, was so startling, that her boss told her, 'You have nowhere to go but down'. Maybe. Nevertheless, she did find true love, and did possess in her few good films an extraordinary screen presence, tough, cool, classy. Off set she was pretty cool and classy as well—of Jack Warner, the all powerful studio boss, she observed, 'He wasn't just a monster—he was a moron'.

She still acts—recently in *The Sweet Bird of Youth*—but people always remember her with Bogey. Forgetting that she was twenty-five years younger than him, they expect her to be either dead or in a wheelchair. Instead she is still one of the world's most glamorous women.[1] And still whistling.

FOOTNOTES

1 Although not, as she never was, one of the world's greatest singers—her voice in *To Have and Have Not* was dubbed by the great Andy Williams.

LAUREN BACALL & FRANK SINATRA

This was not an easy number. Perhaps Frank thought you didn't have to be nice to someone who got their voice dubbed by Andy Williams.

He started dating Lauren while she was still tender over Bogey, and after going out for a while they threw a house party at New Year. It came as a surprise to Lauren when, halfway through, Frank asked her to leave. It was a tricky situation for a hostess, so in order to save the guests embarrassment, Lauren just hung on till the party was over. Which was not to Frank's liking—he completely ignored her for the rest of the weekend, then left himself.

It was weeks before Frank got in touch again. When he did, Lauren got another surprise: the first thing Frank did when he got back in touch was ask her to marry him. Lauren 'hesitated for at least thirty seconds' and then said 'yes'. Perhaps she should have hesitated longer. After the engagement, Frank had to go away for a while, and unfortunately the news about the engagement broke before they had time to announce it and work out plans. Frank rang and said they should lay low for a while. Lauren said fine.

And after that, she never heard from him again.

Several weeks later she saw him in town, and he ignored her.[1]

FRANK SINATRA

This is not the last of Frank's appearances in these lines, where he has done such sterling service. He himself said, about his beloved New York:

'If I can make it there,
I'll make it anywhere'.[2]

On the strength of these lines it looks like, having made it there, he sure did make it . . . everywhere. With almost everyone.

FOOTNOTES

1 See Dai Llewellyn for another way to get out of a drunken proposal.
2 For the expert on popular music, 'New York, New York' is worth another listen to: after 2 minutes 49 seconds Frank sings the longest 'and' in the history of the popular song. It goes on for a good five seconds, and is not so much 'and' as 'aaaaaaaaaaaaaaaaaaaaand'.

FRANK SINATRA & CAROL WHITE

The sad details of Carol's 'big mistake' with Frank are in the Great Communicators line. With all the sympathy in the world, it must be said: 'Thank God, Carol, for your big mistake'. Where would these lines have ever been if Frank had stopped rogering, and just Whited for the rest of his life?

CAROL WHITE

(See the Great Communicators line for her full biography.)

Likewise, for all the final satisfaction it has given her, Carol must have lain back sometimes, stared at the ceiling (or mirror) and said to herself: 'Why am I doing this?' And the answer is: Carol, without you, neither this line, nor the one which binds together Ronald and Tony in coils of steel, would ever have existed.

CAROL WHITE & WARREN BEATTY

There is a chance that this was a very unique roger indeed. Here are the four important pieces of evidence:

1 When she first became famous in *Cathy Come Home*, Carol White was hailed as the 'new Julie Christie'.

2 At that time Carol was living very near Julie Christie in Fulham.

3 Warren Beatty was at that time going out with Julie Christie.

4 Warren is known to be very short-sighted.

It does not take a great imagination to see that this could well be the first and only example in this book of a mistaken identity roger.
Carol denies it.

WARREN BEATTY

It is rather touching to see Warren popping up again in this True Love line, because, despite all his massive efforts, he never has quite managed to hold on to the great loves of his life. Let us hope that he does not grow dispirited, and that he, like the Duke of York and Bogey, eventually finds true and everlasting happiness with someone young, and lovely, and devoted and irresistibly sexy.[1]

FOOTNOTE

1 See Helen Fielding.

WARREN BEATTY & VIVIANE VENTURA

Viviane Ventura likes tall, dark, handsome men with large cheque books, and, unlike so many who just read and dream about them, she actually goes out and gets them. She is, however, determined not to horde the information about how she does it. In her excellent book, 'Viviane Ventura's Guide to Social Climbing' she has generously revealed the secret of pulling men like Warren Beatty.

According to the book, it is first crucial to carry three tennis rackets and some polo sticks around.

Then, when taking a new lover into your bedroom for the first time, it is wise to put a picture of someone famous in a silver frame by the bed—'It makes the newcomer realize what the competition is. That is very healthy. Competition gives you more stamina'.

Obviously, if we may interrupt, Viviane, you should choose your famous person carefully—Prince William, Sir Keith Joseph and Joshua Nkomo are all famous, but they are more likely to send the prospective date running than give him more stamina. Indeed, on reflection, all Viviane's advice suddenly becomes a little suspicious. If Joan Collins' description of four times-a-night Warren is anything to go by, stamina is the last thing he needs. And Warren is so short-sighted that he couldn't see the picture by the bed anyway. And God alone knows what he might think if he did catch sight of that polo stick—he might well assume that he had interrupted something rather personal with another man.

In fact, when all is said and done, it begins to look very much as though the point of Viviane's book is in fact to make damn sure that you don't pick up Warren Beatty, or that if you do, he'll give you such a rogering you never recover.[1]

VIVIANE VENTURA

Born	**1941, in London.**
Occupation	**Actress and Entrepreneuse.**
Hobbies	**Collecting polo sticks.**
Romantically Linked With	**King Hussein of Jordan, Adnan Kashoggi, Omar Sharif, Anthony Quinn, Helmut Berger, Warren Beatty, Victor Lownes,[2] John Bentley, Frank Duggan (m).**
Nickname	**Consort of Kings, Lover of Lotharios.**

The unerringly glamorous Viviane was born in England, but brought up in Columbia in South America, and has always retained an exotic South American air about her. She originally intended to be an actress, but things went badly wrong from the start. Before she was old enough to know what she was doing, she was forced into appearing in a film with Cliff Richard[3] entitled *Finders Keepers* and after that, for a while she just couldn't get back up again. But finally she did get a part in a second film *The Adventures of Gerard*.

To celebrate the great breakthrough, she invited all her influential friends to the film's premiere. It was not a happy event. It turned out that she had been cut from the film altogether.

Viviane decided at that moment that there were better ways of spending her time, and she has since spent good times with a large number of very glamorous men, many of whom were actors. Indeed, taking their fictional parts into account, Viviane Ventura has dated, amongst others, Zapata, Zorba the Greek, Vincent Van Gogh, Aristotle Onassis, Prince Ludwig, John Reed,

Doctor Zhivago and Lawrence of Arabia's best friend. Who's got time for acting when you have that sort of business in hand? If only Viviane had been around to bring joy into the lives of the originals, they might not have fought so many wars and committed so many suicides. Give us a million more beautiful women, and we might just have a beautiful world.

FOOTNOTES

1 Another great rogerer certainly thought he was a fatal weapon. See Alexandre Dumas, who needed more than one mistress just to ensure they survived his passion.

2 The mention of Victor Lownes, once the British representative of *Playboy*, raises one of the most perplexing Great Rogering Mysteries, *The Mystery of Hugh Hefner and The Rabbit*. At its simplest, the mystery can be put this way: What on earth possessed Mr Hefner to believe that men would be more aroused by women the more they looked like rabbits? A quick study of these two illustrations will demonstrate that the actual resemblances between women and rabbits are very slight.

   And yet, Mr Hefner has spent the last twenty-five years disguising women as rabbits, giving them long ears, fluffy tails, and, on occasion, whiskers.

   The obvious answer to this mystery is that Hugh Hefner is either mad or some kind of massive rabbit-fixated pervert. There is, however, a more complex and interesting answer that is now appealing to some erotic scientists. Research reveals that in the animal kingdom it is only the female rabbit and the hermaphrodite snail that can experience orgasm. Now, while the resemblance between women and rabbits is small, the resemblance between women and hermaphrodite snails is clearly even more tenuous.

   The hermaphrodite snail outfit would also be more expensive and difficult to make. It is, therefore, no wonder at all that in his search for the easily fulfilled partner, Mr Hefner lighted, after due consideration, upon the rabbit.

3 Cliff Richard is one of an exclusive band of Men Alone, featuring also Hans Christian Andersen, Edward Heath, Kermit the Frog, and, the leader of the pack, Jesus himself.

VIVIANE VENTURA & OMAR SHARIF

At first sight, it seems astonishing that one girl should have gone out with such a trio as Omar Sharif, Adnan Kashoggi and King Hussein of Jordan. Further investigation reveals however, that it is pretty much the same thing as one girl going out with the three most attractive boys at the school across the road, something which happens in England every day of the week. For Omar, Adnan and Hussein were all pupils at Victoria College, a famous Middle East school.

On Viviane's part, it shows a touchingly artistic desire for unity of style and upbringing amongst her lovers. Also see Viviane Ventura in the King Sized Pair line for advantages of Rogering in the Desert.

OMAR SHARIF

Born	**1934, in Cairo.**
Occupation	**Bridge, gambling, racehorse owning.**
Hobby	**Acting.**
Romantically Linked With	**Barbra Streisand, Viviane Ventura, Anouk Aimee, Catherine Deneuve,[1] Dyan Cannon, Faten Hamama.**
Married	**Faten Hamama.[2]**
Nickname	**Cairo Fred.**

Omar Sharif is one of the greatest sweeties of this book, although not one of the great rogerers—'All my friends have more girls than I've ever had'. He knows what he enjoys and enjoys knowing it. He loves gambling, eating, drinking, playing bridge, racing, having tea in bed and 'spending a little time in my bathroom doing my crossword'. And when he's finished with all that, 'I keep myself perfectly well entertained doing nothing'. For Omar—like Michael Wilding and Roger Moore—is blessed by being one of the few lucky actors who don't care much about their job: he likes acting because 'it fits in with spending time in the bathroom', but is much happier when he's not on the job: 'working gets in the way of living'.

In fact, Omar Sharif is so unbelievably laid back that he's too laid back to be a rogerer—he'd like it all to be just a bit easier than it is, and would appreciate spending less time in the company of highly strung actresses—'I'd love to meet a nice secretary like other men do'. But since it ain't that easy, he has lighted upon a housekeeper to keep him happy. After seventeen years together he says: 'She is everything the perfect wife should be, without the problems'. He still dreams about his perfect woman: 'I hope every day and when I wake up, I haven't given up the idea that maybe today I will find someone whom I am going to fall in love with'. But, what with the hours at the gambling table, over the tea and in the toilet, he just has never got round to it.

Love of leisure has leisured out love.[3]

FOOTNOTES

1 Catherine Deneuve: another of nature's compensatory rogers—to have slept with her is compensation for any other suffering.
2 Faten Hamama, who did or did not overfeed her mother, was the most famous actress in the Middle East, and kept Omar married and faithful to her for ten years. He says of her: 'Just think of it. I was married at twenty-one, an actor, surrounded by pretty girls, and I never once cheated on my wife. Of all my achievements in life, I think that is what I'm most proud of'.
3 Well at least, one hopes it's that, and not some Freudian muck-up. Of which there is a distinct danger. Omar speaking of his mum—'She's not just proud of me. She faints when she sees me. If she were here, she'd want me to sit on her knee'. O—o. (See Appendix: Mothers' Page.)

OMAR SHARIF & BARBRA STREISAND

Omar has never been one for kissing and telling. In 1976, he brought out a book in which the publisher obviously assumed he would do just that. But, talking in a newspaper interview to promote the book, Omar said: 'I know the sort of thing they wanted. But I've always been horrified when I've read books where people talk about their love lives, so in my book, I mention no ladies at all. It's just my impressions of places I've been and people I've met. Frankly, I don't expect a big success. There's no reason for it to do well'. It didn't.

So, if anything is to be known about this roger it'll come from Barbra— and sure enough she claims that not much of a time was had by all—Omar just 'talked incessantly about bridge'. In fact, in the end, it's probably against his will that Omar appears in this book at all. First, he insists that: 'To have an affair with someone doesn't mean you have to go to bed with them'. Then, as if that wasn't a strong enough hint, he muses: 'It is a moment I cherish: to go to bed, have the light on, the book, my cigarette and my ashtray, and read in the silence of the night'. Not much room for rogering there. And if you *were* to break into the smoke-filled sanctum, you would have to be ready for the worst. Omar tells of the time when a lady did indeed burst into his hotel room, and held him at gunpoint demanding he made love to her. She took all her clothes off, and lying on the bed, gun still in her hand, made Omar, good book put aside, take all his clothes off. Despite his protests, she demanded a rogering. Would *not* leave without it. 'Madame', was Omar's truthful reply, once his clothes were dutifully removed, 'as you can see, I can't help you'.[1]

BARBRA STREISAND	
Born	1942, in America.
Occupation	Singer, actress, director, producer.
Hobbies	Singing, acting, directing, producing—'My fun is my work'—and rogering.
Distinguishing Features	Nose and voice.
Romantically Linked With	Elliott Gould (m), Anthony Newley, Jon Peters (m), Omar Sharif, Ryan O'Neal, Richard Gere, George Lucas, Kris Kristofferson, Pierre Trudeau, Warren Beatty.

'I need sex like I need food' is Barbra's attitude to sex, and a frightening attitude it is. You *know* how Americans like to eat. Big breakfasts. Snacks before and after lunch, with a big lunch in-between snacks. Then dinner, then ice-cream, then off to the McDonalds for a late night bite. The exhaustion could be fatal. And that's the optimistic interpretation of Barbra's words—sex as often as food.

For there is an even more terrifying possibility: Jon Peters has said that Barbra's a 'maneater. A ballbreaker'. You can't get more frank than that. And study of the evidence seems to imply that if, while indulging Barbra's desire for sex as often as food, you by chance stray over into one of the food-designated areas, it will be feeding time *whatever*.

Jon Peters continues: 'If you want Streisand, you have to bite the bullet'. And that's what soldiers did in the old days when parts of their bodies were being taken off without anaesthetic. OW!!!! It is no surprise that during his marriage to Streisand, Elliott Gould had a fridge built in their bed, full of coffee ice-cream. To feed Barbra whenever things got dangerous.

Which having been said, the above constitutes no disrespect to the great genius of Barbra Streisand, who has more talent in one of those regularly-used teeth than the rest of us have in our whole bodies and those of all our close relatives. There's an old saying, 'she could eat you for breakfast'. If you don't watch out, Barbra probably will.

FOOTNOTE

1 See Appendix: Great Rogering Excuses.

BARBRA STREISAND & ELLIOTT GOULD

Like the Warren Beatty–Joan Collins rogering, this was an early roger which took place before either of the couple was really famous. Elliott and Barbra met in a New York Jewish musical called *I Can Get It For You Wholesale*, married in 1963, had a son called Jason, and then divorced eight years later. As Elliott never tires of telling, this was because Barbra was totally obsessed with her career: 'She was becoming so successful and independently wealthy that it was a big trap for me. I was faced with the fact that if I held on to her I would have to accept a lifestyle that was not of my own making'. Mmmmmm. Doesn't sound too different from the situation which most married women find themselves in, but still, Elliott was probably right. At least he got out un-eaten, and the inspiration of his wife's success gave him the drive suddenly to become quite as famous as her. Meanwhile, Barbra went on and married her hairdresser, Jon Peters, who obviously didn't find things quite as inwardly tormenting as Elliott had.

Whether or not *I Can Get It For You Wholesale* is a great lost masterpiece of musical theatre, no one really seems to know.

ELLIOTT GOULD	
Born	1939, in New York.
Occupation	Actor.
Hobby	Trying to be sane.
Distinguishing Features	Date with psychiatrist in diary.
Romantically Linked With	Vicki Hodge, Valerie Perrine, Jennifer O'Neill, Bianca Jagger, Barbra Streisand (m), Jennifer Bogart (m. twice).
Nickname	Streisand.

Elliott Gould gives the impression in the movies of being the sanest guy in town. Just the sanest, low-keyest guy on the block. No wool over his eyes, no sirree. This impression is, unfortunately, far from the truth. When asked

about life recently, Elliott spoke of 'a beehive of corruption' and 'irrefutable forces of evil'. Asked to go into detail he only made things harder to understand: 'There are people out there like aliens just waiting for us to open up our minds so they can jump in'.

In response to this quotation, film buffs all over the world set out to discover just who these 'creatures like aliens' were. A strong contender at first seemed to be the American psychiatric profession, but no such thing. The trail suddenly went cold when, speaking of Valerie Perrine, Elliott said: 'What drew us together was the fact that Valerie had emotional problems. I helped her get into psychoanalysis'.

So the 'creatures like aliens' were not psychiatrists. Who could they then be? Fans of *M*A*S*H* and *Bob and Carol and Ted and Alice* would not let it rest.

A study of Elliott's career at last made the answer plain. When he had trouble on a movie called *A Glimpse of the Tiger*, the company responsible for the project had two psychiatrists brand Elliott 'crazy' so they could claim on the insurance. The psychiatrists, early suspects, turned out not to be the aliens, but nice folk *cruelly manipulated*, as so often happens in science fiction movies, by an *outer force*. And that outer force, the essence of pure evil was of course that most frightening of all alien creatures, *the movie industry itself*.

Which makes pretty fair sense, actually, when you consider how little good work we've seen out of the wonderful Elliott since *M*A*S*H*. Horrible, horrible aliens.

ELLIOTT GOULD & VICKI HODGE

Elliott once made the rather puzzling assertion, sounding remarkably like Omar Sharif: 'I believe that you can be lovers, and not go to bed together'. Fortunately, his relationship with Vicki Hodge makes the explanation of the remark clear and sane. The affair lasted ten days, while Vicki was on the bounce from John Bindon, and a lot of it was apparently spent in the back of a white Rolls-Royce. Lovers, you see, without having to go to bed.[1]

VICKI HODGE

Born	**1946, in England.**
Occupation	**Actress, model, tv personality.[2]**
Hobbies	**Spilling beans, going on holidays and rogering.**
Romantically Linked With	**Yul Brynner, George Lazenby, Peter Waller (of Peter and Gordon), David Bailey, John Bindon, Ian Heath (m), John Bentley, Elliott Gould.**
Spent Time in Mustique With	**Prince Andrew.**
Nickname	**The Flying Nun.**

Vicki is the daughter of Baronet Sir John Hodge: their family motto is '*Glory is the reward for virtue*', and Vicki, most nobly, has decided that she will not dedicate her life to the seeking of glory. She has, like Frank Sinatra, lived a life that's full, and travelled each and every by-way, until she finally made her progress up the Royal Mall. In the ultimate kiss and tell, she revealed details in both the press and on tv of her time spent with Prince Andrew on Mustique. A lot of people think she should have kept quiet about it and that describing the Queen's second son as a 'kinky devil' and resonantly announcing, 'I have seen the Royal Bum' is no help at all to the well being of the nation. Such people think that she should have maintained a respectable silence. As we shall now.

FOOTNOTES

1 Margaret Trudeau said of one of her lovers: 'I didn't realise how much space there was in the back of a Daimler'. It is interesting to consider whether car manufacturers take this kind of activity into account when they are making their cars. Or, more importantly, have they ever considered tying it into their marketing policy.

> *Buy the new Volkswagen: Great for Shagging In.*
> *Buy the Renault 87: New Cunnilingus Capacity.*
> *Try a Triumph for Troilism.*
> *The New Metro Five Whore Hatchback: Doesn't Miss a Trick.*

(See Appendix: Unusual Places to Roger.)

2 Vicki gave up tv work after complaining about *Call My Bluff*: 'It certainly requires a lot of brain power'.

VICKI HODGE & PRINCE ANDREW

A respectable silence would have sounded like this.

PRINCE ANDREW

Born	**1960, in England.**
Occupation	**Naval officer, Prince and Duke.**
Hobbies	**Photographing, Selina Scott and rogering.**
Distinguishing Features	**Big, cheerful smile and mother with crown on head.**
Romantically Linked With[1]	**Gemma Curry, Carolyn Seaward, Carolyn Herbert, Vicki Hodge, Clare Park, Katie Rabbett, Koo Stark.**
No Romantic Link With	**Margaret Trudeau.[2]**
Married	**Sarah Ferguson.**
Nickname	**Randy Andy.**

Prince Andrew is now a respectable married man. As the years go by and his jaw and shoulders grow broader, as the decades go by and his heroic exploits by land and sea take up an ever-growing number of pages in *Boy's Annual* and *Biffo*, it may be hard for us to remember the boy who preceded the man. Let this small piece of prose be a tribute to someone who lightened our lives for a while, and then passed on to greater things: the now ghostly figure of Randy Andy.

For once upon a time, in the land of England, there reigned a noble queen in whom all virtue rested. And she bore three sons. And the first, whose name was Charles, waited patiently for the burdens of high office. And the third, Edward, took everyone by surprise by growing up at all. But the second, whose name was Andrew, was an absolute hoot. Big Andy raunched his way round English society with all the priapistic determination of a frying pan: self-consciousness was a mug's game that Andy wasn't playing. Ah me, those were balmy days indeed, when Randy Andy rode rampant through merrie England, and no maiden was safe from his big grin and forthright ways. 'Twas as though the noble Charles had taken upon himself all the burden of introspection and doubt about the sins of the world, while Randy Andy was left merrily to commit them, as big-toothed, big-grinned and big-eye-browed, he sowed his royal seed with all the vigour of a farmer struggling against the worst vagaries of the Common Agricultural Policy.

And there are those who say that on a still clear night, if a young maiden walks alone along a lane, she may just hear the buzz of a ghostly helicopter above her. And if she is foolish enough to stop and look upwards, she may just see a well-built ghost shimmy down a rope and landing by her say, 'Hey, chick, fancy a quick one?' before disappearing as fast as smoke in the breeze. For the ghost of Randy Andy is doomed now to wander the highways and by-ways of England in search of the random roger that can now be no more. But do not feel too much sorrow for him, fair maidens, because like the real Randy Andy he always enjoys having a bash even if there isn't a ghost of a chance he'll get laid.

FOOTNOTES

1 And three cheers for this noble crew who kept us guessing over the years. The Oil of Olay girl, Miss UK, the racing manager's daughter, the racy film-star. Each one played their part with charm, and, except in one case, with discretion. *

2 Said Margaret: 'I found him very sexy—such a handsome, well-built boy. I had to keep reminding myself that he was only sixteen'. Another lucky escape for Andy.

*And a fourth, extra cheer for Koo Stark, whose early film career hadn't left much room for discretion to manoeuvre in, but she still brought it off.

PRINCE ANDREW & SARAH FERGUSON

Sarah Ferguson was a genuine surprise. At first the public asked the question in puzzlement: why with all the girls in the world except Princess Diana to choose from, did Andy plump for Fergie? Finally, however, the answer has become abundantly clear. Beloved Fergie was chosen because she was The Girl with More.

More hair, more laughter, more old flames, more hips, more freckles, more chance of not going mad, more jaw, more parents, more personality, more paternal eyebrows, and, most of all, more experience—how many other girls have lived as Fergie has lived? Has the Queen Mother ever slept on a beach in Paraguay? Have the Queen and Prince Philip ever been photographed rolling an enormous joint? No. Fabulous Fergie has more than most in every department, and before long she'll probably have more 'love of the people' as well.

SARAH FERGUSON

Born	**1959, in London.**
Occupation	**Publishing, Duchessing.**
Hobbies	**Ski-ing, riding, laughing and mucking around with Di.**
Distinguishing Features	**Incredulous smile on face as if she can't quite believe her luck.**
Romantically Linked With	**All put in the shade by Prince Andrew (m.)**
Nickname	**Fergie.**

Sarah Ferguson takes her position now as the last Royal at the very end of the long, long line that has run from Henry VIII. And what a suitable receptacle for that honour, bright bubbly number that she is.

For a start, Sarah would have provided the perfect answer to all Henry's problems. He most certainly wouldn't have been able to execute *her* without a right set-to; one would like to meet the executioner with the sheer brawn to take on Sarah in a cross mood.

Secondly, Fergie is herself the bearer of a royal tradition recently somewhat laid aside, being the first member of the Royal Family since William of Orange to be genuinely orange. Her bright orange hair, bright orange freckles and generally orange shape and demeanour prove her a worthy upholder of another great British Royal tradition.

But thirdly, and most importantly, here, after some fair share of miserable to-ing and fro-ing, executions and heartaches and heartbreaks, the Royal lay lines finally come to rest with a genuine good time girl, someone who would call a roger a roger and not panic about it. Or to put it in her own words, if we can be forgiven a final royal indiscretion, here is the bit they left on the cutting room floor from the very first interview that Sarah and Andrew did together. We join just before the cut:

> SIR ALISTAIR: *Ha, ha, ha. And now tell me, what was it that really attracted you to each other?*
> PRINCE ANDREW: *The red hair. And a good sense of humour.*
> SARAH: *He's pretty good looking too.*
> (Here is where the cut starts.)
> PRINCE ANDREW AND SARAH: (together and very loudly.) *And, of course, we both adore rogering.* (A huge hoot of mutual mirth.)
> (End of cut.)
> SIR ALISTAIR: *And now, on to the wedding dress . . .*

Believe what you will. God bless them both, and all of you.

TRUE LOVE LAY LINE

HUMPHREY BOGART

LAUREN BACALL

FRANK SINATRA

CAROL WHITE

WARREN BEATTY

VIVIANE VENTURA

OMAR SHARIF

BARBRA STREISAND

ELLIOTT GOULD

VICKI HODGE

PRINCE ANDREW

SARAH FERGUSON

' 'Cos you and I,
Have a guardian angel, on high,
With nothing to do,
But to give to me,
And to give to you,
Love for ever true'.

KING SIZED PAIR

FROM	**KING HUSSEIN**
TO	**BARBARA WINDSOR**
IN	**6 ROGERS & A WILD GUESS**

Those who have throughout this book been searching for a deeper meaning in the lay lines will here at last find all their suspicions confirmed, for it contains the most extraordinary of coincidences.

In 1974, there were three major boobs in the world.

Two of them belonged to Barbara Windsor. The third was the Camp David agreement, Jimmy Carter's attempted peace package between Egypt and Israel. *And King Hussein was intimately involved in fighting against it.* The power of the lay line knows no bounds.

KING HUSSEIN

Born	**1935, in Jordan.**
Occupation	**King of Jordan.**
Hobbies	**Writing, trying to stop wars and rogering.**
Distinguishing Features	**Crown on head.**
Romantically Linked With	**Princess Diana,[1] Toni Gardiner, Alia Toukan, Elizabeth Halaby, Viviane Ventura.**
Married	**Princess Dina, Toni Gardiner (Princess Muna), Alia Toukan (Princess Alia) and Elizabeth Halaby (Princess Noor).**
Nickname	**Your Royal Highness.**

It is fitting and right that King Hussein should begin this line in the register of rogering. For he is one of those who dignifies the very act. Tired and disillusioned folk would say that the most that can be expected of the average roger is a little gratification and a good sleep. But King Hussein nobly kicks off this line as a rogerer whose rogers turn girls into the wives of a king, a great and noble tradition that's already been seen with Lady Diana, Wallis Simpson, Mrs Fitzherbert and Priscilla Presley.

FOOTNOTES

1 Not to be confused with Princess Diana, who, of course, only appears on one page in this book. Or two including this one. In fact, more like six because she's at the beginning and end of her line and also in the index at the end and the list of contents at the beginning. And she probably pops up a few other times. So that's perhaps nine. Which should not be allowed to blind the reader to the point of this note. Which was to point out that Princess Diana hasn't slept around. Which you all knew anyway. Sorry.

KING HUSSEIN & VIVIANE VENTURA

The couple met in a restaurant where Hussein was dining with Denis Healey. It was a Saturday, and for the rest of the weekend, Hussein pursued Ventura, eventually discovering her identity and sending her an entire van of roses to coax her favours.[1] The affair did not end, as many of Hussein's have, in marriage, so it cannot teach you how to catch and marry a king. What it does do, however, is offer a serious warning about the kind of mental disorder that may result from having dinner with Denis Healey.[2]

VIVIANE VENTURA

(For full details, see the True Love line.)

Viviane is the link with our last line, and having tasted the exotic pleasures of Omar Sharif is now back between two other desert princes. This would, therefore, seem to be a good moment to examine just what it is about desert conditions that makes them so suitable and tempting for rogering in.

The principle advantages of the desert, according to geoerotic experts, are as follows:

1 The appeal of hot, dry moonlit nights, as opposed to the hot sticky ones encountered on tropical islands. Sex is quite a sticky enough business anyway, without climatic conditions adding to the climactic ones.

2 Hot weather leads to easy access. No need to wear tights.

3 Only in the desert is there a chance of being photographed on top of a camel. Which will really impress everyone back at the office.

4 The chances that the man you are rogering is, unbeknownst to you, a prince are innumerably higher than in England, where there are only about eight princes, most of whom are either married or under five. To add to which, of course, if in England you would recognize the prince in question and, if you didn't, he wouldn't be worth rogering anyway.

The disadvantages can be more concisely expressed:

1 Death by dehydration.
2 Sand in pants.

3 Cactus up bottom.

4 Cactus up worse than bottom.

Taking all of which into account, Viviane is a very courageous lady.

FOOTNOTES

1 See Appendix: Love Tokens.
2 It could indeed be that this 'Dinner with Denis' syndrome is the reason behind all the recent major political scandals: Thorpe, Lambton, Profumo and Parkinson. Certainly it is true that all recent Labour leaders at some stage had dinner with Denis Healey, and they all came to pretty rocky ends.

VIVIANE VENTURA & ADNAN KASHOGGI

The one thing you can be sure of about this coupling is that, whenever it happened, Viviane was *definitely, deeply* in love with Adnan. For as she writes: 'You should always be in love with the man you're sleeping with. It doesn't matter if your love only lasts two minutes'.

Another thing you can be sure of is that Viv gave it everything she's got: her daughter, Scheherezade was once heard observing: 'I don't know where Mummy gets the stamina from'.

ADNAN KASHOGGI

Born	**1935.**
Occupation	**Businessman extraordinaire.**
Hobbies	**Selling arms and shaking hands.**
Romantically Linked With	**Soraya Kashoggi, Laura Biancolini, Viviane Ventura.**
Married	**Soraya Kashoggi.**
Nickname	**Kash.**

Adnan Kashoggi is one of the highest profile international businessmen, and rumoured to be one of the richest men in the world. His American Express Card has a £5 million limit. His annual personal expenses are £120 million, and he earns £600 a minute. Twelve houses, four planes, a 285-foot yacht equipped with Exocets and God alone knows how many pairs of socks are all, to him, bare necessities.

And yet, with this money that can buy him all he desires, Adnan has always been basically a one-woman man. Although he is seen with glamorous girls, they are mainly for aesthetic decoration, since the one woman on whom his heart was set was his wife, Soraya. He met her when she was very young, and took her back to Riyadh as his wife. Once there, he did not fall back on tradition, but actually broke rank and, in a community with only six Westerners at the time, all male, he gave his wife freedom and prominence, letting her share in the responsibilities of his work.

It was pretty bad luck for him then that she didn't really have the staying power, and in the end, demoralized by her reputed promiscuity, Adnan had to let her go. Yet, even now, divorced, he stays friends with his one woman. Vis-à-vis the woman taken in adultery, Adnan is up there with JC.[1]

FOOTNOTES

1 Although not a Christian himself, Mr Kashoggi would certainly have learnt about love and patience from Jesus' famous encounter:

   St John 8.2
   2 Early in the morning he came again to the temple; and the people came to him and he sat down and he taught them.
   3 The scribes and Pharisees brought a woman who had been caught in adultery, and placing her in the midst,
   4 They said to him, 'Teacher, this woman has been caught in the act of adultery.
   5 'Now in the law, Moses commanded us to stone such. What do you say about her?'
   6 This they said to test him, that they might have some charge to bring against him. Jesus bent down and wrote with his finger on the ground.
   7 And as they continued to ask him, he stood up and said to them, 'Let him who is without sin amongst you be the first to cast a stone upon her'.
   8 And once more he bent down and wrote with his finger on the ground.
   9 But when they heard it, they went away, one by one, beginning with the eldest and Jesus was left alone with the woman standing before him.
   10 Jesus looked up and said to her, 'Woman, where are they? Has no one condemned you?'
   11 She said, 'No one, Lord'. And Jesus said, 'Neither do I condemn you; go your way and henceforth sin no more'.

On the other hand, Mr Kashoggi might gain more pleasure from this version of the story, to be found in St Micah, in the Apocrypha:

   Micah 4.22
   22 Early in the morning he came again to the temple; and the people came to him and he sat down and he taught them.
   23 The scribes and Pharisees brought a woman who had been caught in adultery, and placing her in the midst,
   24 They said to him, 'Teacher, this woman has been caught in the act of adultery.
   25 'Now in the law, Moses commanded us to stone such. What do you say about her?'
   26 This they said to test him, that they might have some charge to bring against him. Jesus bent down and wrote with his finger on the ground.
   27 And as they continued to ask him, he stood up and said to them, 'Let him who is without sin amongst you be the first to cast a stone upon her'.
   28 And once more he bent down and wrote with his finger on the ground.
   29 And straightaway did one young man, with short hair and glasses, bend down also and, picking up a large stone, chucked it at the woman.

30 And the Lord was much amazed and said, 'What, art thou then without sin?'
31 And the young man, who was very holy, did reply, 'Yes, master, as far as I know'.
32 And the Lord did give it a moment's thought, and then said, 'Well, come to think of it . . .' and bent down to pick up a great big rock himself.
33 But by this time, the woman, who was a cunning type, had scarpered.
34 And, in fact, Jesus was well pleased with how it had turned out.

ADNAN KASHOGGI & SORAYA KASHOGGI

Unfortunately, great wealth, as well as making it hard for a chap to get through the eye of a needle, also always puts him in danger. And, indeedidoodee, Adnan fell straight into it. For Adnan Kashoggi, along with Howard Hughes, Louis XV, and Edward VIII is a high candidate for that greatest honour of all . . . The World's Most Expensive Roger.

When Adnan did finally sue Soraya for divorce, the great divorce lawyer Marvin Michelson stepped in. In return for separation, Marvin demanded half of Kash's money for Soraya. He was talking about £1000 million.

In the end, Marvin didn't get what he wanted. Soraya finally settled for £100 million: Marvin was ashamed, but for some reason, Soraya didn't seem to mind too much.

SORAYA KASHOGGI	
Real Name	**Sandra Daly.**
Born	**1941, in England.**
Occupation	**Mother of eight, pop group manager, political advisor.**
Hobby	**Rogering.**
Distinguishing Features	**Kash's Cash.**
Romantically Linked With	**Adnan Kashoggi (m), Winston Churchill MP,[1] Jonathan Aitken MP, John Bentley, Jack Jones, David Bailey, Jim Henson, Robert Rupley (m), Richard Coombes (m).**

It is a widely known fact that the character played by Joan Collins in the movie *The Stud* was inspired in part by her close friend Soraya, and the

exploits of this modern day Messalina are a source of permanent wonder. It would, however, take an entire new book with a name like, well, *The Stud*, to tell all Soraya's tales: they run the gamut of romance and divorce and lust and passion and are not at all fit subject matter for a dry reference book such as this.

Nevertheless, just to give a flavour of what kind of excitement we are face to yashmak-ed face with here, it is worth touching on the most remarkable of the tales told, the one about Soraya's stint of work in an escort agency. What makes it so extraordinary is that this is *not* a gruesome tale of early exploitation at all, *not* a tragic story of a pitiable girl in her poverty and weakness, fighting for survival. For Soraya got the urge for escort work when she was at the peak of her wealth and social fame. The woman of pearls would be dropped round the back of an escort agency by her chauffeur, and then would do a good night's work before returning to her millionaire's home.

A lot of strangers have a lot to thank Soraya for. And, of course, all of us in a way have to thank her. For were it not for *The Stud*, Joan Collins might never have been cast as Alexis in *Dynasty*, and life, as we know it, would not be the same: Nancy Reagan, for one, wouldn't be dressing so strangely. Again, the wonder of the power of the roger.

FOOTNOTES

1 The affair almost caused a huge political scandal. See John Bindon, later in this line, for 'Sex and State Security, How It Works'.
2 Another of the Great Rogering Mysteries: What Makes David Bailey Attractive.

SORAYA KASHOGGI & JOHN BENTLEY

On the night of the premiere of *The Stud*, the audience watched, in silent excitement, the 'steamy' scene where Oliver Tobias makes mad passionate love to Joan Collins in the lift of a private house, a scene actually filmed in Soraya's Eaton Square house. Only at one point was the silence broken, and then it was by a loud, fruity guffaw from the throat of John Bentley. He later claimed he had laughed because he recognized the lift.[1]

JOHN BENTLEY

Born	**1941, in England.**
Occupation	**Financier.**
Hobbies	**Reading and rogering.**
Nickname	**Pretty Thing.**
Distinguishing Features	**Pretty Thing, presumably.**
Romantically Linked With	**Mynah Bird, Viviane Ventura, Vicki Hodge, Soraya Kashoggi.**

Vicki Hodge once said of John Bentley that the only two things that he reads are Captain Marvel comics and balance sheets. This goes to prove what has long been suspected, that an intimate knowledge of the history of the English novel, a passing acquaintance with a fair spread of modern poetry and a select overview of Russian literature are almost completely unnecessary if what you want to do is sleep with a lot of girls. On the other hand, a passing acquaintance with Captain Marvel, who spends all his time showing off in a rather complicated kind of underpant, can be nothing but an education to a man who wants to notch up a couple of chicks on his way from cradle to grave.

FOOTNOTES

1 See Appendix: Unusual Places to Roger. Also Britt Ekland and Warren Beatty—love like a lift.

JOHN BENTLEY & VICKI HODGE

This roger did not take place in a lift. Business acquaintances of John Bentley, thinking after the last entry that perhaps they should always go up to see him by the stairs, can breathe again.

VICKI HODGE

(For the facts and figures, see the True Love line.)

This line is exemplary in its demonstration of how rogers can cross all barriers of class, country, religion and wealth. It straddles the huge distances between King and Carry On Girl, between commoner and royalty, between West and

Middle-East, and reduces them to seven simple acts of love, between the sheets, or, in one instance, between the second and third floors. And so it is proper that Vicki Hodge should find herself here, a woman who has promised to the world that she, when it comes to rogering, will not discriminate. When asked what kind of man she liked, top drawer, bottom drawer or somewhere in-between, Vicki magnanimously replied: 'I like the whole wardrobe'.[1]

FOOTNOTES

1 Vicki is, however, worried about what she should do if the wardrobe ever tires of her: in a recent interview she bemoaned: 'I can only hope that something else turns up when my funbags lose their appeal'.

VICKI HODGE & JOHN BINDON

Hodge and Bindon had a stormy affair which had its most famous consummation on the day of Vicki's wedding to Ian Heath, when John and Vicki spent the afternoon before the service in bed together.[1] When the affair finally came to an end, however, John found himself as roughly treated as Ian had been; Vicki ended the affair in the press without telling him. His reaction to the news later that day is one of most moving testimonies of the power of true love to muddle, confuse and break the logic of a once noble mind: 'Vicki has been very depressed since her dog vanished. We've not been having any more rows than usual. She says she'll be back when it stops raining'.

JOHN BINDON	
Born	**1940, in England.**
Occupation	**Actor, novelty artiste.**
Hobbies	**Balancing beer and rogering.**
Distinguishing Features	**Size.**
Romantically Linked With	**Christine Keeler,[2] Carol White, Angie Bowie, Dana Gillespie, Vicki Hodge.**

John Bindon is a classic recent example of the rough trade lover. Although originally an actor, his career has now taken him more in the direction of a novelty act, his speciality being the balancing of four pints of beer on his penis. As a friend of Princess Margaret, it is known that John secretly hopes that he will one day be able to perform this startling act in a Royal Variety

Performance, taking his place amongst such entertainment giants as Roy Hudd.

John actually became a friend of the Princess on the pleasure isle of Mustique, a friendship that thrived despite the fact that the Princess, passing Mr Bindon modelling for a nude photograph, is said to have remarked, 'It's not as good as I expected it to be'. Buckingham Palace sources say that it is not known to what the Princess was at that time referring.

FOOTNOTES

1 Although much was made of this at the time of Vicki's divorce, infidelity on the day of the wedding is not, historically speaking, unusual. In Roman times the priest always deflowered the bride before marriage. In eighteenth-century France and England, the job was done by the lord of the manor. And in certain South Seas islands, *all* male guests at the wedding are expected to roger the bride. (See Appendix: Marriage, Weddings and Wedding Nights.)

The basic theory behind all these customs is to protect the bridegroom from the danger of virgin's blood. Which means that perhaps, on reflection, all this isn't particularly relevant to Vicki Hodge after all.

2 The mention of Christine Keeler here raises the question of 'sex and state security', which has become the staple excuse for the public's intermittent hypocritical hysteria about promiscuity. (Victor Lownes once said: 'A promiscuous person is usually someone who is having more sex than you are'.)

The argument here is that, in the act of rogering, important state secrets may be passed over from one partner to another, and so no person in a responsible position should sleep around.

It is questionable whether this argument really holds water. Let us imagine, to test the theory, a hypothetical situation of the kind imagined.

A minister possesses a state secret, that a nuclear reactor is about to be built in West Hampstead. He is engaged in sex with a girl who also sleeps with a Russian spy. The Russian spy knows that a nuclear reactor is going to be built, but he does not know where. It is the girl's job to find out. Let us now look at the likelihood of her being able to do this: *before, during*, or *after* sex.

BEFORE
GIRL *O darling, I want you, I want you now.*
MINISTER *And I want you.*
GIRL *Quick, quick.*
They undress.
MINISTER *O, the sheets are so cold.*
GIRL *Yes, but I'll keep you warm.*
MINISTER *Yes. Isn't it glorious how warm the body always stays.*
GIRL *Yes, almost as warm as if it were powered by nuclear energy.*
MINISTER *Funny you should mention that, because we've just been having a meeting of the Cabinet today about where to place the new nuclear reactor.*
GIRL *O yes?*
MINISTER *We thought West Hampstead.*
GIRL *O yes, that would be nice.*
LIKELY, OR UNLIKELY?

DURING

MINISTER *O, I love you. I love your soft skin.*

GIRL *O, you're my man. My man.*

She scratches his back hard.

MINISTER *O, I love you, I love you. I love how every move I make, you're there, moving with me.*

GIRL *O God, yes. Stay there. O God, that's it. We fit together, like, O, I don't know, a new nuclear reactor and . . .*

MINISTER *West Hampstead.*

GIRL *Really? O yes. Now, NOW, NOW!!!*

MINISTER *No, stop.*

GIRL *Now, now!!!*

MINISTER *O.*

GIRL *O.*

MINISTER *O.*

LIKELY, OR UNLIKELY?

AFTER

GIRL *O, that was fabulous.*

MINISTER *Short.*

GIRL *Yes, but very sweet.*

MINISTER *O, I love you.*

GIRL *And I love you. At this moment, I feel as though we are the only people in London.*

MINISTER *Well, of course, we would be if there was an accident at this new nuclear reactor that we're going to build in West Hampstead.*

It is just not going to happen: there is no way of passing over detailed military secrets, *before*, *during* or *after* rogering. The fact of the matter is that we members of the public are just jealous of anyone who is lucky enough to have both state secrets and sex at the same time, and do all we can to punish them.

JOHN BINDON & BARBARA WINDSOR

This is our final pairing and the exception that proves the rule. As far as we know, John and Barbara *did not* roger. But both come from London's East End and Barbara did once say, about life before her present husband, Stephen Hollings: 'Before Stephen, I might have had ten geezers a night.' So, if this book proves anything, it must prove that one way or another, a bit of Barbara got to John in the end.

Because, if you've rogered anyone . . .

BARBARA WINDSOR

Born	**1937, in England.**
Occupation	**Actress.**
Hobbies	**Carrying On.**
Distinguishing Features	**Her cockney voice, her high spirits and her boobs.**
Romantically Linked With	**Ronnie Knight, Johnny Brandon, John Reid, and Stephen Hollings (m).**

From a Tudor to a Windsor the long lay line has run, and what more fitting terminal could it have found than Barbara. Henry VIII represents one great British tradition, the monarchy; Barbara represents the other great British tradition, the Carry On films. Through such great British masterpieces as *Carry On Spying, Carry On Abroad,* and *Carry On Camping,* Barbara's high uplifted breasts uplifted the spirits of millions of Britons who found the realities of actual rogering a little more than they could take.[1] There were times, during her career when Barbara was knocked for her knockers, made to feel that they were all she had going for her. But she could always have knocked the knockers for six if she had taken a look at important historical precedents.

Take for example Phyrne, a 400 BC Greek whose breasts were so perfectly shaped that she twice modelled for sculptures of Venus. Phyrne was up in court accused of treason and was to be defended by Hyperides, one of the greatest orators of the day, a John Mortimer, Michael Havers, Bob Geldof figure. Yet, when the time came for the counsel for the defence to speak, Hyperides said not a word. Instead, he simply cast aside Phyrne's veil and displayed her perfect breasts to the jurors. The court was so delighted by them that they decided unanimously to let Phyrne off at once.

FOOTNOTES

1 If this small volume can in any way have served the same service, filled in the odd lonely night, made less unfriendly the odd hotel room, or made less uncomfortable the inevitable British Rail corridor in which you find yourself sitting right on the crack between carriages, then it has done its little job.

KING SIZED PAIR LAY LINE

KING HUSSEIN

VIVIANE VENTURA

ADNAN KASHOGGI

SORAYA KASHOGGI

JOHN BENTLEY

VICKI HODGE

JOHN BINDON

BARBARA WINDSOR

FROM	**FRANK SINATRA**
TO	**ROB LOWE**
IN	**6 ROGERS**

People often accuse Hollywood of being a godless place without roots or tradition. But that's unfair. Look at this line, for instance. Though separated by a span of twenty-five years, six presidents, a major war, and banana-flavoured condoms, these two Hollywood stars are linked in countless ways.

Each spent the early part of his career as a thin, secretly spectacled, teenaged heartthrob; each had embarrassingly disastrous relationships plastered all over the gossip pages; each served as the master of revels for famous friends with similarly overactive egos and a passion for pure alcohol; and each had worked hard and long at linking together as many lay lines as possible.

If that's not tradition, what is? Proving that, old or new, Hollywood is Hollywood.

A ring-a-ding-ding.

FRANK SINATRA

This is Frank's final appearance in these lines.

The authors would like to take this moment to thank Frank Sinatra for making their work so much easier than it might otherwise have been. Frank's personal rogistry serves as a sort of universal "hub" when charting who's had who in Hollywood, spanning generations and linking together a wide array of stars and starlets. For when walking the lay lines of Hollywood, all roads, it seems, lead to Frank.[1]

As for the other, more controversial aspects of Frank's life and career . . . well, a lot of allegations have been made over the years concerning some of his "family" obligations. But considering the high price today of hospital care and the fact that we, the editors, given the choice of a method of execution, would shout 'old age', we'd rather not get into that.

And anyway, the truth is that what Ol' Blue Eyes is really best known for is rogering. (Well, maybe singing. But after that, rogering.) Generations of rogerers have used the seductive powers of The Voice's voice to 'set the mood', and one has to assume that Frank's as good at setting moods in person as he is on vinyl.

FOOTNOTE

1 Frank's dominance in this regard may soon end. Warren Beatty, whose list of probable rogers already stretches from Vivien Leigh to Molly Ringwald (who were born some 57 *years apart*), and who still has a number of potentially productive rogering years ahead of him, could soon become the universal hub to end all hubs.

FRANK SINATRA & NATALIE WOOD

Frank's affair with Natalie is a subject of some debate. It can definitely be carbon dated to the mid-1960s, during the period when Frank was wondering whether or not to marry Mia Farrow, and after Natalie had broken up with Frank's pal R. J. Wagner. However, there're also reports of a roger or two between Frank and Natalie in the late '50s, *before* the breakup with R.J. But Frank would never do a thing like that . . . would he?

Frank had a crucial impact on Natalie's future during the '60s. This was when the great psychedelic wave was just starting to break across the California shore, and one night at L.A.'s Daisy discotheque Natalie met a screenwriter who was an early devotee of LSD. They began to see each other, and the screenwriter convinced Natalie to "drop" acid with him. When Frank found out about this he became furious and made Natalie promise to never take acid again. Then—just to be sure—he hired a bodyguard to tail Natalie and see to it that she never even *saw* the screenwriter again, saving her from a perilous path that might have led to her listening to loud rock and roll or wearing floral and paisley prints.

NATALIE WOOD

For a full biography see America Rampant.

NATALIE WOOD & WARREN BEATTY

Warren and Natalie fell in love while making *Splendor in the Grass* (where, of course, they played lovers), and promptly got written up in every gossip column in America as Natalie and R. J. Wagner's story-book marriage fell apart. The end of Warren and Natalie's relationship wasn't nearly as public, but it was every bit as revealing . . . at least as far as Warren's concerned. He and Natalie had been living together for over a year, and all of Hollywood expected them to soon get married. But then came their fateful final night at Chasen's.[1]

Natalie and Warren were just finishing dinner when Warren excused himself to go to the bathroom. Nothing much out of the ordinary about that, Natalie thought, and nodded her assent. But when an hour passed and Warren still hadn't returned, she changed her mind, deciding that there was something very much out of the ordinary going on.

She was wrong. Warren had ditched Natalie for the restaurant's hat-check girl, ending their love affair with a bang, not a whimper. And hat-check girls were anything but out of the ordinary so far as Warren was concerned.

The obscure connection between hats and laying—as in 'wherever I lay my hat, that's my home'—is thus resolved, thanks to Warren.

WARREN BEATTY

For a full biography, see America Rampant.

Throughout his life, Warren has excelled at a number of hobbies.

Phone calling, for instance.

Few people—even in a town like Hollywood, where business deals, creative meetings, romances, and sometimes it seems *entire lives* are conducted via Ma Bell—can touch Warren when it comes to handling a phone. It's said that he spends hours every day with his ear to the receiver, regardless of where he is or what else he is doing.[2]

Or playing the piano.

In spite of *Ishtar*, Warren was known as something of a musical whiz during his early days in Hollywood, entertaining friends at parties by imitating the piano styles of jazz greats Errol Garner and Art Tatum.

Or . . . yes . . . *rogering*.

Clearly, this is something that Warren has been very good at for a long time. But there's a serious question to be asked here: Is Warren truly a legend in his own time?

Well . . . his favorite come-on line—'What's New, Pussycat?'—became so renowned around Hollywood during the '60s that it inspired the movie of the same name. Not to mention the song of the same title. Not to mention the film *Shampoo*, which—though ostensibly inspired by Jon Peters' life— seems to have more than a bit to do with Warren's as well. Not to mention 'You're So Vain', Carly Simon's hit song inspired by one of Warren's least likable personality traits, and which at the very least implies that he's a legend in his own *mind*. And, finally, not to mention the fact that if Warren's rogering doesn't qualify as legendary, whose does?

And did they live to talk about it?

FOOTNOTES

1 An expensive L.A. eatery known for its famous patrons, its chili, and, apparently, its hat-check girls.
2 Ex live-in lover Joan Collins was particularly annoyed when Warren indulged in a version of love-making that might be termed 'coitus interphonus', wherein the male takes advantage of his position on top to grab the nearest phone and make a couple of quick, mid-roger business calls.

WARREN BEATTY & MICHELLE PHILLIPS

In many ways, this relationship seems like an afterthought for both participants. Kind of like cleaning up what's left on everybody else's plate before you leave the table. By the time they finally slept together, Michelle had already rogered most of Warren's friends, while Warren had probably rogered every woman Michelle had ever *heard* of.

Still, it didn't take long for things to get serious. At least for Michelle. She moved out of Jack Nicholson's pad (with whom she'd been living after leaving Dennis Hopper, whom she had married after divorcing John Phillips, etc.), and settled down with Warren, even getting him to play Daddy for her daughter, China.

This period was at the height of Sabre-rattling between the U.S.S.R. and China. Warren, a noted lover of Russia, may well have felt fatally compromised having to live with China.

Needless to say, it didn't last. Warren sometimes had trouble keeping track of China, explaining that he had never been good with geography. And eventually he and Michelle drifted apart, causing Michelle to complain that Warren 'prefers shallow, meaningless relationships'.

MICHELLE PHILLIPS	
Born:	**1944, in Long Beach.**
Occupation:	**Singer, actress, author.**
Hobbies:	**Rogering, avoiding shallow, meaningless relationships.**
Distinguishing Features:	**Being twice as tall, a third as heavy, and eighteen times prettier than the other Mama in The Mamas & The Papas.**
Romantically Linked With:	**Nearly all of her husband's closest friends.**
Nickname:	**Mama Michelle.**

Michelle Phillips' love-life seems proof positive of the old adage that 'what goes around, comes around'. In her autobiography *California Dreamin'*, Michelle admits to having slept with most of her husband John Phillips' close friends. And that was *before* they got divorced.

Michelle didn't slow down much after the divorce, either, racking up a string of liaisons that reads like a who's who of Hollywood hipdom in the '60s and '70s. Dennis Hopper, Peter Fonda, Bob Rafaelson, Kris Kristofferson, Leonard Cohen, Polanski, Nicholson, Beatty . . .

What was that about shallow relationships, Michelle?

MICHELLE PHILLIPS & ROMAN POLANSKI

Michelle was nearly twenty-five when she and Polanski slept together—a bit long in the tooth for Roman, but then she was the wife of one of his closest friends, so Roman made an exception. Roman never really discussed the affair with John Phillips, who maintained his friendship with Roman and Roman's exquisite wife, Sharon Tate,[1] as if nothing had happened.

But when Sharon was murdered, Roman immediately suspected Phillips, thinking he might have killed her in a jealous rage. Roman asked Michelle if she'd ever told John about their affair. She had. But Roman soon learned that John had nothing to do with the killing, which had been ordered by Old Wild Eyes himself, Charlie Manson—who, thank God, can be found nowhere among the lay lines of Hollywood.

ROMAN POLANSKI

Born:	**1930s, in Poland.**
Occupation:	**Director, actor.**
Hobbies:	**Rogering newly pubescent women.**
Distinguishing Features:	**His height . . . or lack thereof.**
Romantically Linked With:	**Barbara Kwiatowski (m), Sharon Tate (m), Michelle Phillips, Jacqueline Bisset, Nastassia Kinski, various unnamed actresses and models, and a particular unnamed thirteen-year-old.**

Roman is, above all else, a great director. He is also someone who's endured a shattering string of personal tragedies—from surviving the Holocaust to having his wife and unborn child slaughtered by maniacs. But despite all his brilliance and all his pain, Roman is best known for one dubious distinction: breathing new meaning into the old Maurice Chevalier song, 'Thank Heaven for Little Girls'.

There's no doubt about it, Roman likes 'em young—a fact made painfully clear by the charge of statutory rape that sent him scurrying out of the country and forced him to abandon forever his adopted homeland.[2] In fact, there seems to be no record of Roman *ever* rogering anyone who's past the big 3-0. This wasn't much of a problem when Roman was in his thirties. And though not quite legal, it didn't seem hideously offensive in his forties, either. But we have to say, as Roman approaches his *sixties*, it's getting to be a bit embarrassing.

FOOTNOTES

1 Roman formed his friendship with Phillips and other rock stars as part of an effort to become an American hippie. Toward that end he also dropped acid, wore love beads, and once even convinced Sharon Tate to go without make-up on weekends in an attempt to broaden her cultural horizons.
2 There's been a lot of speculation about who that thirteen-year-old girl really was. Personally, we have no idea. And if we did, we couldn't tell you.

ROMAN POLANSKI & NASTASSIA KINSKI

Roman claims to have discovered Nastassia while on a trip to Germany in the '70s.[1] He was on a date with a stunning blonde when he met the young Ms. Kinski, who was going out with a 'friend' of Roman's. In the course of the evening, the 'friend' got somewhat lost in the shuffle, as Roman's tandem became a troika and Nastassia joined him and the blonde in bed.

Shortly after that Roman—now determined to make "Nasty" a star—asked her mother if she (Nasty, of course) could live with him in London. It was only then, Roman claims, that he learned Nastassia was fifteen years old.

He probably thought she was twelve.

NASTASSIA KINSKI

Born:	**1960, in Berlin, W. Germany.**
Occupation:	**Actress.**
Hobbies:	**Herpetology[2].**
Romantically Linked With:	**Roman Polanski, Paul Schrader, Rob Lowe, Keith Carradine, Wim Wenders, Ibrahim Moussa (m).**
Nickname:	**Nasty.**

Although Nastassia has co-starred with some of Hollywood's most romantic leading men, she's probably best known for a poster in which she co-starred with a snake. That pose has forever earned Nastassia a place in the erotic fantasies of millions of young undergraduate males, getting posted in dorm rooms and frat houses across America.

A curious thing about that poster is how *relaxed* Nastassia is with a giant boa constrictor between her legs. Although when you think about it, you begin to realize that while Nastassia's other co-stars may have been warmer-blooded than the boa, none could have quite had that much . . . mass. It's nice to know that in an age when faint-hearts get terrified if their lover wants to see them more than once a week, nice, old-fashioned Nasty embraces a constricting relationship.

FOOTNOTES

1 Roman slightly ignores the fact that Nastassia is the daughter of the internationally famous film actor Klaus Kinski, and therefore was not quite a young Lana Turner sitting unnoticed at the lunch counter of Schwab's.
2 Which means the study of reptiles, not the study of herpes. Although much of the activity chronicled in this book might be described as the *pursuit* of herpes.

NASTASSIA KINSKI & ROB LOWE

Pretty Nastassia and even prettier Rob fell hard and fast for each other while they were making the film *The Hotel New Hampshire*.[1] It was a short-lived affair, and wouldn't have had much impact on the lives of either . . . if it weren't for the fact that actress Melissa Gilbert—Rob's *fiancée*—decided to pay him a surprise visit, catching him and Nastassia doing what a lot of other people do in hotels in New Hampshire without getting caught.[2]

Needless to say, the discovery brought the engagement to a rather sudden end. At least, for a while.

ROB LOWE

Born:	**1964, in Virginia.**
Occupation:	**Actor.**
Hobbies:	**Politics, rogering, making phone calls, wearing glasses, and generally doing everything he can to be the second coming of Warren Beatty.**
Distinguishing Features:	**A face that could probably win him the Miss America contest if his hair was longer.**
Romantically Linked With:	**Melissa Gilbert, Natassia Kinski, Jodie Foster, Demi Moore, Princess Stephanie, and a slew of other likely suspects.**

Rob Lowe has starred in a remarkable number of movies for someone who's still only in his mid-twenties. He's also had a remarkable number of *affairs* for someone who's still only in his mid-twenties, a fact which has probably shaped his reputation more than all of his on-screen performances combined.

Best known among these affairs is the intensely public month he spent with Princess Stephanie, which landed them both on the cover of just about every gossip sheet in the world. That romance, along with his highly publicized on-again-off-again-on-again—oops, off-again—relationship with Melissa Gilbert has caused something of a backlash against Lowe. Critics now accuse Rob of shallowness and—with his highly visible presence at the Democratic National Convention—slavishly aping such rogerer/star/activists of the past as Beatty, Sinatra and Bogart.

Our answer to that is—hey, he's rich, he's famous, he's a knockout, and he's barely twenty-five: we'd be shallow, too, if we had those statistics. And as for Rob aping Beatty *et al.* with his Democratic dabbling, so what? Even if it's only a game, it's a hell of a lot better than golf.

FOOTNOTES

1 It's good that the Kinski/Lowe affair took place on the set of *The Hotel New Hampshire*, otherwise that film would be completely forgotten, as there was certainly zilch to remember so far as the on-screen activity was concerned.

2 Though this may be apocryphal, it's rumoured that Rob tried to convince Melissa he was merely 'checking Nasty for snake bites'.

APPENDICES

UNUSUAL PLACES TO ROGER

One of the definitive facts which emerges from this book is that rogering can be greatly enhanced by the choice of an unusual and stimulating site in which to do it.

Perhaps it was more to the point that they should never have gone up it.

Cars, boats, buses and trains—moving vehicles in general—are widely held to be pleasing choices. Margaret Trudeau was delighted by her experiences with Jack Nicholson in the back of a Daimler, and Vicki Hodge similarly enchanted by Elliott Gould's white Rolls-Royce. Mick Jagger was so aroused by a ride on a bus, that he was moved to roger the girlfriends of both Bill Wyman and Keith Richard on it.

Rogering afloat has always been a popular occupation, right from the days of Elizabeth I when Lord Seymour professed it to be his favourite sport, though this may have had more to do with the sailors than the floating. The Royal Yacht *Brittania* is of course *the* place to have a honeymoon, which presumably has something to do with the gentle rocking motion of the waves. The celebrated Aly Kahn–Thelma Furness roger—one of the Rogers That Changed the World—did, of course, initially take place on an ocean liner.

It is worth remembering that simply being afloat is not, in itself, enough. The presence of a ship, or at least a small boat, is of vital importance. Rafts, for example, when they have appeared in this context, are not a success. Pierre and Margaret Trudeau 'met' on one and the ensuing marriage was an unmitigated disaster. Richard Burton had what must have been his only failed seduction attempt on one, when he tried to roger Joan Collins and she kept her teeth tightly clenched and refused to kiss him. Rogering afloat without any vessel at all is even less of a good idea—as Deborah Kerr and Burt Lancaster discovered when they tried to make love in the Atlantic surf in *From Here to Eternity*. Though perhaps the producer was to blame by insisting that they both keep on their bathing suits.

Finally, if you do want to roger someone in an unusual place, do remember

that this refers to the *location* of the roger, not the place on your partner's body. If there was an appendix on this sort of thing it would be entitled 'Filthy Perversion'.

NAMES FOR ROGERING

(v) = verb (n) = noun

Comfort and consolation between two old friends (n)—as with Britt Ekland and Ryan O'Neal.

Date (v)—*'Jill St John is dating Robert Wagner'.*

Feel like a woman (v)—*'Ryan really knew how to make a woman feel like a woman'* Leigh Taylor Hunt.
'With Richard I discovered what it was like to feel like a woman' Carol White with Richard O'Sullivan.

Meet (v)—*'Carole King wrote a song about a sexy neighbour who she was dying to meet'* Ryan O'Neal.

Open up a can of beans (v)—*'I decided, I'm not going to open up this can of beans'* Joan Collins and Ryan O'Neal.

Play (v)—*'I don't know why, he was just more fun to play with'* Jill St John.

Play around with (v)—*'Leigh didn't like me playing around with other women'* Ryan O'Neal.

Play chess (v)—*'I enjoyed playing chess with Henry Kissinger more than Sean Connery'* Jill St John.

Run after (v)—*'When I'm depressed I drink or run after girls'* Ryan O'Neal.

See a lot of (v)—*'He began to see a lot of Eva Peron'* Porfirio Rubirosa.

Shower (v)—*'It used to be only me who could shower Farrah. Now anyone can do it who buys her shampoo'* Lee Majors.

Slapped by (v. participle)—*'The studio was inundated with letters from fans saying they would like to be slapped by Clark Gable'.*

ARCHAIC NAMES FOR ROGERING

Disrespect for my person (n)
Swive (v)—As used by Elizabeth I.
Long conversation (n)
Be overcome with sympathy (v)—*'James I was overcome with sympathy for Robert Carr'.*
Come in and recognize her again (v)—by Louis XIV.
Fling one's spear into the future (v)—by Franz Liszt.
Tool (v)—Lord Byron.

HOW TO GET RID OF YOUR PARTNER'S PARTNER

This is a traditionally common rogering problem. The best method, as we see from the text, is undoubtedly to be Warren Beatty or, ideally, Ryan O'Neal.

Being Des O'Connor is not so effective in itself, but he did come up with an excellent technique when trying to pull Stewart Granger's girlfriend. Granger rang up, when Des was visiting her flat, and the quick thinking songbird grabbed the phone and said, 'Mr Granger, I'd appreciate it if you never rang my fiancée again'. The completely astonishing thing is that it worked. This is remarkably similar to the method used by Elizabeth Taylor when she decided she wanted Michael Wilding. She simply went out and bought a ring and ordered him to marry her—which he did. He had been going out with Marlene Dietrich at the time.

Frank Sinatra was a little more subtle but no less cunning when he wanted to get rid of Carol White's boyfriend, Paul Burke. He invited the two of them out for the evening and hired two prostitutes to take Burke off and roger the living daylights out of him.

Historically, of course, killing the partner's partner was the blindingly obvious solution, but in this day and age the consequences of such a method must be taken into account. Even when your partner does the killing themselves—as when Andy Williams' wife, Claudine Longet, shot her lover—the whole thing is likely to end up with a lot of messy business with prison or electric chairs which tend to be even worse impediments to happy rogering than partner's partners.

MAD PRODUCERS

Hollywood producers have played a major role in foisting on the twentieth century the image of the perfect man, the perfect woman, and the perfect way to go about rogering. It is therefore alarming and disappointing to discover that a majority of them were quite clearly barking mad, their decisions in forming these giant, far-reaching role models, utterly arbitrary.

Here is an illustrative selection of their great prophetic utterances:

Louis B. Mayer
On Ava Gardner—'*She can't act and she can't talk*'.
On Greta Garbo—'*She's too fat. The American public don't like fat women*'.

Jack Warner
(He was responsible for depriving the world of Natalie Wood's nude scenes in *Splendour in the Grass*.)
On Clark Gable, to a minion—'*Why did you throw away $500 on that big ape? Didn't you see his ears when you talked to him? And those big feet and hands? Not to mention that ugly face*'.

Otto Preminger
On Marilyn Monroe—'*Directing her was like directing Lassie*'.

It was these men, too, who decided that Natasha Zacharenko would sound more sexy if they changed her name to Natalie Wood, and Margarita Carmen Cansino if they called her Rita Hayworth.

When you consider the effect that these dangerous lunatics have had on the rogering lives of each and every one of us, it is hardly surprising that in the 1980s Tony Blackburn is allowed to talk about sex on the radio, beautiful young girls agree to roger Des O'Connor, and the largest appendix in this book is a list of excuses to get out of rogering.

It is all terribly, terribly sad.

DOGS AND ROGERING

There can be little doubt that the extraordinary links between dogs and rogering revealed in this volume must be attributed in part to the Marilyn Monroe/Lassie confusion described in the 'Mad Producers' section. These links, thankfully, have little to do with dogs participating in sexual acts. Let us leave that to the Mexicans. Rather, the conversational topic of dogs, and their doggy habits, proves itself time and time again to be a stimulating prelude to human rogering.

Humphrey Bogart and his first wife, for example, spent much of their honeymoon between rogers discussing whether dogs should eat caviar; whilst Shirley MacLaine and Peter Hamill drove themselves into a frenzy of desire with a conversation about whether dogs have souls.

As we said in the introduction, however, the power of dogs to enhance a rogering career is strictly limited to conversation about them. Never was this more clearly shown than in the case of Howard Hughes who was bitten on the penis by a dog. It is said that the well-meaning animal simply mistook it for a juicy bone.

MARRIAGE, WEDDINGS AND WEDDING NIGHTS

One of the great puzzles of life is the relationship between marriage and rogering. When the rogerers in this book marry and de-marry with such frequency, you cannot help but wonder why they bother to do it at all.

Rita Hayworth was married five times, Elizabeth Taylor six, along with Henry VIII. Artie Shaw, one of Ava Gardner's three husbands, had eight wives, and at the last count Zsa Zsa Gabor had been married eight times. What goes through these people's minds when they say '. . . till death us do part' again? Do they really think that this time they definitely, definitely mean it, or have they simply confused the word 'roger' with 'marry'?

Equally perplexing are the people like Elliott Gould, Jane Wyman, Natalie Wood and Elizabeth Taylor who decide it is a good idea to marry the same person more than once. One possible explanation is they like weddings so much that they want to have as many of them as possible.

Many bizarre and splendid weddings have featured in this book: Aly Kahn and Rita Hayworth's for example, when a thousand little turtles were dispatched across a swimming pool with lighted candles on their backs; and Sir Gordon White's first wedding when all the guests wore white, and the pregnant bride bright scarlet. The success of the wedding, however, is not always reflected in the marriage. Both of these ended somewhat abruptly in divorce. Sometimes the wedding itself is so disastrous that it signals the end from the beginning. At Humphrey Bogart's first one, both the bride's parents were deaf mutes, and the service was conducted in a combination of sign language and a peculiar sing-song whine. The bride found it so traumatic that she had hysterics afterwards. Bogey simply had a stiff drink or ten.

This, however, was as nothing beside the wedding of Princess Marie and the Duke D'Acosta in the eighteenth century, where eight of the participants ended up dead. These included the Count of Castiglione, who fell from his horse and was crushed by a carriage; a visiting prince, who was scalded to death by an exploding boiler; the Lady of the Robes, who committed suicide; the Colonel of the Guard, who got sunstroke while performing his duties, and fell to his death from a balcony; a gateman—suicide again—; the best man, who shot himself; a court official who died of an apoplectic fit; and the station master who was crushed to death by the bride's train.

In terms of the traumatic effect on the bride and groom at the start of their lives together, this wedding can only be matched by those held by the tribesmen of Masamonia. At these occasions the bride is required to roger not only the bridegroom but also the entire assembled company of male guests.

There was a brief and rather diluted attempt to introduce this custom to Great Britain—when Vicki Hodge decided to roger John Bindon on the day of her wedding to Ian Heath—which was not successful. Other than that the custom only exists here in the form of the traditional kiss which the bride bestows on all the guests.

A far cry from a traditional roger it may be, but even so, kissing a series of lecherous old friends of your father is not an attractive prospect for any woman, and it is difficult to understand why marriage continues to flourish and generate enthusiasm as it does.

It is, perhaps, just possible that some people marry because they think it is wrong to have sex without doing so first. In those cases, presumably, it is the wedding night rather than the wedding which is the main attraction. Sadly, however, wedding nights throughout the ages have an alarming tendency to turn out disappointingly: from that of Caroline of Brunswick, whose new husband was seen fleeing from the bridal suite in the middle of the night, pale faced with horror to, more recently, Des O'Connor's wife, who spent hers 'Sipping cocoa and chatting to friends'.

When it comes to marriage there are, of course, a few glowing success stories (see the True Love lines) but—apart from the vague, let's face it rather unrealistic, hope of being one of the lucky few—reasons for going through with all that kissing and pallavah are hard to find. Perhaps the single most convincing one lies in the fact that it is much more fun to roger when you shouldn't be doing it.

Without the noble institution of marriage, people in search of illicit sex would be reduced to rogering their mothers, baby sisters, and Shetland ponies.

LOVE TOKENS

The love token is almost as integral a part of rogering as the Great Rogering Excuse, or even the willy.

What is bewildering about the subject is the wide range of objects which are deemed to be suitable. See:

Aeroplane—*Barbara Hutton to Porfirio Rubirosa.*
Aeroplane II—*Doris Duke to Porfirio Rubirosa (such a bore to get the same love token twice).*
Engagement ring in carton of chopped liver—*Warren Beatty to Joan Collins.*
Pair of Bunny Ears and Tail—*Bunny Girl girlfriend to Tony Blackburn.*
Piddling puppy—*Edward VIII to Wallis Simpson.*

Pink motorbike—*Elvis Presley to Jayne Mansfield.*
Roses, hotel room full—*Frank Sinatra to Carol White.*
Roses, ship's cabin full—*Aly Kahn to Thelma Furness.*
Roses, van full—*King Hussein of Jordan to Viviane Ventura.*
Seventeen dogs—*Hedy Lamarr's first husband.*
200 Marks and Spencer's black nylon brassieres—*Imelda Marcos.*

MOTHERS' PAGE

It would be churlish to leave this account of the world's great rogerers, and their work without some reference to the vast army of mothers who made them so. Producing a major rogerer is a great and mysterious thing, and those mothers who feature in this book distinguish themselves as a noble and spirited bunch.

First there is Eve, who gamely rogered both her sons for the sake of continuing the human race; Rod Stewart's mum, who after thirty years of watching her son wade through a sea of blondes, never gives up hope that he will marry 'a nice Scottish girl'; the mother of Sylvester Stallone who persists in calling his new wife 'that big pig', and instills such fear into her Rocky/Rambo son that bodyguards had to be employed to keep her away from his wedding. Then there is Omar Sharif's Egyptian mama who faints whenever she sees him, and still insists on sitting him on her knee. Favourite of all, though, is the mother of debonair, orange-faced George Hamilton who, in the true spirit of a rogerer's mum recently had an operation to have her boobs lifted. She sent a message to her son saying, 'George, if anything happens to me, please arrange for me to be buried topless'.

Mrs Hamilton is seventy-three.

PULLING TECHNIQUES AND PICK-UP LINES

When so many successful rogerers are gathered together in one volume it is tempting to borrow from and imitate their pulling techniques. There is no harm in this, certainly, but it is vitally important to distinguish between good and bad.

Amongst the good ones (as with 'Getting Rid of Partner's Partner') being Warren Beatty or Ryan O'Neal obviously comes top of the list. This is closely followed by being a king, prince, millionaire and/or film star, or fifteenth century pope.

Fortunately for the ordinary people of the world, poetry and romance can be equally effective weapons. Clark Gable's 'I love you as no man has ever loved woman from the beginning of time', was obviously along the right lines. He tried it on a local shopkeeper before he became famous, and she didn't look at another man for forty-six years.

Carole King pulled Ryan O'Neal by writing a song about him, whilst Orson Welles once got a girl by asking her to pick out a playing card then look at the sky. An aeroplane was passing towing a giant version of the card she had just picked. Obviously these methods are not available to everyone, but it is their basic ingredients—care and concern for the prospective rogering partner, and willingness to make an effort—which are important.

It was just these ingredients which were missing when Robert Mitchum attempted to pull Ava Gardner. He asked Howard Hughes' permission. The answer, of course, was no.

Howard Hughes was equally unsuccessful with his pick-up methods. These consisted of having his chosen beauties followed by private detectives, and locking them in his hotel room. They escaped with commendable frequency.

Neither of these last two techniques should be used by readers at home. It is essential to remember, too, that a method which works for one of the world's major sex objects will not necessarily work in the same way for you.

Still, you never know . . .

AGE DIFFERENCES AND ROGERING

Strange as it may seem at first sight, there is a great deal to be said for rogering, and even marrying, someone of a massively different age than your own. Numerous examples in the book bear witness to this: Lauren Bacall and Humphrey Bogart with their twenty-five year gap are the shining example; then there was Vanessa Llwellyn who exchanged dirty Dai for Gordon White, thirty-seven years her senior. Peter Holme and Joan Collins, Jay Rufer and Des O'Connor, and even Prince Charles and Princess Diana are all living, breathing illustrations of the facts given below:

1 If you are getting rather old and wrinkly, what could be nicer than rogering someone with a lovely new shiny pink body.

2 If you are the lovely new shiny one, the benefit of rogering someone with wealth, success and experience can have an astonishingly smoothing effect on wrinkles.

3 The best way to have a happy relationship with a major sex object is to do it when he's getting too old and tired for runing around. Look, again, at Bacall and Bogey, at Barbara Sinatra who married Frank in his sixties and tamed him beautifully, and Kay Spreckels, Clark Gable's last wife who got him saying, 'I've raised my share of hell in my time. Now I'm more interested in raising kids'.

GREAT ROGERING EXCUSES

Amongst the many interesting facts about rogering are these two:

1 It is widely assumed that everyone likes rogering as much as possible whenever they can get the opportunity. This is NOT TRUE.

2 What *is* true, however, is that rogering is infinitely more fun when you ought not to be doing it.

The combination of these two facts means that one of the most vital pieces of a rogerer's equipment is a bloody good excuse always to hand, either for doing it when you shouldn't be doing it, or for not wanting to do it when the person you are with thinks that you should.

EXCUSES FOR ROGERING WHEN YOU SHOULDN'T BE

This is the most difficult category of all, since when you are caught, on the job *in flagrante*, unless your discoverer is blind, blind drunk, or a complete moron, all the mental agility in the world is not going to convince them you weren't doing what you obviously were doing.

The following examples, the best of the bunch in the book, only serve to illustrate how lame pretty much any excuse is going to sound in this sort of situation:

Harry Killigrew's excuse for rogering Maria Brudenell: 'I had nothing better to do'.

Barbara Villiers, when caught with Jacob the Rope Dancer: 'I wanted to see what he had on under his tumbling outfit'.

Michael Curtiz the film director had slightly more panache when he was caught by his entire cast having his daily blow job from a make-up girl. He looked down at the girl with an expression of horrified surprise and said, 'Oh my God! What are you doing down there? Get off! Get off!'

Chico Marx was massively imaginative, but still unconvincing, when caught kissing a chorus girl. He claimed, 'I wasn't kissing her. I was whispering in her mouth'.

All these efforts are to be praised, however, since to make any excuse at all, however feeble, is infinitely more polite than simply carrying on rogering, pretending nothing has happened.

EXCUSES FOR AVOIDING ROGERING

This is an area where you stand more chance of being believed but still run serious risks. There is, of course, always the risk of hurting your partner's feelings, but far more seriously, the danger of going so over the top in your attempts to put them off, that word spreads like wildfire, and suddenly no one else wants to roger you either. This is the major disadvantage to the otherwise perfect excuse of claiming to have a sexually transmitted disease or to be a dangerous sadistic pervert.

For a practical, no nonsense approach to avoiding rogering, Frances Howard of the sixteenth century is to be recommended. Without beating about the bush she simply inserted a protective device which prevented her horrible husband from putting his willy in. Come to think of it, it probably led to rather a lot of beatings around the bush but it was, at least, infinitely more creative than having a headache.

Imelda Marcos was obviously thinking along similar lines with the two hundred black Marks and Spencer nylon girdles which were found in her palace when she fled. President Marcos, though not a man who oozes sexuality, is quite definitely the violent type. So although, presumably, she rarely needed to wear all two hundred at once, it was handy to have them standing by.

In the more peaceful setting of modern day suburban Britain such extreme measures are rarely necessary. Tessa Wyatt, for example, when married to Tony Blackburn found it sufficient to insist on sleeping alone, in the afternoons, and to refuse to go out with him except in a large party.

The lovely Sabrina Guinness is not a woman who has made much use of excuses to get out of rogering—which is a pity, for if she had done she might have ended up marrying Prince Charles. Her excuse would have been perfect: 'I'm sorry—I'd absolutely love to, but I'm trying to keep in with a chance of being the next Queen of England'.

Presumably this was and still is used with great frequency by Princess Diana, and is, in fact, an excuse which could be used by almost any woman. Do not cry out, 'But Prince Charles is already married'. What about Princes William and Harry? In 1986 it is already very much the thing to roger the older woman. By the time the young princes come of age it will be absolutely *de rigueur* to roger all the most attractive friends of your granny.

There is no doubt that excusing yourself from rogering involves more loss of face for a man than a woman, but when it comes to the excuse the man, in the end, does have the one with which there is no arguing. This was never better illustrated than by Omar Sharif. He shares with Elliott Gould a preference for a good book over a good woman when it comes to bed partners. Both have made valiant attempts to convince the world and their current girlfriends that having an affair with someone doesn't mean you have to go to bed with them—without much success. The lovely Omar, however, tells with great relish a story of the night a girl appeared in his hotel room and ordered him at gunpoint to take off all his clothes. When he had done so she lay on the bed and demanded that he roger her.

'Madam', the great sex object replied, 'as you can see, I can't'.

One final word of warning. No matter how keen you are to avoid a roger it is never, never worth going to the same lengths as an early boyfriend of Nancy Reagan. His excuse for failing to turn up for a date was that he had been run over and killed by a train on the way. Utterly convincing you have to admit, but a little over the top.

ROGISTRY

BIBLIOGRAPHY

Special thanks to:—

Leslie Halliwell *Filmgoer's Companion* 8th Edition Granada
Compton Miller *Who's Really Who* Blond & Briggs
Margaret Nicholas *The World's Greatest Lovers* Octopus Books
Margaret Nicholas *The World's Wickedest Women* Octopus Books
Irving Wallace, Amy Wallace, David Wallechinsky, Sylvia Wallace
  The Intimate Sex Lives of Famous People Arrow Books

and:—

Dulcie M. Ashdown *Royal Paramours* Robert Hale
Donald Barlett *The Life, Legend and Madness of Hughes* Andre Deutsch
Olivier Bernier *Louis the Beloved* Weidenfeld and Nicolson
Caroline Bingham *James I of England* Weidenfeld and Nicolson
Tony Blackburn *Tony Blackburn, the Living Legend* Comet
Lady Blessington *Victims of Society* A&W Galignani
Tina Brown *Life as a Party* Andre Deutsch
Sir Bernard Burke *Romance of the Aristocracy* Henry Colburn
Joan Colllins *Past Imperfect* Fontana
Edward le Comte *The Notorious Lady Essex* Dial Press
Vincent Cronin *Napoleon, Emperor of the French* Penguin
Duncan Crow *Edwardian Women* George Allen & Unwin
Elizabeth Gould Davis *The First Sex* Dent
Britt Ekland *True Britt* Sphere
Ronald Flamini *Ava* Robert Hale
Antonia Fraser *King Charles II* Futura
Frederick Lawrence Guiles *Norma Jean* Mayflower
Geoffrey Haughton-Brown *The Popes, Rome and the Church* Nostradamus
Pearl Hogrefe *Tudor Women* Iowa State University Press
Richard Benjamin Jones *Napoleon: Man and Myth* Hodder & Stoughton
Kitty Kelley *The Last Star–Elizabeth Taylor* Coronet
Peter Kinnell *The Book of Erotic Failures* Futura
Richard Mathison *Howard Hughes, His Weird & Wanton Ways* Robert Hale
Nancy Mitford *The Sun King* Michael Joseph

Nancy Mitford *Madame Pompadour* Penguin
David Ogg *England in the Reign of Charles II* Oxford University Press
Saul K. Padover *The Revolutionary Emperor* Eyre & Spottiswoode
Pears' Cyclopaedia
Frederich de Reichenberg *Prince Metternich in Love & War* Martin Secker & Warburg
Joanna Richardson *The Disastrous Marriage* Jonathan Cape
Joanna Richardson *My Dearest Uncle* Jonathan Cape
Joanna Richardson *Sarah Bernhardt & Her World* Weidenfeld & Nicolson
Mary F. Sandars *Honore de Balzac* Kennikat
Michael Sellers *P.S. I Love You* Fontana
Linda Simon *Alice B. Toklas* Peter Owen
G.L. Simons *The Illustrated Book of Sexual Records* Virgin Books
Christopher Sykes *Black Sheep* Chatto & Windus
Roger Thompson *Women in Stuart England* Routledge & Keegan Paul
David Valentine *Love is for Lovers* William Kimber
Brendan Walsh *The Popes* The Catholic Truth Society

DO YOUR OWN ROGISTRY

If famous people are so deeply and wide rangingly intertwined through their rogering, it stands to reason that any smaller social group of normal healthy adults is riddled with lay lines in a similar way.

Hours of fun are to be had producing a Who's Had Who (or Rogerage) of your own friends and acquaintances (and enemies indeed), both cataloguing old links and, of course, forging new ones where necessary.

HOW TO GO ABOUT IT

(This is a guide to producing a rogerage, not rogering itself. For rogering itself, see 'Where Did I Come From, Mummy?', published by the British Medical Information Council.)

First you need a file of information to start you off. Begin with yourself. Find a clean piece of paper and draw up a list of all the people you have rogered.

Quite soon the paper will look

like this: or like this:

depending on your luck and skill.

Then think of people amongst your friends or enemies who are major rogerers. Make discreet inquiries. Look out particularly for dark horses—the Peter Hamill and Henry Wynbergs of your world, who don't shout out 'Hey, I'm Mr Sex, roger me, baby!', but who have some secret magical charm which means they've quietly clocked up eight of the most attractive people you know, and about 800 others, while everyone thought they were watching *Newsnight*. With all this information, form many lists.

Then take a much larger but equally clean piece of paper, and put all the lists on it. Start to draw lines between the lists, make a few phone calls to fill in gaps, add more names, then more lines, and soon the piece of paper will look like this:

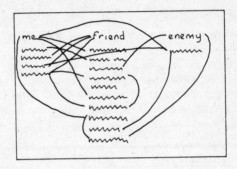

Now take a final piece of cleanish paper, and collate the results, the most testing, but ultimately rewarding, part of the process. You can now create your own lay lines: you can tie yourself to the girl/boy of your dreams whom you haven't got round to, but someone you know has. You can tie your worst enemy to the person they like least. Sometimes you may get stuck but never, never despair; if we can get from Ronald Reagan to Tony Blackburn, you can do it, we know you can.

And soon you will discover that, sure enough, you have slept with everyone you know, or indeed have ever heard of. You are part of the great lay line that is history.

To start the process, in case you can't at the moment find any clean pieces of paper, we supply a chart for you to get going on, from which you should be able to draw your first, hesitant lay lines. Bon Voyage!

ROGERAGE FORM

Me

1
2
3
4
5
6
7
8

Mr/Ms

1
2
3
4
5
6
7
8

Mr/Ms

1
2
3
4
5
6
7
8

Mr/Ms

1
2
3
4
5
6
7
8

Mr/Ms

1
2
3
4
5
6
7
8

Lord/Lady

1
2
3
4
5
6
7
8

MY FIRST LAY LINES